# Children and Drug Safety

## Critical Issues in Health and Medicine

Edited by Rima D. Apple, University of Wisconsin-Madison, and
Janet Golden, Rutgers University, Camden

Growing criticism of the U.S. health care system is coming from consumers, politicians, the media, activists, and health care professionals. Critical Issues in Health and Medicine is a collection of books that explores these contemporary dilemmas from a variety of perspectives, among them political, legal, historical, sociological, and comparative, and with attention to crucial dimensions such as race, gender, ethnicity, sexuality, and culture.

For a list of titles in the series, see the last page of the book.

# Children and Drug Safety

• • • • • • • • • • • • • • • • • • • • • • • • • • • • • • • • • • • • • • •

## Balancing Risk and Protection in Twentieth-Century America

CYNTHIA A. CONNOLLY

**Rutgers University Press**

New Brunswick, Camden, and Newark, New Jersey, and London

Library of Congress Cataloging-in-Publication Data

Names: Connolly, Cynthia A. (Cynthia Anne), author.
Title: Children and drug safety : balancing risk and protection in twentieth century America /
Cynthia A. Connolly.
Description: New Brunswick, New Jersey : Rutgers University Press, [2018] | Series: Critical
issues in health and medicine | Includes bibliographical references and index.
Identifiers: LCCN 2017021379 (print) | LCCN 2017022191 (ebook) | ISBN 9780813575230
(E-pub) | ISBN 9780813563893 (Web PDF) | ISBN 9780813563886 (cloth : alk. paper) | ISBN
9780813563879 (pbk. : alk. paper)
Subjects: | MESH: Drug Therapy—history | Child | Drug Therapy—standards | Drug and
Narcotic Control—history | Health Policy—history | History, 20th Century | United States
Classification: LCC RJ560 (ebook) | LCC RJ560 (print) | NLM WS 11 AA1 | DDC
615.1083—dc23
LC record available at https://lccn.loc.gov/2017021379

A British Cataloging-in-Publication record for this book is available from the British Library.

♾ The paper used in this publication meets the requirements of the American National
Standard for Information Sciences—Permanence of Paper for Printed Library Materials,
ANSI Z39.48–1992.

www.rutgersuniversitypress.org

Manufactured in the United States of America

For Nicholas, Lauren, and my parents

# Contents

1    Drug Therapy: From "Baby Killers" to Baby Savers, 1906–1933    I

2    New Drugs, Old Problems in Pediatrics: From Therapeutic Nihilism to the Antibiotic Era, 1933–1945    16

3    The Child as Drug Development Problem and Business Opportunity in a New Era, 1945–1961    33

4    The Growth and Development of the Therapeutic Orphan, 1961–1979    64

5    A "Big Business Built for Little Customers": Candy Aspirin, Children, and Poisoning, 1947–1976    96

6    Children and Psychopharmacology in Postwar America    124

7    Pediatric Drug Development and Policy after 1979    143

Appendix    163
Acknowledgments    167
Notes    171
Index    233

# Children and Drug Safety

# 1

## Drug Therapy

• • • • • • • • • • • • • • • • • • • • • •

From "Baby Killers" to Baby
Savers, 1906–1933

In 2010 the United States Congress commissioned its advisory research body, the Institute of Medicine (IOM), to collaborate with the Food and Drug Administration (FDA) in studying the success of two 2002 initiatives. The Best Pharmaceuticals for Children Act (BPCA) offered a financial incentive for drug companies to study drugs already on the market. The Pediatric Research Equity Act (PREA) required them to provide dosing and drug safety data for all new children's drugs, which they were already doing for adults.

The first meeting of the IOM committee, comprising internationally prominent pediatricians, researchers, pharmacologists, and ethicists, convened that December 17 with FDA representatives to review their task. Dianne Murphy, director of the FDA Office of Pediatric Therapeutics, began the meeting with a presentation of historical context, emphasizing the era beginning in the 1970s. Her first slide was startling. Although the FDA had been charged decades earlier with assuring that drugs for all Americans, including children, were safe and effective, the slide laid bare a starker reality. "Ignorance is poor public policy," it read, "and yet it best describes what has been the status of our understanding of how best to use therapeutics [medication] in the pediatric population."[1] Although Dr. Murphy also traced the BPCA's and PREA's successes in her presentation, she tempered any celebration with how much was as yet unfinished, lamenting, "[W]e don't even know dosing for most [pediatric] drugs." Dr. Murphy was not exaggerating the problem. Just two years earlier, in 2008, another IOM workgroup expressed concerns that 50 to 75 percent of medications prescribed for children had not received the full panel of tests for safety and efficacy that the committee believed necessary to protect children.[2]

How could this situation have happened? Children's and adults' unique pharmacotherapeutic differences had been emphasized by the founder of modern pediatrics, Abraham Jacobi, in the Civil War era.[3] How could an issue formally identified so long ago remain unsolved so many years later? How could this situation have occurred in a nation in which the FDA, clinicians, and industry had long recognized it as untenable? How especially could this have happened in a nation in which policymakers throughout the twentieth century repeatedly professed agreement that children's health and welfare represented a high national priority?[4]

This book offers some answers to those questions. To do so, it provides a historical overview of drug therapeutics and policy for children in the United States with an emphasis on the period between the founding of the Food and Drug Administration (FDA) in 1906 and the late 1970s, when major stakeholders such as the FDA, the American Academy of Pediatrics (AAP), and leading pediatric pharmacologists, clinicians, and scientists believed—erroneously—that the tools were in place to solve the problems related to children and drug safety. The story is worth telling for multiple reasons. First, most histories of childhood during this era do not have health as their central focus, and they say little about pharmacotherapeutics. Second, studying children, drugs, and drug policy provides a unique lens through which to examine children's health without focusing on a single disease, professional group, or care site such as home or hospital. That the story of children and drugs sits at the interface of the state, business, health care delivery, parenting, and childhood makes it especially intriguing.[5]

Third, the issue situates children at the center of drug regulation and drug development history during these years. There are well-regarded studies of therapeutics and drug policy in American society, yet children are mentioned only in passing, usually as having spurred new legislation or an investigation of some kind.[6] Children's recognized biological differences, the professional structures and specialties governing their care, and their purported protected place in American society as deserving of a healthy start in life have resulted in a different historical trajectory from adults with regard to drug development and policy. Studying this topic in its historical context is critically important because it illuminates the intended and unintended consequences of past policy decisions and offers a framework for considering what alternative directions might have produced different outcomes. The answers to these questions are important today because contemporary policies, and those contemplated for the future, reflect an embedded historical context that suggests certain alternatives as more feasible or consequential than other choices.[7]

Fourth, the twentieth-century history of children and drugs is worth exploring because issues surrounding children's health and social welfare are of profound concern to Americans today, no matter where in the country they live and no matter what their political beliefs. The issues embedded in discussions of children and drugs involve considerations regarding society's obligations to children, evolving understandings of their place and protection in American society, and determinations of who should decide what interventions are in the best interest of the child. These topics are no less relevant today than they have been in the past.

One concern that animated child-focused drug policy reformers in all eras was how to make sure children benefited from new legislation. Some argued that children needed policies crafted just for them, while others maintained that they were better served by being included in broader regulatory actions aimed at all Americans. Similar debates continue today. For example, some maintain that the Children's Health Insurance Program (CHIP), a federal health insurance program enacted in 1996 for poor and low-income children, should be phased out in favor of enrolling these children in the 2010 Patient Protection and Affordable Care Act. Others believe strongly that children's health care funding requires a fundamentally different approach from that for adults, one grounded in a growth- and development-oriented model aimed at maximizing well-being, not just preventing and treating disease. As the 117th Congress prepares to dismantle the Affordable Care Act in 2017, these earlier debates are worth considering.[8]

This topic thus provides an especially rich template to study themes of children's risk, rights, and protection in the United States in the changing contexts of childhood, parenting, and health care delivery. The history of children and drug policy is a particularly valuable case study because the issues unique to children have never been fully addressed, although they have been repeatedly raised by parents, drug companies, scientists, pediatric clinicians, government, and politicians. In the early postwar era, for example, physicians interested in prescribing the newly available penicillin to gravely ill children faced the enduring challenge of how best to approximate children's doses, even as an explosion of postwar research amplified the understanding of the physiologic differences between children and adults and among youngsters of different ages. But in the early 1960s, at a historical moment in time when this new knowledge might have resulted in legislation, and at a high water moment of rhetoric regarding the child-centeredness of the United States, it did not. The adult patient remained the norm in terms of defining official dosage guidelines, formulation, and administration of medications. Why and how did this happen?

History is the only discipline that can capture the complexity of this paradox. A historical lens highlights the ways in which evolving policies, scientific knowledge, and clinical practice solve some problems while creating new ones. It reveals the variables beyond science that shape policy as well as the unexpected consequences of well-intended laws. It also shows how notions of parenting, children, and their place in American society are enmeshed with the regulatory state, science, commerce, parenting, and clinical practice in often surprising ways.

Fifth, the history of pediatric drug development during these years provides a nuanced opportunity to study childhood and children's voices, opening a window into opaque corners of the past. Since the advent of social history in the 1960s and 1970s, capturing the agency of individuals and groups traditionally invisible in historical narratives has received new attention. Children are one such historically underrepresented group. Addressing questions regarding children's influence on events in America is notoriously difficult because they leave few personally generated written or oral records. They have often been viewed as lacking a perspective of their own because, medically and legally, parents or other adults make decisions on their behalf.[9] But this story shows how adults spent much time and energy thinking about how to appeal to children's palate and preferences; thus, children inarguably shaped the postwar drug economy, at least indirectly.

The final reason the history of children and drugs is worth telling is because it is so poorly remembered by scientists, nurses, doctors, pharmacists, parents, and others on today's front lines of pediatric health care, even though it created the context in which they practice. In order to fulfill their obligation to children and families, clinicians need to better appreciate the individuals and events that preceded their era. State-of-the-science studies on pediatric experimentation as well as drug development tend to relegate the pre-1970s era to a few pages or a decontextualized introductory chapter or two. As such, they cannot provide an understanding of the major role earlier events played in constructing the template for late twentieth- and early twenty-first-century pediatric pharmacotherapeutic policy and practice. It is for that reason that this book emphasizes the time period before the 1980s.[10]

Worse yet, the history has sometimes been incorrectly represented. In 2010, for example, the best known and most prestigious pharmacology textbook in the United States, *Goodman & Gilman's Pharmacological Basis of Therapeutics*, updated its section on pediatric pharmacotherapy. The authors who drafted the section briefly traced a few pediatric drug-related disasters such as thalidomide. Before moving on to discuss recent regulatory changes, they stated, "Before the 1970s, children and pregnant women were routinely excluded from drug studies."[11]

This statement was incorrect. In researching this book, I learned that at some historical moments it had been considered in children's best interest for them to participate in drug trials, sometimes with their parents' knowledge, sometimes without it. At different junctures in the past, children were barred from such research in an effort to protect them. In other words, the ethics regarding how best to evaluate drugs in the pediatric population has been dynamic and contingent. Balancing the potential benefits of more pediatric data against the need to expose children to as little risk as possible remains a vexing problem, as do questions about who makes those determinations and how they do so.[12]

Our contemporary sound-bite culture favors descriptions of greedy drug companies or bumbling federal regulators. One of the most fascinating parts of this story, to me, is how far from the truth those labels are. Organizations such as the AAP and the American Pharmaceutical Association (APhA), along with the pharmaceutical industry, the FDA, Congress, and individual scientists, pharmacologists, pharmacists, and pediatricians devoted considerable time, attention, and resources to issues surrounding children and drugs over the years. Almost all were well intentioned, but the same or similar problems arose again and again. As I drew on surviving primary sources, events, and people to weave the larger social, cultural, political, and economic context over time, I have been able to examine the successes, missed opportunities, and consequences—intended and unintended—of decisions made in the past with regard to American children, thus providing guideposts for better decision making in the future.

This book problematizes the issues of children and drug development and safety for both minor and serious conditions. My study does not include a lengthy explication of vaccines, vitamins, or drug development and testing in pregnant women because their historical trajectories differ from those of pediatric medications. Where there is overlap, however, I do address topics related to these concerns.[13] Drugs for children with cancer receive mention where appropriate, but they are an extremely small part of this story because, as I explain, the funding structures governing cancer therapeutics differed from other drugs with much more widespread use in children, such as antibiotics.[14]

My goal is to generate a meaningful synthesis of a broad topic, requiring compromise and omissions. As with all historical research, the data set is incomplete. I have chosen representative events and seminal moments in an effort to provide fidelity to the history and I focus on the United States only. That is not to say that many of the issues raised in this book were not occurring elsewhere. They were, although the narrative and stakeholders differ from country to country; forms of government, regulatory structures, clinical practice, and cultural issues surrounding children, parents, and experimentation

vary widely. A comparative history of pediatric drug development and pharmacotherapeutics in industrialized countries is very much needed.[15]

## Chapter Outlines

The book is organized both chronologically and thematically. Chapter 1 provides an introduction to the book, presents research questions and themes,
and details relevant historical context. It traces late nineteenth- and early
twentieth-century baby- and child-saving, using concerns about widespread
use of opium-laced "soothing syrups" in infants as a case study. Media campaigns referred to these agents as "baby killers" and helped create the FDA in
1906, ushering in the modern era of drug regulation. Soothing syrups also provided the major justification for the subsequent 1914 Harrison Narcotic Act.
This introductory chapter also provides historical background, sketching the
rise of experimental science and pharmacology and the evolution of pediatrics as a medical and nursing specialty. It concludes with an exploration of the
shifting context of American childhood and child health and social welfare
policy debates from the early twentieth century until the early 1930s.

Chapter 2 explores attempts in the 1930s to improve pediatric drug knowledge amid escalating tensions between the American Medical Association and
the American Academy of Pediatrics regarding which organization should
speak for children on this topic. It charts the rise of the modern era of therapeutic medicinal chemistry in the United States with the advent of the sulfonamides. These new agents profoundly changed the treatment of common,
often fatal pediatric conditions such as meningitis and pneumonia. Despite
the new drugs' potential, however, innovation sometimes brought risk. In
1937, the product Elixir Sulfanilamide, which contained the sweet-tasting
but poisonous diethylene glycol, resulted in dozens of deaths. Because many
of those who died from the tragedy were youngsters, child protection rhetoric helped forge a new law, the 1938 Federal Food, Drug, and Cosmetic Act.
This statute stipulated that manufacturers had to provide the FDA with data
about drug safety before marketing or selling their products. This chapter also
examines sulfa drugs and penicillin in actual use for children during the 1930s
and 1940s. This close analysis not only reveals the evolving transformations in
medical and nursing practice, hospitals, parental expecations, and the childhood illness experience brought about by these drugs; it also shows how and
why the template for pediatric drug discovery, testing, dosing, and monitoring
of adverse reactions evolved the way it did.

Chapter 3 traces the way antibiotics dramatically reduced pediatric morbidity and mortality in the early Cold War era, a time rife with discourse regarding American commitment to child well-being. At the same time, the absence
of formal rules for informed consent engendered a "trial and error" approach

to pediatric drug research, just as with other medical experimentation during this era. The ongoing debates about how to systematize pediatric drug knowledge and what group should take the lead stalemated any potential for an easy solution. This chapter also explores antibiotics' unintended consequences. For example, as media coverage announced penicillin's successes, parents began to demand antibiotics for their children, bringing unprecedented challenges to physician authority. The introduction of broad-spectrum antibiotics demonstrated how important the drug industry believed the pediatric market was to a full product line in a competitive marketplace. Yet the discussion of the two pediatric chloramphenicol catastrophes of the 1950s reveals the inability to protect children from risks of some antibiotics, the most widely used drugs for children in this era.

Chapter 4 begins in the early 1960s, chronicling how reformers used the thalidomide disaster, the sleeping pill linked to birth defects, to mobilize support for the bill that became the landmark 1962 Kefauver-Harris Amendments to the Federal Food, Drug, and Cosmetic Act. This legislation codified evaluation standards for measuring drug efficacy and mandated new rules for research ethics. The statute arrived at the same time that rhetoric about the importance of the child to American society soared. Within the year, however, fears that the new law was not fulfilling its safety promise to children led pediatrician and pharmacologist Harry C. Shirkey to coin an evocative and Dickensian term, calling children "therapeutic orphans." The FDA could approve a new drug application submitted without pediatric data, even if there was reasonable expectation that the drug would be prescribed to children. Pediatricians and others treating children were then required to modify the adult dosage for children, using whatever method they chose.

Shirkey argued that the lack of formal consideration of children's needs disenfranchised them. Other leading pediatric pharmacologists and physicians agreed with Shirkey, as did the AAP, FDA staffers, and some drug company representatives. A number of national conferences and meetings brought stakeholders together in an attempt to resolve the pediatric drug discovery and testing issues. The 1970s ended on a high note, with optimism that everything was in place to generate better pediatric drug knowledge and safety going forward.

Chapters 2, 3, and 4 focus almost exclusively on prescription drugs, especially antibiotics, the most widely used prescription drugs in children during this era. But analysis of these drugs does not tell the full pediatric story. Chapter 5 moves from a largely chronological order to examine the over-the-counter pediatric drug market, using as a case study the postwar creation, distribution, and marketing of an old chemical agent, aspirin (acetylsalicylic acid), in a small dose flavored to appeal to a child's palate. Advertisers of "candy aspirin," as it was often called in the 1950s and 1960s, strove to convince mothers (any emphasis on fathers is notably absent) that parental competence was linked to the purchase of a particular aspirin brand. Tactics were often grounded in racial, class, or gender stereotypes. But the popularity of candy aspirin quickly resulted in a dramatic increase in the rate of children's aspirin poisoning. One perceived solution, child safety caps, fomented much contentious debate, resulting in decades of stalemate. The 1966 Child Protection Act Hearings, which debated safety cap legislation, weighed the benefits to youngsters' health from such a mandate against the aspirin industry's resistance to greater governmental intrusion into private enterprise. This case study reveals what can happen when recommendations for reducing risks to children's health challenge corporations' economic well-being.

Chapter 6 begins in the 1930s with the discovery that amphetamines calmed children with behavior disorders, rather than stimulating them the way the drugs did in adults. It interweaves the history of pediatric psychopharmacology into that of child psychiatry in the United States in the years between the late 1930s and 1970s. The chapter also analyzes the similarities and differences in drug development, testing, and use when the agents in question were to be used for a child considered to be suffering from a "mental" disease and not a "physical" one. Using the research of Leon Eisenberg and Lauretta Bender as case studies, it also traces the different ways prominent child psychiatrists perceived the role of drugs in diagnosing and treating the behaviorally disordered child. Finally, given the lack of diagnostic specificity in child psychiatry for most of this time, pediatric psychopharmacology also provides a lens through which to study cultural anxieties regarding the "normal" American child and the ways the use of mood altering agents in children encoded prevailing notions of race, gender, social class, and ethnicity.

Chapter 7 begins in the late 1970s, when the FDA, AAP, and other stakeholders believed that technical, scientific, and ethical processes were in place to improve pediatric drug safety. But their optimism quickly faded as drug companies continued to submit new drug applications to the FDA without pediatric data and the agency approved them. At the same time, the political context shifted as a result of the antiregulatory philosophies of the newly elected President Ronald Reagan. But in what came as a surprise to many, President Reagan did sign the 1983 Orphan Drug Act (ODA). The ODA offered companies who manufactured and sold drugs for conditions with relatively few sufferers lucrative patent extensions. The law benefited children disproportionately because so many rare diseases afflict youngsters. Interestingly, while the AAP and FDA played important roles in helping enact the ODA, it was parental activism, particularly that of one mother, Abbey S. Meyers, that made the difference.

Chapter 7 also summarizes the changing context of American childhood in the 1980s and 1990s, when the imperative to address the problems of children and drugs began to accelerate. In an era in which parents were becoming more fearful regarding child safety, the rising incidence of chronic illness in children and the growing use of behavioral drugs meant that more children received drugs on a regular basis than in the past, a trend that began to receive significant attention in the 1990s. This phenomenon coincided with the acquired immunodeficiency syndrome (AIDS) epidemic. Activists successfully strove to hasten the drug approval process and increase adults' access to experimental therapies. Whether this course of action was or was not in the best interests of children with AIDS weighed heavily on families, clinicians, activists, and the FDA. Also during this decade, the market supremacy afforded to children's aspirin for fever and pain was challenged again. But this time it was not in the context of concerns about aspirin poisoning. Rather, by the early 1980s, aspirin became linked to a terrifying condition, Reye's syndrome. The aspirin industry responded by employing all the tactics it had been drawing on since the early 1950s.

Food and Drug Administration rules crafted in the 1990s created what became known as the "Pediatric Rule," mandating manufacturers to conduct studies and provide adequate labeling for use of the products in children. When the FDA's authority to write such a guideline was successfully challenged in federal court, stakeholders, among them the AAP and FDA, pressured Congress to write new legislation. This effort culminated in the 2002 Best Pharmaceuticals for Children Act (BPCA) and the Pediatric Research Equity Act (PREA). In 2012, President Barack Obama signed legislation making these laws permanent. Chapter 7 closes with a description of these laws, their impact on pediatric drug safety and knowledge today, and an analysis of what we can learn from this story.

## Baby Killers, Child Saving, and Regulation

The August 27, 1900, edition of the *Pittsburgh Press* carried an advertisement for a new medicine, Dr. James' Soothing Syrup Cordial. The language was designed to capture parents' attention in an era of expanding literacy. "Little Folks Love it," the promotion proclaimed. Touted as a "cure" for cholera infantum, an antiquated term for infectious diarrhea, the elixir, promised the ad, also "relieves colic, corrects sour stomach, [and] eases the pain of teething," common ailments suffered by almost every baby at one time or another. For the parent who worried about safety, the ad reassured in big letters:

Clear as crystal,
No laudanum.
Nothing that could
Possibly harm.

Just a pure wholesome
Cordial, that soothes the
Little nerves and gives them natural rest.[16]

Dr. James' Soothing Syrup may not have included laudanum, an opiod compound such as morphine or codeine, sometimes blended with alcohol—but it did contain heroin. Synthesized in 1897 by a scientist from the German company Bayer, heroin attracted great attention in both Europe and the United States. Within a year Bayer marketed it as a more effective cough suppressant than codeine. Another benefit, the company claimed, was that heroin was not habit-forming.[17]

Today we know that heroin is an addictive and dangerous substance, and, as such, Dr. James' Soothing Syrup caused the same high rates of infant death as the other opiate-laced soothing syrups did. Like Dr. James's, these sweetened narcotic products were advertised as treatments for a number of minor conditions. Parents could purchase soothing syrups at local stores or from trained apothecaries, who began calling themselves professional pharmacists in the latter part of the nineteenth century. They could even order them through mail-order services.[18] The soothing syrups were so widely available and penetrated culture so thoroughly that, in 1879, composer Edward Elgar named a composition for the well-known Mrs. Winslow's Soothing Syrup.[19]

FIGURE 1 Advertisement for Mrs. Winslow's Soothing Syrup for Children, 1885. (*Credit*: Courtesy of the National Library of Medicine.)

Some reformers argued against direct selling of soothing syrups to parents, but there was no consensus on the issue. The controversy over how best to balance ideals of free enterprise with consumer protection resulted in a rift in the nineteenth-century feminist movement. In their women's rights periodical, *The Revolution*, editors Elizabeth Cady Stanton and Susan B. Anthony, warned women about patent medications, especially those dangerous to children, such as soothing syrups. Cady Stanton and Anthony could not keep *The Revolution* profitable, however, and Laura Curtis Bullard, whose large family fortune relied on the invention and successful marketing of Mrs. Winslow's Soothing Syrup, purchased the journal, and the product subsequently received aggressive promotion in its pages.[20]

Physicians also worried about the indiscriminate sale of narcotics, although they, too, often recommended them liberally for young children. But just as with all drugs, they worried about how to titrate doses for children of different ages and sizes. One doctor, Abraham Jacobi, argued that nowhere were the differences between children and adults more profound than when it came to considerations of drug therapy. As early as 1861, he maintained that "for the purpose of attending the diseases of children, it is not sufficient to diminish and sweeten the doses administered to adults."[21] Although he could not articulate quite how, Jacobi believed that children's needs were more complicated than the age- or proportion-based dosing schemes such as Young's Rule, which dated to at least the early nineteenth century.[22] Pioneers in the evolving field of experimental pharmacology also struggled to understand what children's small size relative to adults might mean in terms of their ability to process or metabolize drugs.[23]

By the 1870s and 1880s a small number of children's specialists, led by Jacobi, institutionalized pediatrics as a specialty within medicine. They founded a pediatric section within the nation's leading physicians' organization, the American Medical Association (AMA). Some practitioners from the newly inaugurated nurse training schools also focused their efforts around the needs of sick children. Like Jacobi, nurses and doctors who specialized in pediatrics believed that children needed their own health care providers because youngsters were wholly different in terms of disease presentation and course, rather than just "miniature men and women."[24]

Soothing syrups were just one of the numerous health threats to children in the early twentieth century. An industrializing economy led many rural Americans to relocate to overcrowded and polluted cities to work, sometimes alongside their children, in factories or textile mills. Many of them, as well as a large influx of new immigrants, resided in tenements on the narrow, dirty streets of cities such as New York, Philadelphia, and Chicago, where diseases spread quickly, especially among the youngest, most indigent children. The growing trend to track vital statistics in the latter part of the nineteenth century documented the frighteningly high infant mortality rate, making the problem increasingly visible to scientists and public health reformers.[25]

One hope to reduce morbidity and mortality from infectious disease lay in preventive measures such as vaccines. But after a number of pediatric deaths from smallpox vaccine and diphtheria antitoxin (an antibody treatment aimed at neutralizing the bacteria), public health reformers insisted that biological agents be manufactured according to set standards to protect the public. They persuaded Congress to pass the Biologics Control Act of 1902. Under this law, the Hygienic Laboratory of the Public Health Service oversaw the manufacture and distribution of biological agents such as vaccines.[26]

Advocates of the Biologics Control Act effectively used child protection to build support for the law, and those who sought new drug and food safety laws took notice. Over the course of the next few years, muckraking journalist Samuel Adams Hopkins and the women's magazine *Ladies' Home Journal* railed against the risks to infants from soothing syrups. Hopkins's polemical 1905 *Collier's* magazine articles, subsequently published in book form as *The Great American Fraud*, strengthened public support for new laws to protect consumers from unsafe drugs and adulterated foods. Within a year of Hopkins's blistering exposé of the patent drug industry, Congress passed the Federal Food and Drugs Act, which in 1906 created the modern FDA.[27] The AMA, too, framed its support for the 1906 law in terms of child advocacy, at least in part. The organization's periodical, the *Journal of the American Medical Association* (*JAMA*), published letters from physicians who described infant deaths from soothing syrups. In the wake of the Federal Food and Drugs Act's success, the AMA became a major broker in American pharmaceutical policy. Its Council on Pharmacy and Chemistry, comprising expert physicians in pharmacology and therapeutics, advised the FDA and served as physicians' primary drug resource through its regular *JAMA* updates.[28]

The new law, however, did not actively ban soothing syrups, nor did it require premarket approval from the FDA before a medicine could be sold; it merely stipulated that drugs needed to be labeled correctly and meet specified standards. If they did not, the FDA considered them misbranded. For example, opium-containing products had to be manufactured in compliance with the standards of strength and purity set by the United States Pharmacopeia (USP) and the National Formulary (NF). Any variation from the USP-NF–approved formulation needed to be noted on the label. Therefore, opium needed to be correctly labeled but was not prohibited.[29]

Although members of the public could still legally purchase opium for themselves or their children whenever they chose, the 1906 Federal Food and Drugs Act also stipulated that manufacturers could not make false or misleading statements. In other words, in addition to quantifying the amount of heroin in Dr. James' Soothing Syrup, Bayer could no long maintain on the label that it contained "Nothing that could possibly harm," since physicians and public health reformers had widely documented the risks of opiate overdose in infants and young children. The FDA could take legal action against any company continuing to advertise the safety of opium products for children. But building a case against an individual company and bringing that case to court took time and resources. Some companies simply flouted the law and, in the short term, opium-laced products marketed for children remained readily available.[30]

The attempt to protect children from soothing syrups and other dangerous patent medications between the 1890s and World War I, a period of structural change and bureaucratic expansion known today as the Progressive era, was one component of a much larger "baby-saving" or "child-saving" movement. Child-saving causes spanned a range of issues, from infant mortality prevention to mandatory schooling, juvenile justice reform, and a ban on child labor. The movement's early twentieth century high water moment arrived in 1909, when, after an intensive lobbying effort by professional and lay child savers, President Theodore Roosevelt sponsored a White House Conference that brought together hundreds of specialists across a number of disciplines to study the needs of orphans and children whose parents were too poor to keep them at home.[31]

Capitalizing on momentum from the 1909 conference and societal enthusiasm for child saving, public health reformers in a number of cities began educational campaigns that attacked soothing syrups as "baby killers." Hoping to heighten parents' awareness of their dangers and to counter manufacturers' aggressive advertising, they posted placards that implored, "Don't make a dope fiend of your baby." The next year, prominent doctors and nurses gathering in Baltimore to discuss ways of reducing infant mortality in the United States made a point of denouncing soothing syrups.[32] The FDA also worked to educate the public about soothing syrups. In addition to publishing articles in *Good Housekeeping* and other women's magazines, FDA staff used the mostly agricultural periodical, the *Farmers' Bulletin*, to issue one of its earliest public warnings about addictive medications, noting that "soothing sirups [*sic*], naturally occupy the first place" on any warning list of habit-forming drugs.[33]

The ongoing activism from initiatives such as these helped spur another law, the Harrison Narcotics Act of 1914, which codified the amount of opium a proprietary drug could contain. It further mandated that the public could obtain legal narcotics only through physician sanction, that is, a prescription. The newly created Federal Trade Commission would file suit in the event of violations.[34] Despite these laws, educational efforts, and health care provider activism, at least some mothers remained confused by proprietary drug manufacturers' advertising tactics. They wrote letters to a new federal agency, the Children's Bureau, revealing their confusion regarding claims made on behalf of medications such as soothing syrups.[35] The bureau joined the fight against soothing syrups, adding information about their dangers in educational pamphlets written by its nurses and doctors.[36]

At the same time that reformers worked to protect children from soothing syrups and other dangerous drugs, new understandings of infant and child physiology and biochemistry began to improve the fluid and electrolyte management of acutely ill infants and young children. Potentially life-threatening clinical problems such as dehydration, for example, could now be more effectively managed, even in newborns. Outcomes for acutely ill, hospitalized children began to improve by the 1910s and 1920s. Better treatments helped children's hospitals transition from facilities aimed at providing moral and environmental care to indigent children who were often well but had no place to live to institutions that increasingly emphasized technologically driven care to acutely ill youngsters from all social classes.[37]

The 1921 Sheppard-Towner Maternity and Infancy Act created a federal role in maternal, infant, and child health in the United States. The federal funds distributed to states through Sheppard-Towner enabled communities to screen thousands of children for health defects and deliver well-child care, considered by pediatricians, public health, and school nurses essential to their well-being.[38] But the Sheppard-Towner Act fomented controversy within the AMA when, in the late 1920s, the law needed reauthorization. The pediatric section strongly supported the initiative, but the organization's policymaking House of Delegates did not. The AMA broader membership worried that the law, with its public funding for health promotion and disease prevention, represented an "imported, socialistic scheme unsuited to our form of government" and, as such, was anathema to the AMA's preferred private practice, fee-for-service health care delivery model.[39] The disagreement resulted in two AMA resolutions regarding the reauthorization, the pediatric section in favor and the House of Delegates in opposition. The AMA leadership ended the impasse by reminding the pediatricians that they could not issue independent policy endorsements. Partly as a result of the AMA's intense lobbying effort, Congress allowed Sheppard-Towner funding to expire in the late 1920s. In response, in 1930, a small group of outraged pediatricians broke away to form a new group, the American Academy of Pediatrics. Its central mission included political engagement on children's behalf.[40]

While there was less controversy among physicians about the need to remove unsafe drugs from the market, most American courts through the 1920s set a high bar to prove fraudulent claims of drug safety. This hampered efforts to remove potentially dangerous products from the market and led some to believe more stringent drug laws were needed.[41] One significant expansion of FDA authority came in 1927, when Congress enacted the Federal Caustic Poison Act. Focused largely on protecting children, the law mandated warning labels for potentially dangerous household products such as cleaning agents.[42]

The onset of the Great Depression in 1929 dampened enthusiasm for new drug legislation. President Herbert Hoover's administration, however, forged ahead with a White House–sponsored children's conference scheduled before the economic downturn. Whereas the 1909 meeting had largely addressed issues surrounding indigent and orphaned children, the 1930 White House Conference on Child Health and Protection focused on the needs of all American children. Its most visible outcome was the nineteen-point manifesto of children's rights, the Children's Charter. But delegates to the conference carefully avoided taking a position on whether the obligation of fulfilling the charter, which focused heavily on health, fell to parents, the government, voluntary organizations, or some combination of the three. The tangible results of the 1930 conference were nominal and overshadowed by the deepening financial crisis.[43] But the combination of the 1930 White House Conference and the founding of the AAP did make an impact on a group of pediatricians in Philadelphia. They decided the time was right to amplify their long-standing baby- and child-saving efforts by focusing on an issue they monitored with mounting alarm—the lack of pediatric dosing and drug safety information.[44]

## 2

## New Drugs, Old Problems
## in Pediatrics

• • • • • • • • • • • • • • • • • • • •

From Therapeutic Nihilism to
the Antibiotic Era, 1933–1945

By the early 1930s, pediatric drug knowledge had advanced little beyond
Abraham Jacobi's nineteenth-century declarations that children were not just
miniature adults. When J. P. Crozer Griffith and A. Graeme Mitchell published their state-of-the-science *The Diseases of Infants and Children* in 1933,
they lamented the weaknesses of nineteenth-century metrics for pediatric dosing. The authors, prominent pediatricians at Children's Hospital of Philadelphia, nonetheless recommended these proportion-based rules in the absence
of any more meaningful rubric. They considered the risks to children from
the drugs available so great, and their potential benefit so minimal, that their
use could not be justified. Griffith and Mitchell cautioned that for most children "little medicine of any sort is required, and the careful attention given to
hygiene and diet is sufficient."[1]

Other pediatricians, particularly those trained and teaching at elite medical schools, agreed. Famed Harvard University pediatrician Charles A. Janeway noted that when he graduated from medical school in 1935, "there were
only about six drugs I needed to know how to use; all the others were basi-
cally ineffective."[2] Similarly, pediatrician Thomas E. Cone, who would become
professor of pediatrics at Harvard and chief of ambulatory services at Boston
Children's Hospital, later recalled, "I didn't feel that what I was doing was that

much different than thirty years before. . . . We had little to work with. We tended to be therapeutic nihilists, I think," and trusted in "[t]he old aphorism about the healing power of nature."[3]

As a more nuanced understanding of children's physiological and pathological differences from adults evolved in the 1910s and 1920s, the paucity of pediatric drug and dosing information became more glaring. By 1933, leading members of the venerable Philadelphia Pediatric Society (PPS) were particularly concerned that the standards for drugs, the United States Pharmacopeia (USP) and the National Formulary (NF), had no pediatric representation, especially since many of the drugs listed were "employed extensively in treating disease in infants and children."[4] The Philadelphia doctors' worry was especially acute because so few American children in the 1930s ever interacted with a pediatrician. Many did not see a doctor regularly at all and, when ill, received care from a general practitioner who often had little or no training in pediatrics.[5]

The PPS doctors wanted to discover whether pediatricians around the country shared their concern that "the committees of the USP and NF have never felt it sufficiently important to secure the advice of pediatricians."[6] The results of the survey they sent to a carefully selected group of their colleagues throughout the United States, showed near-unanimous agreement with the PPS position.[7] Next, the Philadelphia pediatricians sent their findings to the newly founded American Academy of Pediatrics (AAP). The PPS sought the AAP's assistance in securing pediatric representation on the committee that oversaw the decennial USP revisions, next scheduled to be published in 1940. The PPS also wanted the USP to appoint a permanent pediatric panel to strengthen the evidentiary base for pediatric practice.[8]

Looking for opportunities to develop its activism as a voice on behalf of children, the AAP was immediately supportive of the PPS idea. Leaders saw this endeavor as a way to shore up pediatricians' role as the primary, if not sole arbiter of whether a child should receive medication. Pediatricians wanted all recommendations for children's drug treatment under their professional domain and away from public health nurses or pharmacists, both of whom frequently made such suggestions to parents. The AAP's inaugural president, Isaac Arthur Abt, was especially enthusiastic about making sure that physicians oversaw all medication-related decisions. He had worked in an apothecary as a teenager in the late nineteenth century and remained troubled that the store's clerk had dispensed medical advice along with drugs.[9] His primary goal, as stipulated in comments in the *Journal of Pediatrics* in 1934, was that the AAP, through USP representation, could "reestablish the use of drugs and remedial agents prescribed by physicians in place of the use of proprietary products. A further purpose is to put dosage for children on a sound and satisfactory basis."[10]

The AAP formed a Committee on the Revision of the Pharmacopeia, and Abt appointed himself chairman. Because of the professional rivalries and tensions between pharmacists and physicians, the USP allowed a set number of representatives from each group. The AMA selected the physician members. Thus, in order for the AAP to seat its own representative, the AMA would need to agree to cede one of its slots, diminishing its authority.[11] It was certainly improvident that Abt was the individual who approached the AMA to discuss the issue, for he had been one of the leaders of the AMA breakaway group that had chartered the AAP several years before. When he broached the topic with Olin West, secretary and general manager of the AMA, West, clearly rankled, was not receptive to the idea. Perhaps he was still miffed about the AAP rejection of the AMA several years before, or feared that doing so might result in other specialty groups seeking a place at the table, which could lead to a dilution of AMA authority. Whatever the reason, West was not about to help. Abt dejectedly noted West's response, "I am inclined to the opinion that if the pediatricians of the country really desire to be represented in the Pharmacopeia convention, that they may of their own effort, obtain such representation through the procedure of bringing the necessary pressure to bear upon the officers of the Pharmacopeia convention."[12]

West's advice to the AAP was disingenuous, however, since the USP was unlikely to change the balance of power between physicians and pharmacists by adding a new physician. The powerful AMA Council on Pharmacy and Chemistry considered itself the medical profession's single voice on all matters related to drugs, and the USP had little wish to alienate the group. The council's "New and Nonofficial Remedies," published as a regular *Journal of the American Medical Association* (*JAMA*) section, represented the chief source of physician knowledge about drugs, dosing, and toxicity for every drug on the market, and drug companies competed with one another for the council's financially advantageous Seal of Acceptance. The AMA did usually include a pediatrician as part of the council, but the AAP wanted to oversee the selection process, and the wall of interprofessional politics among physician groups was impossible to overcome.[13]

Faced with defeat, the AAP Committee on the Revision of the Pharmacopeia looked for other ways to become relevant on matters pertaining to children and drugs. The group decided to gather in one place all the pertinent data related to pediatric pharmacology. This resource would include "a study of vehicles and other means of administering therapeutic remedies, with the thought of improving unpleasant-tasting remedies for use in infants and children, . . . a study of dosing standards by age [and] body weights, . . . [resulting in a] manual that serves as supplement to USP and NF with indications for the use of such drugs [and] method of administration."[14] Their goal was to assure that physicians caring for children would have ready access to state-of-the-science pharmacology information. This initiative was especially ambitious because it aimed to make suggestions for every age range, from infancy to adolescence, and for all drugs—from each of the many pediatric laxatives on the market, for example, to the powerful heart stimulant digoxin. Support from the AAP executive board was tepid, however, perhaps because such a plan represented an entirely different agenda from the Committee on Revision's original charge. The board may also have believed there were other, more important, issues facing children during the height of the Great Depression, especially considering the paucity of drugs pediatricians considered useful in children. With these obstacles and lack of board support, the Committee on Revision soon disbanded.[15]

The federal Children's Bureau, a group that might have been a strong ally in the AAP's efforts to secure a place for the 1940 USP revision, seems to have been silent. The work of the AAP, the FDA, and the Children's Bureau overlapped in multiple areas: promoting food and milk safety, developing growth standards for children, and promulgating the importance of good nutrition, vitamins, and immunizations. Given the prevailing opinion among pediatric leaders that even sick children rarely benefited from drug therapy, perhaps the bureau saw little reason to devote time and energy to an idea that would presumably benefit only a few youngsters.

It is more likely that the long-standing tensions between leading academic pediatricians, who were more likely to view medicine as a private business enterprise, and the Children's Bureau's social workers, nurses, and physicians, who favored governmental involvement in health care delivery, also played a role. The bureau's leadership may have felt that the AAP was attempting to undercut its role as a voice for children, not just within the federal government, but within society as well. Finally, more than just philosophical differences regarding government's role in the delivery of health care may have prevented cooperation between the bureau and the AAP on this issue: gender may also have been a factor. Children's Bureau physicians were almost all women and the early AAP leadership was almost exclusively male. Women physicians in this era faced a number of barriers within medicine, such as limited access to training at elite hospitals that served as pipelines for medical school professorships. While some male physicians were involved in the Children's Bureau, it became a key organizational voice for female pediatricians who lacked other avenues to rise to positions of power.[16]

Despite the efforts of FDA reformers, pediatricians, and the AMA Council on Pharmacy and Chemistry, the patent medicine industry flourished in the 1930s.[17] A growing consumer movement, nurtured by the FDA and accompanied by New Deal activism, offered hope for legislative reforms to rein in proprietary drug manufacturers. The FDA, for example, sponsored lectures and a series of exhibits at agricultural and state fairs around the country aimed at building public support for new food and drug laws in the United States. At the same time, the nonprofit organization created to provide the American public with reviews of a wide variety of commercially available products, Consumers' Research, Inc., published a monograph enitled *100,000,000 Guinea Pigs*. Its central argument was that Americans were at risk because of weak federal regulations for foods, drugs, and cosmetics.[18]

In 1933, Senator Royal S. Copeland, a homeopathic physician from New York, placed a muscular bill on the docket of the U.S. Senate Commerce Committee, which he chaired. The proposed law placed strict new regulations on patent manufacturers' labeling and branding practices. Like earlier drug industry reformers, rather than emphasize its regulatory features, Copeland stressed the way his proposed law would provide a measure of protection for vulnerable "women, babies, and children."[19] But his bill and subsequent related legislation stagnated over the next few years amid intense opposition. The Proprietary Association and the Institute of Medicine Manufacturers, representing the patent drug industry, convinced congressional Republicans that the proposed law placed undue burdens on the American free enterprise system.

Meanwhile, the FDA kept up its pressure tactics. In 1936, FDA information officer Ruth deForest Lamb published the polemical book *American Chamber of Horrors*. Demonstrating an astute understanding of how to use children to play on public sympathies, Lamb included a letter from a ten-year-old child, Hazel Fay Brown, to President Franklin Roosevelt. In her letter Hazel informed the president that her mother had been blinded by the dye in a brand of mascara. She pleaded with the president to "help my mother" and "to get the law across."[20]

## The Sulfonamides and Children: Promise and Peril

A dramatic challenge to the notion that drugs offered a great deal of risk, but dubious benefit, to children occurred in 1936. At the International Congress of Microbiology in London, Eleanor A. Bliss and Perrin H. Long, researchers at the Johns Hopkins University medical school, heard riveting reports of a new agent's ability to cure postpartum infection or "childbed fever." The drug, Prontosil, worked amazingly well against the streptococcus bacteria in researchers' experiments. After returning home, Long and Bliss procured a supply from DuPont and Company and began investigations with streptococcus-infected mice, confirming that the drug worked on almost all the mice treated. The two researchers were naturally eager to try Prontosil on a human subject, and later that fall their opportunity arrived in the form of a seven-year-old child at the Johns Hopkins Hospital's pediatric center, the Harriet Lane Home, very ill with a high fever from a raging streptococcal skin and tissue infection known as erysipelas.[21]

The child had not improved with conventional supportive therapy, in which nurses sponged her with tepid water to reduce her fever, elevated the infected area to reduce swelling, and encouraged her to drink to prevent dehydration. Doctors disappointedly noted that the little girl also did not improve with serum therapy. Serum worked in one of two ways. Some, such as diphtheria antitoxin, worked against the poisons produced in the body by bacteria; others contained antibodies that destroyed the bacteria itself. The production of antibacterial serum therapy was labor intensive and expensive. First, it required a laboratory for identification of the bacteria afflicting the ill person. Next, a skilled technician needed to inoculate an animal (typically a horse or rabbit) with the bacteria, then harvest the resulting antibodies from the blood, which would then be injected into the child to help fight the infection. Additionally, the serum was highly perishable and often produced serious side effects, including fever, joint pain, rash, and even fatal allergic reactions.[22]

Because serum was administered subcutaneously, intravenously, or intraspinally (injected into the spine), it was an uncomfortable procedure. The treatment also posed challenges unique to the pediatric patient. Its administration almost certainly frightened young children who could not understand what was happening to them, which undoubtedly was upsetting to their parents as well. Moreover, infants and very young children who experienced an allergic reaction to serum could become critically ill much more rapidly than adults. Their smaller blood vessels also made serum administration more challenging than for adults.[23] Bliss and Long arranged for the child to receive Prontosil. Despite the fact that she was critically ill, within twelve hours of her first dose, the child's doctors and nurses reported excitedly that her fever had disappeared and she was improving. The *New York Times* noted the "triumph" in a feature story entitled "Conquering Streptococci."[24]

Bliss and Long next sought to try the drug on a different streptococcal infection, scarlet fever. Baltimore's Sydenham Hospital, a municipal infectious disease facility affiliated with Johns Hopkins, offered a ready supply of children suffering from the condition. According to physician trainee Elinor Fosdick Downs, Long arrived one day in late 1936, explaining to the young doctors that Sydenham's sickest youngsters with scarlet fever were to receive the Prontosil he carried with him in a small glass bottle, mixed in orange juice to disguise its taste. Children received the drug four times a day until the limited supply was exhausted. Everyone was "incredulous" when, "within a few hours," the youngsters' fevers disappeared. Five days later, children were "smiling" and well enough to go home.[25]

Research soon began using Prontosil's therapeutically active component, sulfanilamide. Prontosil's expense, set by its manufacturer, Germany's I.G. Farbenindustrie, led a number of investigators to create a new, more cost effective formulation. The first American pediatric trial of sulfanilamide occurred in a youngster with streptococcal meningitis, a bacterial infection of the membrane that protects the brain and spinal cord, at Sydenham Hospital.[26] Before serum therapy, almost all of the children with this type of meningitis at the Harriet Lane Home or Sydenham Hospital died. Through bedside trial and error, by the 1930s Sydenham doctors developed a serum treatment protocol they believed worked best. Children received repeated doses of serum both intravenously and intraspinally. Doctors regularly drew spinal fluid and continued serum injections until the fluid was free of bacteria. This approach lowered the mortality rate to about 30 percent. But serum was no panacea because children often suffered life threatening allergic reactions and treatment progressed slowly. Many of the youngsters who received serum for meningitis and survived subsequently developed hearing loss, brain damage, or other aftereffects of protracted infection.[27]

Because of meningitis's high fatality rate and serum therapy's side effects, Johns Hopkins and Sydenham pediatrician Francis F. Schwentker was ready to try sulfanilamide for meninigitis. Although the mortality rate had decreased using serum, one fatality for every three of his pediatric patients was too many. Another reason was that he was having difficulty procuring the same quality serum for Sydenham as was available at the Harriet Lane Home, possibly because Sydenham, as a public hospital, had less money to spend on the product. After obtaining a small supply of sulfanilamide from two chemical companies, DuPont and Winthrop, Schwentker readied a supply for testing in Sydenham children with meningitis.[28]

The first child with meningitis to receive sulfanilamide arrived at Sydenham Hospital on December 4, 1936, with a high fever, headache, and stiff neck, all suggestive of bacterial meningitis. Laboratory tests confirmed the deadly diagnosis: streptococcal meningitis. The child received serum, with no response. Death seemed imminent until she received sulfanilamide, at which point her doctors noted with amazement that she "showed rapid clinical improvement."[29] Not only did sulfanilamide have the potential to be more effective than serum, Schwentker concluded that it could be administered orally after an initial intraspinal, intravenous, or intramuscular injection. It had the added benefit of being much less expensive and less perishable than serum. The little girl returned home on Christmas Day, the first person ever to survive at Sydenham from streptococcal meningitis.[30]

Because 80 percent of Sydenham Hospital's patients were children, the institution provided a ready population of youngsters with bacterial infections on which to study the new class of drugs.[31] When, in February 1937, Schwentker presented his latest research to the Medical Society of Kings County, New York, he also reported on sulfanilamide therapy for meningitis patients infected with a different bacterium, the meningococcus. Meningococcal meningitis was even more fatal than streptococcal meningitis. Eleven Sydenham patients with meningococcal meningitis received treatment with sulfanil-amide. Only one patient, an adult African American male desperately ill on admission, died. The other ten, seven of whom were children, survived, much to the astonishment of the physicians.[32]

Notably, the records indicate that Schwentker and his colleagues were more concerned with distinctions among infectious organisms than with patients. They included more children in their research because these comprised the bulk of the hospital's population, and they did not privilege access to the sulfonamides according to race. This by no means implies that Sydenham offered equal access to black and white children. The historical record is clear: between 1909 and 1924 no African Americans were admitted to Sydenham, despite the fact that infant and child infectious disease mortality in Baltimore was much higher in black children than white during these years.[33] The institution maintained racial exclusion until it moved to a new and larger location in 1924. Physicians' interactions with one another document the normative racism that framed their clinical thinking. For example, on his return from a trip to study public health infrastructure in other Southern areas, physician and Sydenham superintendent Myron G. Tull explained to a colleague his surprise when he learned that every "colored" child in Jacksonville, Florida, had been immunized against diphtheria. Tull concluded that the success was because "the Negroes do what they are told in the south," not that the African American physicians and nurses overseeing the effort had done a better job than their white counterparts. But with regard to the early pediatric sulfonamide studies at Sydenham, there is no evidence that Schwentker and his colleagues used race as a criterion for receiving the drugs. Rather, they sought children of any race harboring the particular bacillus they were testing for response to sulfa drugs.[34]

Sulfanilamide quickly spread to other leading pediatric centers of care, and the results were similar to those at Sydenham. Physicians at Boston Children's Hospital, for example, praised sulfanilamide as a "remarkable substance," one that was clearly in a new category of therapeutic agent, since it was "neither a vaccine, nor a serum, but is a chemical drug."[35] Recognizing that they were practicing at a historically significant moment, one Children's Hospital pediatrician noted that sulfanilamide's "efficacy . . . has definitely changed the entire procedure which we were accustomed to use in the treatment of meningococcal meningitis. No longer is it necessary to subject children to repeated and painful lumbar puncture and to the injection of a foreign serum."[36]

But even as Schwentker and his colleagues in Boston marveled at sulfanilamide's curative potential, they, like their counterparts who treated adults, began documenting its troubling adverse reactions in some recipients: rash, fever, anemia, and kidney complications. Some side effects were dose-related, presenting a particular problem for the pediatric patient, since infants and children came in so many different sizes that estimating how much sulfanilamide to administer represented a challenge.[37] Nonetheless, they calculated that sulfanilamide's risks were worth taking because serum therapy's cure rate was so much less and its side effect profile was even greater.

The race was now on to decipher sulfanilamide's metabolism and excretion in children of different ages and sizes to determine dosing protocols. This effort also provided clues that there were important differences in the way infants and young children processed drugs relative to adults. In one of their earliest publications about sulfonamides, Long and Bliss observed with surprise that children with severe infections sometimes needed a higher proportional dose than adults to achieve the same serum concentration of the drug. Their observations suggested that dosing requirements for the sulfonamides were not necessarily linear according to children's size, a finding that would later have great clinical significance.[38] Sulfanilamide also provided a stark example of how using age or weight as the sole rubric for calculating children's dosages was profoundly inaccurate. This concern notwithstanding, Sydenham publicized its achievements with the new class of drugs now known as sulfonamides. As child after child survived after receiving sulfanilamide, the *Baltimore Sun* exulted about the victory over the "child-killing" bacteria and happily concluded that "Medical Science Conquers a Foe."[39]

While Schwentker, Bliss, Long, and Boston Children's Hospital doctors successfully employed Prontosil and then sulfanilamide on youngsters in 1936 and early 1937, those working on drug law reform on Capitol Hill grew increasingly frustrated. Opposition to Senator Copeland's bill to expand the FDA's powers kept it from progressing through the legislative process.[40] But in the fall of 1937 reports of more than one hundred fatalities from sulfanilamide treatment brought drug safety questions in the United States onto the pages of American newspapers. In one November article that spurred panic, for example, the *New York Times* proclaimed that a particular sulfanilamide brand was not a life saver, but rather a "Death Drug."[41] The crisis began because some adults, and almost all young children, had difficulty swallowing sulfanilamide in pill form. A sweet-tasting liquid formulation of the drug produced by the S. E. Massengill Company, called Elixir Sulfanilamide, seemed an ideal solution, especially for the pediatric patient. A Massengill pharmacist had discovered that diethylene glycol dissolved sulfanilamide, and the company rushed the drug into production and distribution. Because no one owned a proprietary stake in sulfanilamide, any company could manufacture its own version. Getting to market quickly and differentiating one's product from others was essential to making a profit. Massengill considered diethylene glycol's sweet taste a bonus, one that would make its addition to sulfanilamide more palatable for the pediatric patient.

Unfortunately, however, diethylene glycol was also a highly poisonous substance, analogous to antifreeze, that could cause severe kidney damage, agonizing pain, and death. Many of Elixir Sulfonilamide's 107 victims were children. As Daniel Carpenter and Gisela Sin have shown, the public face of the disaster became a white child, Joan Nidiffer.[42] The congressional report in response to the investigation of the Elixir Sulfanilamide disaster included a letter written to President Roosevelt from the girl's mother:

> Two months ago I was happy and working, taking care of my two little girls, Joan age 6 and Jean age 9. Our byword through the depresson was that we had good health and each other. . . . [Joan] was given the Elixir of Sulfanilamide. Tonight our little home is bleak and full of despair. All that is left us is the caring of that little grave. Even the memory of her is mixed with sorrow for we can see her little body tossing to and fro and hear that little voice screaming with pain. . . . [I]t is my plea that you will take steps to prevent such sales of drugs that will take little lives.[43]

The document included Mrs. Nidiffer's full letter to President Roosevelt, as well as a smiling picture of the little girl.[44]

The specter of children dying spurred new energy for legislative reform. Although the AMA was supportive, ultimately it was the FDA-mobilized advocacy of women's and consumer groups that made the difference. Working together under the umbrella organization the Women's Joint Congressional Committee, sixteen women's groups—including the National League of Women Voters, American Medical Women's Association, American Nurses Association, and National Congress of Parents and Teachers—joined FDA officials, sympathetic congressmen, and consumer organizations to mobilize public and congressional support for better drug laws. The resulting 1938 Federal Food, Drug, and Cosmetic Act amplified the FDA's mission and expanded its regulatory powers. Not only did the statute codify and formalize many FDA procedures that had evolved since 1906, it also mandated drug safety testing before the sale and marketing of any drug. Going forward, whenever manufacturers developed a new medication, they were mandated to submit "full reports of investigations which have been made to show whether or not such drug is safe for use."[45] Additionally, companies needed to provide clear information about drug dosing, administration, and other important recommendations regarding its use. The 1938 law also created a regulatory category known as "new drugs," meaning those that needed physician oversight. New drugs such as the sulfonamides required a physician prescription to be purchased. But neither the law nor its subsequent regulations provided clear guidance for how to determine a drug's category of prescription or nonprescription.[46]

With regard to children, Copeland's original bill addressed drug safety for youngsters specifically. The final approved bill did not include any child protection language for the new drug category, for reasons that remain unclear. Most likely reformers and policymakers believed that the broad language regarding safety included youngsters, so there was no need to mention them by name. It may not have seemed necessary because although the Elixir Sulfanilamide crisis involved a number of children, the problem was not dose-related (or even drug-related, since it was the additive, not the therapeutically active compound that caused the problem), nor did the event spotlight the unique challenges involved in determining pediatric drug safety. Moreover, when the law was finalized, sulfonamides had been in use for slightly over two years, and their therapeutic benefits were still unfolding. The notion that medications would be recommended regularly was just emerging, even among physicians.[47] And, as the Philadelphia Pediatric Society had noted years earlier, there was no stakeholder involvement in the policymaking or advisory process charged to represent children's drug-related interests, or to point out that the trial and error process for determining the best administration route, dose, and length of treatment was riskier and took much longer in children because they lacked adults' relative size uniformity.

## Sulfapyridine and the Pediatric Patient

With the 1938 law, the United States entered a new era in drug regulation. The FDA now needed to sanction a drug's safety before it could be sold, and efforts were underway to determine what kind of documentary evidence the agency needed to make those judgments. Three months after President Roosevelt signed the Federal Food, Drug, and Cosmetic Act, Merck and Company approached the FDA for permission to distribute its new sulfonamide, sulfapyridine, and the agency decided to use it to design the evaluation standard to which all new drug applications would be held.[48]

Sulfapyridine held particular promise for the treatment of a major pediatric killer, pneumonia, for two reasons. First, despite the success of sulfanilamide in killing some bacteria, that drug had a limited effect on the one that caused many pediatric pneumonias, the pneumococcus. Second, the serum therapy that had reduced pneumonia's morbidity and mortality in adults and older children by the 1930s was of limited value in infants and young children, for whom pneumonia was especially fatal. The disease was also a prime reminder of the fundamental ways, beyond size, in which infants and children differed from adults. Babies and young children often suffered from "mixed" pneumonias, meaning they harbored more than one bacterial subtype. As a result, they needed multiple types of sera, exponentially increasing the risk of an allergic reaction or other side effect. Given their small size, allergic reactions were more likely to result in a medical emergency or death.[49] Moreover, even identifying the microorganism when the patient was an infant or toddler posed a challenge because obtaining a sputum culture to confirm the causative bacteria required patient participation. Most adults could follow instructions to cough up a sample of sputum for laboratory testing, but young children could not. The most common method for obtaining sputum from young children, aspirating stomach contents in the morning before the youngster had eaten, was notoriously unreliable. For all these reasons, physicians were reluctant to employ serum therapy in infants and young children with pneumonia even as its use in adults grew, deeming the benefits "questionable."[50]

As a result, for infants and young children, pneumonia therapy remained what it had been in the 1910s and 1920s before serum therapy: ice caps and baths in an effort to reduce fever; steam heat to make breathing easier; and, if a child was unable to take fluid orally, hydration with subcutaneous or peritoneal fluid injections known as clysis. Where available, supplemental oxygen helped them breathe. The pharmacological remedies discussed in the pediatric medical literature through the 1930s addressed comfort rather than cure: codeine or phenobarbital for severe coughing, digitalis or whiskey for a weak or irregular pulse, opium-laced Dover's powder to promote rest and sweating, and regular enemas to manage the resulting constipation.[51]

Merck's new drug application to the FDA for sulfapyridine included data from Great Britain, where the drug had been developed, as well as its preliminary testing on animals. As part of its evaluation, the FDA sought to obtain more data from investigators who were using it in trials with their patients in the United States. Companies were allowed to distribute new drugs to researchers and clinical investigators for testing before their product received FDA approval in order to generate safety data. Among the early subjects who provided pediatric data were a number of very ill Sydenham children who received it under the oversight of Sydenham's new head pediatrician, Horace L. Hodes.[52] One of the first Sydenham youngsters to receive the drug was a thirteen-month-old African American infant admitted Christmas Eve 1938 with post-measles pneumonia. Her high fever and labored breathing made her situation a dire one. But within twelve hours of receiving "sulphpyridine," she "improved very rapidly. . . . [Her] temperature came down to normal and remained normal until discharge."[53] In case after case, children recovered dramatically. For example, another severely ill thirteen-month-old who received the drug could be found "sitting up in bed entirely well" a day after treatment with sulfapyridine.[54] An eighteen-month-old girl who had the added complication of an ear infection showed "rapid improvement" when she received the drug.[55] Another child, a nineteen-month-old boy who was febrile and short of breath on admission, showed a "prompt and striking recovery in less than twenty-four hours after sulfapyridine."[56]

Whereas no children with post-measles pneumonia survived at Sydenham before the mid-1930s, after the introduction of sulfapyridine almost half did, an "astonishing recovery rate," trumpeted the *Baltimore Sun*.[57] Such was sulfapyridine's success for Sydenham's pediatric patients with pneumococcal infections that Hodes and his colleagues subsequently declared that, although research was underway to develop a pneumonia vaccine, "infants and children respond so readily to treatment with sulfonamides that it does not seem advisable to attempt mass immunization of children against these organisms."[58] But like sulfanilamide, sulfapyridine provided clues that dosing metrics were not always proportionally based. Cincinnati Children's Hospital pediatricians Glenn E. Cullen and Armine T. Wilson noted with frustration, the variables relevant to dosing the pediatric patient were "not fully understood."[59] In other words, a child 10 percent the size of an adult did not necessarily need 10 percent of the dose relative to a full-grown person. Sometimes it was more, other times less. Cullen and Wilson observed that Perrin Long's recommended dosing rubric, tracking serum levels, was risky for the pediatric patient because of the drug's narrow safety margin: "[W]e realize that it is necessary to have some program for determining the preliminary dosage for patients of various ages and sizes."[60]

Sulfapyridine received national attention as its use became more widespread in the United States, raising hopes that bacterial pneumonia was headed for extinction. The *Los Angeles Times*, for example, ran a story in 1939 proclaiming "Pneumonia, America's No. 1 Killer, Declared Conquered," and quoting Harvard pediatrician Charles F. McKhann: "The medical profession has whipped pneumonia."[61] The media celebrated this vital breakthrough in the treatment of infectious diseases in the popular science literature, news journals, and newspapers. An article in the *New York Times* in 1941 announced "Sulfa Drug Saves Baby," concluding with a quote from the attending physician that it was "the first time in his knowledge that the 'miracle' drug had been used on a newborn child."[62]

The paucity of surviving evidence makes it difficult to get a sense of how sulfonamides may have changed the experience of sick children or their parents at Sydenham or elsewhere. It is reasonable to assume that parents rejoiced at improving survival rates, and youngsters appreciated receiving the drug orally, unlike serum's intraspinal or intravenous route. But unintended consequences followed both sulfanilamide's and sulfapyridine's introduction at Sydenham. The institution needed to scramble to quickly build a modern laboratory on site, because doctors needed ready access to one so that patients' bacteria could be identified and urine and blood samples could be monitored for drug side effects. Additionally, the drugs heightened Sydenham's already acute nurse staffing problem. While some children improved immediately after receiving a sulfa drug, others remained ill for long periods of time or developed complications from the infection or medication-related side effects. Often these problems required oxygen, intravenous fluid, or mechanical ventilation and intensive medical and nursing monitoring. Within a few years, Hodes lamented that these factors were driving up Sydenham's costs exponentially. They also played a major role in completing the transformation of the children's ward or hospital from a homelike environment to a medicalized, technologically driven space.[63]

Despite the 1938 law, it soon became clear that children remained especially vulnerable to drug-related problems. For example, in March 1941 the Massachusetts Department of Public Health contacted the Boston FDA office with ominous news. A three-year-old girl had slipped into a coma after receiving the newest sulfonamide, sulfathiazole. An investigation revealed that the machine that compressed sulfathiazole powder into pill form sat next to one for a potent sedative, luminal, and the medications had become mixed.[64] Despite this tragedy, however, the sulfonamides dramatically changed the therapeutic landscape for both children and adults. Over the course of the next few years, drug companies made capital investments, building laboratories and hiring chemists and researchers to develop and test new sulfa drugs. As a result, dozens of new sulfonamides poured into the market. One after another they were tested in Sydenham's youngsters in the early 1940s.[65]

## Penicillin

Penicillin's discovery is one of the most widely known medical history narratives of the past century. Scottish biologist Alexander Fleming's 1928 observation that no bacteria could grow in the vicinity of *Penicillium notatum* mold in culture intrigued scientists. But the substance did not yield therapeutic results until 1940, when Oxford scientists Howard Florey and Ernst Chain described its chemical structure, prepared an extract, and successfully treated mice they had infected with streptococci.[66] Just after America entered World War II, the congressionally chartered scientific advisory group, the National Research Council, established the Committee on Chemotherapeutic and Other Agents (COC) to allocate the small amount of penicillin available for civilian use. The equipment, commercial techniques, and other infrastructure necessary to generate penicillin in large amounds did not yet exist.[67] Perrin Long served as COC chair for a short time before accepting a commission in the U.S. Army Medical Corps; the role then went to a former Johns Hopkins Hospital trainee, Massachusetts Memorial Hospital's Chester S. Keefer, who became known as the nation's penicillin "czar."[68]

The first pediatric patient to receive penicillin in the United States was a child at the University of Minnesota Medical Center. By July 1, 1942, Merck and Squibb had produced enough penicillin for human trial. A few days later,

University of Minnesota infectious disease physician Wesley W. Spink admitted a seven-year-old girl suffering from an overwhelming staphylococcal infection of the blood, lungs, and bone. When she did not respond to sulfonamide therapy, Spink wired Merck and, with Keefer's permission, soon received a small supply of penicillin via airmail. Spink's access likely came quickly because he was one of Keefer's former students, but the child in question benefited because the COC was especially interested in staphylococcal infection, which was responsible for a high percentage of soldiers' wound infections.[69]

By the time the penicillin arrived, the little girl's condition was grave. She was convulsing, cyanotic, and disoriented with a fever of almost 106 degrees Fahrenheit. Although Perrin Long had recommended, based on his animal research, that children receive 5,000 units of penicillin every four hours intravenously, Spink instinctively doubled the dosage because the child was so ill. Within a few hours, he was amazed to report that the child seemed to feel and look better and was even asking for food. The next day an astonished Spink reported that his patient sat up in bed and played with paper dolls. But in the days that followed, Spink struggled to understand whether the child's subsequent course of jaundice, nosebleeds, swollen liver, and other symptoms was related to the penicillin dosage he administered or her infection. When he sent his report to Keefer a few weeks later, Spink emphasized that administering penicillin intravenously to a child was significantly more complicated than for an adult. In his response, Keefer readily agreed that it represented a "very great" problem.[70] Two weeks after Spink's patient began therapy in Minneapolis, a second child, this one a four-year-old white male at the Johns Hopkins Hospital's Harriett Lane Home, received penicillin. Doctors had diagnosed this little boy with a sulfonamide-resistant pneumococcal infection and an empyema, a collection of pus in his pleural cavity. Perrin Long himself sat at the child's bedside and oversaw the case. After several days of empirically titrating the child's dose according to his clinical response, trying different routes of administration, he reported that the child was "convalescing nicely" and was discharged a few weeks later, his doctors marveling that he was "much improved."[71]

The success of penicillin treatment for these and other patients spurred a race to generate as much penicillin as quickly as possible. But the shortage continued until drug companies could fully industrialize production and increase manufacturing capacity—and the war ended, removing the urgent need to treat soldiers' wounds. One Harvard pediatrician, Thomas Cone, later recalled that when his infant daughter developed a severe ear infection, he used his connections to acquire experimental penicillin through the military distribution channels. But the substance was so precious that he resorted to reusing what he gave her by collecting her urine. "Whatever was not absorbed would come out in the urine and we would use that again, it was so rare."[72] In 1943 Keefer distributed the drug to twenty-two of the best-known infectious disease researchers in the United States.[73] Civilians infected with a bacterial type often seen in soldiers remained the highest priority. Children received a disproportionate share of the civilian stock of penicillin, but not necessarily due to their privileged status as vulnerable, innocent, and deserving candidates. Researchers quickly realized the advantages of testing on children—more subjects could be enrolled in trials since lower doses were required. In this case, it was the drug that was especially precious, rather than its young recipients.[74]

Although penicillin was more effective than the sulfonamides for some bacteria, much less was known about how it was metabolized and its toxicity. In 1943 alone in the United States, almost six hundred scientific papers about sulfonamides' physiological action were published in the medical literature. Clinicians possessed a more robust knowledge base for the sulfonamides upon which to base pediatric dosing and understand adverse reactions and toxicity, benchmarks that had yet to be identified for penicillin.[75] One confusing difference between the two drugs was that penicillin was metabolized and excreted quickly, making it difficult to maintain constant concentrations in the blood, a therapeutic goal with sulfonamides. It would take years of research to ascertain that the consistent blood levels necessary to see a response from the sulfonamides (which were bacteriostatic compounds that inhibited the growth of new bacteria) were less important when treating with penicillin, a bacteriocidal drug (agent that destroyed bacteria). For penicillin, relatively infrequent peak blood levels sufficed, meaning that the drug needed to be administered only several times in a twenty-four-hour period.[76]

Penicillin's early formulations could also not be administered orally, a major setback to those who had been excited about this benefit of sulfonamide over serum therapy.[77] Thus children who received it required more intensive nursing care, as leading pediatric nurse Stella Goostray noted in her 1945 administrative report for the Boston Children's Hospital's nursing service. "The use of penicillin with its frequent administration by hypodermic is a striking example of a time-consuming treatment which is required in the Hospital today," she wrote. "To give the amount and quality of nursing care necessary will mean a material increase in staff nurses."[78]

Finally, abandoning sulfonamide therapy to try this new agent on critically ill children seemed risky to some. By 1943, for example, sulfonamides had reduced mortality from meningococcal meningitis at Sydenham to less than 8 percent.[79] Replacing a useful drug with one that might be more efficacious but about which less was known was a high-stakes problem. Physicians needed to consider whether to use established therapy or to test unproven but potentially more beneficial treatments in ill children, and nurses needed to adapt technology to figure out how to get the drugs into youngsters.[80] This challenge notwithstanding, it was clear that the sulfonamides and penicillin had changed American childhood and parenting within a few short years. As World War II ended, American children stood a better chance of surviving once-fatal infections than they ever had before.

# 3

# The Child as Drug Development Problem and Business Opportunity in a New Era, 1945–1961

• • • • • • • • • • • • • • • • • • • • • •

As servicemen returned home from World War II, they married and started families in unprecedentedly large numbers, beginning what became known as the baby boom. The benefits of two generations of improved nutrition such as milk pasteurization and public health measures as well as antibacterial and antibiotic drugs redefined maternal and infant mortality as an unusual tragedy for most families, especially those in the growing middle class, rather than as a lamentable but commonplace occurrence.[1] As a result, the influential architect of early postwar science policy in the United States, Vannevar Bush, observed that science (and funding) was moving on to new problems: "This reduction in the death rate in childhood has shifted the emphasis in medicine to the middle- and old-age groups, and particularly to the malignant diseases and the degenerative processes which are prominent in the later decades of life."[2]

But the American Academy of Pediatrics (AAP) leaders believed that children needed much more from their doctors and nurses than infectious disease prevention. While well child care for poor children remained spotty or even nonexistent, by the end of World War II, pediatricians had convinced middle-class Americans that even healthy children needed regular medical check-ups to monitor their growth, administer immunizations, and identify and manage problems early. When ill, their treatment could be subsidized by the growing number of employer-based insurance programs. A major infusion of federal dollars for hospital construction through the Hill-Burton Act also meant that pediatric illness care would be more hospital-based than ever before.[3]

Only in hospitals, pediatricians argued, could children receive round-the-clock access to the sophisticated medical and nursing care they often required. Because of antibiotics and better pediatric fluid and electrolyte management, many youngsters who contracted acute bacterial infections such as pneumonia could now be cured. Those with chronic conditions such as cystic fibrosis or sickle cell anemia could survive the infections that often accompanied the disease. Corrective surgery for congenital anomalies was less risky with antibiotics to treat postoperative infections. As a result, drug therapy was increasingly central to the therapeutic management of the sick child. Katharine F. Lenroot, head of the Children's Bureau, acknowledged these advancements in 1950, when she extolled the "valuable tools" in the pediatrician's armament including the sulfonamides and penicillin. Furthermore, diagnostic technologies and drugs could work in synergy with one another: Lenroot argued that the electroencephalograph, a diagnostic tool that helped diagnose epilepsy, should be celebrated primarily because it facilitated the development of "new drugs for its control."[4]

But for the increasingly complex, more corporatized drug companies, funding pediatric research was not nearly as profitable as identifying new drugs targeted for use in the adult population, such as antihypertensives. Even though the number of children in the United States was growing as a result of the baby boom, the percentage who might be prescribed drugs was small relative to adults. This mattered because drug development had grown more expensive as a result of the 1938 Federal Food, Drug, and Cosmetic Act, which required companies to present safety data demonstrating the drug's safety in order to receive approval.[5]

The AMA Council on Pharmacy and Chemistry published the FDA's requirements for new drug applications in its journal, the *Journal of the American Medical Association* (*JAMA*), so that industry and academic investigators had a sense of the evidentiary criteria the FDA sought. The guidelines emphasized the collection of animal and other laboratory data about mechanisms of action, toxicity, and other variables as preliminary steps. They also noted the importance of "establish[ing] the effective dosage range for different age groups," but said nothing about how investigators might accomplish that outcome. Should pediatric data, for example, accompany the new drug application or should pediatric dosing and pharmacodynamics data be based on clinical observations and reported to the FDA after the drug's approval? Congress had been silent about this point in the law.[6]

No recorded discussions about amending the 1938 law to address the specific issue of pediatric drug safety exist in the public record. Why is unclear, but it may have been because Americans remained deeply ambivalent about what many saw as too much governmental intrusion into private life, and children's issues and health care were no exceptions. While the 1930 Children's Charter outlined a manifesto of rights for American children, it was vague on whether its ambitious goals would be met with public funds, private dollars, or a combination of the two. The class-based approach to children's health meant that some very poor or disabled children qualified for certain health care programs under the Social Security Act, and middle-class youngsters were increasingly covered through their parents' employer-based programs. But access to health care for all youngsters remained spotty, especially for poor children, who were disproportionately African American, Native American, or Hispanic. Two ambitious pieces of legislation during the Truman administration—the National Child Research Act, which would have funded developmental research, and the Children's Act of 1949, a health insurance bill that would have covered all children—failed to pass in Congress in part because reformers believed their needs could better be met by broader laws that benefited all Americans.[7]

Although neither law would have funded pediatric drug development or related research, both bills were a step toward a national policy for child well-being. Both recognized children's unique health and medical needs, and they might have provided a future model for such a policy. Instead, systematic considerations for how to obtain the general information regarding dosing, metabolism, excretion, and other measures for the pediatric patient remained unaddressed. While the federal government in the early postwar era was heavily involved in funding for more hospital beds for children, financing for pediatric medical education, and targeted investments into specific pediatric diseases, it did not take a primary role in drug-related research for either children or adults. This responsibility lay within the purview of the private sector, which responded to any suggestion that government become more directly involved in the development of therapeutics with claims that such control augured the beginning of socialized medicine, a contentious charge in an increasingly heated Cold War context.[8]

## Attempts to Develop Systematized Pediatric Drug Knowledge

Consequently, physicians who treated children faced the enduring challenge of how best to approximate pediatric doses, even as the postwar explosion of research continued to document the many physiologic differences between children and adults, and, increasingly, between children of different ages. As new drugs poured onto the market over the the next decade, millions of children began to receive them. But the FDA had no explicit statutory authority to regulate dosage standards, formulation issues, or administration practices as part of the approval process in order to make sure drugs were safe for children.

With the pediatric patient in mind, FDA officials Robert Stormont, chief of the FDA drug division, and medical officer Irvin Kerlan approached the AAP in 1947. The agency had already contacted the organization once before, in 1944, when representatives asked AAP president-elect Joseph A. Wall for assistance with proper pediatric dosing recommendations for several drugs. That effort had not progressed beyond a discussion. This time Stormont and Kerlan flew to AAP headquarters in the Chicago suburb of Elk Grove Village, Illinois, to speak to the executive board.

They asked the AAP to help the agency in two ways: to provide expert advice on Federal Trade Commission (FTC)-related prosecutorial matters and to "undertake studies" on drugs being used in children.[9] Companies that misbranded their products by recommending a drug for children's use without providing warnings and directions violated the law, and the agency needed pediatric experts to provide testimony in court. It also needed pediatricians to provide scientific evidence to help evaluate pediatric labeling provisions for new drug applications because manufacturers were not required to submit pediatric safety data. In their attempt to convince the board that this assistance should be a priority for the AAP, Stormont and Kerlan lamented the fact that the FDA did not have enough scientific information to recommend a dosage range for penicillin in children, despite the fact that the medication was already widely prescribed for millions of them throughout the United States.[10]

Acknowledging that the FDA lacked "scientific people in the field of pediatrics on our staff," Kerlan outlined the problem for the executive board: "[I]f we obtain a new drug for which recommendations are made for use in children and for which an actual dose schedule has been provided, we want to know whether that is safe for children. . . . Manufacturers . . . should provide actual directions for use and warnings against misuse. . . . Warnings must be provided for use in children."[11] Stormont and Kerlan also suggested that it might be in the AAP's interest to partner with the FDA, pointedly remarking that several drugs and devices in which FDA laboratories had found safety-related problems had been openly advertised in booths at the 1945 AAP convention as well as the organization's *Journal of Pediatrics*.

With the mention of drug advertising, Kerlan and Stormont had, intentionally or unintentionally, exposed an issue about which the board and the journal editors were clearly not in full agreement. George F. Munns, board member and professor of pediatrics at the Mayo Clinic, detailed his worries about pharmaceutical advertising in the *Journal of Pediatrics*: "Many of [the drugs being advertised] are still in the experimental stage. There will be a paper about the use of a certain remedy with a favorable report, and the next thing we know the company that is sponsoring the piece of work is advertising in the advertising section of the *Journal*."[12] The ensuing discussion exposed the tensions within the group regarding the way in which advertising decisions

should be made in the *Journal*. It also highlighted the fact that medical journals had interests beyond science: the revenue generated by advertising played
an important role in the journals' financial viability.

Having made his point, Kerlan now steered the discussion to the concrete
assistance the FDA sought. The FDA wanted advice and, if necessary, expert
testimony on specific instances. In the past, the FDA had been hard-pressed to
find pediatricians who would consult for the agency because, for physicians in
private practice, time not spent with a patient was lost income. Citing a specific case, Kerlan pleaded with the board:

> [I]n that particular instance we had four or five men lined up, and each man in
> testimony would not contribute more than a half hour. The products must be
> scientifically sound to be approved by the Food and Drug Administration. We
> feel that the only people who can give us information in the field of pediatrics
> are the pediatricians. . . . We want some cooperative organization, like the Acad-
> emy, to come and say what the feeling of the Academy is and to go on record for
> or against products.[13]

The board, disappointed that Stormont and Kerlan offered no financing to
help the organization develop a meaningful consultative role, deliberated the
financial implications of partnering with the FDA. Just as they had when
the AAP first approached the AMA about pediatric representation at the USP
in the 1930s, scientific issues collided with organizational politics. In the postwar era, the AAP goals were very ambitious, focused heavily on enhancing the
pediatric curriculum across all medical schools and increasing the number of
pediatricians in the United States. In 1949 more than 80 percent of American
children still received their medical care from general practitioners, half of
whom had never received training in the care of hospitalized children. Only
2,600 board-certified pediatricians practiced in the United States, and two-
thirds of them were located in Massachusetts, New York, or Pennsylvania.
Although the AAP convinced policymakers of the need for public investment in pediatric medical education, children did not receive a larger share
of federal dollars. Rather, funds were largely redirected from the Children's
Bureau.[14]

Although the board expressed ambivalence regarding Stormont and Kerlan's request, members did agree to help and immediately created the Committee to Cooperate with the FDA, placing eminent pediatrician Waldo E.
Nelson in charge.[15] Unfortunately, the partnership was unsuccessful: the
records indicate the group convened only a few times. Another effort to
improve drug dosage knowledge began in 1950, when influential pediatrician Harold K. Faber, in a letter to the AAP executive board, explained that
the lack of meaningful data concerning dosage, particularly in infants, was

no longer tenable. The resulting Committee on Drug Dosage spent much of its time surveying pediatricians about how they used specific drugs in their practices. After publishing a few features in pediatric journals, the committee either disbanded or stopped keeping any formal records.[16]

## The Growing Pediatric Antibiotic Market

In 1949, drug companies began introducing a new class of drugs known as broad spectrum antibiotics, so named because they attacked a number of bacteria. A number of broad spectrum antibiotics came onto the market in rapid succession: Parke-Davis introduced the first one, Chloramphenicol (chloromycetin), in 1949, followed quickly by Lederle's Aureomycin (chlortetracycline). A few months later, in 1950, Pfizer made Terramycin (oxytetracycline) available, and in 1953 Lederle started advertising Achromycin (tetracycline). These drugs represented a major therapeutic advance because, first of all, they attacked a wider range of microorganisms than did penicillin and the sulfonamides alone. The broad spectrum antibiotics saved time, money, and lives by increasing the likelihood that the drug would kill the bacteria making the person ill.[17]

Additionally, the broad spectrum antibiotics generated profits for drug companies. Previously, any company could create its own formulation of the active compound that served as the basis for both the sulfonamides and penicillin because they had not been patent protected. But because the broad spectrum antibiotics were proprietary—owned by the companies that had funded their creation, either in their own labs or in those of academic scientists whom they had supported—they produced profits on a scale not seen in the past. The introduction of broad spectrum antibiotics ignited an explosion in competition and advertising to doctors. And in order to make sure a busy physician heard about the latest one and its advantages, companies hired more "detail men" (sales representatives) to educate doctors about their drug and provide free samples to them. Given the increasingly crowded antibiotic marketplace and the growing number of children in the United States, companies set out to compete with one another to develop liquid formulations that tasted good to children and were easier to swallow than pills.[18]

The broad spectrum antibiotics arrived at a propitious moment in the history of American childhood, when children's emotional and developmental needs received unprecedented scientific and political attention. The tremendous reductions in infant and child mortality, accompanied by a growing number of immunizations and antibiotics to prevent and treat infectious diseases, had given Americans the luxury of focusing on other dimensions of child well-being. A discussion of child cognition and related issues became the central topic of the 1950 White House Conference on Children. The 60,000 individuals in attendance debated the variables needed for America to provide "For Every Child a Healthy Personality." This theme of the conference—the importance of developing the American child's unique personality and maximizing the potential to create his or her own destiny—and a focus on nurturing emotional and social development, stood in stark contrast during the early Cold War period to characterizations of Soviet youngsters growing up in an oppressive nation in which they had little opportunity for individual growth.[19]

*The Common Sense Book of Baby and Child Care* by pediatrician Benjamin Spock added to this rhetoric, as he urged parents to move away from the rigidity and harsh discipline recommended in earlier eras and replace them with a more nurturing approach. Nurses and physicians, too, drew on the work of developmental theorists such as Erik Erikson and Jean Piaget in the planning and delivery of their care.[20] No longer was it enough for clinicians merely to treat a child's physical condition; by the 1950s creating a nursing or medical plan of care that took into account, for example, the security needs of an infant and the fear of pain in a preschooler was important. Since a foul-tasting medication might cause unnecessary distress to a very young child, the company that created one children favored stood to be amply rewarded financially. Flavored medication captured both the cultural and economic moment perfectly. One humorous example of how seriously companies took the issue of palatability in children can be seen in Eli Lilly and Company's 1953 marketing program, in which its "Juvenile Board of Judges" weighs in on medication flavoring.[21]

Originated by the company's product development team, the initiative's purpose was to "Let the kids decide for themselves what flavor they like" by "giving them a taste of their own medicine." For example, when formulating the combination penicillin and sulfonamide drug Sulfa-Neolin (benzethiacil with sulfonamide) the company wanted to know whether children preferred "chocolate-mint, butterscotch, or custard" flavored medicine. Employees' children as well as those drawn from a local school and hospital were solicited for the jury and the company was careful to obtain parental consent before beginning the testing. A registered nurse administered the various samples and the Eli Lilly product development team assessed children's responses carefully. While the youngsters liked the taste of custard, chocolate-mint concealed the medication's aftertaste. As a result, the product came to market with the two flavors combined. Youngsters also had strong opinions about color, texture, and odor, all of which the company measured.[22]

Drugs joined a growing number of products marketed for children as the baby boom continued and as family income rose in the postwar economic expansion in the United States. Trade magazines such as *Advertising Age* and *Business Week* now regularly reminded their corporate readers that "Babies Mean Business," and that those rapidly expanding ranks could bring

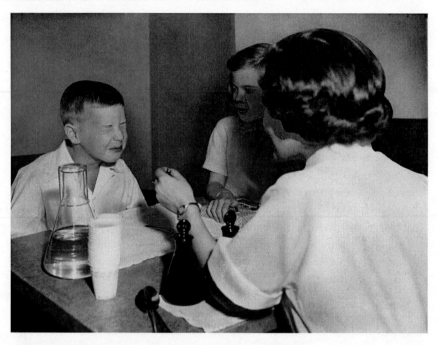

FIGURE 2   Eli Lilly & Company Juvenile Board of Flavor Judges, 1953.
(*Credit*: © Copyright Eli Lilly and Company. All Rights Reserved. Courtesy of Eli Lilly &
Company Archives.)

companies "Two Million New Customers a Year."[23] In addition to enhancing
profits, a focus on children's needs also served another purpose for the drug
industry. A pediatric formulation could be used as evidence of a company's
beneficence toward children. During a Capitol Hill hearing on pharmaceutical industry practices, for example, Philip I. Bowman, president of Bristol
Laboratories (a division of Bristol Myers), defended the company's intensive
research in developing its own version of a drug already available, marketing it
heavily, and setting the price to garner a profit by arguing that the company's
actions "benefit[ed] the public." In his testimony, Bowman recounted Bristol's
motivations in the early 1950s as child-focused: "Take, for instance, a good-
tasting pediatric suspension. Now, probably all of you at one time or another
have had the problem of getting medication into children. . . . We were able
to make an oral suspension that was relatively good-tasting, and I know that
with our children, and with the children of many of our friends, we found that
the problems of getting the medication down were solved with this product."[24]
Although adults did not enjoy bitter-tasting medication, the issue of palatability was much more important for young children. The research and marketing efforts of drug companies to address flavor illustrate the indirect power of

children as well as the kind of financial investment they were willing to make when they believed doing so would pay off financially.

In 1950, Pfizer microbiologist Gladys Hobby partnered with famed Harvard Medical School and Boston City Hospital antibiotic researcher Maxwell Finland. Their goal was to develop a pleasant tasting pediatric formulation for the broad spectrum antibiotic Terramycin. Explaining that "We are anxious to move these pediatric dosage forms in the near future in view of the fact that we are obtaining many requests for them," Hobby sent Finland ten vials of cherry mint-flavored diluent along with the antibiotic for use in Finland's pediatric patients.[25]

Although Hobby sought data regarding the drug's ability to kill bacteria, she stressed that she also wanted to know whether children thought the product tasted good. When Finland reported that, not only was it easier to get young children to swallow the syrupy liquid than a capsule, but they also liked it, Hobby wrote back within twenty-four hours, letting him know she would send a large shipment to him for further testing. The competitive nature of the broad spectrum antibiotic market is clear in the letter: Hobby reminded Finland—for the second time in several weeks—that the company desired a pediatric formulation "as promptly as possible."[26] And she wanted enough information to satisfy the FDA, which was clearly trying to track pediatric data. "The FDA has asked us to give them data concerning its tolerability for children and some information concerning its therapeutic efficacy," she explained.[27] But this pressure from the FDA came after the drugs had been approved; they were not premarket mandates, so companies were not required to submit such data along with their new drug application.

Within a few days, Finland wrote that four children with pertussis had received the flavored Terramycin in doses his laboratory had calculated would be enough to kill bacilli. He reported that the dosage range he used had produced no side effects and that "clinically children showed gradual improvement as they had with other types of Terramycin."[28] But generating a sound pediatric dosing metric remained a challenge even for one of the nation's leading antibiotic researchers. A few months after Finland sent Hobby his recommendations for pediatric dosing, Ray A. Patelski, coordinator of clinical investigation for Pfizer, informed Finland that the company had doubts about the accuracy of his dosing instructions: "Judged by the rash of letters that we have received from practicing physicians in various parts of the country, our recommended dosage schedules for Terramycin for infants and children under 20 kg in weight appear to be higher than necessary."[29]

Companies quickly realized the pediatric broad spectrum antibiotic market was financially significant enough to warrant a close watch on FDA activities that might influence sales. For example, when the FDA asked the AMA and the AAP in 1954 whether the labels on drugs should include specific directions for use by children under six years, the influential drug industry newsletter *F-D-C Reports* characterized the request as "bearish" and noted it on page 1, under the anxious title "Children's Medication Products Face Imminent Danger."[30]

By the middle of the 1950s, antibiotic makers considered pediatric formulation essential in order to offer a full product line to doctors, pharmacies, and hospitals. For example, in March 1955 Pfizer sales representative Robert Bittner summarized for his supervisor, H. R. Stewart, the data he had gathered and scrutinized from two pharmacies in Knoxville, Tennessee. It is "very obvious the physician prefers ready-mix pediatric broad spectrum antibiotics" because they are the "favorite" with pediatricians. "I sincerely hope that Pfizer will have a ready-mix oral suspension for us in the very near future," he concluded.[31] Another memorandum, this one from the Pittsburgh sales representative, Howard J. Taylor, argued that it was hard for Pfizer to increase market share for specific antibiotics without a pediatric formulation. As a result of its cherry-flavored suspension, Taylor warned, Lederle was "taking over the broad spectrum market" with the "hottest prescription" drug in the United States, Achromycin. He recommended strongly that "our number-one job" should be to develop a "comparable product to compete" with Achromycin.[32] And Lederle representatives followed Pfizer's efforts just as closely. Internal Lederle correspondence in 1951 referenced a popular comic strip that had run in at least one newspaper in the South. The cartoon featured a nineteenth-century medicine show traveling west on horseback, stopping to receive an inquiry from a stereotypically depicted Native American mother seeking help for her infant's cough. The "medicine man" is shown recommending Terramycin over Lederle's product. Lederle representatives were clearly concerned by the way Terramycin had penetrated popular culture and the free marketing benefiting Pfizer.[33]

The impact of pediatric formulations on sales appeared at times to astound even companies' own salesmen. According to one Lederle field report, a sore throat and fever "epidemic" in Detroit, Michigan, resulted in "remarkable sales" in Achromycin syrup in the region, a particular feat since the city's most influential pediatricians often received drugs free of charge.[34] In addition to its concerns about Pfizer, Lederle also worried about competition from Squibb, which soon had its own pediatric broad spectrum antibiotic available. The 1956 "Dear Doctor" marketing letter that accompanied Squibb's tetracycline formulation stressed its use in children, spotlighting that the medication was "liquid and so palatable, it is readily suited to your young patients."[35]

Although drug companies were prohibited from advertising their prescription products directly to the public, they were allowed to promote their company's contributions to postwar American society in a general way. As a result, by the 1950s, almost every issue of family-oriented magazines such as the *Saturday Evening Post*, *Life*, and *Parents* carried messages from major pharmaceutical companies such as Parke Davis, Ciba, Lederle, and Eli Lilly, attesting to the ways in which the pharmaceutical revolution in general, and their particular company specifically, had benefited Americans. The advertisements frequently included children, who made good advertising copy. For example, many issues of *Parents* magazine in the years between 1945 and 1960 carried promotions by major pharmaceutical houses featuring a healthy child. A list of the drugs made by a particular company and the ways in which the agents had improved Americans' health adjoined the photograph. Although the ads did not suggest that parents request the products for themselves or their children, the message that drug companies' efforts saved children's lives was clear.[36] They also celebrated white middle-class suburban life and the nuclear family, tapping into cultural anxieties about the growing complexity of raising a healthy child in the postwar era. While subtly reminding parents of the dangers that had befallen American children before the pharmaceutical industry had brought them vaccines and antibiotics, they celebrated American capitalism and the ways it kept children safe.[37]

A *Life* magazine advertisement in March 1956, for example, featured relaxed mothers at a children's birthday party. When one mother complained about her child's health care costs, the other admonished, "Oh, but actually, sickness costs *less* today—and many more children get well," followed by text that highlighted the the example of a child suffering a chronic ear infection that could inflame the nearby mastoid bone in the skull. The advertisement noted that before antibiotics, surgeons could sometimes drain the infection and save the child's life, often at the cost of the youngster's hearing. But "nowadays" the child could be cured with "potent new medicines" as an outpatient, "represent[ing] one of the really extraordinary bargains of your life."[38] Annual reports and other materials companies sent to shareholders also heavily emphasized drugs' pediatric benefits.[39]

Some concerned pediatricians did seek to monitor manufacturers' promotional statements to parents. Allan M. Butler, professor of pediatrics at Harvard's medical school and senior doctor at Boston Children's Hospital, helped found the National Council on Infant and Child Care in 1956. Ostensibly, the council's purpose was to approve any advertising to parents in lay periodicals, virtually offering a stamp of approval from the leading pediatricians who constituted the group. But its goals were also protectionist for the medical profession, reminding advertisers that specific suggestions with regard to child-rearing, nutrition, or health "should remain the responsibility of the physician. Promotion influencing the parent to assume these responsibilities or creating concern regarding the physician's recommendations is not acceptable."[40]

## An Increasingly Vocal Actor in Therapeutic Decision Making: Middle-Class Parents

Almost as soon as the public could obtain antibiotics, physicians began to worry about how they might change medical practice. In 1945, for example, physician Leslie A. Falk expressed concern that the availability of an inexpensive and widely available "magic" therapy like penicillin might result in sloppy medical care, less careful history taking on the part of physicians, or over-prescription of the new drug.[41] And what if bacteria developed a way to fight off the medicine? The latter fear, at least, was not unfounded, since the first reports of drug resistance came directly on the heels of the sulfonamides' and penicillin's success.[42] By far the most prevalent fear of many pediatricians was the potential for overuse. The popularity and palatability of broad spectrum antibiotics made parents demand them, sometimes aggressively. Former AAP president Isaac Abt had issued one of the first warnings that the balance of power between mother and physician was shifting, observing in 1944: "[T]he mother of long ago was, in general, easier to work with than the mother of today. Although she was often garrulous, she was quick to observe deviations from the normal and report them exactly, permitting the doctor to interpret the facts. She said 'baby sniffles every night and has a rattle in his throat.' The modern mother, on the contrary, is inclined to make her own diagnosis."[43] At the 1948 Annual Meeting of the Medical Society of the State of New York, physician John Craig also complained about this new type of mother to his colleagues, "Any number of times a mother has told me that after a moderate fever her child has been cured by two doses of sulfa. This, of course, is not true."[44]

Physicians were right to be worried about the potential overuse of antibiotics. So commonly did doctors prescribe penicillin by 1950 that, as one physician reported, American children created a playful chant:

Mother, Mother I am ill!
Call the doctor from over the hill!
In came the doctor, in came the nurse,
In came the lady with the alligator purse.
Penicillin, said the doctor,
Penicillin, said the nurse,
Penicillin, said the lady with the alligator purse![45]

Managing parents who "demanded" antibiotics and were "responsible to a large degree for the indiscriminate use of antibiotics," as one pediatric researcher, Hattie Alexander, characterized it, became a challenge.[46] Startled by the growing assertiveness of parents during the health care encounter, one doctor sent his own annoyance through the media. Professor of pediatrics at Yale School of Medicine Milton J. E. Senn, writing in *Woman's Home Companion* in 1953, devoted an entire monthly column to educating parents about their place. His title, "It's the Doctor's Job: Let Him Do It," admonished parents not to overstep their bounds. In great detail Senn scolded that "too often parents label a doctor old-fashioned if he doesn't administer the drugs for even mild illness" and "pressure him" to do so.[47]

One emboldened, more knowledgeable mother reportedly even helped shape the use of the laboratory in her city. Pediatrician Milton Markowitz recollected one home visit he made in Baltimore in 1951 or 1952 when he diagnosed strep throat in a youngster. As he prepared a penicillin injection, the mother startled him by asking, "Wait, aren't you going to do a throat culture?"[48] Markowitz explained to the mother that this would delay treatment since it required sending a swab from the child's throat to a hospital laboratory. The mother was unimpressed with this information, having "just moved from Rochester, New York, where her pediatrician . . . did his own throat cultures."[49] Markowitz called the upstate New York pediatrician, who gave instructions on how to build his own incubator, and he did so. Thus, according to Markowitz, plating and growing samples in a private practice outpatient setting "spread through the city and beyond."[50]

## The USP Tries to Bring Order to Pediatric Drugs

As steroids and antihistamines joined broad spectrum antibiotics in the late 1940s and early 1950s, the standard-setting body for drug strength and purity in the United States, the United States Pharmacopeia (USP), turned its attention to children. In an undated memo from this era, Lloyd C. Miller, director of the USP committee overseeing revisions to the standards manual, scrawled a handwritten reminder to himself that the group needed a better roadmap for the "problem of children's doses."[51] The FDA associate commissioner, John L. Harvey, equivocated, however, on whether the USP should take on the issue of children's doses. Absent a uniform system for pediatric dosage calculation, he argued that it might be "impracticable" to seek consensus among leading pediatricians on this topic.[52] Without more knowledge, specific dosing recommendations were difficult to establish, and without established dosing recommendations, clinicians were frequently forced to make determinations based on suggestions from colleagues, their own experience, or the detail man's often heavy-handed sales tactics.

The USP and the FDA ultimately decided to collaborate on a pediatric effort. After a careful search, in November 1950 the USP board asked University of Iowa School of Medicine professor of pediatrics Philip Charles Jeans to oversee the project. Jeans's charge was to convene a panel of experts that would, first, identify children's "special requirements" with regard to drug therapy and, second, generate a list of the drugs used in pediatrics, including the drug name, dosage, dosage range, and mechanism of action.[53] Jeans was an ideal choice for this assignment because his undergraduate degree was in chemistry, his medical education had been at the top-ranked Johns Hopkins University medical school, and he had completed clinical training at Boston Children's Hospital. His service on the Food and Nutrition Board of the National Research Council had brought him to the attention of the FDA, where staffers respected him for his efforts to fortify milk with vitamins.[54]

Jeans invited four pediatricians with an interest in pharmacology to join him on the committee.[55] The challenge inherent in pediatric drug issues became clear immediately. As the panel debated the dosage range for calcium chloride, a potentially dangerous drug used in infants with metabolic problems, their frustration centered on the lack of data needed to recommend a safe dosing regimen.[56] Just as the committee's work was getting underway, Jeans died abruptly. After a number of eminent pediatricians declined the chairmanship, the USP's Miller turned to Harry C. Shirkey, the most junior member of the panel, who immediately and enthusiastically accepted the appointment.[57] His new USP role drew on all Shirkey's prior professional experiences and interests. A 1939 graduate of the University of Cincinnati's School of Pharmacy, he practiced as a pharmacist at the city's children's hospital while he worked his way through medical school. After graduation, he served a stint in the military and undertook a pediatric residency before joining a private practice in Cincinnati in 1950. Just thirty-eight years old when he received Miller's letter, Shirkey was eager to make his mark at the national level of pediatric medicine.[58]

Miller admitted to Shirkey that "in the past, we have not paid much attention to children's doses, assuming they could be approximated satisfactorily from the Usual [adult] Dose" on the basis of some general factor involving the "weight of the child."[59] He framed Shirkey's potential role optimistically, suggesting that as a pediatrician and a pharmacist he had the opportunity to "break new ground," although he was vague as to how he might do that.[60] But politics were already complicating Shirkey's job, although he did not yet know it. This time, the issues were not between which medical organization, the AAP or the AMA, had the right to set drug standards for children, but whether the USP's actions with regard to children might be perceived by the AMA as overstepping its bounds. In his personal notes surrounding the Shirkey appointment, Miller scrawled a note to himself acknowledging that USP president Windsor Cutting felt that, with regard to bringing order to children and drugs, "the difficulty is too great to work out right now."[61]

Aside from the scientific problems associated with drug safety and dosing in children, pediatric concerns also raised potentially contentious issues—and

FIGURE 3  Undated photograph of Harry C. Shirkey.
(*Credit*: Courtesy of Cincinnati Children's Hospital Medical Center.)

territorial boundaries—between the AMA's and the USP's respective roles, which the USP probably wanted to avoid. Did the USP, for example, have the authority to create a dosing manual for doctors? Even though it maintained a working group on posology (dosing), Miller was not sure, as his personal notes from a meeting with Cutting show. Dosing determinations, he mused, are the "MD's concern and the USP is not a manual of therapeutics"; as such, it did not need to delve substantively into dosing-related issues for any group. Pharmacists, he determined, "were responsible only for knowing the adult dose."[62] The two men decided the best course of action was a politically expedient one, allowing the organization to avoid any immediate controversy with the AMA or any other group. The USP would "continue to study the pediatric issue" in preparation for the 1960 USP revision, almost seven years away. This approach allowed the USP to neither reject nor embrace a leadership role in this endeavor.[63]

Because Miller's and Cutting's discussions had not included Shirkey, he had little knowledge of their decision to move slowly and he clearly had an agenda for an activist committee. His vision included a publication from the USP with pediatric information for both pharmacists and physicians, and he promptly informed Cutting that the USP manual should be more therapeutically oriented to effect this initiative.[64] Miller acknowledged cautiously that some FDA staffers had suggested that the USP "could render the greatest service" by providing some guidance in pediatric pharmacology, especially since the new drugs coming to market were often used for reasons that differed from adults.[65] Antihistamines, for example, might be used to treat allergies in children, just as they were in adults; yet their antispasmodic properties also showed promise in treating colic, a common infant problem that distressed parents and vexed many pediatricians. But neither he nor any USP official responded to any of Shirkey's specific ideas or proposals.[66]

In 1957, disappointed that the USP had taken no further action on his ambitious ideas, Shirkey decided to do so himself. He wrote to Miller that "the problem of drug dosage in children is one which is becoming ever more increasing and important" to the pediatric USP panel.[67] He and a colleague at Temple University medical school, William P. Barba, had decided to take concrete action. They aggregated as much information as they could find on drugs widely used in children. Published as a section in Waldo Nelson's 1959 *Textbook of Pediatrics*, it became, in effect, the most comprehensive postwar manual of pediatric therapeutics to date. For the first time, a readily available synthesis of drugs, dosing, metabolism, and other useful metrics for clinicians was placed in the same text as the diseases they were used to treat.[68]

As Shirkey grew more confident in his USP role, he became more assertive in advocating his positions. For example, Merck and Company leaders had written to the USP to influence the way the data for the company's cough suppressant Nectadon (noscapine) would be presented in the USP manual (Merck had submitted new data to the USP that the company believed demonstrated an improvement over the earlier formulation).[69] Shirkey noted for the official record that members of his panel had not had adequate time to study the data or its implications for children, yet in his personal comments to Miller about Nectadon, he dryly commented that pediatricians had found the drug "rather useless" in the past and suspected that any new formulation would not move it into the category of "absolutely necessary drug or one for which we have been awaiting with outstretched arms."[70]

The USP also asked its pediatric workgroup for recommendations regarding the new tranquilizer Compazine (prochlorperazine), Shirkey took the opportunity to suggest that the USP recommend to its manufacturer, Smith, Kline, and French Laboratories, that the company create a pediatric formulation. He thought, on balance, that Compazine was safe, although he did express concern to Miller about the side effects he had observed in some youngsters at Cincinnati Children's Hospital. Without indicating the number of cases or age of children who received the drug, Shirkey noted that eight youngsters had experienced "moderately adverse reactions" such as "catotonic" [sic] and "Parkinsonian" symptoms such as muscle tremors and spasticity.[71]

He also mentioned that these reactions were well known to Smith, Kline, and French through his exchange of letters and telephone calls with the company's representatives. Both he and the company "hope[d]" that the reactions were a "problem of dosage," but he reminded the USP that the issue of working out that dosage fell to individual doctors.[72] Shirkey commented that whether a pediatric warning should accompany the Compazine's listing in the USP was "open to question" but that the decision "primarily should be the responsibility of the company."[73] It is unclear what Shirkey meant by this statement. He certainly believed that more clarity regarding pediatric dosing was critically important. Perhaps his comment reflected an acknowledgment that, no matter what the intent of laws and the wording of FDA regulations were, the balance of power in terms of marketing decisions remained weighted in favor of industry, not the FDA and certainly not his panel.

The extent to which his comments mattered to anyone is unclear. The AMA Council on Drugs reported on Compazine in *JAMA* in 1958, before Shirkey's panel had debated its pediatric safety and utility. Smith, Kline, and French had already developed a pediatric formulation, and the article included a pediatric dosing schedule. The *JAMA* summary noted that side effects were "dose-related," but presented no supporting pediatric data.[74,75] It is easy to understand why Smith, Kline, and French had decided to find as many uses for Compazine for both children and adults as rapidly as possible. Introduced in 1956, the drug showed promise treating nausea and vomiting, and as a result it was an overnight success, boosting company profits almost immediately. Partly as a result of Compazine, the company's consolidated net sales reached over one hundred million dollars for the first time in 1956. Clearly, the lack of supporting pediatric data had not hurt sales. Pediatricians and other physicians using the drug in children were growing used to modifying the adult dose for children through trial and error.

## Pediatric Drug Research and Testing in the Early Postwar Era

The growing enthusiasm for biostatistics and randomized controlled trials strengthened the relationships between drug companies and pediatricians.[76] Partnerships between companies and influential private practice physicians—such as Smith, Kline, and French's with Shirkey—or university researchers—such as Pfizer's with Finland—were, of course, not new. They had evolved during research into antitoxins, vitamins, and commercialized serum therapies that accelerated in the 1920s and 1930s. For example, Edwards A. Park, chair of pediatrics at the Johns Hopkins University School of Medicine and its Harriet Lane Home, had worked closely with Pfizer and other companies on pediatric serum research for meningitis and pneumonia during the interwar period.[77] In the postwar era, pediatric departments in medical schools were even more invested in relationships with drug companies because of a growing need for external funding to support their research mission. Although the federal government, through its National Institutes of Health, dramatically ramped up its support for disease-related research and medical and scientific training in the early postwar era, pharmacological research remained largely the province of industry.

As the numbers of drugs used in children increased and the body of knowledge differentiating pediatric subgroups expanded, these pediatrician and drug company partnerships deepened and intensified. In addition to bringing revenue from drug companies to the physician's institution, the relationships conferred professional authority to physicians who undertook the research. When researchers published their findings in the clinical literature, thought leaders like Shirkey used the information in their overviews of pediatric drugs and as the basis for their recommendations to the USP and FDA. Partnerships with the right pediatricians not only gave companies access to large numbers of children, it also substantially affected sales.[78]

In the early 1950s Horace Hodes, the young pediatrician who had played a foundational role in pediatric sulfonamide research at Baltimore's Sydenham Hospital, developed a model of industry and academic pediatrician partnership. Hodes's pediatric research at Sydenham on the sulfonamides, penicillin, infant diarrhea, and other topics had made him one of the nation's most highly regarded pediatric researchers by the late 1940s. When Sydenham Hospital closed in 1949, Mount Sinai Hospital in New York City recruited Hodes to become director of pediatrics. The informal personal exchanges between Hodes and drug company representatives trace the easy familiarity between pediatric researchers who controlled access to the children recruited for the drug trials and the companies that often provided their products free of charge for research purposes.[79]

Wyeth Laboratories funded Hodes in 1952 to test the antibiotic Bicillin (penicillin G benzathine) at a rheumatic fever and chronic disease hospital called Irvington House in Irvington, New York. Hodes gathered pediatric data about the drug's dosing, side effects, and other information requested by Edward F. Roberts, Wyeth's director of clinical investigation. And because children received Bicillin by injection, he also measured another parameter, pain, important given the growing focus on children's emotional well-being. Hodes's work was yet another instance of the way clinicians increasingly drew on developmental psychology to consider children's differential fears and responses to injection, as well as how their anxiety could be reduced through age-specific interventions. Soon, Roberts asked Hodes to gather pediatric dosing and efficacy data that the FDA had asked the company to provide for another new antibiotic, dipenicillin G.[80]

Children who suffered from chronic conditions such as rheumatic fever or who required a prolonged convalescence sometimes resided at congregate institutions such as Irvington House. Others were there because they had neurological conditions such as cerebral palsy or developmental disabilities that left them cognitively impaired, and the facility was considered better equipped to care for them than their homes. Children at Irvington House were a captive population with a nursing staff to gather research data twenty-four hours a day, and their parents were rarely on hand to oversee what was happening or to intervene. Even if their families visited regularly, they were often easily intimidated because many were poor or felt stigmatized for having what they had often been told was a defective child. In many instances, parents may no longer have had the legal authority to provide consent for participation in research because, in order to receive care at state-sponsored institutions, their child had to become a ward of the state.[81]

Permission to experiment on children in institutions often came from state or local health departments. For instance, one of Hodes's early 1950s experiments measured the benefits of penicillin G administered intramuscularly at birth, a treatment to replace the standard practice of silver nitrate drops to the eyes. Silver nitrate treatment was a long-standing practice used in newborns to prevent blindness from gonorrhea, which could be unwittingly transmitted from their mothers during labor. Hodes had written permission for this experiment, but it came from New York State and from the New York City Department of Health. Although he may also have secured parental consent, no mention is made of him having done so. Unlike today, this fact was not regularly noted in research reports or publications.[82]

Formal parental approval for children's research participation was not a standard practice in this era. Questions regarding whether consent for children's participation in research should be sought—and if so, from whom—were not new. They had been raised early in the twentieth century in the context of institutionalized children's participation in nontherapeutic research involving the testing of vaccines, as well as other experiments such as, for example, pediatrician Alfred F. Hess's 1914 induction of scurvy in healthy infants in order to better understand the disease. In the 1950s, decisions about research ethics were usually grounded, as they had been in the past, in a researcher's mandate to follow his or her own conscience regarding the subject's risks and benefits of participating in a research project, and physicians policed one another for violations As Susan E. Lederer and Sydney Halpern have shown, the norms governing research participation grew out of a paternalistic tradition of physicians serving as primary decision makers for ill patients, especially in life or death situations. Moreover, the boundaries between treatment and research were often indistinct, and no clear standard for informed consent, for either children or adults, existed.[83]

New guidelines for informed consent and research protections had been codified into what became known as the Nuremburg Code, developed shortly after World War II, when the world learned about the Nazi atrocities involving vulnerable populations that were undertaken in the name of research. But the Nuremburg Code had little effect on the subsequent research practice of American pediatric clinicians, who framed their decisions about how and when to use new drugs in terms of their potential to save the lives of sick children and not in any way subject to the Nuremberg-derived ethical principles.[84]

The infant who first received the new steroid adrenocorticotropic hormone (ACTH) in 1950 at Columbia-Presbyterian Babies Hospital in New York City is a particularly well-documented example of the vague boundaries between research and treatment in this era.[85] Born prematurely and weighing less than three pounds, the baby was the child of a senior biochemistry professor whose wife had experienced six miscarriages before delivering a live infant. Experience at the bedside suggested that supplemental oxygen helped newborns with immature lungs stay alive, yet the baby's doctor, one of the founders of modern neonatology, William A. Silverman, knew that oxygen could be a double-edged sword because the high doses required could also hurt premature infants' retinas.

Nevertheless, he treated the professor's baby with the extra oxygen, and, as expected, the infant's lungs improved and he began eating and gaining weight. But soon an ophthalmologist documented the ominous irregularities in the baby's retinal vessels that signaled inflammation. Would the treatment that had saved his life now cause blindness? Preliminary evidence had suggested that steroids had the potential to reduce retinal damage and save babies' vision while they received the oxygen they needed until their lungs matured. Although no infant had ever received ACTH, Silverman wanted to try it. He recalled:

I couldn't imagine what the dose should be. We quickly looked at some animal work to extrapolate a dose. Unbelievably, within days after beginning ACTH, wild retinal vessel proliferation subsided! . . . We promptly reduced the dose because the side-effects were horrendous. The infant became ravenously hungry, extremely irritable, and weight gain ceased. But, when the dose was reduced, the retinal changes flared up. We increased the dose, and the vascular changes again subsided. The infant was now in pathetic condition; crying constantly and look-ing horrible with all the signs of adrenocortical hyperactivity. We tried again to reduce the dose of ACTH, and this time there was no retinal flare-up. We stopped the ACTH and the eye changes returned to virtually normal. . . . The whole medical center applauded our daring exploit.[86]

But Silverman and his colleagues quickly realized they had a "difficult dilemma."[87] Although ACTH seemed to be a "miraculous treatment" for the problem of potential eye damage from oxygen, one case did not provide defin-itive evidence of its benefit.[88] Silverman and his colleagues had recently "got religion" and were now "devotees" of the randomized controlled trial, rather than the observational or case study, for determining whether a drug or treat-ment worked.[89] Because of ACTH's "horrendous side effects," they wanted to know whether it was worth the risks to babies.[90] As he recalled,

This was the end of 1950. We went to see the chairman of the pediatric depart-ment, Rusty McIntosh. We laid out this dilemma in front of him. We told him we were frightened about the side-effects of ACTH, and we had no concurrent controls. What we would like to do, we told him, is to carry out a randomized clinical trial, a method that had never before been used in studies of human infants. It grew extremely emotional, the idea of withholding a cure for infants simply to test it. All of the issues that we now understand are obvious, but this was the very first experience. . . . Remember, this was years before ethical review committees . . . [when] the chairman of the department decided everything that was done or not done in his department.[91]

After securing McIntosh's approval, Silverman consulted a textbook to develop a randomization strategy, which suggested he first fill a bowl with two different colors of marbles. The protocol stipulated that the nurse caring for a baby in the study close her eyes, reach into the bowl, and choose either a white or a blue marble. Depending on the color she selected, the child was enrolled in either the experimental group that received supplemental oxygen or the control group that did not. Unbeknown, at first, to Silverman and his col-leagues, the head nurse kept pulling out marbles until she found the color that suited her assessment of what a particular baby needed, and this unanticipated human factor foiled the randomization technique. The power of randomized clinical trials, in which experimenters did not know which patients received a treatment or a placebo, became clear to him when the study showed no statistical difference in retinal change between the treated and untreated groups. In fact, the ACTH group had a higher death rate from infection, a finding that ran counter to Silverman's clinical observations. He later recalled his epiphany when he realized that researchers were not neutral observers; they sometimes drew conclusions based not on data, but on what they hoped to find.[92]

These kinds of experiments that aimed to identify dosing regimens using both healthy and ill children were common as new drugs poured onto the market in the United States in this era. For example, at approximately the same time that Silverman undertook his ACTH research, a young physician named Julius B. Richmond published the results of his drug investigation. Richmond and his colleagues administered sulfonamide therapy orally and subcutaneously to fifty-seven healthy infants at the University of Illinois Hospital to determine the appropriate treatment regimen. They studied dosage in terms of body weight, rate of excretion of the drug, and other measures that would be useful in caring for sick infants. The experiment, published in the *Journal of Pediatrics* in 1950, entailed the babies receive frequent blood drawing and medication injections and, in keeping with the era's norms, the report did not mention parental consent.[93]

In another drug experiment a few years later in 1956, Samuel O. Sapin, Ephraim Donoso, and Sidney Blumenthal of the Mount Sinai Department of Pediatrics in New York City studied fourteen healthy infants under the age of six months to ascertain how much of the powerful cardiac stimulant drug digoxin (administered intramuscularly) was necessary to produce side effects and changes to heart rhythm.[94] Doctors desperately needed this information because babies born with congenital heart disease often needed the drug's heart-strengthening qualities. But the pediatric dosing metric for digoxin had long been, as Cornell medical school faculty member Harry Gold noted in 1947, an "unsettled" problem.[95] Many of the babies in the Sapin, Donoso, and Blumenthal study experienced one of digoxin's most common side effects, vomiting. In a number of the infants, electrocardiograms documented potentially dangerous changes to their heart rhythm from the drug. One even developed a more severe, potentially dangerous disturbance of the heart's electrical functioning known as heart block. Sapin, Donoso, and Blumenthal did not explain the rationale for conducting the experiment on healthy babies, and, in fact, they noted that their findings could not be "directly transferred to babies with diseased hearts."[96] Nonetheless, *Pediatrics* published the study, which, too, lacked any mention of parental consent.

In this trial, as well as Richmond's sulfonamide research a few years earlier, the investigators probably felt they could defend their research because they were confident in their ability to manage any drug-related complications.

Perhaps because they assumed they could reverse any negative effects of the drugs in healthy infants, the physicians believed they were ethically justified in subjecting healthy infants to the research because they were generating knowledge that might save the lives of ill, much more fragile babies. Moreover, no one had proffered a better way of deriving pediatric drug-related information. The publication of their research in leading journals implies that most of their colleagues probably agreed. These drug studies were clearly welcomed by the institutions and academic settings in which they took place and helped advance the careers of the physicians who oversaw them.[97]

It was in this era that New York University pediatrician Saul Krugman began research at Staten Island's Willowbrook State School that later became infamous. Krugman investigated whether injections of antibodies protected uninfected children from the hepatitis virus. He and his investigators had observed that young children housed at Willowbrook, almost all of whom had profound cognitive impairment, often contracted hepatitis early in their stay. These children, they observed, suffered a less severe form of the condition than did older ones or adults. In another study, the investigators deliberately infected newly admitted youngsters who had received antibodies with the virus. A control group received the antibodies but were not infected with the virus. Children whose parents consented to have their child infected with hepatitis received expedited admission to a unit that had a higher nurse-to-patient ratio.[98]

Ethical standards were even less clear when the research took place outside the United States. At the 1957 Fifth Antibiotic Symposium, held in Washington, DC, one of many conferences held throughout the decade to synthesize the rapidly growing body of antibiotic research into therapeutically manageable guidelines, Elmer H. Loughlin, Louverture Alcindor, and Aurele A. Joseph, faculty at New York Medical College, informed colleagues of their research on children in rural Haiti, undertaken to ascertain the pediatric effects of long-term use of Pfizer's antibiotic Terramycin. They wanted to know whether the drug influenced children's growth. Beginning in October 1956 and continuing through 1957, the doctors administered varying doses of Terramycin to at least 240 schoolchildren and reported at the conference that the same kind of "growth-stimulating effects" that had been noticed in farm animals who received antibiotics could be observed in Haitian children.[99] Finding "no toxic or untoward effects," Loughlin, Alcindor, and Joseph proposed a potentially novel use for Terramycin. They hypothesized that the drug might be useful in treating "undernutrition" in "tropical children," especially since "correcting the undernutrition by supplying diets rich in high quality proteins, including milk, has not been economically practicable because foodstuffs are unavailable or too expensive."[100]

When drugs saved lives, the payoff in terms of scientific advancement and children's lives could be profound—as they had been with the sulfonamides in the 1930s and penicillin in the 1940s. One of the most significant postwar pediatric success stories came in the area of cancer. With the founding of the National Institutes of Health (NIH) in the 1940s, the federal government made a major investment in cancer-related research and treatment. The collaboration between the government, industry, scientists, and clinicians became one of the primary justifications for a public-private partnership in the U.S. approach to funding science and medicine. Lederle, for example, sponsored research by Boston Children's Hospital pediatric pathologist Sidney Farber, who was convinced that he could find a more successful way to treat pediatric leukemia than the traditional modalities of surgery or radiation, tools that did little for a blood cancer. Based on his laboratory research suggesting that folic acid played a role in nourishing cancer cells, he and his colleague Louis Diamond had tried a new agent, Aminopterin, on children very ill with leukemia. Their May 1948 report in *New England Journal of Medicine*, which outlined their ability to achieve temporary remission, created a sensation.[101]

Subsequent pediatric clinical trials in the 1950s and early 1960s yielded data that increased remission periods for youngsters, especially those with acute lymphocytic leukemia (ALL). There was little debate about whether or not to experiment using these new therapies because children with ALL died in such large numbers. As researcher Emil J. Freireich argued to his superiors at the National Cancer Institute when he sought permission to use what became known as chemotherapy on his young patients, "I've got children on the ward right now that are dying, who have no hope for living. What harm is there in doing it?"[102] By the next decade the industry, academic, and government partnership paid off as combination chemotherapy—a timed cocktail of multiple drugs, each with a different mechanism of action—began to reduce mortality in children with ALL substantively.

## Chloramphenicol and Children in the 1950s:
## High Stakes Problems

Although the popular press reported the Elixer Sulfanilamide and sulfathiazole disasters, most stories in the media about drugs and their development in the early postwar era celebrated the advances emerging from pharmaceutical companies. When safety issues did arise, the power of drug companies could hamper the investigation as it did in the example of chloramphenicol. Chloramphenicol had quickly proved itself to be extremely profitable for its manufacturer, Parke-Davis and Company, which sold it under the trade name Chloromycetin. Within a year of its 1949 release, the firm sold more than twenty-seven tons of the drug, and it had earned the company a quarter of its more than 100 million dollars in sales by the end of 1950. By 1951 the company was well on its way to achieving its goal of number-one position in the American market, sales having risen by 30 percent in the previous year, in large part as a result of chloramphenicol's success.[103]

Many physicians favored chloramphenicol for pediatric use because, first, it appeared to have fewer side effects than the sulfa drugs, penicillin, or streptomycin and, second, Parke-Davis had figured out how to formulate the drug in a vanilla-custard-flavored liquid popular with children.[104] All seemed to be going well until 1951, when the FDA and Parke-Davis received reports that chloramphenicol could cause a potentially life-threatening condition in both children and adults. The condition, known as aplastic anemia, resulted in the bone marrow producing an insufficient number of oxygen-carrying red blood cells.[105]

In 1952, Albe Watkins, a California physician, and his wife Geraldine, a nurse, watched in dismay as their nine-year-old son James, who had received the drug for a urinary tract infection, developed aplastic anemia and subsequently experienced a gruesome death. Watkins, like most other physicians, learned about the latest drugs on the market from the companies' detail men. As historian Thomas Maeder recounted, the Parke-Davis sales representative had provided Watkins with a wealth of information heralding the therapeutic benefits of chloramphenicol. After James's death, Watkins wrote to Parke-Davis, sure that the company would want to know of his son's aplastic anemia. Their indifferent reply suggested to him that they had little interest in what had happened to James. The company's response made Watkins so angry that he loaded his family in the car and headed to Washington, DC, to talk to the FDA directly about the drug and his son's death.[106]

During their cross-country odyssey, the family stopped briefly in Chicago, where Watkins sought out AMA president Austin Smith. Watkins believed that Smith, too, showed little concern for the absence of any warnings about aplastic anemia in Parke-Davis's marketing literature. The frustrated father began his own informal epidemiological investigation as the family continued its trip east. Each evening when they stopped to rest in a particular town, he called colleagues with whom he had trained to discuss chloramphenicol. In areas where he knew no one, he looked up physicians' names in the phone book and cold-called them to inquire about their experience with the drug. He identified new cases of aplastic anemia in both children and adults all along the way. Watkins was so anxious to present his findings to Henry Welch, director of the FDA Division of Antibiotics, that the family did not even check in to their hotel when they finally reached Washington. His wife and surviving children waited outside in the car while Watkins showed his data

to an amazed Welch, who could not believe that Watkins's informal epidemiological investigation closely approximated what his agents were beginning
to find.[107]

Partly as a result of Watkins's tenacity, the resulting investigation became
one of the FDA's largest up until that point. It exemplified what many saw as
a glaring problem with drug regulation in the United States, that the companies that stood to profit from the drugs were also expected to play a major
role in tracking any side effects, adverse reactions, and negative outcomes that
might threaten their bottom line. Watkins and others whose family members
had become sick or died from chloramphenicol-related aplastic anemia would
later bitterly note that physicians had begun informing the company of the
side effect within a few months of the drug's release. Indeed, the AMA's own
*Journal of the American Medical Association*, noted the side effect. The 1952
*JAMA* article even cited a case, published just a few months after chloramphenicol's release, from an Australian journal that mentioned that the drug
had caused aplastic anemia in a child.[108] Chloramphenicol's relationship
to aplastic anemia had particular cultural resonance in Cold War America,
where nuclear tests were rapidly increasing. It seemed incredible, a *Los Angeles Times* article noted about the Watkins family's saga, that one of the new
infectious disease-fighting "wonder drugs" could cause a condition "that
depletes the blood structure and attacks bone marrow in the manner of atomic
radiation."[109] Although Watkins, as a physician, possessed enough political
and economic clout to bring his findings directly to Welch and the FDA
leadership, he was only one of many parents who contacted the FDA about
chloramphenicol. For years after aplastic anemia's link to chloramphenicol
came into public consciousness, letters from other family members, especially
parents, who felt betrayed by Parke-Davis, the FDA, or the doctor who prescribed the drug to their child arrived at the FDA or Capitol Hill.[110]

Parke-Davis soon faced another chloramphenicol-related disaster, this
one affecting very young infants exclusively. Doctors had begun treating a
newborn with the drug when a mother developed a fever while in labor or
when her water had been broken for an extended time before the baby's birth.
Both conditions were considered risk factors for neonatal infection, and doctors were optimistic that administering a broad spectrum antibiotic such as
chloramphenicol as a preventive to such infants might avert a life-threatening
illness. By the late 1950s, however, doctors in Alabama, Ohio, and California
had observed that mortality rates in some nurseries in which babies received
antibiotics were going up, not down. A young Los Angeles pediatrician, Joan
Hodgman, noticed the same thing and decided to investigate how and why
this was happening. She and her team randomly assigned 126 premature newborns into one of four groups: Group One, no antibiotic; Group Two, chloramphenicol; Group Three, procaine penicillin and streptomycin; and Group

Four, all three antibiotics. Chloramphenicol's toxicity became obvious when the group that received it exhibited a high mortality rate.[111]

Although 41 percent of the infant subjects in the overall trial died, it was the comparative deaths between the groups that was the most shocking. The mortality rates for babies who received no treatment or the procaine penicillin and streptomycin combination were 19 and 18 percent, respectively. But 60 percent of the babies administered chloramphenicol and 68 percent of the procaine penicillin-streptomycin-chloramphenicol group died.[112] Hodgman's study confirmed what was being observed elsewhere empirically. After a few doses of chloramphenicol, some infants developed respiratory distress and turned a dusky gray. The death rate was highest for premature infants because they often lacked the necessary enzymes to metabolize the drug adequately in their liver.

Hodgman later expressed regret about parts of the study to an interviewer regarding what quickly became known as gray baby syndrome:

> We discussed stopping the study early, and the decision was made—I was a junior faculty member at that time, working under the chief of the premature service, and the decision was not altogether mine, though I wasn't against it—that unless you have convincing evidence, nobody's going to believe you. We had to convince more than ourselves. We had to convince the public that the standard practice and the recommended doses were wrong. We weren't Harvard: we were a county hospital. So we continued the study as it had been designed. . . . We would do it better now.[113]

But she also reported somewhat bitterly in a 2004 oral history about the bind in which individual physicians found themselves. Unless a company requested information about the performance or dosage for its products, doctors were largely on their own, with no financial or statistical support, to answer important clinical questions such as Hodgman's. Moreover, Hodgman had gone beyond the ethical practices of many of her colleagues because she had received written informed consent from the parents of the children in the untreated group. She recalled: "[A]t the time, other people were killing half their preemies with chloramphenicol and not appreciating it. But we did it carefully, and we had permission from our research committee. We didn't have permission from all the families because we were giving them standard doses, but we did get permission from the untreated group," considered, in a sad irony, to be more at risk by the investigators than the babies who received an antibiotic.[114]

Hodgman was certainly correct about chloramphenicol's widespread use at other institutions, even the most prestigious hospitals. Surviving records from the Harriett Lane Home at the Johns Hopkins Hospital, for example, reveal that almost 75 percent of infants under the age of two months who received the drug in the late 1950s died.[115] Chloramphenicol became the first drug to carry a warning label with regard to its serious, potentially life-threatening side effects, what today is referred to as a "black box" warning.[116] The episode also added to the growing body of information about the ways in which untoward reactions from drugs could sicken and even kill people. Physician Robert H. Moser, for example, added chloramphenicol to his new compilation of unforeseen consequences to novel technologies and drugs known as *Diseases of Medical Progress*.[117]

The reaction by at least one Parke-Davis drug metabolism expert, Anthony Glazko, to the infant deaths reflected his interest in the adverse events caused by chloramphenicol. In 1960 Glazko wrote to Maxwell Finland, explaining the way gray baby syndrome had stimulated him to become "interested in the question of proper dosage in children" from a scientific perspective. He ended his letter to Finland emphasizing another reason his preoccupation with "pediatric problems" in drug development had recently taken "a more practical turn." His wife had just given birth to a baby boy.[118] Through Finland, Glazko had connected the previous year with a physician at Boston City Hospital, Rudi Schmid, who was caring for a two-year-old patient with a liver condition that caused him to metabolize drugs similarly to a premature infant. Believing that research on this child's unusual metabolism might provide useful information, he expressed no concern about its potential untoward effects to the child despite its connection to aplastic anemia and gray baby syndrome.[119]

## Trying to Find a Way Forward

The FDA's efforts in pediatrics remained at a very basic level. As late as 1957, for example, FDA staffers were still debating at what age infancy ended in the context of developing rubrics for evaluating drugs.[120] This operational definition was not unimportant in terms of drug labeling, but the drug-information needs of pediatricians were acute and clearly went far beyond this issue.[121] As a result, individual physicians stepped up their efforts to investigate drugs in children.

With funding from the AAP, for example, Massachusetts General Hospital's chief of pediatrics, Allan M. Butler, and his colleagues made their own study of children's dosages, which the hospital used in its formulary. Interestingly, doctors at the nearby Boston Children's Hospital were engaged in similar research, and the efforts of the two institutions appear to have operated parallel to one another, even though they were in close geographic proximity and most of the senior doctors at both hospitals served on Harvard's medical school faculty. Despite their common affiliation, they did not cite one another's work, nor were they collaborating; it seems clear that both hospitals were jockeying for preeminence in pediatric therapeutics. Theirs is an instance of professional competition, one that also showcased the changing role of the hospital pharmacy in pediatrics.[122]

In 1960, according to its chief pharmacist, Arthur Thompson, the role of the pharmacy at Boston Children's Hospital was virtually unrecognizable from what it had been two decades earlier. It had expanded to a new, much larger space for storing and dispensing medications. Thompson noted that, although the drugs decreased the number of days many children needed to stay in the hospital, cost savings from their use were elusive. Unfortunately, the reduction in nursing time afforded by a pharmacy that prepared prepackaged drugs in a pediatric formulation was offset by the larger pharmacy staff required to make that happen. Pharmacists' workload at Boston Children's Hospital was so heavy because, according to Thompson, "most pharmaceuticals are manufactured for adults with little or no attention directed to pediatrics."[123] Unless industry saw potential to make significant profits on pediatric formulations—such as with the broad spectrum antibiotics—it had no financial incentive to do so. As a result, Boston Children's Hospital needed to purchase whatever dosage forms were on the market and then use a hand-operated capsule machine to compound its own pills.

Thompsons's and his colleagues' role at Boston Children's Hospital was now as an outlier in the world of pharmacy, more akin to their predecessors in decades past. At the beginning of World War II, for example, 75 percent of the drugs doctors prescribed needed to be compounded, a process in which the pharmacist mixed chemicals and prepared the drug prescribed by the physician. By the late 1950s more than 95 percent of all prescription drugs came to a pharmacist ready-made. The pharmacist's role in general practice increasingly became that of dispenser, transferring the number of pills ordered by the doctor from a large container to a small bottle. But at premier pediatric institutions such as Boston Children's Hospital, the labor-intensive process of compounding drugs for children because of their many different sizes remained the norm. According to Thompson, the need to prepare drugs on site did have one important benefit. Pharmacists could use the capsule machine to efficiently and quickly compound investigational drugs provided by pharmaceutical companies free of charge to doctors and the hospital.[124] Despite its modernized and larger space, however, Thompson complained that the new pharmacy was already out of date. For example, any volatile solvents needed to prepare drugs had to be stored in the cellar and brought up and down using a "hand-operated, antiquated elevator" before being brought to and from the pharmacy on a "dangerous spiral stairway."[125] Thompson wearily noted how his department was stretched thin: "[T]he staff is hardly adequate to accomplish all that is necessary."[126]

Another variable that reduced any nursing cost-savings brought on by more robust pharmacy support at Boston Children's Hospital was the increasing complexity involved in administering medications and caring for the children who received them. While the expanded pharmacy saved nurses preparation time when their young patients required an oral medication, more and more children required an intramuscular, subcutaneous, or intravenous injection. Many of these drugs arrived on the ward in a powdered vial into which nurses needed to inject sterile water or saline to reconstitute it, calculate the amount of medication to be drawn into a syringe, and then administer the agent to the child. In addition to managing children's and parents' anxiety and educating them about the drug in a developmentally appropriate manner, late 1950s procedure manuals for the hospital detailed the expansive medication-related nursing protocols.[127]

At the national level, Harry Shirkey continued encouraging the USP to take a leadership role in knowledge dissemination for pediatric drugs. In 1959, the same year he accepted a position as medical director at Birmingham, Alabama, Children's Hospital, Shirkey eagerly sought reappointment as chairman of the USP Panel of Pediatrics.[128] The committee revealed its ongoing frustration in 1959 as members contradicted one another in their debates about dosing and safety, even about potentially dangerous drugs such as the cardiac drug digoxin and the sedative chloral hydrate. The panel's notes to one another included comments such as the one by University of Colorado pediatrician Henry Kempe, who opined that the USP's "doses for digitalis preparations are completely inappropriate for children and particularly infants."[129] An attempt to provide a pediatric dosing regimen for the sedative chloral hydrate was impeded when Boston Children's Hospital pediatrician Robert Haggerty noted the limitations of weight-based criteria: "Here again is the problem of children's doses and use. . . . If this adult [dose] is scaled down, it would be too little."[130] Shirkey himself reversed his own earlier opinion on one of the formulations of Compazine (prochlorperazine edisylate) he had supported a year earlier. Subsequent clinical experience now led him to believe unequivocally that it was "bad for children."[131] It is unclear what, if any, formal action Shirkey or the USP took to communicate the information about Compazine to Smith, Kline, and French. The drug remained on the market with indications and company-recommended pediatric dosing schedule that Shirkey now did not support.

Almost three decades after the Philadelphia Pediatric Society had first proposed the idea to the AAP, there was a growing consensus that the organization should play a central role in advising government and the USP when it came to questions of drugs for children. USP president Windsor Cutting noted as much in 1960 when he proclaimed that the AMA judged the worth of drugs "in all instances except for pediatric patients," where that responsibility fell to the AAP.[132] Shirkey hoped that together the USP and AAP could address the pediatric scientific and policy issues generated by the plethora of new drugs continuing to flood the market. The AAP executive board agreed, and in October 1960 the organization allocated funds for a new Committee on Drug Dosage, with Harry Shirkey as chair.[133] Sensing that the time was right, Shirkey doubled the size of his USP pediatric committee in 1961, adding a number of interested and activist pediatricians, making the Panel on Pediatrics larger than any other USP specialty group. Moving ahead with his agenda of including pediatric therapeutics and dosing in the USP manual, in 1961 he reminded the organization's leadership with growing force that his panel was of the "very strong opinion that Pediatric dosage is still in a chaotic situation."[134] At the same time, individual physicians increasingly pressed the FDA to take a more visible role with regard to children. As leading pediatrician William L. Nyhan argued, "suppliers of drugs should be required to establish, before marketing, the presence or absence of differential toxicity in the very young."[135]

Shortly afterward, the FDA, which had increased its internal discussions about drug safety in children, hired its first pediatrician in the New Drug Division, Washington, DC, pediatric cardiologist John Nestor. Recognized as the "key man" in the FDA's "intensified pediatric program" by the trade journal *F-D-C Reports*, Nestor was at the center of the agency's "new pediatric emphasis."[136] Warily characterizing him as a "strong-willed, crusading, pediatrician," the *F-D-C Reports* article signaled to the drug industry that Nestor had significant influence.[137] More stringent federal oversight of drugs as they related to children seemed imminent as industry representatives were informed that "All NDAs that may have pediatric implications are now routed to Dr. Nestor for special scrutiny. He is the FDA staffer with whom the pharmaceutical MDs have to discuss pediatric drugs, implications, and dosages."[138] Any company submitting a new drug application was now supposed to submit pediatric data; if it did not do so, the agency might require a disclaimer, "not for pediatric use," on the label.[139] Left unsaid was what the consequences of such a label would mean, since a physician could prescribe any drug off-label, meaning a dosage or purpose outside that approved by the FDA.

Simultaneous to Nestor's hiring, interest on Capitol Hill was growing in this now major sector of the American economy. Senator Estes Kefauver's Antitrust and Monopoly Subcommittee was focused on practices such as questionable pharmaceutical industry advertising, potential price gouging, and companies' outsized profits. Although Kefauver was not uninterested in children's issues—he had chaired 1954 hearings investigating whether comic books could harm children's psyche and even induce them to become juvenile delinquents—his committee's interest in 1961 had little to do with children. Neither pediatricians nor the FDA had reason to believe that would change.[140]

# 4

# The Growth and
# Development of the
# Therapeutic Orphan,
# 1961–1979

• • • • • • • • • • • • • • • • • • • • •

By 1961, Harry Shirkey was the nation's most strident and recognized advocate for children's drug policy. That year he suggested that the United States Pharmacopeia (USP) work with the American Academy of Pediatrics (AAP) Committee on Drugs (COD) to address pediatric drug safety.[1] His proposal coincided with a time when rhetoric trumpeting U.S. investments in child well-being was arguably at its most vocal. The largest generational birth cohort in American history, the baby boomers, showed no signs of slowing down. More and more children were being born every year, an ever larger percentage of the population of the United States. In 1940, for example, youngsters under the age of eighteen years made up less than one-quarter of the population; by the early 1960s they comprised more than one-third.[2]

Beyond their numbers, proclamations regarding Americans' commitment to children's well-being symbolized strength and power to the rest of the world. The Golden Anniversary White House Conference on Children and Youth convened in 1960 personified this ideology. Like its predecessors, held roughly a decade apart since 1909, the conference drew together experts from the worlds of science, health care, politics, and culture. Conference leaders extolled the ways in which new drugs, especially antibiotics, had improved children's lives. The progressive, linear narrative accompanying scientific discussions in the three-volume manifesto arising from the conference and pediatricians' first-hand reports signaled that the decade of the 1960s would bring even more positive change to the lives of children and families.[3]

The nation's new president, John F. Kennedy, himself the father of two very young children and a third that did not survive its premature birth while he was president-elect, added to the spotlight on children by professing a robust governmental commitment to children. Soon after his January 1961 inauguration, and at the urging of his sister, Eunice Kennedy Shriver, President Kennedy proposed the first National Institutes of Health (NIH) branch dedicated to a life stage—the National Institute of Child Health and Human Development (NICHD), which would focus its attention on the developing child. One acknowledged aim of the new institute was to generate more pediatric-related research and provide funding to train children's specialists.[4]

By the early 1960s, the impact of the explosion of new drugs—resulting in a much more pharmaceutically oriented disease economy for both children and adults than in the past—was readily apparent. A staggering 90 percent of the medications physicians now prescribed had not been available just two decades earlier.[5] Analysts estimated that more than four thousand prescription products had come onto the market in the years between 1951 and 1961. Seventy cents of every dollar spent on drugs in 1961 went toward an agent not available ten years earlier. Pediatric products were central to this rapidly growing economic sector, because of children's growing numbers and their symbolic importance to the postwar American ideal.[6] Newborns and premature babies were now not the only subcategory within pediatrics who metabolized drugs uniquely, according to research. In the case of toddlers and the cardiac drug digitoxin, for example, evidence suggested that children sometimes required as much as a 50 percent higher dose than adults based on body weight.[7]

Nevertheless, little consensus existed, even among elite pediatricians, that more federal oversight of the drug industry specific to children was desirable. At the 1961 Conference on Perinatal Pharmacology, Charles D. May, the influential editor of *Pediatrics* and a member of the AMA Council on Drugs, expressed his sympathy for the drug industry. His primary fear was that too much regulation might cause manufacturers to "panic" and "take drugs off the market," thereby making new agents unavailable to children.[8]

Another AAP subgroup, the Committee on the Fetus and the Newborn, supported Shirkey and disagreed with May, taking a vocal stance in the wake of the gray baby syndrome crisis. Under the chairmanship of William A. Silverman, who was now a national leader of the new pediatric subspecialty known as neonatology, the committee pushed for more "extensive preclinical investigation than is being carried out at the present time," because "there is increasing awareness" of the necessity of making "more than a quantitative distinction between infants and children. The fetus and the newborn infant often behave so differently as to warrant consideration as separate categories of the human species." Silverman's adrenocorticotropic hormone (ACTH) research on retinal damage in premature infants receiving oxygen a few years earlier had turned him into an activist for better research into their needs.[9] The warnings from the Committee on the Fetus and the Newborn proved horrifyingly prescient within a few short months when the *Washington Post* broke the thalidomide story, bringing it to the forefront of legislative debates in 1962. The tragedy also ended the unbridled optimism for a boundless future of health improvements from an ongoing stream of new wonder drugs that had begun with the sulfonamides in the late 1930s.[10]

## Thalidomide and Its Aftermath: A New Era of Safety for Children?

A tranquilizing and antinausea agent widely employed in Europe and Japan, thalidomide had been under consideration for FDA approval since September 1960, but a newly hired FDA physician and pharmacologist, Frances O. Kelsey, stalled the application.[11] Under the 1938 law, the FDA had sixty days to review a new drug application. If the agency took no action during that time frame, the product was automatically approved. Kelsey reviewed the submission, concluding that the supporting evidence for thalidomide was weak. She decided to use an FDA loophole that delayed an incomplete application until the distributer supplied the requested information. She waited until two days before the end of the sixty-day review period to send a letter demanding additional toxicity data from the William S. Merrell Corporation of Ohio, which hoped to become the U.S. distributor of thalidomide under the brand name "Kevadon."[12]

Although Merrell and her superiors pressured her to approve the drug, Kelsey refused to buckle and sent five more such letters requesting more data. She grew more worried about thalidomide, particularly after meeting in February 1962 with John Nestor. Nestor informed her that one of his professors from Johns Hopkins, pediatric cardiologist Helen Taussig, had just returned from Germany, where she had consulted on what appeared to be an epidemic of congenital heart defects and other anomalies.[13] Kelsey and Nestor traveled to Baltimore to learn what Taussig had found. Taussig's report convinced Kelsey that the many defects, most notably the frightening long-bone malformation known as phocomelia (Greek for "seal limb"), that she observed in hundreds of German children could be attributed to fetal exposure to thalidomide. Kelsey contacted Merrell to warn them about Taussig's finding. Although the FDA had not yet approved thalidomide for sale in the United States, she knew that under the 1938 law drugs could be administered to patients without FDA approval so long as they were labeled as investigational and the company maintained records of its studies. Her fears that at least a few pregnant women in the United States had been prescribed thalidomide were confirmed when she learned that more than 1,000 physicians had been supplied with the drug.[14]

When reports of Taussig's investigation reached Estes Kefauver and his staff, they leaked the thalidomide story to the media. Kefauver saw the chance to attract attention to his concerns regarding the U.S. drug industry, and he made sure Taussig testified on Capitol Hill.[15] Taussig herself saw the thalidomide crisis as an opportunity to broaden the political discourse beyond Kefauver's primary focus on advertising, increased competition, and stronger antitrust rules to more explicit protections governing drug safety in pregnant women, fetuses, infants, and children. Moving quickly, Taussig presented findings from her German trip to the academic pediatricians who comprised the American Pediatric Society (APS) conference, and she contacted leading pediatricians all over the country, asking them to mount a letter-writing campaign to pediatric organizations and the FDA in support of more stringent monitoring of the pharmaceutical industry.[16]

But despite the thalidomide crisis, some American medical leaders still disagreed about the need for new legislation. Philip S. Barba, associate dean at the University of Pennsylvania medical school, for example, explained to Taussig in July 1962 that he remained "fearful of writing things into laws."[17] Well-known physician Morris Fishbein, editor of *Medical World News* and former editor of the *Journal of the American Medical Association* (*JAMA*) even wrote a letter to the *New York Times* attacking those who testified at the Kefauver hearings as "mavericks" and "scientific Leftists."[18] He took Taussig to task by name, claiming that her call to test drugs in pregnant animals before their approval would escalate costs. He also derided her as not "qualified as an expert in drug research, development, or promotion, or in the laws regulating these activities."[19] Since brokering decisions about drug efficacy traditionally fell within medicine's province, both Barba and Fishbein probably worried that increasing the government's authority would ultimately supersede or replace that of physicians.

Fishbein was no match for Taussig's sophisticated media strategy, however, as she announced warnings about thalidomide specifically and spoke out on the need for pediatric drug safety in general in numerous radio, television, magazine, and newspaper interviews, speaking out in ways that Kelsey and Nestor, as government employees, could not do publicly. At the same time, she worked closely with Kefauver and his staff to add what she hoped would ensure broader and more meaningful safety protections for fetuses, infants, and children into the bill.[20] One of her most effective tools was showing legislators pictures of thalidomide-maimed children. She riveted them with a gendered appeal, not as legislators but as American fathers: "I am quite sure that if any of your wives had given birth to a child with this type of malformation, you would want to exert all the influence you possibly could to prevent the occurrence of another similar tragedy."[21]

Once she had policymakers' attention, Taussig argued for new protections for children: "[S]afety and efficacy go together. . . . [A] drug cannot be assumed to be safe for infants and children because it is safe for adults. . . . [I]t is not sufficient to merely state in tiny print somewhere at the end of the advertisement of a drug: 'Warning: this drug may not be safe for children (or for pregnant women) because this aspect has not been tested.' . . . [S]afe should mean safe for all ages and all groups of people."[22]

The cumulative efforts of Kelsey, Nestor, and Kefauver yielded talking points for the FDA leadership. In June 1962, the director of its Bureau of Medicine, Ralph G. Smith, gave a speech at the National Meeting of the Drug and Allied Products Guild, wherein he warned: "[E]xperts in the field of pediatrics have pointed out that infants and children may react to drugs differently from adults. . . . It is no longer considered safe to derive children's doses from safe adult doses by age or weight formula. Safety of new drugs for infants and children must be shown by actual use in the various age groups."[23]

Just as agency staffers had warned companies the previous year in *F-D-C Reports*, the FDA was trying to get the drug industry to undertake, or at least voluntarily underwrite, pediatric testing. But some senators wanted government to play a stronger role than simply encouraging industry from the sidelines. As legislators delved deeply into the pharmaceutical industry during the Kefauver hearings, their concern at the lack of communication between different branches of the federal government increased. Minnesota Democrat and pharmacist Hubert Humphrey, for example, expressed shock on the Senate floor that his staffers had found a complete lack of "basic collaboration" regarding issues of fetal drug safety between the Children's Bureau, NIH, and the FDA.[24]

By the time President Kennedy signed the Kefauver-Harris Amendments to the Federal Food, Drug, and Cosmetic Act in October 1962, Kelsey was a national heroine, and the FDA received sweeping new responsibilities, involving it in all phases of the drug development process.[25] Both pediatricians and politicians were optimistic that the new law would improve pediatric drug safety. The FDA now supervised all clinical testing for any new drug, setting standards that affected every aspect of drug company operations, such as, for example, the type of records they needed to maintain and the manufacturing guidelines they needed to follow. Other significant changes governing the drug approval process included new informed consent provisions for clinical trials that the FDA deemed "adequate and well-controlled." Manufacturers filing a new drug application also needed to supply evidence of a drug's efficacy; that is, the drug had to "have the effect it purports or is represented to have . . . for the use intended."[26] In other words, a company that applied for FDA approval needed not just data that the drug was safe, but also evidence to support its curative or ameliorative effect on the condition it was prescribed to treat.

Harry Shirkey convened an urgent ad hoc meeting on October 28, 1962, at the American Academy of Pediatrics annual conference. Gathering just eighteen days after President Kennedy signed the Kefauver-Harris Amendments, the twenty attendees included many of those who had campaigned actively for the new legislation, such as John Nestor and Helen Taussig. Multiple AAP subcommittees sent representatives to the meeting, as did the Pharmaceutical Manufacturers Association (PMA), a drug industry trade organization. The mood was celebratory as Shirkey led the group in crafting recommendations they believed necessary to implement the new law, such as mandatory testing in pregnant and infant animals before human clinical trials could begin; stronger pediatric pharmacologist representation in FDA decision-making; development of protocols for clinical testing that incorporated the metabolic and physiological specifics of the developing child; and procedures for assuring pediatric clinical drug trials prior to FDA approval.[27]

Ongoing congressional hearings were scheduled for March 1963 in order to investigate existing FDA procedures for a broad range of drug-related issues—including those concerning pregnant women, neonates, and children—in the wake of the new law. Hubert Humphrey prepared exhaustively for his leading role, one that drew on the pharmaceutical knowledge he possessed and most legislators lacked as well as his deft political skills. He requested written summaries about pediatric drug-related issues from stakeholders such as the AAP and invited comments from a number of scientists, pediatricians, drug researchers, and FDA thought leaders. Humphrey asked them all to address the same questions, which reflected his belief in the power of government to effect positive change:

> Has the U.S. Government, including the Food and Drug Administration, done all that it should have done in cooperation with your profession and the pharmaceutical industry in the interest of the well-being of infants and children? If not, what should it have done earlier? Whether or not the past record was satisfactory, what should the Federal Government be doing now and what should it do in the future with respect to drug safety and efficacy?[28]

Humphrey also wrote to Surgeon General Luther Terry in early March 1963, expressing his frustration and "deep personal feelings" that a research grant application that aimed to investigate the effects of drugs on newborns, particularly premature babies, had not been funded by the NIH, and warning that he intended to spotlight this decision at his forthcoming hearings.[29]

He proclaimed in the letter, "[t]o me, it is shocking that as of March 1963 in this, the leading medical Nation on earth, funds have been so lacking that this indispensable concept"—that is, the study of drugs in children—"is still only in the proposal stage."[30]

As the hearings began on March 21, Humphrey called an eager John Nestor to Capitol Hill, asking him to explain publicly the insider's perspective he had already provided to Humphrey's staff in great detail. Nestor's remarks unequivocally set the hearing's tone: "In the past, adequate recognition has not been accorded to the problem of drug therapy in infants and children. There has been a failure to recognize that the metabolism and action of drugs often differs both qualitatively and quantitatively in this special group."[31] Nestor began his testimony by explaining the informal manner in which he became an FDA consultant. "Upon reading in a medical magazine of the problems of FDA in obtaining and retaining qualified physicians," he made an appointment with the FDA commissioner and "offered my services."[32] Believing that the agency sought his "frank and open" opinion, he accepted a position, but he quickly became disenchanted:

> Unfortunately, although my frankness was acceptable before I was hired, after joining the organization I found that any medical opinion that raised issues that involved reappraisal of past decisions, past policies, or past commitments to the pharmaceutical industry would be challenged—not in a healthy scientific atmosphere, but rather, with indifference, disapproval, or even hostility. This, unfortunately, was frequently the case with drugs for pediatric use.[33]

Pointedly reminding the congressmen that he was the first board-certified pediatrician ever hired by the FDA, Nestor appeared to hold nothing back, excoriating the agency's operating procedures in general and citing a number of instances in which he alleged incompetence. He painted a damning portrait of the FDA regarding pediatric policies, claiming that staffers involved in pediatric-related decisions lacked an appreciation of the latest scientific research relevant to children. As such, they possessed "a failure to recognize that the metabolism and action of drugs often differ both quantitatively and qualitatively in this special group" and a "disregard of the long- and well-established medical principle that infants and children often react differently to disease and drugs than do adults."[34]

Moreover, according to Nestor, the FDA did not seem concerned about its ignorance regarding children, stipulating that "the standard the FDA aspired to" with regard to children was "perfunctory and meager":

> Applications were approved for [pediatric use] . . . despite the fact that the testing had been carried out in only a few children and very few infants in many

instances. There seemed to be a general disregard for the need to establish the safety of the use of the drug in the pediatric age group. What may be regarded as an "established" drug and therefore, not a "new" drug in adult medicine is often a new type of treatment for adults and children, raising all the questions of rationale, risks, and usefulness.[35]

In other words, he was trying to explain in lay terms that children and adults often received the same drug for different purposes; for example, antihistamines were used for treating allergies in adults and for treating colic in infants. Nestor concluded by hinting at fraudulent activity on the part of industry, which, he claimed, was ignored by a complaisant FDA.[36]

Charles May, now professor of pediatrics at New York University School of Medicine and former editor of *Pediatrics*, followed Nestor's testimony and provided his views as an expert with outsider status relative to governmental processes. May was much less inflammatory than Nestor and, interestingly, said nothing about his 1961 remarks at the Conference on Perinatal Pharmacology, in which he had voiced weak support for any new regulation. Perhaps as evidence of just how tepidly he supported the Kefauver-Harris Amendments to the Federal Food, Drug, and Cosmetic Act, however, he put the blame for the lack of data about newborns and pharmacology not on industry or government regulations, but on pediatricians who had not "given sufficient attention" to the problem.[37]

Although May's testimony was surely a relief to FDA leadership, the damage from Nestor's accusations required a response. Agency commissioner George P. Larrick sent a letter to Humphrey that same afternoon, rebutting each of Nestor's charges. With regard to Nestor's claim that FDA staff not only ignored children but lacked a basic understanding of how they differed from adults, Larrick cited multiple cases to demonstrate the reverse. For example, he provided the text of a speech in which Bureau of Medicine director Ralph G. Smith detailed the latest understanding of newborn physiology and pharmacodynamics. Larrick particularly faulted Nestor for not making clear that almost every one of the instances he cited had occurred before the Kefauver-Harris Amendments became law. But none of this seemed to matter to a furious Senator Humphrey. He responded to Larrick's rejoinder with his own "Initial Rebuttal to the Rebuttal."[38]

The focus of the hearings now turned away from the past and toward considerations for the future, such as how best to evaluate drugs according to the new rules for safety and efficacy, as well as the pressing need for more qualified investigators to undertake pediatric drug research. Witnesses and congressmen expressed considerable optimism about the new NIH branch, the NICHD, and its potential role in training the investigators necessary to generate new science as well as to teach clinicians about pediatric pharmacology.[39]

Alaska Senator Ernest Gruening, a doctor who had worked as a journalist before he entered politics as a New Deal reformer, emphasized two issues he felt needed to be addressed immediately. First, the NIH had no obstetricians and only one pediatrician on its grant-making staff, and, second, with the exception of poison prevention and treatment, not one of the 6,200 hospitals involved in the FDA system for reporting negative drug outcomes was a children's hospital.[40] Gruening believed that the answer to children's underrepresentation in pharmaceutical development lay in the NICHD's potential to expand the science and increase the number of researchers necessary to address these issues. He expressed his hope for such a plan when introducing Stanford University biochemist and pediatrician Norman Kretchmer, who had recently published an editorial in *Pediatrics* in which he had championed these very thoughts.[41] Kretchmer did not mince words when it came to accountability for safety and efficacy. He argued that the "responsibility is on the manufacturer to take particular care to comprehend and document the entire range of action of a drug when it is to be used in the treatment of the young infant."[42] Provocatively, he dryly suggested that if pharmaceutical companies took the money they put into advertising and used it to support clinical pharmacology, they would have ample funding to assess drug effects for infants and children.[43]

Humphrey also presented data that documented a meager $3.7 million in current NIH funding for twelve pediatric drug-related studies. Although he did not say so for the record, the former pharmacist surely saw a glaring issue in investigations receiving NIH support. The majority of them focused on a narrow population. One study, for example, looked at the way growth hormone affected developmentally disabled children; another focused on pediatric cancer treatment.[44] None of them studied metabolism, distribution, absorption, excretion, and other metrics for the drugs most commonly used in children, information increasingly referred to by the term *pharmacokinetics*.

Finally, Humphrey introduced into the congressional record a number of letters to the government from parents and doctors. Some of these expressed heartfelt gratitude to Kelsey, but others detailed the worrisome side effects of drugs their children had taken. One parent, for example, explained a reaction her ten-year-old son experienced as a result of Compazine. "His eyes became fixed in his head. He couldn't move them. His facial muscles became rigid. His body began to twist and pull until he had no control."[45] The letter writer assumed her son was allergic to the medication, but later found a magazine article that acknowledged this potential side effect from the drug. Upset that no one had informed the family, she beseeched Humphrey to "help make this fact known so that parents may become aware of the harmful effects of these drugs."[46] Letters such as these provided the evidence Humphrey wanted to show that the American parents demanded more governmental oversight of drug industry practices.

## The Birth of the Therapeutic Orphan

Shirkey increasingly saw his job as getting all stakeholders for pediatric drugs to "communicate the same message" to industry and policymakers.[47] In an effort to accomplish this aim, he added membership on the AMA Council on Drugs to his USP and AAP appointments. "When anything came up, I brought those three together and made them work it out," he wrote.[48] The AAP executive board had endorsed Shirkey's request to broaden the COD charge to one that encompassed all issues surrounding children's drug testing, safety, policy, and physician education.[49]

In the wake of the Kefauver-Harris Amendments, Shirkey was at first optimistic that structural changes in pediatric drug development and regulation would be forthcoming. Within the year, however, he saw ominous signs that the legislation might not protect children in the ways he hoped it would. He noted disappointedly that drug companies circumvented the additional pediatric drug safety information the law mandated by adding labels that declared, "This drug is not indicated for children."[50] Because this practice became the norm, individual companies were not at a competitive disadvantage. Without a specific requirement that anyone systematically gather new evidence through a clinical trial or critique already extant pediatric data, by 1964 Shirkey felt children were being left out of the safety and efficacy improvements already benefiting adults. He described this phenomenon with a memorable, Dickensian phrase—*therapeutic orphan*—which would become his mantra in his critique of American pediatric drug policy.[51]

The FDA acknowledged the problem Shirkey was working so hard to publicize at one of its meetings in 1965. In response to a request from the AMA Council on Drugs for how to indicate on a drug label the lack of pediatric data, eight FDA staffers drafted a statement: "This drug ordinarily should not be used in children since safety and effectiveness information on its use is not available."[52] The FDA, however, took no further action, most likely because at that moment the agency faced a much broader problem than pediatric drug safety. The Kefauver-Harris Amendments assigned the FDA the daunting task of overseeing an efficacy review, determining whether the thousands of drugs brought to market since the 1938 Federal Food, Drug, and Cosmetic Act had the effects their manufacturers claimed. In 1966 the agency contracted with the newly created Drug Research Board of the National Academy of Sciences to plan a review of each drug. Over the next three years, the thirty panels of the Drug Efficacy Study Implementation (DESI) program analyzed evidence surrounding 4,000 drugs in the hopes of quantifying their therapeutic utility.

Although pediatricians served on a number of the panels and Harry Shirkey played a leadership role because of his appointment to the study's Policy Advisory Committee, the DESI initiative added little new information specific to children. Operationally, the thirty panels were organized by drug class (such as anti-infective) or organ system (such as cardiovascular), rather than by life stage or other classification. Pediatricians were dispersed through the various panels, making conversations about children difficult. More problematic, however, was that the quality of scientific data for pediatrics just did not exist. It was already clear to Shirkey by 1966 that participants lacked a "firm body of knowledge upon which to base a scientific opinion" about pediatric efficacy in a meaningful way as mandated by the 1962 Kefauver-Harris Amendments.[53] Ultimately, the vast majority of research in the published literature or the drug houses that met DESI requirements included adult subjects only.[54]

To generate the necessary evidence to appraise pediatric drug efficacy using randomized trial data, the few available investigators encountered formidable barriers. No one was really sure how to design a study with meaningful endpoints in a child, an evolving physiological target. Under what circumstances could adult data be extrapolated to children? Which animal models translated to humans? Were drug studies needed for each pediatric subpopulation (premature babies, newborns, toddlers, preschoolers, school-age children, adolescents)? What was the best metric to use in terms of dosage calculation? Should the scientific template be predicated on percentage of adult weight, on body surface area, or on an entirely different model? Given the paucity of scientists or clinicians with the necessary training, who was qualified to develop, conduct, and analyze the investigations?

The NICHD had initiated a developmental pharmacology program to address the scientific issues regarding the fetus, infant, and child, but the institute leaders acknowledged that it would take years for the investment to pay off. Stakeholders could not even agree about pediatric pharmacology's place within the medical specialty substructure, a decision with both philosophical and reimbursement implications. If, for example, pediatric pharmacologists were situated in medical school clinical departments, revenue streams from grant funding accrued there, and not in the basic science departments that often trained investigators and designed the studies. Finally—and critically—who should incur the cost burden of pediatric drug development? Government? Industry? Parents? Insurers? Hospitals? Medical schools?[55]

Furthermore, the tensions within traditional sources used to guide clinical practice—medical journals—became increasingly suspect as pediatricians scrutinized advertisements in these journals with a more critical eye, using the 1962 safety and efficacy criteria. Journals needed advertising to stay in business, but advertisements did not go through the peer review process the way scientific articles did, and problems ensued. For example, in a 1966 letter to the editor in *Pediatrics*, pediatrician Arthur Eidelman expressed his dismay that the journal had accepted an advertisement from Merck and Company. The promotion claimed that the steroid Decadron (dexamethasone) was a useful therapeutic for croup. Eidelman argued that the journal's acceptance of an advertisement "implies de facto endorsement by the Academy of the safety (if not the efficacy) of the particular product or mode of therapy."[56] He complained that the copy did not explain the drug's utility for different types of croup (e.g., viral vs. bacterial), and he was upset that it had not noted that Decadron's use was "still controversial."[57] Finally, he criticized the fact that the journal's editors had accepted the paid promotion because "What is obviously needed . . . is a large, well-controlled, double-blind (and probably inter-hospital) study to clarify its efficacy in the management of the different types of croup."[58]

A somewhat chastened editorial response by Clement A. Smith did not disagree with Eidelman's charges, yet he attempted to reassure readers that advertisements were carefully vetted. According to Smith, *Pediatrics* had turned down twenty-five drug- and food-related advertisements and forced twenty-eight others to change their language. He conceded, however, that the journal's system was "not infallible" and that in this instance an error may have been made.[59] Smith reminded readers of the journal's policy warning pediatricians to make clinical practice decisions based on "scientific reports . . . rather than from other sources."[60] In other words, *Pediatrics* tacitly recommended that its subscribers read advertisers' claims with a skeptical eye. There is no evidence that Eidelman's complaint—or others like it—made their way to the FDA for follow-up.

Another challenge to the traditional practice of physician-determined estimations of risk versus benefit analyses as the primary criterion for children's participation in a drug trial, was the mandate included in the Kefauver-Harris Amendments that stipulated informed consent for all research subjects, although exactly what that meant was still under debate. Moreover, the ethics surrounding human experimentation were not confined to the United States. In 1964 the World Medical Association, a group of national medical organizations, published research principles known as the Declaration of Helsinki. These guidelines distinguished between therapeutic and nontherapeutic research, stipulated that all research undergo independent ethical review, and mandated informed consent. With regard to children, the declaration supported the rights of parents to enroll their child in a research study, without restrictions. In other words, a parent's consent absolved investigators of ethical concerns, even if the study brought risk to an individual child, such as a study undertaken to increase scientific knowledge that brought no potential for benefit to him or her.[61] By the mid-1960s the FDA required that companies and researchers secure patients' consent before they received an investigational drug. Researchers, however, found a loophole that they could use if they so chose. The FDA Statement of Investigator form required consent "from subjects, or their representatives, except where this is not feasible or, in the investigator's professional judgment, [doing so] is contrary to the best interests of subjects."[62] This qualifier effectively permitted investigators to substitute their own judgment for parents whenever they chose.

All these issues—lack of qualified investigators, research design, consent, funding for pediatric drug research, and advertising debates—needed to be considered in the context of tectonic shifts in health care economics occurring in the mid-1960s. More American families had health insurance through private employer-sponsored plans. The elderly and indigent could look to new public programs, Medicare and Medicaid. The old, largely self-pay or charity-supported health care model in which patients often participated in research or acquiesced to medical care without question was waning.[63]

A signal that ethical norms in the United States were in transition arrived in 1966 when Harvard anesthesiologist Henry Beecher published a damning critique of contemporary biomedical research ethics.[64] In his article, Beecher described twenty-two research studies from the mainstream medical literature that he judged ethically troubling, four of which included children. One article Beecher condemned was emblematic of the type of research undertaken in earlier decades by Hodes, Richmond, Finland, and other investigators. The article, published in the prestigious *New England Journal of Medicine*, explained that Wyeth Laboratories had funded Howard E. Ticktin and Hyman J. Zimmerman, George Washington University medical school faculty members, to study the effects of the antibiotic Triacetyloleandomycin (TriaA) on institutionalized "mental defectives" or "juvenile delinquents" at the Laurel, Maryland, Children's Center.[65] The participants, some as young as thirteen years old, were healthy except for their acne. The study was undertaken to "determine the incidence and type of hepatic dysfunction" from TriA.[66] More than half of the fifty patients in the study experienced signs of liver problems from the drug, at which point they were subjected to an invasive liver biopsy; several individuals required more than one such procedure. Liver function tests eventually returned to normal in all subjects.[67]

As soon as Beecher's critique was published, he began receiving letters from physicians. While not drug-related, one exchange between Beecher and a young pediatrician at the University of Rochester medical school reveals how difficult it could be to initiate a dialogue about ethical concerns. The pediatrician, Evan Charney, told Beecher about an episode that had been troubling him since his training days at Boston Children's Hospital three years earlier. In

1963 he had written to A. Ashley Weech, editor in chief of the *American Journal of Diseases of Children*, expressing concern about a recent study in which newborn female infants were restrained, had a catheter placed in their umbilical vein, and received an intravenous infusion for a study of newborn water balance. Charney pointed out that this experiment was undertaken to generate knowledge, not to benefit the children enrolled. As such, he believed the study "a debatable case of medical judgment which requires careful scrutiny."[68]

Charney included his back and forth correspondence with Weech in the materials he sent to Beecher. Weech replied to Charney explaining that he would not publish his letter because it might "do a great deal of harm to the scientific reputations of a group of young men."[69] Weech also commented in a patronizing tone that when he was a junior doctor like Charney, he, also, was "too young at the time" to understand the importance of some investigations.[70] Instead of publishing Charney's critique, Weech offered to contact the lead physician on the study, T. C. Panos at the University of Arkansas. Weech subsequently forwarded to Charney his correspondence with Panos, in which the latter acknowledged the difficult balance between risk and protection. Nonetheless, Panos agreed with Weech about Charney's concerns and motivations: "[T]here is the danger . . . of confusing ethics with self-righteousness."[71] In Beecher's reply to Charney, he made clear that Panos's research was just the type of study he had been criticizing. He bluntly told Charney that the *American Journal of Diseases of Children* should be "downright ashamed of itself for the attitude it took."[72]

## National Conferences on Pediatric Pharmacology, But Little Progress

Progress on pediatric drug safety seemed stalled. Clinicians could rely only on their own judgment or the published literature. For example, in 1967 the FDA investigated the case of an eight-year-old child who had died from an Eli Lilly and Company drug used to treat parasitic infections. The doctor prescribed the drug, Delvex (dithiazanine iodide), according to the unnamed resource he consulted. Delvex had not received FDA approval for use in children, so there were no FDA-sanctioned pediatric dosing guidelines. The suggested dosage published in the manual was most likely predicated on clinical trial and error and, in this case, proved fatal to a child.[73] Worse yet, the paucity of pediatric drug knowledge was becoming normalized in the pharmacology literature. For instance, Louis S. Goodman, the renowned professor of pharmacology at the University of Utah, authored many editions of a definitive textbook, *Pharmacological Basis of Therapeutics*, with Yale University medical school pharmacologist Alfred Gilman. The authors' notes and correspondence for the volume throughout the 1960s—a period in which there was a tremendous expansion of knowledge in other areas of pharmacology—barely mention pharmacokinetic issues specific to children[74]

Discussions regarding how to move forward on children's drug safety and efficacy issues now pervaded research, clinical practice, industry, FDA, and NICHD discourse. The National Academy of Sciences, FDA, NICHD, and the National Institute of General Medical Sciences (NIGMS), which oversaw pharmacology research training programs, decided to sponsor an invitational conference in 1967 in an effort to help the FDA "fulfill its responsibility ... [and] ... approve recommended dosages for drugs and directions for their safe use" in the pediatric population.[75] By bringing together academic pediatricians, industry, and the FDA, the conference leaders aimed to promulgate a set of regulations governing children and drugs.

If Harry Shirkey attended the conference, no documents record his participation. In fact, his name does not appear in the list of attendees invited, a curious omission for a pediatrician with his credentials.[76] Perhaps he was absent because he was then serving as a visiting professor at Honolulu's Kauikeolani Children's Hospital, far from the conference site and planners in Washington. Perhaps the organizers at the FDA found Shirkey's term *therapeutic orphan* unnecessarily inflammatory or confrontational, and expected his participation to follow suit. Or perhaps tensions among the few pediatrician-pharmacologists on the national scene had become heightened. A reorganization of the AAP Committee on Drugs (COD) resulted in Shirkey's chairmanship going to Harvard-trained Sumner Yaffe, a pediatrician at the State University of New York at Buffalo medical school. Finally, it may have been that Yaffe's basic science research training and experience (as well as his close affiliation with NICHD) embodied the pedigree the conference conveners sought.

The meeting began optimistically and ambitiously, with the stated goal of addressing issues of safety and efficacy that the FDA could use to quickly generate a regulatory template. When Eli Lilly and Company's Charles N. Christensen spoke for the drug industry, however, he offered a sobering perspective. First, he sought to mute expectations, explaining that instead of presenting an "ideal" program as organizers had requested, he wanted the group to consider what was "practical" instead.[77] He argued that "before we get to the question of how to do it [study pharmacokinetics in the developing child], we must consider, are we going to do it?"[78] Christensen did agree with the broad statement that "we need more and better evaluation of drugs in infants and children."[79] His solution, however, left all the control and decision-making about how and whether to test with industry, advocating for an advisory group to consult with drug companies and the FDA "[i]nstead of a stringent set of 'this you must do for every drug' rules."[80] Christensen also stressed what industry saw as a barrier to complying with the Kefauver-Harris Amendments as the law related to children: too few trained researchers and a lack of pharmacokinetic guidelines.

Physician Charles F. Weiss, representing Parke Davis and Company, agreed with Christensen, characterizing what he saw as an "emotionalism" surrounding pediatric experimentation that heightened the risk for industry and investigators.[81] He believed the stakes were high, that the negative public relations consequences of a study that harmed children would likely be worse than for other groups. On the other hand, Weiss pointed out, because children occupied a symbolic place in the United States as deserving innocents who needed protection, there could be a payoff in public goodwill for any company that successfully developed a new pediatric medication. Weiss also acknowledged that children could serve as evidence of companies' beneficence, noting that charities do not "put up the picture of an old alcoholic or prostitute on its posters to get money. Instead they use the picture of a little child in braces."[82]

Pediatrician Charles U. Lowe from the University of Florida medical school outlined the objectives for the final panel, one that considered ways in which the media could aid "in convincing the public about the need to enroll children in drug studies in order to generate the necessary data."[83] But this session, too, revealed that there would be no easy resolution to how best to move forward on issues concerning pediatric drug knowledge. Panelist Mildred Spencer, medical editor for the *Buffalo Evening News*, reminded attendees that their access to research participants was likely to decline in the wake of Medicaid because the indigent could no longer be pressured to do so in exchange for charity care. She ominously synthesized the challenges ahead, ones that could not be fixed easily by a public relations campaign:

> The public today has taken the attitude, and it is my attitude, that nothing should be done on someone else's child that we would not want done to our own children. . . . The press cannot create a climate of favorable public opinion for you. We tell the story. The reaction of the public depends on what you do. . . . It may be that [institutionalized mentally retarded] children are not as valuable as the future citizens the drugs may save, but I do not think the public is going to accept using them as test subjects. And I do not think anything the press can say will make the public accept it.[84]

In the wake of the conference, the AAP COD developed a formal liaison relationship with the FDA and an advisory role to the Pharmaceutical Manufacturers Association. Committee membership doubled and the group began meeting more frequently, publishing an ongoing commentary about pediatric drug-related issues in *Pediatrics*. Additionally, Sumner Yaffe successfully convinced the AAP executive board that there was need for a new workgroup, the Section on Pediatric Pharmacology, which would address educational issues pertaining to drugs. The COD, however, would remain the official AAP voice for drug policy. The revamped COD now included a place for industry representation and added two of the more vocal attendees at the recent conference, Charles H. Christensen and Charles Weiss. Even though Shirkey had left the COD, he remained an ex officio presence because of his affiliation with the AMA Council on Drugs. An FDA representative, medical officer Jean Lockhart, filled the final committee position.[85]

All the issues present at the 1967 conference resurfaced in May 1968, when infant formula maker Ross Laboratories sponsored a pediatric pharmacology symposium. The Ross meeting began with frustration and finger-pointing, unlike the positive tone that characterized the start the previous year. Conference chair Alan K. Done of the University of Utah medical school opened the gathering by expressing his frustration that "concern and talk" about pediatric drug safety had not, as yet, yielded "progress and practical solutions."[86] Next, neonatologist William A. Silverman posed a blunt question that signaled his impatience with the status quo: "What is the FDA doing to stimulate research in pediatric pharmacology?"[87] Daniel Banes, FDA associate commissioner for science, responded reluctantly that the agency's primary role was, thus far, that of a "gadfly to induce industrial firms and universities to conduct research" because it lacked grant-making authority.[88]

When it was his turn, C. Joseph Stetler, president of the Pharmaceutical Manufacturers Association, expressed industry's belief that "needless and arbitrary limitations on drug development" put in place a few years earlier in the wake of the thalidomide disaster made it harder for them to do business.[89] Speaking in general terms, and without discussing pediatric issues, he stressed the increased costs companies faced because of the Kefauver-Harris Amendments, the results of which, he argued, were slowing the pharmaceutical development juggernaut that began in the 1940s. The only area in which industry and FDA reached consensus at the meeting was that too many pediatricians refused to undertake the necessary clinical research, even with drug company sponsorship. Shirkey did attend the Ross conference and spoke eloquently about the growing "unreality" of the situation.[90] He also pointed out the way physicians were put "in a very difficult legal position" because "drugs which ultimately will be used in infants or children" include instructions "stating they should not be so used."[91] A second conference ended with no real consensus or forward movement.

The FDA received a number of queries around this time from individual pediatricians whose concerns over the impasse echoed Shirkey's. For example, Melissa A. Warfield, medical director of the Children's Hospital of the King's Daughters in Norfolk, Virginia, sought guidance about the antiemetic drug Tigan (trimethobenzamide hydrochloride), specifically about the label's "Not for use in children" warning. Given that her institution cared for children from birth through eighteen years, how should she interpret this guideline for her hospital's formulary? In internal memoranda, FDA staffers debated the definition of a child in the context of Warfield's letter. In his reply to Warfield two months later, B. Harvey Minchew, acting deputy director of the FDA Bureau of Medicine, suggested that she consider that Tigan was approved for use in those over the age of twelve years. He indicated his displeasure that the manufacturer had not provided more precise data, pointing out that the FDA "generally recommend[s]" that companies do so. He also reminded Warfield of her right to use drugs off-label, meaning that a doctor could prescribe the drug for a purpose or a dosage he or she chose. The physician, he noted pointedly, had the right to use "commercially available drugs in a manner which his knowledge and experience indicate to him is in the best interest of his patient."[92] Although no further correspondence between the two exists, it is probable that this delayed reply, one that put the onus of deciding safety and efficacy back on Warfield, did not provide the guidance she sought.

In 1968, in a speech at Harry Shirkey's Children's Hospital in Birmingham, Alabama, FDA commissioner James L. Goddard publicly and frankly acknowledged the agency's frustration about therapeutic orphans. Situating the agency's work in the context of increased funding for maternal and child health services proposed by President Lyndon B. Johnson that year, he informed those in attendance of the FDA's general efforts in the approval, monitoring, and regulatory processes for drugs. Goddard expressed his concern that the FDA was not receiving investigational plans from drug companies for children. But he also articulated the agency's limitations. "Unless such data is submitted to us," he said, "it is not legally possible for the FDA to permit anything else [other than a label stipulating the drug has not been established as safe for children] on the label of a marketed drug other than that prohibitive clause."[93] He asked his audience of pediatricians to take ownership of the problem because he was "loath to believe that all the tough questions must be passed on to the Government for final answers. Surely this issue of drug use in children—the prohibition in the labeling being based on the void in the clinical back-up—surely this issue can be examined and resolved by physicians themselves."[94]

Goddard had admitted that the problem might seem "insoluble," although he did try to end optimistically, claiming he remained "confident" of a solution, one that accounted for children's "moral, ethical, and medical issues."[95] He assured the group he believed that children—"who are now receiving such comprehensive attention in health" from President Johnson's Great Society programs—should not "be literally deprived of useful drugs."[96] Undoubtedly Shirkey, if not others, could hear that Goddard's speech sounded remarkably similar to one ten years earlier by prior commissioner Paul B. Dunbar: celebratory, focused on generalities, and lacking operational details.[97] In the late

1960s, FDA staffers repeatedly lamented the growing knowledge gap between pediatric and adult pharmacology, but their meetings yielded no concrete plan of action.[98] As they had in the past, they debated how to define the age ranges for pediatric categories—for example, neonates, infants, children, and adolescents. But their central question remained as to how the agency should proceed when the drug under consideration held "a clear possibility for use in children" and "data on safety and efficacy are extensive in adults but meager in children"?[99]

The situation was no better for the AAP COD. Its meeting minutes and discussions in this era are conspicuous for what they avoid—who should pay for pediatric testing? Members spent a great deal of time on the wording of statements about the importance of pediatric testing and drug safety and the merits of particular therapeutic agents, but the critical issue of just who should fund drug testing was never discussed for the record.[100] As a subcommittee within the AAP, of course, the COD was not free to advocate independently from its parent organization. Members faced the difficult balancing act of focusing attention on issues surrounding children and drugs without overtaking the agenda of the larger organization. For the AAP executive board, pediatric pharmacology was just one of many issues. At that point in time, for instance, the AAP sought congressional support for pending bills related to child abuse, and for increases in funding for pediatric medical training and social welfare programs.[101] By design, the AAP had mandated the COD to advocate but not agitate—a very tenuous position. It could serve as an "authoritative body" in terms of the "science and practice of therapeutics as it relates to the pediatric patient."[102] It could consult with the FDA, monitor legislation, issue commentary on particular drugs, and study drug-related issues, but it could not independently weigh in on potentially controversial, but critical, issues such as who, exactly, should provide funding for and oversight of the process.

As the decade ended, with no concrete outcomes from either of the pediatric pharmacology conferences and little progress within the FDA, Shirkey grew even more worried. In private correspondence in 1969 to Cleveland, Ohio, pediatrician Irwin A. Shaefer, he was so frustrated he romanticized the pre-1962 Kefauver-Harris Amendments era: "Before the drug amendments of 1962," he complained, "there was some pediatric testing *before* a drug's release and its use by a physician for a child."[103] While Shirkey blamed industry, he was also upset with pediatricians for not accepting responsibility to undertake research. He was also irritated with the FDA, explaining to Shaefer the way he had "put this issue squarely" commissioner Herbert Ley at a National Research Council Policy Advisory Committee meeting for the DESI program:

> He [Ley] had mentioned the poor data which comes from industry. I enlarged this to suggest that he expand his criticism to us in the "scientific community"

since only we can get data. Then, I brought the criticism back 360° to his organization which approves new drug applications *without* study in a large segment
of the population (infants and children) who cannot speak for themselves. Truly
all of us have orphaned the children.... [T]he situation in which practicing
physicians find themselves is deplorable.... Is the group in which the greatest
catastrophes have occurred to be placed in further jeopardy?[104]

It is also likely that Shirkey was increasingly discouraged by the confusion surrounding consent and pediatric research. Henry Beecher spotlighted
the pediatric specific issues regarding informed consent and research ethics
for children as part of his ongoing critique of medical ethics. He and lawyer
William J. Curran published their analysis of legal precedents, risks, benefits,
and, ultimately, their recommendations for children in a 1969 *JAMA* article.[105]
Beecher and Curran believed that parents and older children should have a
great deal of deciding power with regard to participation in research, a position subsequently challenged by Princeton University religion professor Paul
Ramsey and NIH lawyer Edward Rourke. Ramsey and Rourke wanted to limit
children's participation in any research deemed nontherapeutic for that child,
even if they and their parents gave permission, arguing that exposing youngsters to risk without direct benefit to them was simply immoral. Pediatricians,
too, were divided on this issue.[106]

The FDA's informed consent guidelines in the late 1960s gave parents full
consenting authority for any research, medication, or treatment, therapeutic
or nontherapeutic, a stance with which the COD appears to have been in full
accord since it published the guidelines in *Pediatrics* in 1969 with positive
commentary. The FDA rules allowed physicians to abstain from informing
a parent, guardian, or child if he or she thought it best. If, for example, the
physician deemed it "impossible or 'not in the child's best interest'—a situation which the attending physician must determine with great care," he or she
could order the drug be administered without permission.[107] In other words, it
fell within the purview of physicians to determine when, and in what circumstances, parents and children should be brought into the discussion.

## Who Speaks for Children?

In 1970, in an attempt to break the stalemate and stimulate industry to take
ownership of children's drug development- and safety-related issues, Marion J.
Finkel, the new deputy director of the FDA Bureau of Drugs, brought stakeholders together to discuss pediatric-related issues. An internist, Finkel joined
the FDA in 1963 as part of its post Kefauver-Harris Amendments expansion.
She rose through the ranks quickly, and by 1970 she was the agency's highest-
ranking woman. Finkel signaled industry that the FDA might not approve

new drug applications if the product had a potential pediatric use and lacked the necessary pharmacokinetic and dosing information. At a meeting in November 1970, she asked industry, FDA, and COD attendees for guidance regarding whether all drugs needed to be tested in pediatric subgroups such as neonates, infants, toddlers, and older children. The meeting resulted in just one concrete outcome, a decision to convene a National Academy of Sciences advisory group to address pediatric drug research.[108]

Finkel believed that companies should fund pediatric studies, an idea that received strenuous objection from the PMA representatives in attendance. Eli Lilly and Company's Charles Christensen warned that such a policy might result in a firm's deciding against developing a much-needed medication. Such veiled threats did not deter Finkel, whose remarks were publicized in the trade journal *F-D-C Reports*: "We [the FDA] . . . feel that [the therapeutic orphan] . . . situation requires correction. . . . Accordingly, we are adopting the policy that it is possible that an NDA for a drug that would have considerable therapeutic utility in children . . . in the absence of adequate investigational studies in children will not be approved unless the necessary studies are performed."[109]

Finkel's bold stance came as pediatricians' requests to the FDA were growing more pointed—and exasperated. Pediatrician Robert Warren from Richmond, Indiana, for example, wrote to the agency in early 1971 concerned about the lack of pediatric drug data. "As a practicing pediatrician I am in a position of making a dosage decision which is avoided by those with far more information," he complained.[110] He received a weak response from staffer John W. Winkler, "regretting" there were no data to give him.[111] An aghast and angry Warren penned another letter to Winkler challenging the moral logic of the situation in which he found himself: "[M]y basic question . . . was why should a practicing physician decide appropriate dosage [for a child] under the age of three years when neither the manufacturer nor the FDA will give guidelines. . . . Doesn't the law now require demonstration of effectiveness as well as safety?"[112]

In an effort to keep the discussion going, in February 1971, Sumner Yaffe and the rest of the COD, joined by industry representatives Charles Weiss, Charles Christensen, and Schering executive John Leer, put together a proposal aimed at convincing drug companies to underwrite pediatric pharmacology centers. After soliciting thirty-two companies for contributions, Leer dejectedly reported that only six had agreed to donate an unspecified amount of money. Unfortunately, those six companies also stipulated that a majority of their remaining twenty-six competitors join them or their offer would be voided. Given this lack of support, Leer and Christensen told Yaffe that funding from industry would not be forthcoming.[113]

Another conference, this time sponsored by the National Academy of Sciences in November 1971, included all the familiar stakeholders: the COD with its clinical and research knowledge in the form of its pediatrician experts; the NICHD and NIGMS both charged with training investigators and funding research into developmental pharmacology; and industry, the source or financial sponsor of most drug development.[114] The invited guests worked in groups and focused on a set of specific questions, almost all of which were similar to those raised in the past, although the difference this time was that attendees evinced significantly less optimism. Rather than trying to develop a concrete action plan to address pediatric drug development, pharmacokinetic, and efficacy-related issues, participants devoted the bulk of time lamenting the problem. Significantly, no one addressed Finkel's demand that industry submit, if not fund, pediatric research. A frustrated Harry Shirkey beseeched stakeholders to break the impasse and called for some group to take leadership, if not ownership, of the problem challenging: "Who speaks for children?"[115] No one, however, replied. Shirkey lost most of his influence the next year when the AMA abolished its Council on Drugs because most of its duties now fell within the purview of the FDA. Refusing to give in, Shirkey led a discussion at one of the council's final meetings on the many "problems" in generating the necessary pediatric "research and experience."[116]

Three major conferences, numerous internal FDA meetings, and several attempts to stimulate industry funding and interest in sponsoring the necessary studies had all failed to generate an action plan that addressed the issue of the therapeutic orphan. Although the NICHD was making progress in training pediatric clinical pharmacologists, the numbers were still very small. Moral, legal, and ethical issues surrounding informed consent for drug testing in children remained unresolved. And despite a major expansion in FDA hiring after 1962, by 1972 only eighteen of the 118 medical officers in the agency had pediatric training and just two specialized in pediatric pharmacology. A sign of the discouragement felt by all participants was the resigned comparison Charles Weiss made when introducing a new section for the journal *Pediatrics*, called "Pharmacology for the Pediatrician," by comparing the discipline to "an underdeveloped country."[117]

In this context, FDA commissioner Charles C. Edwards took the stage at the AAP annual convention in October 1972. He began his speech by reassuring pediatricians that the FDA took the therapeutic orphan problem seriously. He referred to the phenomenon as "an anathema to every concept of modern care" and a "dangerous double standard" that needed "immediate attention."[118] He acknowledged that "between 1969 and 1971 more than half of all systemic drugs approved with a potential for use in children carried a label disclaimer for pediatric use. But many of these drugs are used in children, and, in too many cases, the physician has no choice" but to risk using them because they might relieve a child's suffering.[119] Edwards emphasized the joint FDA-AAP efforts and, like his predecessors, shared his optimism that meaningful guidelines for pediatric drug testing were on the horizon. He warned, however, that "although he was not interested in pointing a finger," in order to be "successful there must be a total effort on the part of the medical profession, industry, and the FDA. To date, we have not had this total effort."[120] He did not provide details of what a solution would look like, nor any ideas for how it might be achieved.

Pediatric drug safety and efficacy arose again in 1973 at hearings sponsored by Wisconsin senator Gaylord Nelson that focused on a number of drug-related issues, chief among them safety and affordability. While Nelson's efforts would not result in the sweeping changes Kefauver's had a decade earlier, the senator did pressure industry concerning a number of issues, among them drug costs.[121] When Shirkey testified at the Nelson hearings, he turned the tables on the senator and his colleagues, pressuring them to ensure Edwards fulfilled his recent promise to improve pediatric drug knowledge and safety.

Shirkey demanded that Congress force the FDA to live up to its mandate of assuring drug efficacy and safety for all, including infants and children.[122] He argued that ownership of the "blame and the shame" lay with the "big three"—industry, pediatricians, and government.[123] In his most blunt public statements thus far, he made a series of provocative statements. He began by focusing on the FDA, arguing that the agency had "a legal responsibility, a charge by Congress, not exclusively a charge to protect only the mature. They cannot arbitrate in favor of the needs of adults just because studies in mature subjects are easier and less costly. Time is running out: They must ultimately withhold approval of any New Drug Application in which realistically a potential use for adults and children exists. The FDA must 'speak' for children for new drugs."[124]

He and a surprised Senator Nelson sparred through a series of contentious exchanges, repeatedly interrupting one another. Nelson challenged Shirkey to defend the ethics of withholding drug approval for an agent known to benefit adults until the completion of pediatric testing. Although he did not mention the term "drug lag" by name, clearly his staff had briefed him on the concept. Some industry sympathizers in the medical community had become increasingly concerned about delays in getting drugs to market, arguing that the additional complexity and costs required by the Kefauver-Harris Amendments hampered drug development. As a result, they maintained that the numbers of new pharmaceuticals lagged behind what they would have been without the law. Fears surrounding drug lag pitted two constituencies, children and adults, against one another. Solving the therapeutic orphan problem the way Shirkey,

Yaffe, and others desired almost certainly meant new laws and potentially more complex regulations surrounding the statutes already in place.[125]

Shirkey showed little patience for Nelson's worries about drug lag, explaining the "untenable" problem from the pediatrician's perspective and rejecting the senator's framing as a children-versus-adults problem:

> He has a patient with an illness for which a certain drug has been most efficacious in adults, and let us say the patient is a child 11 years of age. That age we would call a child. Is he to withhold the use of this drug from this 11-year-old when it has been perfectly successful in a 15-year-old? . . . If he withholds a valuable drug, he is a criminal. If he follows the package insert, which says there have not been adequate studies, and then there is an adverse reaction, . . . then he has used a drug which has been clearly contraindicated for the use of children. He is damned if he does and damned if he does not.[126]

Back and forth the two men sparred:

> SENATOR NELSON:  But you would not object to marketing a drug that had only been tested adequately in adults if it were a lifesaving . . . new drug entity?
>
> DR. SHIRKEY:  Senator, I should think if it is a lifesaving drug, it should be tested in children.
>
> NELSON:  But you would then delay its marketing, even though studies showed that it was safe and efficacious in adults and critically important. You would still withhold it from those adults during the period of time you tested it on children.
>
> DR. SHIRKEY:  No. I would not withhold it from those adults. I would make certain a drug this valuable was tested on children so that it could be released for the children. . . . This is the thesis of my whole presentation.[127]

Answering his own question regarding who spoke for children, Shirkey stressed that the way industry did so was clear: "Industry can 'speak.' Industry has been 'speaking' and financially supporting the present level of drug knowledge for children. I contend this is inadequate."[128] He also presciently warned Nelson that if the government did not provide funding for pediatric testing, then the decision-making about which medications to test in children lay solely with drug companies. In Shirkey's mind, industry would, as it always had, continue to focus on developing pediatric drugs they believed would be most profitable, not necessarily ones clinicians believed were most needed.[129]

Finally, in a brilliant attempt to capture the zeitgeist, Shirkey charged that the lack of pediatric drug information represented a form of discrimination against children as a vulnerable minority. He proclaimed the time nigh for "children's liberation" from a normative practice in which drugs were regularly approved without pediatric safety and efficacy data.[130] Shirkey's testimony occurred at a high-water mark for rhetoric in the 1970s surrounding what society owed all American children. His words echoed those of reformers who nested their advocacy in the language used by other political movements, such as those seeking to end discrimination based on race or gender. Their efforts achieved new prominence in 1973, when civil rights attorney and activist Marion Wright Edelman founded the Children's Defense Fund, a private, not-for-profit advocacy focused on health, education, protection, and other issues affecting child well-being.[131]

## Child Protection in a New Era: Weighing the Risks and Benefits in Pediatric Drug Development

The United States in the early 1970s was a nation in cultural transition. Youth unrest and the civil rights, feminist, and antiwar movements were challenging and fracturing the country. At the same time, a number of voices joined the Children's Defense Fund in urging greater protections for children. But what did that mean in 1973? While child-saving was never a monolithic movement, advocacy on youngsters' behalf in the first part of the twentieth century had more unity than it did in the second half. Most progressive era child-savers' efforts centered around problems such as high rates of infant mortality and child labor and for mandatory education and juvenile justice laws. But reformers' causes were more diverse in the 1970s.[132] For example, to some, child protection meant legislating what had long been considered a social problem, child abuse, resulting in the first federal legislation to address the problem, the 1974 Child Abuse Prevention and Treatment Act. For others, child protection meant making sure all poor children benefited from new Medicaid rules that paid for well-child care and developmental screening. For the increasingly vocal parents of disabled youngsters, child protection included pressuring government to make sure they benefited from a free public education.[133]

For the most ambitious activists, child protection in the early 1970s meant supporting broad legislation that recognized children's unique needs as a population, such as the 1973 Comprehensive Child Development Bill (CCDB), designed to draw together programs interspersed throughout the health care, education, and social welfare governmental sectors for all children, poor and non-poor. While targeted laws for child abuse and broad access to public education for all children, including those with special needs, proved popular, the notion of a unified, cross-class, federal approach to children's health and social welfare proved much less so. The proposal received little bipartisan support and some charged it would "Sovietize" American youth. As the president, Richard M. Nixon, emphasized in his veto of the bill, "For the federal government to plunge headlong financially into supporting child development would commit the vast moral authority of the federal government to the side of communal approaches to child-rearing as against the family-centered approach."[134]

For Shirkey, child protection meant that children received medications for which there was robust evidence to support a prescribed dosing regimen and rationale for their use. But the politically contentious debates surrounding the CCDB showed the limits of political will for expansive child-focused legislation, especially laws that placed new mandates on American free enterprise. And even if a law did somehow pass, there was little consensus regarding how pediatric drug safety data could be generated without putting some children at risk as part of the testing. All concerned agreed the need for experimentally based data to address the problem, but both scenarios—testing and not testing drugs on children—were fraught with potential problems. Extrapolating dosages from adults was often not accurate and research put at least some youngsters in jeopardy from the testing. Some feared that the most vulnerable, indigent, and especially minority children would bear the bulk of the risk. So concerned was Marian Wright Edelman about the issue of medical experimentation that she made it one of the Children's Defense Fund's six areas of emphasis.[135]

In an attempt to address the scientific issues related to pediatric drug testing, members of the COD in 1973 worked through four drafts of the FDA-contracted *General Guidelines for the Evaluation of Drugs to Be Approved for Use during Pregnancy and for Treatment of Infants and Children*. When the *Guidelines* were finalized early the next year, they cogently synthesized the state of the science in pediatric pharmacology, even though the recommendations were surely more tentative than the COD chair, Sumner Yaffe, or the workgroup's consultant, Harry Shirkey, wanted. Although the document affirmed that drugs that had potential use for children should be tested in them for safety and efficacy, the committee had acknowledged the political reality that necessitated striking a balance between what was "desirable" and "necessary" because data "concerning pharmacokinetics which is desirable may not be feasible because of economic considerations or ethical questions."[136] Importantly, the *Guidelines* provided the clarity for pediatric stages the FDA had been seeking for years, defining the neonate, infant, toddler, child, and adolescent. It discussed issues specific to each age group, known toxicities, and challenges to determining efficacy or safety. Finally, the *Guidelines* outlined research methodological issues as well as those related to experimental design with particular relevance to the pediatric patient.

The *Guidelines* addressed consent only briefly, in recognition "that the ethics of 'drug testing' in minors is currently being debated."[137] Medical ethics became a national debate when news of the Tuskegee Study broke. Beginning in the early 1930s, the Public Health Service studied syphilis by observing its effects in indigent African American men in Tuskegee, Alabama, who were neither informed of the nature of the research nor offered penicillin when it became available in the 1940s.[138] In response to the resulting scandal, Senator Ted Kennedy, chair of the Subcommittee on Health of the Committee on Labor and Public Welfare, convened hearings in February 1973 to investigate experimentation-related issues such as how best to balance issues of safety and consent, especially in vulnerable populations.[139]

A number of morally questionable studies spotlighted by the media during Kennedy's congressional hearings involved the use of institutionalized children as research subjects, leading to a broader discussion of how best to assure the protection of all youngsters in medical experimentation. Research that had not been deemed ethically troubling at the time now came into question. For example, Joan Hodgman's late 1950s chloramphenicol research, in which a number of babies died after receiving the drug, became characterized as rogue researchers' misuse of vulnerable subjects.[140]

Early on the hearings' first day, FDA commissioner Edwards professed his understanding of the need for more pediatric drug-related data. When Pennsylvania senator Richard S. Schweiker pressed him to provide more detail, Edwards deferred to Henry E. Simmons, director of the Bureau of Drugs, who responded cautiously that FDA regulations regarding children were "evolving."[141] Simmons assured the senator that the FDA intended to mandate pediatric testing for a drug that might be used in children, but neither he nor Edwards provided an action plan for how this would occur.[142] As the hearings progressed throughout the first half of 1973, Congress, Edwards, and the most tireless champion for children's drug safety and efficacy, Harry Shirkey, discovered that the pediatric drug–related scientific and ethical issues got even more complex, as discussions surrounding pediatric drugs became entangled in the politics of legalized abortion.

## Pediatric Drug Research in the Aftermath of *Roe v. Wade*

In January 1973, just a month before the Kennedy hearings began, the U.S. Supreme Court affirmed a woman's right to terminate her pregnancy for any reason. Although the *Roe v. Wade* decision allowed states to set limits on second- and third-trimester abortions, in all fifty states abortion was now legal during the first trimester (twelve weeks). The dust had not yet settled on the Supreme Court ruling when a complicated question arose: If a woman planned to terminate her pregnancy, could the aborted fetal tissue be studied in an attempt to generate valuable data that might enhance drug pharmacokinetic knowledge? Supporters reasoned that this information could then be used to help the fetuses of those women who planned to continue their pregnancy.[143]

Shirkey quickly realized that legalized abortion further complicated the issue of pediatric drug research. In a 1974 speech in Buenos Aires, Argentina, at the International Congress of Pediatrics entitled "Ethical Limits of Pharmacological Research in Children," he expressed his frustration at what he saw as the latest challenge to addressing pediatric drug safety. A woman's right to choose, he said, had created "a great deal of emotionalism about the whole subject of abortion, and fetal research has been swept in with it."[144] He worried that, as a result, "vital fetal experimentation" might be restricted or banned.[145] He also saw how it could confound pediatric research consent-related issues. After all, he noted, if mothers had the right to terminate a pregnancy, why should there be any limits to their authority in terms of enrolling their already born progeny in research, even if it engendered significant risk to them? Shirkey's strategy was to try and tease apart the issues surrounding abortion and pediatric drug development. He argued that no matter what one thought about the issue of legalized abortion, "[t]he present status of pediatric pharmacology" represented a "crime against children."[146]

The discussions on Capitol Hill in 1973 and 1974 involving research protections, informed consent, and fetal tissue research resulted in the National Research Act, which created the National Commission for the Protection of Human Subjects in Biomedical and Behavioral Research. Congress charged the eleven-member panel with developing national guidelines for human experimentation. Although a number of physicians served on the commission, they were also joined by theologians, philosophers, and others from the emerging field of bioethics. Over the next several years, the group engaged in intense discussions regarding how to protect vulnerable populations such as mentally ill and disabled children from exploitation by researchers. They also debated issues such as what age a child might be developmentally capable of providing research participation assent, even if the law gave legal decision-making authority to parents or guardians.[147]

The AAP moved quickly to ensure that the commission heard the organization's perspective on all issues related to children and medical experimentation. It created the Pediatric Research, Informed Consent, and Medical Ethics (PRIME) task force, and invited Horace L. Hodes, who now had almost forty years of experience in pediatric medical research, to serve as chair. Although the task force's mission was broader than just drugs, the COD strove to make that topic the core of PRIME's efforts.[148] The COD had its own perspective on consent-related issues, and had a powerful vehicle through which to share its voice, given that it was under contract with the FDA to recommend ethical guidelines for pediatric drug research to complement the group's recently completed research standards. Members saw the rights of vulnerable populations on a continuum, with children needing more protection than, say, prisoners.

In a November 1974 letter to the NIH that summarized the COD's thoughts regarding ethical standards governing research, Sumner Yaffe stressed that some experimentation on prisoners was "essential" to garnering new knowledge about pharmacokinetics and toxicity that could benefit children.[149]

Meanwhile, the drug industry sought an alliance with the PRIME task force and the COD in the wake of the Kennedy hearings. In November 1974, Thomas C. Smith, director of clinical pharmacology for Parke Davis and Company, wrote a gossipy letter to the AAP, proclaiming his dismay at the "demagoguery" and "rude and disdainful" manner in which he thought Senator Kennedy had treated the FDA leadership.[150] After all, he snidely noted, more governmental oversight was not likely to provide protection to vulnerable populations, since it was the Public Health Service, not the drug industry or the American medical establishment, that bore the guilt for Tuskegee.[151] Given the growing challenges to physician authority made manifest by the Kennedy hearings, the company may have hoped a partnership with the AAP would help stave off any new legislation unfavorable to industry. In written documents and testimony before the National Commission, several organizations—the PRIME task force, the COD, and the research-oriented American Pediatric Society—supported the need for protections for children and for clarity surrounding parental proxy consent. However, they opposed what they viewed as a "precedent-shattering" effect on practice if fetal research was banned.[152] Rather, physician groups hoped such decisions could be made on a case-by-case basis as a joint decision between parents and physicians.[153]

In 1975 the National Commission issued its *Report and Recommendations: Research on the Fetus*, dashing the hopes of physician groups that decision-making would be left largely to them and their patients and families. The recommendations stipulated that fetal research must not carry more than "minimal risk" to the fetus, that is, the risks of daily life.[154] They made no distinction between fetuses in which the mother planned to abort and those in which she did not. Although researchers could petition for an exemption for a specific study, this ruling had the effect of shutting down almost all fetal research.

## A Collective National Stalemate and Innovation on the Ground

In 1975, 70 percent of the drugs listed in the *Physician's Drug Reference*, a major repository of drug-related information, lacked safety, dosing, pharmacokinetic, adverse reaction, or efficacy information for the pediatric patient.[155] The government seemed unclear what steps to take next. Caspar Weinberger, secretary of Health, Education, and Welfare, publicly admitted as much in February 1975, when he said he felt "on the horns of a dilemma" because he lacked procedures and consensus on who should pay for pediatric testing "to insure . . . safety, efficacy, and correct dosage among children."[156] Although twelve years had passed since the 1962 Kefauver-Harris Amendments, Weinberger acknowledged that the law was not in practice as it related to children: "There is no way to abide by the Harrison-Kefauver Act [*sic*] as it applies to drugs for children without first having a clear mandate on the ethical issues of testing drugs on children as subjects."[157]

And even the bravado that had animated the FDA's Marion Finkel a few years earlier, when she warned that new drug applications lacking relevant pediatric data might not receive approval, seemed to be waning. In October 1975, she disappointedly informed the COD that, although the agency sought better pediatric data, it lacked the leverage to change the status quo.[158] At the same time, a burgeoning health consumer movement was bringing new challenges to governmental authority. In 1975, for example, the FDA received many letters from parents about situations in which they questioned the safety of drugs they or their children had been prescribed.[159]

The stalemate and "handwringing," as one COD member called the conversations in early 1976, also impeded a pediatric perspective on broader drug policy issues of importance to many families, given the growing cost of medications in the United States.[160] One potential solution to reining in costs included encouraging companies to compete with one another by formulating and marketing "generic" drugs once a patent expired for a chemical entity. In order for this practice to be safe, however, scientific evidence needed to show that the generic version was bioequivalent, meaning that it possessed enough chemical similarity to the more expensive brand-name drug to work the same way.[161] The COD argued that children's biological exceptionalism complicated any discussion of generic drugs for children. Ultimately, the committee determined that "the data which would allow the pediatrician to prescribe generically and expect consistent therapeutic results does not exist."[162] As a result, "until suitable bioavailability data in children are determined, . . . the physician should continue to prescribe the products which have shown significant clinical effectiveness in his hands or in published clinical trials."[163]

Despite, or perhaps because of, the policy paralysis regarding pediatric drug safety at the national level, intellectually entrepreneurial physicians and scientists were taking action at their individual institutions. The Department of Clinical Pharmacology at Boston Children's Hospital, for example, secured funding from the Burroughs Wellcome Fund and the FDA to build an evidentiary base for pediatric drugs. Pediatrician Allan A. Mitchell and his colleagues created the Pediatric Drug Surveillance (PeDS) program in 1974. Their efforts began to inform clinical practice almost immediately. Within two years, 1,300 youngsters on the inpatient wards at Boston Children's Hospital had contributed data about the hundreds of FDA-approved drugs for which pediatric data were lacking. Mitchell and his team also began trials for new drugs, and, because the National Commission had not yet issued its pediatric report, the hospital continued to follow its own review process in terms of research ethics. It had created its first ethical review board, the Committee on Clinical Investigation, in 1969.[164]

Mitchell's prospective epidemiological study engaged nurse monitors to track a large volume of detailed information—adverse effects, toxicity, dose responses, and other pharmacokinetic metrics—on individual children in an effort to develop a comprehensive pediatric drug therapy database, exactly the type of evidence Taussig, Shirkey, Yaffe, and others had been demanding for years. The study was also aided by emerging computer technology, which facilitated the management and manipulation of large amounts of data in ways not possible in the past. The PeDS program's interdisciplinary nature also proved extremely valuable because the team-based approach allowed nurses, physicians, pharmacologists, and pharmacists to discuss issues related to medication prescription, formulation, and administration across disciplines in ways that synergized knowledge and improve patient care.[165] Others began on-the-ground attempts to generate pediatric drug knowledge, as well. For example, Sumner Yaffe left the University of Buffalo in 1975 for the University of Pennsylvania medical school and its affiliated pediatric clinical site, the Children's Hospital of Philadelphia (CHOP). Drawing on seed money from Johnson and Johnson, Yaffe developed a pediatric pharmacology research program that focused on several different diseases. Each child served as his or her own control for the study of specific drugs to treat the condition.[166]

Pediatric drug knowledge advanced rapidly in the area of cancer treatment in the 1970s, as the governmental, industry, and academic pediatric partnership for pediatric cancer established early in the postwar era continued to enhance survival rates, especially for those suffering from acute lymphocytic leukemia (ALL). But the pediatric cancer model did not translate well to children suffering from non–life-threatening conditions. Families with extremely ill children often believed new drugs were worth their potential risks. But there was less justification to exposing a child suffering from an ear infection who needed an antibiotic to an untried agent if there was already one available. Often the older drug, while potentially less effective, had a great deal of empirical evidence behind it.[167]

In 1977, the National Commission for the Protection of Human Subjects of Biomedical and Behavioral Research published *Research Involving Children*, a report that drew heavily on the work of the PRIME task force as well as the COD recommendations to the FDA. *Research Involving Children* affirmed the importance of pediatric drug research and described a series of recommended procedures for weighing risks and benefits and for obtaining informed consent from parents and assent from children if they were deemed cognitively able to provide it. Critically, the report also distinguished research from therapy and included explicit rubrics for doing so. The commission, however, could not reach consensus about one issue: Should children, even with parental consent, be permitted to enroll in a study offering little or no benefit to that particular child? This controversy had divided the pediatric community for at least a decade. Beecher and others had debated the ethics of enrolling healthy children in intervention-based studies. Two commission members, one of whom was the father of two profoundly disabled children, thought doing so was coercive and immoral. Finally, in 1979, the National Commission issued its report, which codified values such as autonomy and individual rights. It outlined three ethical principles to guide research—beneficence, respect for persons, and justice. The report also highlighted pediatric-specific research issues.[168]

Another hopeful note that year came from an internal FDA study reporting that the number of pediatric drug company–sponsored clinical trials appeared to be on the rise.[169] The FDA's Marion Finkel took this as a positive sign. She, like everyone else, was cheered that the National Commission had promulgated an ethical road map for research and that the FDA had issued scientific guidelines for pediatric drug research based on the work of the COD.[170] COD members surely reacted with excitement on hearing Finkel's proclamation of the new FDA regulation stipulating that any pediatric indications included on the label needed full description and must be accompanied by dosing and administration information based on research in children.

All these developments seemed to indicate that the time might finally be right for pediatric drug knowledge to move ahead significantly. With Sumner Yaffe as its guiding force, pediatric clinical pharmacology had emerged as a recognized medical subspecialty. A number of pediatric pharmacology training programs were in place and plans for two scholarly journals were underway. Under the auspices of NICHD, a new generation of scientists trained as pediatric pharmacologists were rising in the ranks of industry and academia. In 1979, Yaffe, head of the growing pediatric pharmacology unit at Children's Hospital of Philadelphia, completed the inaugural edition of the first pediatric pharmacology and therapeutics textbook. His introduction celebrated his optimism that the technical, ethical, and scientific issues necessary to assure better and safer drugs for children had been addressed, especially satisfying, he opined, given the year's designation as the International Year of the Child.[171]

# 5

## A "Big Business Built for Little Customers"

• • • • • • • • • • • • • • • • • • • •

Candy Aspirin, Children, and
Poisoning, 1947–1976

One area of the pediatric drug market that remained robust and immune to the other regulatory changes affecting the prescription drug industry was in over-the-counter drugs.[1] Most had been on the market for decades and brought huge profits to the companies that sold them, none more successful than St. Joseph Aspirin for Children. Its history reveals the advantages and challenges of this pediatric drug market sector. In 1947 the Plough Company, founded by Memphis pharmaceutical entrepreneur Abe Plough several decades earlier, successfully reformulated an old, off-patent medication—aspirin—into a flavored, small-dose chewable tablet designed to appeal to children's palates.[2] Plough had made his fortune by buying failing proprietary drug companies such as St. Joseph and marketing their products aggressively. Although Plough purchased St. Joseph in 1921, by the 1940s he had yet to see much profit from his investment in the crowded, competitive aspirin market. The explosion of births that began immediately after World War II provided him an opportunity to fill a niche in the market for fever- and pain-reducing drugs. Plough put St. Joseph chemists to work developing a pediatric aspirin formulation attractive to children in both color and taste.[3]

In September 1947, the company released the bright orange-colored St. Joseph Aspirin for Children amid a wave of creative marketing. Advertising to children and their parents was not new, nor was formulating patent medicines and other substances to appeal to them. Plough was not even the first entrepreneur to create a flavored aspirin; the Food and Drug Administration (FDA) had already flagged an aspirin "lollipop" marketed for use after tonsillectomy to ensure it was not promoted as candy.[4] But Plough was the first to draw direct attention to a reduced-dosage pill tailored especially for the pediatric patient, and it quickly became known as candy aspirin. And he did so at a time when demand for children's products reached unprecedented levels, the beginning of the baby boom era.

Advertisers increasingly targeted not just parents but children themselves, recognizing their potential to influence family purchases. In line with the trend toward child-sized furniture and foods marketed specifically for children such as sweetened cereals, there was now an aspirin tablet formulated just for them. At the same time, an unprecedented array of toys, games, and books aimed at children entered the market. Health was a visible theme in some of those new products. The Little Golden Book series, for example, included a bestseller that normalized the idea that children regularly took medication. One series character, Nurse Nancy, always had her "handy candy pills" for any

FIGURE 4  Undated fair trade drug price list at drug store of A. W. Boston, Providence, RI. (*Credit*: "Windows—Babies," Folder *Drug Topics*, Photograph Collection, American Institute of the History of Pharmacy, University of Wisconsin School of Pharmacy.)

playmate who wanted them. Toy versions of doctor and nurse bags included syringes and vials that could be filled with pretend tablets and liquids, and the companies who produced them benefited from robust sales.[5]

Although Plough used radio and, later, television to sell his products, he relied heavily on newspapers and magazines such as *Life*, the *Saturday Evening Post*, and *Woman's Home Companion* to attract the attention of consumers, particularly mothers.[6] No publication received more of Plough's advertising dollars in the late 1940s and 1950s than the venerable *Parents* magazine. Created in the 1920s by businessman and social worker George Hecht, *Parents* aimed to teach middle-class mothers about all aspects of child rearing. By the late 1940s its advertisers reached nearly one million homes in which at least one child resided.[7] Plough's efforts to attract consumers through *Parents* were remarkable for their size and sophistication. Whereas many ads in the magazine were half- or quarter-page black-and-white sketches, Plough's were full-page color displays with sophisticated illustrations and memorable copy.[8] Like the articles they surrounded, the families and scenarios in the St. Joseph ads presented an idealized, Madison Avenue vision of the American family, replete with overt gendered and classed messages. Mothers in well-appointed living rooms chatted with one another while girls played with dolls and boys with trucks or action toys. The messages were also racially coded: without exception, the children in St. Joseph ads in *Parents* in this era were white.[9]

Occasionally St. Joseph ads carried endorsements by celebrities such as movie and television stars with young children. Testimonials from mothers designed to appear unsolicited framed others. Mrs. Donald Crow from Houston, Texas, for example, appears to have been so pleased with St. Joseph, the ad copy implies, that she sent Plough a picture of herself with her two little boys along with the following note: "My sons hated to take ordinary adult aspirin. There's no fuss now that I give St. Joseph Aspirin for Children. They like its pure orange flavor." Because of physicians' unchallenged status as America's health care authority, many versions of the Plough ads carried a promotion from a physician—always white and male—assuring mothers that there was nothing better they could do for their hurt or febrile child than administer St. Joseph Aspirin for Children.[10]

Although the race, class, and gender messages in these ads were homogeneous, their cultural messages were contradictory. Mothers appeared relaxed, but the copy implied that parenting was stressful and difficult. The ads were designed to tap into mothers' anxieties by persuading them that postwar parenting was much more complex than it had been in the past. As a result, children could face danger if a mother made poor or ill-informed decisions by purchasing a product that had not been scientifically formulated to accommodate their children's physiological and psychological needs. Featured ads for St. Joseph Aspirin for Children throughout the early 1949 *Parents* issues, for example, emphasized the way the product was tailored for youngsters. "Mother: Here's the Aspirin Tablet that 'Fits' your Child's Needs" was proclaimed in January that year. The accompanying illustration demonstrated the way a product designed for an adult would not work for a child by showing a little girl trying to put on an evening gown. The next month, a St. Joseph ad showed a little boy putting his legs into pants sized for an adult man.[11] St. Joseph Aspirin for Children's promotional materials also emphasized the way the flavored, small-dose aspirin tablet reduced medication-related stress. Concern for children's emotional needs and cognitive development became increasingly important in the early postwar era, so much so that these issues became the central focus of planning for the1950 White House Conference on Children, as discussed in Chapter 3.[12]

Plough's new product achieved blockbuster status almost immediately. In 1949, less than two years after the launch of St. Joseph Aspirin for Children, the *Wall Street Journal* reported on the company's growth and prosperity. This success was attributed, in large part, to children's aspirin, his "Big Business Built for Little Customers," as one article in *American Business* lauded.[13] By the early 1950s, surveys of physicians suggested that aspirin was the most common drug used in pediatrics, spurring Bayer and other manufacturers to launch competing versions of reduced-dose, flavored aspirin.[14] Their products, too, sold well and their promotional materials featured the same happy, healthy, white children and relaxed suburban mothers. Plough, though, had a distinct knack for capturing attention, one that helped him break all the company's sales records.[15] First, he sought to cultivate brand loyalty by reminding mothers that his company's version was the first—and, as such, the best. He also sought novel ways of capturing potential customers' attention; for example, he distributed free copies of the company's St. Joseph 1954 calendar, which featured the Civil Defense Air Raid Instruction Chart do's and don't's for making sure one's family survived an atomic bomb attack. According to company legend, Plough used another potent marketing strategy. The company hired groups of women posing as mothers to request St. Joseph Aspirin for Children in drug stores in small Southern towns. Once the druggist began stocking it, the women moved on to another area and demanded the product there.[16]

But Plough's success relied on more than a growing customer base, brilliant advertising, and a product that captured the cultural zeitgeist. St. Joseph Aspirin for Children's sales also benefited because parents needed no physician prescription to purchase it, in contrast to the broad spectrum antibiotics, steroids, and tranquilizers entering the market at the same time. Although the Federal Trade Commission regulated Plough's ads in terms of the kinds of claims the company could make, Plough was able to appeal to consumers directly; prescription drug makers could advertise only to physicians.[17] And it was not just parents who were convinced by Plough's promotional campaigns.

FIGURE 5  Advertisement, St. Joseph Aspirin for Children, *Parents Magazine*, January 1949.
(*Credit*: Courtesy of Foundation Consumer Healthcare.)

FIGURE 6 Advertisement, St. Joseph Aspirin for Children, *Parents Magazine*, February 1949.
(*Credit*: Courtesy of Foundation Consumer Healthcare.)

Doctors increasingly recommended aspirin for children with minor pain or fever. This was a new trend. Before the advent of St. Joseph Aspirin for Children, for example, the drug was almost never prescribed for children with pneumonia or meningitis at Baltimore's Sydenham Hospital, no matter how high their fever. Until 1949, the last year the institution remained open, ice collars, tepid baths, and other nonpharmacologic treatments remained the primary fever therapeutic. Aspirin was only employed in Sydenham youngsters with rheumatic fever–related inflammation and pain[18] Within a few years of Plough's introduction of St. Joseph Aspirin for Children, the Committee on Toxicology for the American Medical Association (AMA) recognized its escalating popularity and charted the growing use of the "children's size" aspirin for minor pain and fever in the pediatric patient.[19] Even Benjamin Spock was not immune: he did not mention children's aspirin in the 1940s editions of his book, but by the middle of the 1950s he gave it prominent acknowledgment.[20]

## Candy Aspirin's Unintended Consequence

By the 1950s, low-dose, flavored aspirin was the number-one drug ingested by children, far outstripping its chief competitor, penicillin.[21] Plough's profits increased by double digits throughout the decade, in some years by as much as 50 percent. Prescription drug manufacturers took notice of Plough's success, competing with one another to create a palatable pediatric formulation for the broad spectrum antibiotics.[22] If the narrative had ended here, in the early 1950s, the candy aspirin story would be a reification of American capitalism's dynamism and societal benefits. But an unintended consequence to candy aspirin's popularity appeared within a few years of its introduction—the incidence of aspirin poisoning in young children increased dramatically. Accidental poisoning in children was, of course, not a new problem. Prescribing manuals as early as the 1880s at the Children's Hospital of Philadelphia, for example, included instructions for purging children of dangerous substances they had ingested. Accidental poisoning in children led to one of the more important additions to FDA authority between the 1914 Harrison Narcotic Act and the 1938 Federal Food, Drug, and Cosmetic Act: the 1927 Federal Caustic Poison Act. This statute mandated that household products include packaging and warning labels, specifically with child protection in mind.[23]

The first suggestion that aspirin poisoning in young children was a significant problem arose in 1952. The American Academy of Pediatrics (AAP) newly created Committee on Accident Prevention began its work by surveying 3,000 pediatricians around the country about mishaps involving young children in the home. The committee's chair, George M. Wheatley, a pediatrician with many years of injury prevention work from his job as vice president of Metropolitan Life Insurance Company, sounded an alarm regarding

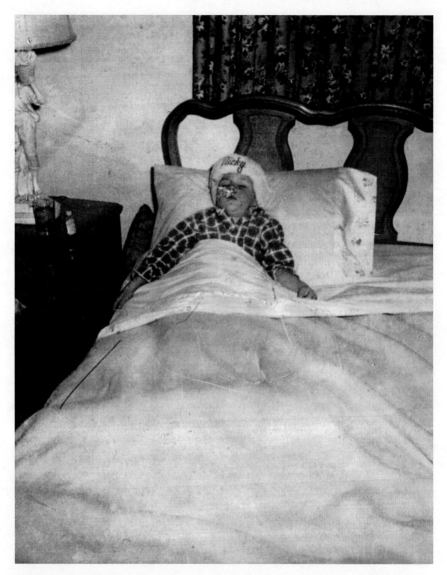

FIGURE 7 Beginning in the late 1940s, a bottle of children's aspirin could be found at the bedside of many sick youngsters. Four-year-old boy with mumps, 1968.
(*Credit*: Courtesy of Nicholas Connolly III).

its major finding, the surprisingly high rates of poisoning in young children, especially from aspirin.[24]

Plough's marketing strategy had clearly worked: children loved the taste of St. Joseph Aspirin for Children. But nothing in Plough's advertisements mentioned the importance of keeping it out of the hands of toddlers and pre-schoolers, and many parents may not have realized that an overdose could be life-threatening. They were undoubtedly horrified to learn that soon after ingesting a toxic dose of aspirin, children could experience ringing in the ears accompanied by sleepiness, rapid and deep breathing, vomiting, and vision problems. An especially high dose could result in seizures, coma, and even death.[25] Parents themselves even sometimes inadvertently overdosed children. There was no mandate for a standardized children's aspirin preparation. Each company decided how many milligrams of acetylsalicylic acid to put in a tablet. Plough's St. Joseph, for example, sold a 1.25 grain tablet (80 mg), whereas Bayer's was 2.5 grains (160 mg). Parents needed to read the label on each brand carefully. This confusion worried the Committee on Accident Prevention, which publicized the problem. As soon as Wheatley reported that 50 percent of accidents in children were poison-related, interested pediatricians, nurses, and public health officials began tracking all accidental ingestions in children, regionally at first, then nationally. In most instances, aspirin topped the list for medication-related household poisonings.[26]

In 1954, leaders at the FDA began hearing about aspirin poisoning in children from field agents, regional inspectors who served as the agency's eyes and ears on the ground. With regard to drugs, in addition to monitoring factories where they were manufactured, field agents responded to queries and concerns within their geographic area of jurisdiction. In June 1954, field agent W. H. Moses filed a worrisome report with his superiors in Washington, sounding an alarm that pediatric aspirin poisoning was a real problem in his southern region. Not only had his own nephew overdosed, a Texas doctor informed Moses that his hospital "alone had more infant deaths from ingestion of aspirin than the entire city of San Antonio had had from polio over the last two years."[27] By likening aspirin overdose to America's most frightening children's epidemic at that time, the doctor was clearly trying to convince Moses that the issue was a serious one. He pressed Moses regarding the agency's plans to address the problem, since "babies eat it like candy" and "someone should do something to stop these deaths."[28]

Despite the evidence mounting in the news media and professional literature, the aspirin industry, with Plough in the lead, denied that any safety problem with children's aspirin existed. In a 1954 letter to the AAP (with a copy to the FDA), Plough executive vice president Harry B. Solmson challenged the data, claiming that the company had sold thirty-five million packages of St. Joseph Aspirin for Children since 1947 without a problem. "[W]e do not have knowledge of a single instance wherein serious results have accrued," he wrote, "even though we have been made aware of several instances of a young child taking a whole bottle."[29] A piqued Solmson stressed that low dose, flavored aspirin had been created with youngsters' best interests in mind and that he could produce 25,000 letters from consumers thanking the company for its product. If any action was needed at all, he argued, it was simply parental education.[30]

Others companies that competed in the now crowded children's aspirin market agreed that inadequate parenting was the culprit in aspirin overdoses—if, in fact, any problem existed, which they did not concede. A. Dale Console at Squibb also made sure the FDA received a copy of his letter to the AAP's Wheatley about aspirin safety. In it, he stated that more parents should follow his own example: "I personally make it a practice to place [aspirin] . . . on a high shelf . . . and to twist the screw stopper tight enough that it is virtually impossible for my children to open it."[31] Another aspirin industry executive, Jerome F. Grattan from Carroll Dunham Smith Pharmaceuticals, also wrote to Wheatley and copied the FDA, charging that the "fault lies not with the pharmaceutical manufacturer but with the guardians of the children involved."[32]

Just as the tobacco industry had begun to do by the middle of the 1950s with regard to health risks from cigarettes, aspirin manufacturers shaped the debates concerning aspirin poisoning using similar tactics. Any problems resulting from use of the product was the fault of the individual, not the product. In the case of aspirin, this meant poor parenting. And like the tobacco industry strategy, Solmson denied scientific data and promulgated what he claimed were facts that challenged reports from the AAP, health departments, and FDA with regard to aspirin poisoning and children.[33]

## The Conference on Accidental Aspirin Poisoning and Its Aftermath

Growing concerns about candy aspirin poisoning led the FDA to convene a meeting about the problem in February 1955, one of the first times it brought stakeholders together to discuss an issue specific to the pediatric population.[34] The FDA staffers overseeing the gathering, physician and assistant medical director Irvin Kerlan and director of public information Wallace F. Janssen, knew they faced an uphill battle getting industry even to acknowledge aspirin poisoning was a public health problem. Manufacturers' recent letter-writing campaign to the FDA and AAP had made that clear. In his scrawled planning notes for the meeting, Kerlan mused that he hoped to balance what he thought was an ideal solution with what might be "feasible" in terms of manufacturer cooperation. Kerlan was undoubtedly aware that just a few years earlier the Public Health Service had lost its battle to force manufacturers to package household-cleaning products more securely to prevent child access.[35] Wheatley agreed with Kerlan. The AAP Committee on Accident Prevention minutes before the FDA meeting documented his "considerable correspondence" with manufacturers of "candy-coated aspirin" and his frustration that they were reluctant to admit any problem resulting from the medication.[36]

The FDA, AMA, and AAP leaders who attended the February 1955 conference, accompanied by vocal supporters from the American Public Health Association, hoped to obtain an affirmative response on two major issues from the eleven manufacturers who agreed to attend, Plough among them. They wanted aspirin makers to place a label on aspirin bottles warning parents to make sure the bottles were kept away from young children. They also sought manufacturer agreement for a standard dosage across the industry for what constituted a child-size tablet to minimize consumer confusion.[37]

Aspirin makers arrived at the meeting harboring a very different agenda than the FDA. The drug industry trade journal *F-D-C Reports* had outlined their strategy. They wanted to forestall with their presence "drastic and unrealistic measures"—such as banning flavored aspirin, which had been proposed by some physicians, particularly pediatricians.[38] The aspirin industry got its wish. Despite heavy pressure from FDA staffers and pediatricians, the only concrete plan arising from the conference was a recommendation that industry voluntarily consider different packaging. While there was tentative industry agreement for an aspirin warning label, no timeline for how this might happen was outlined nor any wording specified.[39] With relief, the *F-D-C Drug Letter* reassured its readers the week after the conference that the FDA would "go slow" and that the agency probably lacked the legal authority to mandate a standardized dosage per pill.[40] But through their discussions at the conference, aspirin makers also realized that a voluntary parental education campaign on their part could also work to their advantage: "From a PR [public relations] standpoint, a general program involving all medications could have the result of converting the suggested salicylate warning statement from a potential liability into an industry-wide asset . . . and might forestall any potential govt. or MD program that would overemphasize the 'poisoning' aspect of the situation."[41]

The absence of any immediate and meaningful action from the conference is interesting, given the 1950s rhetoric surrounding children and their protection. Fears that potentially negative messages in comic books and other popular media might lead to juvenile delinquency and social unrest, for example, figured prominently in the national news around the time the aspirin conference occurred. Legislators and others who expressed concern about reports that portrayed American youth as anything less than happy, healthy, and safe saw a threat to the image of the nation's ideological superiority to the Soviet Union. So it was ironic that Congress convened a subcommittee on juvenile delinquency, spending three years investigating the potential ways popular culture might harm youngsters, yet showed no interest in legislating safety protections for children stemming from aspirin, despite how extensively the new poison control centers, FDA staff, and AAP leadership documented the problem.[42]

The AAP said little publicly about its disappointment with the meeting's outcome. But in private correspondence Wheatley expressed his frustration to the organization's executive secretary, E. H. Christopherson.[43] His letter reveals that the fault lines that appeared at the FDA conference were some of the same ones that had led to the AAP's founding. Some on the AMA Committee on Toxicology—primarily non-pediatricians—agreed with aspirin manufacturers that what was needed was better parenting. Perrin Long, the eminent Johns Hopkins infectious disease specialist and pharmacologist, for example, expressed his opinion in the immediate aftermath of the aspirin meeting that it was overly indulgent postwar child-rearing practices that created the pediatric aspirin poisoning problem. Although clearly exaggerating, he nonetheless expressed nostalgia for an earlier era of parenting in which little thought was given to whether children liked the taste of their medicine: "[F]rom the beginning of this discussion I have been opposed to candy-coated medication. This business about physical and psychic trauma leaves me cold. In a nation of essentially undisciplined children who have been conditioned in this respect by ethnologists, social anthropologists, and doting psychiatrists, the answer is 'Take this cod liver oil, you little brat, or I will beat hell out of you.'"[44] While some pediatricians agreed with Long, most clinicians by the 1950s underpinned their assessments and interventions using developmental psychology. Drawing on this framework, they viewed youngsters' resistance to foul-tasting medications as normative, given that they lacked the cognitive ability and emotional maturity to understand why they were necessary.[45]

Despite Long's opposition to flavored medication, several months after the FDA-sponsored aspirin conference the AMA Committee on Toxicology published a report in *JAMA* acknowledging that, in addition to aspirin, manufacturers of antibiotics, sulfonamides, barbiturates, antihistamines, and vitamins increasingly sought to appeal to children's palates. Because aspirin was the most widely used medication in children, however, available in most homes, its candy formulations caused the highest number of accidental ingestions. The statistics they cited seemed irrefutable. Whereas 20 percent of aspirin fatalities in prewar America occurred in preschool-age children, by 1951, three years after St. Joseph Aspirin for Children became available, this age group represented 80 percent of aspirin deaths. The committee attributed this fivefold increase to candy aspirin. Their review of data from Chicago's poison control center revealed that in seventy-three of the eighty-four recent pediatric aspirin poisoning cases, children's aspirin was the culprit.[46]

Plough's and other manufacturers' chemists had done their work well. Children simply loved its flavor and marketing campaigns that emphasized its similarity to candy. As Chicago physicians Robert B. Mellins, Joseph R. Christian, and Herman N. Bundesen, observing the new phenomenon of children's aspirin poisoning, commented: "Children who were old enough to verbalize invariably reported that they sought out and ate the 'aspirin' because they liked the taste. Thus, although the poisoning was *accidental*, the ingestion was clearly *intentional*."[47] According to their analysis, the problem was not that some parents did not read the directions on the bottle; rather, youngsters aggressively hunted for it in medicine cabinets or on counters. As a result, an extraordinary amount of parental diligence was necessary to prevent access to the drug by the determined toddler or preschooler.

As the numbers of aspirin-poisoned children continued to grow, one North Carolina pediatrician at Duke Medical Center, Jay M. Arena, decided to take action. By the 1950s, Arena was one of the nation's leading pediatric poison experts, having recently founded the hospital's poison control center. After two children under age five died in one week from an overdose of "candy aspirin," a frustrated Arena picked up the telephone and called Abe Plough himself at the company's Memphis, Tennessee, headquarters.[48] Bluntly describing the deaths to Plough, he informed him that St. Joseph Aspirin for Children was a "fine product, but I think it's a dangerous product. . . . And you have to do something about it."[49]

Plough was initially reluctant, admitting to Arena he was "scared to death" that taking any action would negatively affect sales for his leading product.[50] Arena responded with an appeal to Plough's marketing sensibility, explaining that St. Joseph Aspirin for Children could differentiate itself from competitors by demonstrating a commitment to child well-being. Arena suggested that Plough could even promote its financial investment for a protective barrier that made it difficult for children to open the bottle as proof of the company's largesse.[51] Plough agreed and assigned one of his employees, Ray L. Sperber, the head of marketing, to work with Arena on a prototype for what would become known as a safety cap. The collaboration began with Arena informing Sperber about his most recent study in the Durham, North Carolina, area. His survey of eight local pediatricians indicated that fifty-six children had overdosed on children's aspirin in a six-month period. Arena informed Sperber that the poison rate was likely even higher than his numbers suggested, however, since 35 to 40 percent of Durham's 70,000 residents were African Americans and he had no data about poison rates in this segment of the population.[52]

It is unclear from Arena's letter to Sperber why poison-related information in African Americans was not possible for him to obtain. Perhaps the health department did not track aspirin overdoses in them, making it difficult to access any data. More likely, the eight pediatricians from whom he obtained information did not accept African American children in their practices, the norm in the segregated South. It is also possible that Arena, like many others, considered blacks so different from whites genetically, physiologically, and behaviorally that he believed trying to gather aspirin poisoning information about black children would complicate his ability to draw conclusions from his sample. Either way, his matter-of-fact comments provide a clear example of how racialized norms influence research questions in ways that appear invisible to those involved. Nothing in Arena's writings or biographical materials suggests that he was any more racist than other Southern physicians of his era.

Sperber funded Arena's work in 1956 and 1957 to study a few potential safety closures in North Carolina children. Arena eventually concluded that one cap seemed to require more cognitive skill and manual dexterity than the others. He recommended that Plough choose his preferred closure device to be mass produced and affixed to its children's aspirin bottles.[53] In the first advertisement for the safety cap–protected St. Joseph Aspirin for Children, in the December 1958 issue of *Parents*, the company featured it prominently.[54] Within a year Bayer was advertising its safety-capped children's aspirin in *Parents*.[55] Despite the advent of the safety cap, however, mortality rates in young children from aspirin poisoning continued to rise. The determined toddler or preschooler with enough time could overcome the barrier. In an effort to educate parents about this fact, the FDA, poison control centers, and pharmacists' associations instituted public health campaigns focused on aspirin poison prevention.[56]

Rising concerns about childhood accidents, including poisoning, were featured prominently at the 1960 White House Conference on Children and Youth.[57] The problem of children's aspirin poison even arose during one of Senator Estes Kefauver's unrelated hearings into issues surrounding price fixing in the pharmaceutical industry. Kefauver's committee reviewed a letter from outgoing FDA physician Barbara Moulton in which she opined, "Baby aspirin still is one of the biggest killers in spite of our aspirin warning, and in spite of the new closure. In my opinion, the only solution is to ban candy-flavored aspirin completely."[58] The AAP journal *Pediatrics* now regularly called for packaging changes to children's aspirin or even its removal from the market.[59] But some physicians continued to debate whether aspirin poisoning represented a public health problem or an individual failure. Boston Children's Hospital pediatrician Roger J. Meyer, for example, argued that a large segment of aspirin-poisoned children hailed from families with "working mothers," "broken homes," and other types of "family pathology."[60]

Those who sought legislative action to address aspirin poisoning were hopeful in 1960, when Congress passed the Hazardous Substances Labeling Act. The law authorized the FDA to require warning labels on products considered dangerous to young children. The statute, however, did not include drugs. Policymakers determined that any such authority should come through drug-related, not poison legislation.[61] Although manufacturers had, by now, agreed to standardize the amount of aspirin (81 mg) in one

FIGURE 8 Passaic County Pharmaceutical Association Poison Prevention poster, 1954. (*Credit*: Located at the National Library of Medicine. Courtesy of the New Jersey Pharmacists Association.)

children's aspirin tablet, they refused to budge on another issue of importance to the AAP, FDA, and poison control centers: limiting the number of pills per bottle. Poison activists believed that keeping the total dosage contained in one bottle to less than the fatal amount for a preschool-aged child saved lives. But in the context of the thalidomide crisis and other concerns about the pharmaceutical industry ultimately addressed by the Kefauver-Harris Amendments of 1962, the regulatory energy surrounding children's aspirin fell by the wayside in the short term.[62]

## "Politics in the Pantry and in the Bathroom Medicine Cabinet"

The aspirin issue roared to life again a few years later. First, in 1964, the respected periodical *Consumer Reports* publicized its concern about "candy aspirin" poisoning.[63] The next year Missouri Democratic Representative Leonor K. Sullivan, learning from one of her constituents that a child had died from a children's aspirin overdose, introduced a bill that prohibited its interstate sale. According to Sullivan, mothers and grandmothers from around the country contacted her with "hair-raising" experiences about the safety cap's inability to prevent ingestions.[64] Sullivan's efforts received publicity, putting the issue back in the legislative spotlight. A few weeks after Sullivan's impassioned remarks on the House floor, prominent investigative journalist Jack Anderson validated her concerns in his *Washington Post* column, noting that his two nieces had just nearly died from flavored aspirin overdoses.[65]

Although Sullivan's proposed statute stalled in the House, South Dakota Senator George McGovern soon introduced his own aspirin-related legislation, the Children's Aspirin Amendment of 1965. He had been alerted to the problem of pediatric aspirin ingestion in young children after a neighbor's child, followed quickly by a staffer's toddler, overdosed. McGovern's measure was less restrictive than Sullivan's in that it did not ban flavored aspirin entirely; rather, it limited the number of tablets in a bottle as poison control activists wanted.[66] Although Jay Arena supported McGovern's bill, it failed to garner endorsement from all poison control leaders, including the AAP Subcommittee on Accidental Poisoning. Several subcommittee members wanted a more restrictive bill, while others saw little reason for a legislative battle because they believed the industry was already working on aspirin-poisoning issues voluntarily.[67] As a result of these divisions, an opportunity for partnership between a powerful senator and one of the nation's leading advocacy groups for children's health, the AAP, faded.

By the mid-1960s, in a trend that surely dismayed the aspirin industry, leading pediatricians' aspirin research focused less on its therapeutic uses and more on its poisoning risks in young children.[68] Meanwhile, the evidence of its dangers to young children accumulated. In 1964, the Division of Vital Statistics of the Public Health Service attributed 125 deaths in children under five years to aspirin or salicylate poisoning. In 1965, the National Clearing House for Poison Control Centers received 34,483 accidental drug ingestion reports by children under five, of which 16,328 (47 percent) involved aspirin or other salicylates. In 1966 poison control centers documented that 88 percent of the nearly 11,000 children under age five treated in an emergency room for aspirin ingestion had overdosed on a flavored formulation.[69] Prominent papers in large cities such as the *Los Angeles Times* increasingly reminded readers of "sugar-coated" aspirin's risks.[70]

In this context, FDA staffers Kerlan and Janssen moved to enhance the agency's regulatory control over children's aspirin.[71] The FDA was still struggling to establish a clear role for itself regarding the broader problems of children and drug safety, specifically as it juggled the controversial issues of proxy consent, discussions regarding the scientific benchmarks for pediatric drug research, and funding studies in children. But Kerlan and Janssen believed that a consumer education campaign focused on poison prevention was not only noncontroversial, it also unquestionably fell within the agency's purview and provided an opportunity for the FDA to provide leadership for a major child safety-related issue. They convinced the FDA to commission the popular cartoonist Hank Ketcham to create a child safety story line for his "Dennis the Menace" characters. The resulting "Dennis the Menace Takes a Poke at Poison" comic strip soon found its way into doctors' offices and health departments around the country.[72] But Kerlan and Janssen did not believe voluntary educational campaigns for children regarding aspirin ingestion were enough. As Janssen later recalled, the mortality figures from flavored aspirin provided the major stimulus for agency support for several bills expanding federal control over hazardous substances. A series of hearings regarding the Child Safety Act (soon renamed the Child Protection Act) were scheduled for 1966. Among the many new powers the law, if enacted, would provide to the FDA was statutory authority to regulate all aspects of manufacturing, bottling, and labeling of children's aspirin.[73]

## The 1966 Child Protection Act Hearings: In Whose Best Interest?

Any hope that children's aspirin makers harbored for avoiding negative publicity from the Child Protection Act hearings was dashed on March 21, 1966. On that day President Lyndon Johnson issued a statement in which he directly addressed the makers of children's aspirin. Although most of his remarks concerned the benefits of more careful scrutiny of toys and other "children's articles," he called specifically for "limit[ing] the amount of children's aspirin available in retail packages" and "requir[ing] certain potent drugs attractive to children to have safety closure caps," exactly the type of federal oversight industry had successfully avoided for many years.[74] The president's statements received heavy coverage in the media. The *New York Times*, for example, featured his comments on page 1, accompanied by details regarding the epidemiology of children's aspirin poisoning.[75]

Aspirin makers seemed stunned by the negative attention. On May 18, at the annual meeting of the Proprietary Association, an industry trade group, James F. Hoge warned his colleagues that the enhanced regulatory power the Kefauver-Harris Amendments had given the FDA over prescription drugs might now envelop over-the-counter agents. Hoge conceded that the makers of proprietary drugs needed to accept that they lived in a "revolutionary time," on the "ascending scale of federal supervision" that had resulted in "limitless boundaries of the welfare state."[76] Nonetheless, he called his colleagues to a "rendezvous with destiny" and draw the line at any new restrictions on children's aspirin packaging, labeling, and marketing.[77]

Hoge suspected that the Child Protection Act hearings in the House of Representatives, scheduled for the summer of 1966, spelled trouble for him and his colleagues. And as he feared, the debate surrounding the need for more federal oversight of children's aspirin became the focal point in five days of riveting testimony and interchange that spanned from June to September 1966. The hearing's only agreement regarding aspirin occurred on the first day, when everyone involved—members of Congress, industry representatives, FDA officers, and pediatricians—agreed to act in a way that benefited children.[78] But it was quickly clear that children were valuable and negotiable political property; there was little consensus among stakeholders for what constituted children's best interests and how that should be determined.

One of the first witnesses, the FDA's crusading new commissioner, James L. Goddard, aimed to set the hearings' tone. After summarizing the escalating pediatric morbidity and mortality from aspirin, he intoned that "every three days a child dies from an overdose of children's aspirin."[79] Goddard stressed the importance of making decisions about the drug's packaging based on aspirin poisoning's pediatric epidemiology. He argued stridently that toddlers and preschoolers were best served by mandating safety caps and limiting the number of pills in a single bottle of aspirin to an amount considered unlikely to be fatal for a child three years of age or younger. Although he acknowledged the broad range of potentially toxic household products beyond aspirin, he was adamant that robust data suggested that "the greatest danger [to children in the home] is posed by the flavored children's aspirin."[80] No doubt to provide a memorable accompaniment to his testimony, Goddard made sure his staff supplied the committee with a number of different types of safety caps to practice opening.[81]

Representative Sullivan also testified, imploring her colleagues not to heed the numerous forthcoming witnesses from the aspirin industry. Both she and Goddard made sure legislators heard that young children overdosed on aspirin in a ratio of four to one relative to other medications. They provided clinical case reports of aspirin-poisoned children with gruesome stories of stomach pumping and other treatments. Policymakers received articles drawn from the popular and scientific literature, along with poignant letters from parents beseeching them to make it harder for their children to overdose.[82] Wisconsin Democratic representative Lynn E. Stalbaum summarized supporters' argument, reminding his colleagues of President Johnson's admonishment that "Children must be our first concern."[83] He concluded his testimony by arguing that there were many things parents could not protect their children from in 1960s America, but an aspirin overdose was not one of them: "We are powerless to guard our children against many of the hazards of 20th-century life. However, thousands of young victims of aspirin poisoning would be alive today if the quantity of aspirin in each container did not constitute a lethal dosage, or if drug containers were secured by safety closures."[84]

Lobbyists for aspirin manufacturers and related trade organizations such as the Pharmaceutical Manufacturers Association (PMA), the Proprietary Association, and the glass and packaging manufacturers that would be affected by mandatory safety closures and package size restrictions also testified. C. Joseph Stetler, president of the PMA, put forward the central pillars of the industry's case for why the aspirin component of the Child Protection Act did not serve children, parents, or the American people. First, Stetler implied that it was industry, not children, who needed protection. Aspirin makers needed to be safeguarded from unwarranted governmental intrusion into their practices because the law would grant the FDA "virtually unlimited authority" to mandate safety caps on any product it chose.[85] The pharmaceutical industry should be celebrated, he proclaimed, because the products manufactured by PMA companies "prolong and save lives."[86] In other words, Stetler insinuated that no new regulations were needed because the industry already acted in children's and the nation's best interest without them.

Richard E. Fisher, director of public affairs for the Glass Container Institute, began his testimony by protesting the need for a safety cap mandate, bolstering Stetler's claim that industry already aggressively protected youngsters: "nowhere has . . . [the safety of children] been given greater priority than in our industry."[87] Attempting to sideline the bill's safety cap mandate for all aspirin bottles, he stipulated that further study was necessary. Finally, he lamented that the voluntary public-private partnership that, in his memory, had worked so well as a result of the 1955 FDA-sponsored aspirin conference, could not be employed again.[88] Fisher's recollections of the 1955 meeting, of course, differed substantially from recollections of the FDA and AAP participants who attended that event. According to Fisher, the aspirin manufacturers came to the meeting gladly and voluntarily and promptly made changes requested by the FDA. Fisher, of course, did not mention that one reason that Child Protection Act supporters felt so strongly about legislating the number of tablets in a bottle of children's aspirin was because, even eleven years after the meeting, not all manufacturers had followed the 1955 total dosage per unit of sale recommendations.

Aspirin makers, led by Plough, the company with the largest market share, testified next. Plough executive vice president Harry B. Solmson emphasized each of Stetler's and Fisher's points, especially the importance of voluntary action on industry's part. Solmson pointed out to the committee his company's beneficence, reminding them that St. Joseph Aspirin for Children, voluntarily and before any other manufacturer, safety cap-protected its product. He declared that Plough wanted to cooperate with the government, but this "highly controversial bill containing broad new regulatory powers"—it gave the FDA the authority to mandate safety caps on all types of aspirin— went too far.[89] He challenged legislators' claim of public support for the Child Protection Act aspirin provisions by countering that he could produce evidence from consumers who liked St. Joseph Aspirin for Children exactly as it was manufactured and labeled. Plough clearly feared that new aspirin-related mandates could set a precedent for other regulations that the company might not be as willing to enact as the safety cap.[90]

Maurice L. Tainter, vice president of Sterling Drug, the maker of Bayer Children's Aspirin, reiterated and extended his colleague's comments. Just as his predecessors had argued in the past, Tainter maintained that even if pediatric aspirin poisoning was a bona fide health issue, the problem lay not with those who manufactured the product, but with parental negligence. He also warned that safety caps and limits on pill bottle size might increase the numbers of small children accidently overdosing on aspirin because new restrictions could make adults more complacent, leading them to leave the pills where youngsters could access them.[91] Next, he presented a chart entitled "Recorded Ingestions in 2–5 Year Group Where Age and Dosage Are Known," the data in which, he suggested, showed that children needed to ingest much more than Goddard maintained in order to die.[92] Tainter professed that this was because: "aspirin is different from many other drugs or hazardous substances in that it does not damage the vital organs in such a way as to leave significant permanent injury after such overdosage. Recovery from overdosage is therefore usually prompt and complete."[93]

Tainter went further still. How could anyone even know what an overdose was, he charged, since leading pediatric pharmacologist Harry Shirkey suggested that the weight-based dosing rubrics used to determine dosing guidelines for most pediatric drugs might not be as accurate as using a child's body surface area as a basis for the calculation? With this argument, Tainter was intimating that perhaps all pediatric drug knowledge was predicated on faulty metrics. If so, his tenuous logic reasoned, aspirin was no less safe than any other drug.[94] But Tainter's words undercut the basic principles behind his product. If Sterling was not sure that the 81 milligrams of aspirin in each Bayer's children's pill was appropriate for a toddler, then why did the company so prominently advertise its safety in *Parents*? Finally, Tainter ended his testimony with a truly audacious ploy—blaming not just parents and the "family environment," but toddlers and preschoolers themselves for the problem of aspirin poisoning. If there was a problem with children's aspirin ingestion, Tainter's interpretation of the scientific literature was that it might be due to "repeaters" with a "psychological urge" to overdose.[95]

The last witness to testify against the legislation was Proprietary Association president James Hoge, who drove home the all the themes expressed by Stetler, Fisher, Solmson, and Tainter. He warned the subcommittee that "under the heart-stirring' banner of 'child safety,'" the proposed laws, if enacted, would give "unlimited delegation of authority to the Food and Drug Administration."[96] Hoge begged Congress to slow down on what he saw as the most important piece of legislation to affect over-the-counter drugs since 1938. He maintained that aspirin companies "don't need to be policed. They are very law-abiding people, and very high minded, and very much interested in the public health."[97] He ended with his trump card—that the bill was anti-American because instead of "encourag[ing] private initiative and enterprise," the proposed legislation moved "far beyond child safety, envelope[d] controversial medical opinion, escalate[d] legal liability, and constrict[ed] industrial independence."[98]

Industry participants had also come armed with their own letters of support from physicians, albeit not the experts in poison control from the American Academy of Pediatrics and the American Public Health Association that the bill's advocates inserted into the congressional record. Virginia pediatrician Archibald R. MacPherson did not support the aspirin component of the Child Protection Act because he agreed with those who attributed children's aspirin poisoning to poor parenting. He informed Congress that aspirin's packaging and labeling "seem adequate to me" and in the event of an accidental ingestion, "the children's parents are the ones at fault."[99] And manifesting the enduring struggle for power between the AAP and the AMA as the spokesperson for children's health pertaining to pharmaceuticals, AMA executive vice president F.J.F. Blasingame questioned whether a single pediatric aspirin-related death had ever occurred. Blasingame agreed with MacPherson that, if any children had died from aspirin ingestion, it was a problem that could not be solved by legislation because the phenomenon "must be traced to parental ignorance, carelessness, or indifference."[100]

By the time the aspirin industry's testimony was over, subcommittee members who had previously supported the FDA's position now felt angry and betrayed by the FDA. New York Democratic representative Leo O'Brien declared that Goddard's original testimony had affected him profoundly: "I would like to say that I attended the first hearing on this bill, and we heard the representatives of the Department [FDA], and I think that before we were through, that most of us were close to tears, weeping for the little children who apparently were being killed in vast numbers by consuming those colored aspirin."[101]

Clearly, O'Brien now felt Goddard had manipulated him. Under the "guise of child safety," he suspected that the FDA was trying to increase the agency's power, exactly what Stetler, Solmson, Tainter, and Hoge had asserted.[102] O'Brien demanded to hear from Goddard again, this time "minus the emotional impact," before we "rewrite a very broad segment of the drug laws."[103] In case anyone on the subcommittee still needed convincing, Hoge interjected a final volley, imploring them not to "rewrite the whole food and drug law under the pretense we are protecting children," which would actually permit the "wanton, unbridled delegation of [FDA] authority."[104]

The tone was very different when Goddard returned to the Hill. Industry had successfully shifted the issue from discussing how best to use the epidemiological evidence gathered by pediatricians, health departments, poison control centers, and the FDA to protect young children, to the need to reign in a rogue federal agency. Goddard's detailed, point-by-point rebuttal to the aspirin industry's charges mostly fell on deaf ears. For example, he explained what he and his staff saw as Tainter's flawed interpretations in his "Recorded Ingestions in 2–5 Year Group Where Age and Dosage Are Known" chart.[105] Analyzing the same data, the FDA concluded that more children did not die from aspirin ingestion not because of its wide safety range, but because of prompt clinical intervention in the form of stomach pumping, blood transfusions, and other "heroic therapy."[106] An annoyed Goddard maintained, "The fact that more lives are not lost hardly proves there is no risk."[107] But there was little congressional follow-up to Goddard's rejoinder to industry. Although Congress did pass the Child Protection Act, the proposal to limit the number of tablets in a bottle of aspirin and other aspirin-related mandates such as safety caps were dropped. Policymakers declared that the problems could be addressed with a voluntary FDA-industry conference, exactly what industry representative Richard E. Fisher suggested in his testimony.[108]

## Mandating Safety Barriers: Industry, FDA, Pediatricians, and Congressional Negotiations

The Child Protection Act congressional hearings showed how easily industry had shifted the terrain from protecting children from aspirin poisoning to safeguarding industry from the federal government. But aspirin manufacturers now faced more negative press from consumer advocates. *Consumer Bulletin*, for example, accused manufacturers of trying to hide aspirin's risks to children in the wake of the hearings, warning parents not to be "disarmed by advertising that shrewdly implies that aspirin is harmless."[109] Nonetheless, the mood was celebratory a few weeks later, in early December 1966, at a Proprietary Association meeting. In the past year, Plough and other aspirin makers had fended off the aspirin regulations in the Child Protection Act and embarrassed FDA commissioner Goddard on Capitol Hill. Joseph M. Pisani, Proprietary Association medical director, extolled the way industry had stalled governmental oversight and "placed the matter in proper perspective" for legislators.[110] While his group had agreed to attend the FDA-sponsored aspirin conference scheduled for early 1967, he dryly signaled his tepid support for labels that alerted parents that flavored aspirin posed a significant poisoning risk to young children: "The label I suggest for 'Safety in the Use of Home Medicines' is read: 'Active Ingredients: Common Sense, Integrity, and Alertness. Warning: *Keep yourself within reach of your children*.' Advertising Copy to accompany this label: 'Use this product as directed and you will keep the American home safe!'"[111]

As with the 1955 FDA-sponsored aspirin meeting, the 1967 conference included representatives from groups active in the poison control movement, aspirin manufacturers, and the FDA. Because of its FDA consultative role, the AAP Committee on Drugs played a central role; as COD leader, Harry Shirkey served as chair. For Shirkey, of course, aspirin poisoning in young children constituted just one piece of what he saw as the much broader issue of inadequate attention to pediatric drug dosing, pharmacokinetics, and other safety metrics.[112]

In his opening remarks at the 1967 aspirin conference, FDA commissioner Goddard admonished stakeholders that he would not hesitate to return to Congress if he determined industry was not participating in good faith. He had been assured, he warned aspirin maufacturers, that "if the problems that had arisen at the Child Protection Act hearings regarding whether or not safety caps should be mandatory and limiting the numbers of tablets in a container could not be solved on a voluntary basis, that [Congress] would be willing to entertain legislation at a future date."[113] Perhaps fearing that Goddard would make good on his threat, industry quickly reached consensus regarding a pills per bottle industry standard for children's aspirin. After Jay Arena entreated companies to sell safety with the same alacrity that they marketed their products, companies agreed to support a national poison education campaign. Finally, the industry also acquiesced to the FDA request to fund a subgroup of conference attendees, the Subcommittee on Safety Closures, to determine an ideal safety device that all manufacturers could agree to adopt.[114]

The Subcommittee on Safety Closures began its work in April 1967 by first compiling all the information members could find about the fifty barrier devices already patented in the United States. The group also designed research tools to assess the benefits of available closure devices. Some of the data they wanted to collect, however, seemed tangential to their task. For example, some subcommittee members thought it important to gather information on the marital status of mothers enrolled in the studies. Because their central aim was to identify a closure device that would allow ready access for adults, but not children, they understandably sought parental data, but the committee recorded no discussions about why they thought marital status might be relevant. Perhaps some members saw it as a proxy for intelligence, social class, or maternal competence. The subcommittee also did not reach consensus regarding whether to include institutionalized children in their data set. It does not appear those harboring worry about their involvement had ethical concerns. Rather, some subcommittee members believed the data would be skewed because because institutionalized youngsters were probably not a representative sample of toddlers and preschoolers in terms of intellectual and motor development.[115]

Aspirin manufacturers used their participation in the aspirin conference and support for the Subcommittee on Safety Closures in their public relations campaigns. Soon after the conference, for example, Wyeth Laboratories issued a press release informing consumers about its "Safer Packaging for Aspirin Aims To Curb Accidental Poisonings."[116] For its part, the FDA had agreed to a demand from industry to work with the Public Health Service to generate better data regarding the brand and type of aspirin on which children overdosed.[117] This time-consuming task, however, offered little new therapeutic knowledge. Given the increase in aspirin poisoning in the pediatric population after the introduction of children's aspirin, it was already clear that taste mattered. And knowing which brand had hurt a child provided no useful therapeutic information, only an advertising weapon manufacturers could use against one another.

While the Subcommittee on Safety Closures sought to learn more about the demographic characteristics of families in their study, there was little mention of race. This omission is curious, given that a 1968 Public Health Service (PHS) epidemiological study on aspirin poisoning found that more white than black children overdosed on aspirin. No one seemed interesting in following up on this finding. Was this difference because cases of aspirin poisoning in black children went unreported to the National Clearinghouse for Poison Control Centers? Or was it because black families did not purchase children's aspirin, or restricted access better than white families? The study's lead investigator, John J. Crotty, associate director of the Poison Control Branch of the PHS, did not offer a hypothesis.[118]

Between 1967 and 1971, the Subcommittee on Safety Closures met formally on eight occasions. The group oversaw a series of industry-funded studies that enrolled hundreds of young children, mothers, and older people with the goal of identifying a safety cap that prevented children from opening the bottle but made it as easy as possible for adults to do so.[119] At least some Americans followed the effort closely. The FDA received a number of letters from citizens submitting their safety closure suggestions, drawings, and prototypes.[120] One Oregon mother, for example, summarized her ideas based on the unspecified observation and testing she had done with her own children. The return letters from FDA staffers reveal the agency's frustration at its perceived powerlessness. One FDA response explained to its writer that "the bill was not passed"—that is, the section of the Child Protection Act authorizing FDA to mandate safety caps—so "we have no authority" to oversee the Subcommittee on Safety Closure's efforts.[121]

The FDA and members of the Subcommittee on Safety Closure came to Capitol Hill in October 1969 to report their progress during the Senate Commerce Committee hearings for a new bill, the Poison Prevention Packaging Act. If enacted, the statute would empower the FDA to set "standards for packaging designed to prevent young children from obtaining harmful amounts of hazardous substances found around the home."[122] Alan K. Done, a University of Utah medical school professor and pediatric expert in poison control, attempted to explain the scientific issues to impatient senators who wanted the subcommittee to complete its task. The safety cap issue, he stressed, was not one that could just be solved by engineering:

> We have been surprised on numerous occasions when we have developed an
> innovation that we were absolutely certain would be childproof and the children
> would fool us. We had one cap, for example, which we specifically designed
> on the basis of previous failures, to get around the effect we thought existed in
> the earlier closure. It was absolutely foolproof; you could not get it off. Adults
> couldn't get them off either unless they knew what to do. The children, in their
> frustration, quickly learned that if they turned the bottle upside down and hit it
> on the table one time, the cap would crack and they could immediately get
> it off.[123]

In a number of ways, the pediatric experts who testified at the 1969 hearings rehashed earlier positions. Some, such as Done, while strongly supportive of safety closures, preferred a voluntary effort on the part of manufacturers rather than a legal mandate. For his part, Harry Shirkey hoped to use the aspirin poisoning issue to justify the need for broad new pediatric drug safety measures.[124] And aspirin manufacturers used the same arguments they had honed in the past—challenge the data, emphasize the benefits of voluntarism, slow the process, and blame aspirin poisoning on nonindustry sources. At the 1969 Poison Prevention Act hearings, Sterling vice president Maurice Tainter, for example, was again eager to blame "Mother's inadequate awareness of safety requirements in the home over which she presides" and "Dennis the Menace" children, "well known to the psychologist, psychiatrist, or pediatrician."[125]

Beyond aspirin, the issue for many over-the-counter drugs was not the risk of poison, but dosing confusion, just as was occurring with prescription drugs. This was most problematic for very young children under the age of three years. In their case, most proprietary drug labels instructed parents to contact their physician in advance of administration. In fall 1969, one irate pediatrician, Robert T. Kostello of Chico, California, articulated the bind in which this placed him. In a letter to Phillip Lee, assistant secretary for health and scientific affairs at the Department of Health, Education, and Welfare, Kostello complained: "I object to being consulted about medications which I do not prescribe. . . . This statement puts me in the position of endorsing the medication when a patient calls. . . . I have two choices, either to suggest a dosage, or to advise them I do not use this medication. . . . If the schedule of medication is such that the pharmacist or the drug house dispensing the medication does not know the appropriate dosage, why should the private physician be called regarding this?"[126]

Kostello's letter eventually reached John M. Gowdy at the FDA Bureau of Medicine, who sent a reply that Kostello surely found frustrating because it elided his concern and, indeed, punctuated his point. After quoting the portions of the laws pertinent to nonprescription drugs, Gowdy informed him that drugs safe for adults may have "special toxicity in children" because youngsters "vary in weight and maturity."[127] He ended the letter by telling Kostello that "you are perfectly right to suggest a more suitable medication if you believe such a measure appropriate."[128] But Kostello's concern was that he, as a private practice pediatrician, had no scientific way of making this determination and needed guidance from the manufacturer, government, or some official source.

## Success—The Poison Prevention Packaging Act

The Poison Prevention Packaging Act stakeholders were able to cobble together enough support to pass legislation requiring all potentially toxic household products to carry child safety closures within a specified period of time. Aspirin was the first product covered by the new law, and the packaging needed to go into effect by August 1973.[129] The Poison Prevention Packaging Act was only one of several new child safety laws in which the FDA was involved. A year earlier, in 1969, President Nixon had signed the Child Protection and Toy Safety Act into law. Like the Poison Prevention Packaging Act, an FDA division was charged with overseeing compliance with the law—in this case, the Bureau of Product Safety (BPS). Division staff in the six-member Toy Safety Review Committee traveled to toy fairs to study prototypes for playthings, evaluating fifty kinds of toys a week. In 1971 alone, BPS director Malcolm Jenson noted that the agency removed five hundred toys from the market.[130]

As FDA commissioner Charles Edwards observed, as a result of the Child Protection and Toy Safety Act, the agency faced a dramatically expanded workload because of the "hundreds of thousands of products" for children it now needed to monitor.[131] The FDA annual reports for the early 1970s reveal the increased time and resources devoted to overseeing child safety packaging and potential problems in toys, clothing, furniture, and other children's products. The Toy Safety Review Committee oversaw the 83,000 toys produced by 1,200 American toy manufacturers. Sixty-seven million children played with these items, resulting in seven hundred thousand injuries every year. The workload and complexity of tracking all children's products quickly became so overwhelming that in October 1972, President Nixon signed legislation establishing an independent federal agency, the Consumer Product Safety Commission (CPSC), to free the FDA from this responsibility.[132]

Undoubtedly not lost on the agency itself was the fact that, before toys, furniture, and other children's products moved to the CPSC, the FDA had authority to protect youngsters from the Do-It-Yourself Bomb Kit toy, which it removed from the market in 1968, but no clear ability to oversee prescription drug safety and efficacy in children.[133] Although the 1962 Kefauver-Harris Amendments theoretically provided the FDA statutory oversight of prescription drugs, the agency had not been able to fully execute those powers when it came to children because no one could figure out who should bear the cost burdens for the additional testing necessary for children and the scientific and ethical issues.

By the mid-1970s, aspirin mortality rates in young children had declined significantly. When Richard Simpson, director of the CPSC, testified on Capitol Hill about the new agency's successes, he proudly highlighted that safety caps and other poisoning preventive measures had resulted in a "fairly remarkable decline" in aspirin poisoning in young children.[134] Despite reluctance and delay on the part of many in the aspirin industry, the safety cap campaign is remembered today as a "model for accident prevention in children."[135] Aspirin makers, too, learned valuable lessons in terms of how to respond to the threat of new legislation: challenge the problem's existence and the data underpinning the science; deflect blame; and mount a public relations campaign to confuse the public. These tactics would be used again in the 1980s in the face of a new pediatric threat from aspirin.[136]

# 6

# Children and
# Psychopharmacology
# in Postwar America

• • • • • • • • • • • • • • • • • • • • • • •

What little historical scholarship exists on children and mood-altering drugs focuses largely on the rise in the stimulants for what has been variously known since the early twentieth century as minimal brain dysfunction, hyperkinetic reaction of childhood, and attention deficit hyperactivity disorder. While these drugs play an important role in the history of pediatric psychopharmacology, they are only one part of a broader story.[1] This chapter interweaves the history of other psychoactive agents into that of stimulants. It analyzes the ways in which psychotropic drug-related issues were similar to—and different from—those for other prescription drugs for the child patient. The history of pediatric psychopharmacology also provides a unique lens through which to consider temporally derived political and social definitions of "normal" and "abnormal" children, parenting, and family life and the role drugs have played in those determinations.

Like all pharmacotherapeutic agents, the development, testing, and use of mood-altering drugs in children is at once a story of commerce, research, technological and scientific change, politics, and evolving parental and societal expectations regarding the medical encounter and American childhood. Unlike other medications such as antibiotics, however, psychotropic drugs treated more contested, and relative to infectious diseases, poorly defined conditions. By the 1930s when the sulfonamides came to the market, for example, experts agreed on the major diagnostic criteria for bacterial pneumonia and its clinical presentation in an infant or child. Differentiating child mental illness from neurological problems such as epilepsy or developmental disorders remained less clear until much later.

In some ways, the story of pediatric mood altering drugs is a very old one. Arguably, Mrs. Winslow's Soothing Syrup, which arrived on the American market in the 1830s, represented one of the nation's earliest domestic blockbuster drugs. Heavily advertised for its success at quieting the crying, restless infant or young child, the narcotic-laced product and its many competitors generated millions of dollars in profits. But there is only a superficial similarity between soothing syrups and their mid-twentieth-century successors. Soothing syrups were not targeted at children believed to be suffering from behavioral disorders.[2]

Like elite pediatricians in the 1930s, those who specialized in the emerging field of child psychiatry largely eschewed pharmacological therapy. Leo Kanner, for example, who originated the nation's first child psychiatry department in 1930 at the Johns Hopkins Hospital's Harriet Lane Home, did not sanction their use. When, in 1935, he published the first child psychiatry textbook, he advised against the use of drugs. But his reason differed from that of J. P. Crozer Griffith and A. Graeme Mitchell, who argued in their 1933 text *The Diseases of Infants and Children* that few drugs benefited youngsters. Rather, Kanner reasoned that children's behavior often reflected parental "carelessness" or "overindulgence."[3]

Child and adult psychiatry evolved differently from one another. Although certainly influenced by Freudian psychoanalysis, child psychiatry was solidly rooted in the early twentieth-century child-saving and juvenile justice movements. The field also reflected the thinking of pioneering developmental psychologists such as Arnold Gesell, who argued that universal and timed patterns defined normative emotional, social, and cognitive maturation in children. Interest in child mental health by the Children's Bureau as well as private foundations such as Rockefeller, Grant, and the Commonwealth Fund in the interwar period provided resources to unify these ideological threads. The "child guidance clinics" that emerged emphasized a team-based approach that brought together nurses, social workers, psychologists, and psychiatrists in ways not common in general pediatrics.[4] Nonetheless, child psychiatry was heavily influenced by pediatrics' growth as a medical specialty. Pediatricians' emphasis on universal well child care did not just provide a referral base for psychiatrists, it offered a roadmap for how the specialty could achieve legitimacy. Just as pediatricians could make use of height and weight tables to chart children's physical development, Gesell's research yielded a parallel set of tools believed to differentiate the child maturing normally from one harboring psychopathology.[5]

The modern history of pediatric psychopharmacology begins in the 1930s. It was then that psychiatrist Charles Bradley alerted his colleagues to a finding that surprised him. Smith Kline & French's amphetamine, benzedrine sulfate, calmed many of his young patients at the Emma Pendleton Bradley Home in Providence, Rhode Island. Children Bradley diagnosed with "neurological and behavioral disorders" improved after receiving amphetamines for headaches associated with one of their medical procedures.[6] The "spectacular" change he documented in many of the children was "paradoxical" because, rather than "stimulating" them as the drug did adults, it had the opposite effect.[7] They appeared to learn better after receiving amphetamines, behavior that disappeared as soon as Bradley withdrew the drug.[8]

Another foundational event in the history of pediatric psychopharmacology included the 1946 National Mental Health Act. The growing federal interest in hospital funding and medical research extended to mental health. This important legislation led to the creation of the National Institute of Mental Health (NIMH) and the first large-scale public investments in training and research for mental health-related issues.[9] Organizers for the 1950 White House Conference on Children capitalized on the founding of NIMH and its initiatives by setting as the conference's main theme the mental and emotional well-being of American children.[10] While few in number in the early 1950s, child psychiatrists argued that pediatricians' expertise did not extend to managing the mentally ill child or one with severe behavioral problems. As such, a small group of them founded the American Academy of Child Psychiatry in 1953. But these early leaders also recognized that they faced a challenge that their pediatrician and general practitioner peers who treated children did not. Kanner's descriptions of "autistic differences of affective contact" and its symptomatology, for example, lacked the diagnostic specificity of cancer, pneumonia, or other diseases considered physical in nature.[11] Moreover, few psychiatric conditions included age as a relevant variable in assessment or diagnostic criteria, so there was less evidence to justify the need for a pediatric focused specialty within psychiatry. The new resource for classifying and defining psychiatric conditions published in 1952, *Diagnostic and Statistical Manual of Mental Disorders*, for example, made no distinction between children and adults.[12]

## The Child Patient and the Psychopharmacology Revolution

One of Kanner's former colleagues, Lauretta Bender, grew fascinated by childhood schizophrenia which she characterized as a maturational disorder of the central nervous system. By the time Bender published her first description of the condition in 1942, she was already famous for her Bender-Gestalt Visual Motor test, a measure of neurological and cognitive damage. As lead psychiatrist at New York City's large public Bellevue Hospital Child

Psychiatric Division, Bender oversaw both its outpatient clinics as well as its inpatient unit.[13]

Bender was also influenced by her mentor at Johns Hopkins, psychiatrist Adolf Meyer, especially his conviction that biology played an important role in psychopathology. Like Bradley, Bender too experimented with stimulants in children. As she grew more interested in psychopharmacology, Bender hypothesized that psychoactive medications served as both a diagnostic and a therapeutic tool in children. She believed that a child's response to a drug revealed important clues about the disordered developing brain. This thinking bound her less to child psychiatry's child-saving roots and more to Meyer's psychobiology framework.

Bender must have realized another benefit to psychopharmacology. While she did not state this point explicitly, it was clear by the ways in which she described drugs' importance that she also appreciated that they differentiated her practice from that of psychologists. Psychopharmacology validated child psychiatrists' claim that they possessed a unique body of knowledge because prescription medications fell solely in physicians' domain. While the clinicians on her unit included nurses, social workers, teachers, and psychologists just as in the child guidance model, Bender's enthusiasm for drugs meant that the Bellevue unit operated firmly within a biomedical model that placed physicians at the top of the hierarchy. As tranquilizers started pouring onto the market in the 1950s, Bender and her trainees prescribed them to their children. Her unit soon developed a reputation as the nation's premier site for pediatric psychopharmacology research and therapy.[14]

The inpatient Bellevue Child Psychiatric Unit's fifty beds housed children under the age of twelve years. Bender estimated that she had enrolled 350 children into her drug studies by the middle of the 1950s. They arrived at Bellevue through different pathways and with a variety of symptoms, but most were poor. In 1950, for example, 24 percent of children came through social service agencies, 23 percent came from the juvenile justice system, and 17 percent had been brought to Bender directly by their parents. The rest were referred by schools or transferred from hospitals or other institutions.[15] Like other 1950s psychiatrists, Bender was struck by the transformation wrought by the new tranquilizer Thorazine (chlorpromazine). The drug's manufacturer, Smith, Kline, & French, stressed its potential uses for troubled children and juvenile delinquents. All Bender's patients carried one of these broad labels, and she started using Thorazine as soon as it became available in 1954.[16] Just as it did for adults, the drug transformed the care of the most behaviorally challenging children at Bellevue. Until Thorazine, Bender later recalled, children's "severe tension states might become so uncontrolled that they would be put in the adult ward temporarily to prevent danger to themselves or to others."[17]

But after receiving Thorazine, their behavior could be managed on the pediatric unit.

In 1955 Bender, along with Alfred M. Freedman and Abraham S. Effron, colleagues at New York University's medical school, where she held a faculty appointment, published the first pediatric psychopharmacology review article in the United States. The physicians reported their three-year study in which they had randomly assigned boys between the ages of seven and twelve years admitted to Bellevue to receive one of six new psychiatric drugs. Another group of boys received only a placebo. One of the major benefits of an inpatient unit was that staff could completely control children's environment. Bellevue's nurses and teachers spent months monitoring children for side effects and drugs' impact on symptoms such as anxiety, agitation, or attention. Freedman, Effron, and Bender concluded that all the drugs influenced behavior on the 195 youngsters in some way, leading them to conclude excitedly that "Pharmacological agents have an indisputable role in the management of children in a psychiatric hospital setting."[18] They did not tease out the impact of particular medications on specific disorders. Nonetheless, they concluded that psychiatry was about to benefit from pharmacology in the same way as had other areas of medicine, noting enthusiastically: "in the last two decades advances in pharmacological therapy in medicine have been noteworthy and, in certain instances, spectacular. Antibiotics, sulfonamides . . . have wrought impressive changes in clinical practice. . . . Yet the application of this new information has had, until very recently, very little utilization in the field of psychiatry."[19]

But Bender faced challenges her general pediatrics colleagues did not in terms of her drug studies. First, unlike many of her colleagues, she lacked ready access to a comparison group of healthy children. Second, a disproportionate number of her patients were boys. Where concern existed regarding behavior problems in female children, it was usually in those who were pubertal and considered to be acting out sexually.[20] Because Bellevue did not accept youngsters over age twelve, the unit admitted few girls. Without acknowledging the ways in which gender, race, and class may have influenced her diagnostic patterns, Bender pathologized those behaviors that did not fit her preconceived expectations. For example, she thought that many Puerto Rican and African American children cared for in New York City's child guidance clinics had low IQs and "development problems" associated with "hereditary and family patterns."[21] She also believed that Jewish children were overrepresented in the city's psychiatric centers, hypothesizing that the reason was that Jewish parents were overly anxious: "About one-third of the clinic population would be Jewish children brought in very young by very concerned parents, both parents coming and absolutely devoted to their children and seeking medical advice as early as they possibly can because their child is not 'achieving.' This is the major problem with the Jewish child in New York City."[22]

Bender presented more of her Bellevue pediatric drug research the next year at the 1956 annual meeting of New York's state medical society. By now she estimated that at any given time multiple investigations exploring four or five different drugs were underway on the ward. She provided great detail with regard to her research procedures: "Some medications were deliberately discontinued at the height of clinical improvement to produce changes" in an effort to understand how the drugs worked.[23] In other words, Bender blurred her roles of researcher and physician, making no real effort to differentiate between them. In this way she differed from most others who undertook pediatric drug research in this era. While Julius Richmond administered sulfonamides to healthy newborns to better map out dosing patterns, there is no evidence that he or any other pediatric antibiotic researchers in this era stopped the drug in an ill child to see what happened. But Bender was far from alone in her research endeavors on testing mood altering drugs in children. As one eminent psychologist later noted about this era, "any drug that happened to be used [in adults], we thought we should try with children."[24]

Within a year of Thorazine's 1954 availability, another drug, Miltown (meprobamate), arrived on the market. Miltown hailed from the drug class called minor tranquilizers because it treated conditions such as anxiety rather than psychosis like Thorazine, classified as a major tranquilizer. Manufactured by Wallace Laboratories, a division of Carter Products, Miltown was quickly recommended for children. A 1955 *Cosmopolitan* magazine feature story extolled the new drug as "not habit-forming" and benefiting "restless, tense children with behavior problems."[25] After trying Miltown on some of his young patients, Brooklyn, New York, physician Harry R. Lichtfield reported to his colleagues that he found the agent useful in "one of the foremost pediatric challenges," treating the "markedly restless, irritable, aggressive, or tense child who has become a problem both to himself and to his family."[26]

Although Lichtfield did not specify the frequency with which he prescribed Miltown, such a broad description of its benefits suggested he used it to treat a wide range of normative behavior in the healthy infant or child. Wallace Laboratories' promotional materials targeted physicians like Lichtfield, emphasizing that many company-funded pediatric studies demonstrated the drug's success with children. One summary, for example, concluded that "delinquent" youngsters "showed continued improvement on prolonged meprobamate therapy."[27] According to the company, another study suggested Miltown was "the drug of choice in child psychiatry."[28] In an attempt to capture the pediatric market, Wallace Laboratories formulated a small sugar-coated tablet "especially suitable for use with children" that could be crushed and placed on children's cereal.[29] Interestingly, the FDA-approved label for Miltown in 1956 makes no mention of its potential uses for children with behavioral problems, despite the fact that the company included pediatric dosing guidelines in its published guidelines.[30]

Other psychiatric drugs also quickly found their way into general pediatric practice. New York pediatrician Milton W. Talbot alerted his colleagues to the fact that he found the antipsychotic drug reserpine useful for the "unhappy infant, with its accompanying problem of distraught and unhappy parents," a problem he saw in his practice "all too frequently"[31] Psychoactive drugs also showed promise in treating pediatric conditions considered to have both a psychiatric and nonpsychiatric component. Miltown, for example, was suggested as a therapy for the child who wet the bed.[32] Finally, some argued that tranquilizers had an important role to play in the nation's civil defense plan in terms of child protection. Lists of stockpiled supplies families needed to keep handy in their bomb shelters included tranquilizers to keep rambunctious children calm during the weeks the family would need to spend underground in the event of a nuclear attack.[33]

How and when to use the new mood altering agents in general practice reveal the era's cultural anxieties about what constituted the normal child. On the one hand, Americans differentiated their country from the Soviet Union by maintaining that the culture nurtured children's individuality in ways the communist nations did not. On the other hand, the child who did not conform behaviorally risked becoming labeled a juvenile delinquent or behaviorally disordered. Marketing materials for Miltown, for example, capitalized on worries about the normal child by urging physicians to study the behavior of children and parents in their practices and make such assessments. Wallace Laboratories compiled a litany of pediatric symptomatology for which the drug might be prescribed, including children with sleeping problems and those with uncooperative behavior. But left unclear, and exacerbated by the unstable diagnostic categories characteristic for pediatric mental illness in this era, was how to determine when children's sleeplessness met the threshold of a condition needing treatment with a powerful medication. That most of the physicians prescribing the drugs were pediatricians or general practitioners, not child psychiatrists, arguably led to even more confusion.[34]

## The 1958 Child Research in Psychopharmacology Conference

In October 1956, the American Academy of Child Psychiatry and the American Psychiatric Association tried to bring more intellectual coherence to child psychiatry as well as the issues regarding psychotropic drugs for the pediatric patient. With funding from the National Institute of Mental Health and U.S. Public Health Service, the two organizations convened a conference. Perhaps implicitly acknowledging that psychiatrists could exert little control over their non-psychiatrist colleagues, the meeting focused on children

admitted to inpatient child psychiatry wards. As director of the nation's largest such unit, Bender was invited to detail her therapeutic programs. While
she described the many interventions she employed to treat children, she
reserved special enthusiasm for psychopharmacology and how Bellevue had
"pioneered" its use.[35]

That same year, Congress appropriated funding to establish a Psychopharmacology Service Center (soon renamed the Psychopharmacology Research
Branch or PRB) within NIMH to help organize testing for psychiatric drugs
arriving on the market.[36] In October 1958, the Institute sponsored an invited
conference, "Child Research in Psychopharmacology."[37] Echoing Abraham
Jacobi and, by now, generations of pediatric leaders, director R. H. Felix
stressed in his opening remarks that he understood that the child was not a
"miniature adult."[38] He also admonished the pediatricians, child psychiatrists,
psychologists, pharmacologists, and one social worker in attendance that
"these drugs when used with children may not only be tools of tremendous
value but also may contain elements of danger."[39] Felix and PRB staff believed
clinicians needed better measurement tools to assess the need for, and response
to, psychoactive drugs in the pediatric population.

Divisions among the child psychiatrists in attendance about how and when
to employ drug therapy became clear from the conference's start. Johns Hopkins Hospital psychiatrist Leon Eisenberg expressed concern about what he
saw as the overuse of mood-altering agents in children. Eisenberg was certainly not averse to medication. He and his mentor Leo Kanner had just published an article summarizing their pediatric tranquilizer experiments.[40] But
Eisenberg was very worried about the loose prescribing practices of physicians such as Lichtfield and Talbot. He believed better research design would
provide guidance to help doctors with drug-related decision-making. At the
same time, he believed that pediatric psychopharmacology research presented
challenges, a number of which he synthesized in his remarks. First, since the
child "comes to [psychiatric] attention because of his family's or his community's initiative," not on his or her own, he pointed out that it could be hard
to identify whether the disturbance was in the child, parent, or family. Second, "the lack of a commonly agreed upon system of classification" within
child psychiatry, other than labeling children "emotionally disturbed," made
it difficult to compare treatments or define "improvement" in ways that met
an agreed upon standard.[41] Third, too often "clinical investigation can proceed
without a theoretical commitment" or is undertaken to "see what happens."[42]
All these factors made it hard for the psychiatrist to have a firm sense of what
he or she was treating as well as to interpret the drug response, "Is the child
improved . . . only because he is less troublesome to others if he is in a chemical straitjacket?"[43] Without better diagnostic criteria and pediatric behavioral
measurement rubrics, he believed it was difficult for physicians to interpret

children's responses to psychoactive medications. Eisenberg argued that the best solution to the problems was for psychiatrists to embrace randomized controlled trials just as their colleagues in other areas of medicine were doing.

Lauretta Bender, a former Kanner colleague herself, responded to Eisenberg. At this point in their respective careers, Bender had significantly more seniority. She had just moved from twenty-two years as Bellevue's director of child psychiatry to an advisory position with the New York State Department of Mental Hygiene. She also served as research scientist in child psychiatry at Creedmoor State Hospital in Queens, New York. Bender bristled at what she perceived as Eisenberg's criticism of her approach to pediatric psychopharmacology investigations. She questioned his reliance on the idea that research questions needed to be theoretically framed or hypothesis driven, "wonder[ing] whether one man's biases are not the other man's theories."[44] But Bender saved her harshest words for Eisenberg's call for randomized trials in pediatric psychopharmacology. In a patronizing tone, she characterized his speech as having "dutifully emphasized the importance of research methodology," but revealing his lack of experience because "we cannot fool ourselves by designing standardized medical research and matching controls among human beings, especially children."[45] Bender maintained that drug research approaches that worked in other areas of medicine could not be translated to child psychiatry. She believed that randomized trials in pediatric psychopharmacology introduced "error" because such research was inherently reductionistic, and, as such, an anathema to studying the child as a "unique" individual.[46]

Other speakers avoided directly weighing in on the controversy, but seemed to agree with Eisenberg that psychoactive drug "misuse" was occurring in at least some American children.[47] Yale School of Medicine child psychiatrist Milton J. E. Senn emphasized this point when he concluded the conference by urging the drug companies in attendance (no names were provided) to be more judicious in terms of their sales tactics, "I think the drug houses are aiding and abetting this [over-prescription of mood-altering agents in children] by their looseness of advertising and by the frequency by which they send out literature and samples."[48] He acknowledged that pediatricians faced a dilemma because parents' expectations of pediatricians had evolved from earlier eras. Now they were "often called upon to deal with children who are not psychologically sick in terms of mental illness," but whose parents were concerned about their conduct or demeanor.[49] Senn indicated that pediatricians sometimes faced pressure from parents, teachers, and society to medicalize children's behavior: the "pediatrician and the nonpsychiatric physician are now attempting to use drugs as short cuts they have been seeking for years to bring about changes in behavior that parents expect the physician to bring about."[50]

## The 1960s: New Frontiers in Pediatric Psychopharmacology

Felix and others at NIMH clearly supported Eisenberg, not Bender. Soon after the conference ended, the Institute funded Eisenberg to undertake the first randomized controlled trial in pediatric psychopharmacology.[51] In keeping with the casual norms of informed consent during this era, one of Eisenberg's earliest NIMH-funded studies compared children with behavioral disorders who were followed at Johns Hopkins Hospital. Youngsters received one of three different treatment regimens, Miltown (meprobamate), Compazine (prochlorperazine), or a placebo in addition to their psychotherapy. Eisenberg did not inform families that they and their children were enrolled in a research study. Rather, parents were told that the drugs had been prescribed to help their children "feel better" or "make the world seem happier."[52] A frustrated Eisenberg found the results difficult to interpret because of subjects' disease heterogeneity. He considered another experiment more successful. For this study he enrolled institutionalized African American youngsters labeled delinquent. The stimulant dextroamphetamine significantly improved many boys' scores on behavioral rating scales, encouraging him to express cautious optimism that drugs might treat juvenile delinquency.[53]

As the 1950s ended, some Americans began to criticize the widespread use of tranquilizers and other mood-altering agents. One Chicago mother wrote anonymously about her experiences in the February 1960 issue of *Ladies Home Journal*. She characterized her ten-year-old son as a "normal, bright, healthy boy."[54] Because he "occasionally had bad temper tantrums" she and her husband took him to see a child psychiatrist for advice.[55] Aghast that the doctor wrote a prescription for tranquilizers, the mother traveled to a medical library and read whatever she could find about them. She wanted other *Ladies Home Journal* readers to know what she found. Mood-altering drugs could cause numerous side effects of which her doctor had not informed her and she felt betrayed. She warned other mothers that no long-term data existed as to how tranquilizers might affect the developing brain. Her findings led her to wonder "Is this the kind of medicine to give to a child—*any* child?"[56]

In 1961, one of Bender's former child psychiatry trainees, Barbara Fish, took charge at Bellevue. Like Bender, Fish ardently believed in psychopharmacology, administering Thorazine and similar drugs to youngsters between the ages of one and six years, for example, to observe their behavior as part of her early research into severe childhood mental illness. Unlike Bender, however, Fish believed in randomized controlled trials and the importance of designing investigations that employed structured, state-of-the-science research methodologies. This embrace brought her a large NIMH grant for Bellevue's program. Renamed the Children's Psychopharmacology Research Unit, Bellevue became the only federally funded psychopharmacology research unit with a dedicated pediatric focus.[57]

At about the same time, Bender embarked on what many would later consider her most controversial research, studying children's responses to lysergic acid diethylamide (LSD). While a number of investigators were experimenting with the agent on adults, Bender and her colleague Gloria Faretra at Creedmoor State Hospital were interested in its effects on children.[58] Bender believed that LSD might have a therapeutic impact on children with autistic or schizophrenic symptoms because it increased cerebral vascular tone. She hypothesized that "in childhood schizophrenia, all boundaries are lost, not only of the psychological and personality experiences, but also those of the visceral functions, autonomic nervous system, vascular tone, muscular tone, and perception."[59] As such, Bender reasoned that an agent that made the brain's blood vessels less permeable might help them, or at least reveal data to extend her knowledge of the condition. She acknowledged that the New York City commissioner of the Department of Mental Hygiene initially opposed her plan to experiment with LSD on young children, but ultimately acceded when she lobbied him vigorously. In one of her earliest pediatric LSD studies, in 1961, children between the ages of five and eleven years received it every day for up to several months. Staff administered the agent daily to at least a few youngsters "for a year or two."[60] Based on her personal observations and those of the Creedmoor staff, Bender concluded that the children seemed to have a "general improvement in well-being, appearance and lift in mood."[61] In addition, they "all showed a tendency to become 'high' and lively," although LSD had been withdrawn in two children who became "panicky and anxious."[62]

In another study, the team first subcutaneously injected epinephrine and pilocarpine, potentially risky agents known to stimulate and inhibit vascular tone, into thirty boys between the ages of seven and twelve years. Bender used these drugs to better understand individual children's baseline vascular functions. Next, youngsters received either LSD, Sansert (an investigational LSD derivative developed by the Sandoz company), or psilocybin (a psychedelic compound produced by mushrooms). All three drugs affected children's blood pressure, pulse, and respiration. Bender and her team repeated this study in ten younger (five to ten years old) boys whose psychological tests revealed they were sicker than the first group. After seven weeks of therapy using LSD, Sansert, or psilocybin, Bender reported a broad range of encouraging results, among them "improvement in interpersonal relationships, more awareness and response to their environment."[63] Taken together, these investigations convinced Bender that such agents stimulated mentally ill children's central nervous systems in a way she deemed "remarkable."[64]

Bender later estimated that she prescribed LSD to eighty-nine children in the years between 1961 and 1965.[65] Although most of her funding for the research came from the New York state health department and Sandoz, she did manage to obtain one small NIMH grant in the wake of late 1960s reports that LSD could cause chromosome damage. Since she had administered it or the Sandoz investigational LSD derivative for a protracted period of time to so many children, Bender had a ready supply of subjects on which to study this hypothesis. She and her team studied cells harvested from children who had participated in her experiments. They found no chromosomal breakages and concluded that they had not suffered any ill effects from LSD. Interestingly, in the publication resulting from this research Bender claimed she had administered LSD or Sansert to some children for as long as three years, not the two she had previously stipulated. She also wrote that her work had ended in 1966, not 1965, as she noted elsewhere.[66] For years after she was forced to cease her LSD-related work because she could no longer obtain the agent from Sandoz by the mid-1960s, Bender expressed hope that it could be resumed because "it is one of the most effective methods of treatment we have for childhood schizophrenia."[67]

There was little likelihood that Bender's methods at Creedmoor would be questioned by hospital employees. Her research staff managed the unit, overseeing the nurses and other staff who carried out the protocols. Although she never disavowed her LSD research, perhaps in an effort to stem criticism as ethical norms evolved, Bender included details omitted from her publications in an extensive, but unpublished, 1968 summary of her Creedmoor research. For the first time, Bender went out of her way to stress that her work had been approved by the unit's "Research Committee and [had received] informed parental consent."[68] She did not, however, describe these processes further. Although largely forgotten today, Bender's work was no secret at the time. She published widely in prestigious journals without challenge. No colleagues whose questions and comments accompanied many of her published presentations seemed concerned. Nor did the *New York Times*, which reported on Bender's work in 1963: "LSD Drug Found to Aid Children."[69] This is not surprising given that most Americans during this era knew little about LSD, and the publicity surrounding its use by members of what became known as the youth counterculture had not yet occurred.

At the same time Bender undertook her LSD-related work in the early 1960s, Eisenberg, joined now by psychologist C. Keith Conners, continued to build his NIMH-funded program of pediatric stimulant research. In the late 1950s, Eisenberg became Leo Kanner's successor as chief of child psychiatry at Johns Hopkins Hospital.[70] Just as Harry Shirkey, Helen Taussig, John Nestor, and others sought to use the thalidomide crisis to move policymakers to consider a broader set of pediatric-related drug safety issues, so, too, did Eisenberg, who wanted to draw legislators' attention to questions specific to mood-altering agents in children. During Hubert Humphrey's post-thalidomide

Capitol Hill hearings into how to improve federal oversight of American drug policy, Eisenberg wrote to the senator reiterating the concerns he had raised at the 1958 conference. Informing Humphrey that he was "impressed with the discrepancy between the wide use of these [tranquilizers] drugs in pediatric practice and the meager evidence of their value," Eisenberg argued for new regulatory protections for children.[71] He also warned Humphrey about the "extensive advertising campaign of the drug companies," whose claims regarding psychoactive drug safety and efficacy fell "just short of open deception." The letter found its way into the published hearings but with no formal comment from Humphrey.[72]

In an effort to reach practitioners outside child psychiatry, Eisenberg expanded on these and related concerns the following year in the Children's Bureau periodical, *Children*. Without identifying Bender, but surely with her in mind, he lambasted "physicians who consider drugs *the* agents of choice."[73] In lay terms, Eisenberg outlined the issues as he had to Humphrey. He also walked readers through the ways in which research into child mental illness differed from other pediatric research. Describing the paucity of child-focused measurement tools, he lamented the fact that he lacked a "psychiatric thermometer" to assess youngsters' mental health.[74] Officials at NIMH clearly agreed with Eisenberg. In the years following its late 1950s and early 1960s support for him and Bellevue's Barbara Fish, the Psychopharmacology Research Branch ceased supporting any new pediatric drug studies. Staffer Ronald S. Lipman acknowledged that the "hiatus . . . reflected not an absence of applications" but "the unsophisticated state of methodology in pediatric [psycho] pharmacology."[75]

Eisenberg and Conners both left Johns Hopkins for Harvard in 1967 and were by then well on their way to establishing the efficacy of stimulant medications for what was now called hyperkinetic reaction in childhood. They had also just successfully petitioned the updated version of the *Diagnostic and Statistical Manual of Mental Disorders*, published in 1968, to include the diagnosis.[76] Recognizing the need for better pediatric psychometric tools and assessment rubrics, NIMH funded Conners to develop them. Significantly, Eisenberg's and Conners's success at defining diagnostic criteria for hyperactivity, validating assessment measures, and quantifying situations in which the stimulants worked made this area of research the most attractive to NIMH. When it once again approved pediatric psychopharmacology research grants in the late 1960s, most of the successful applicants aimed to extend the work of Eisenberg and Conners in some way.[77]

The second half of the 1960s also saw a number of legislative and policy discussions surrounding child mental health in which psychopharmacology had no direct immediate role. As part of President Johnson's War on Poverty and other Great Society initiatives, the government launched new programs aimed at studying and addressing ways in which poverty affected children emotionally and academically. The National Institute for Child Health and Human Development (NICHD) funded research and training programs related to developmental disability (often referred to in that era as mental retardation), a condition frequently confused with mental illness in children. Within NIMH, new centers for child and family mental health and juvenile delinquency received robust support. As the decade ended, NIMH drew together leaders in child mental health, creating the Joint Commission on Mental Health of Children. The Commission aimed to synthesize a cohesive national action plan for child mental health in the 1970s.[78]

## Pediatric Psychopharmacology: Conflict and Consensus in the 1970s

The ways in which the climate surrounding the use of mood-altering drugs in children had shifted since the 1950s became evident early in 1970, when the Commission issued its report, *Crisis in Child Mental Health: Challenges for the 1970s*. Whereas Bender had once been considered a leader in pediatric psychotropic drug research, she was now an outlier. Although the report did not mention her by name, it included pediatric LSD research in its examples of "fringe" practices.[79] The Commission said very little about medication as a therapeutic modality for mentally ill children. In only one place was there mention that, under the right circumstances, drugs could supplement individual child or family therapy.

In summer 1970, just as the Commission's report was published, the *Washington Post* featured an article that attracted widespread public and congressional attention. The piece alleged that as many as 10 percent of Omaha, Nebraska, school-aged children, many of them poor and black, had been prescribed "behavior modification" drugs, especially Ritalin (methylphenidate hydrochloride).[80] The newspaper noted concerns by parents who felt pressured to medicate their children. They and community leaders alleged that the aim was to "drug black children into quiet submission."[81] A few days later, the *New York Times* followed the *Post* story with one of its own. The article in the *New York Times* presented a more sympathetic view of stimulants. It emphasized Eisenberg's and Conners's research and quoted Eisenberg, who reassured parents that when used in the right circumstances, the drugs helped youngsters and was "remarkably safe—even safer than penicillin."[82] Extending the antibiotic analogy, the story cited pediatric neurologist Eric Denhoff, who observed that some called stimulants the "penicillin of children with learning disabilities."[83]

The dueling newspaper stories only fueled the controversy. Within a few weeks, New Jersey Democrat Cornelius E. Gallagher convened a hearing in the House of Representatives seeking a "full public discussion" about "prescribing speed for children."[84] Referencing the drug catastrophe everyone remembered, Gallagher mused that the nation might be facing a "mental thalidomide" situation.[85] He questioned whether prescribing stimulants sent mixed messages to American youth at a time when adults increasingly worried about substance abuse in the younger generation. Was it illogical, he queried rhetorically, to steer junior high and high school students away from "speed" at the same time their younger siblings were having it prescribed to them?[86] Gallagher also wanted to initiate a national conversation about what constituted normal behavior in the average American child and who made that decision. How, he pointedly asked Ronald Lipman, an FDA clinical studies section chief, did one differentiate the child with "hyperkinesis" from "just a bored, bright, creative pain-in-the-neck kid?"[87]

The thoughtful overviews of hyperkinesis and stimulant research summarized by NIMH and FDA staffers somewhat mollified Gallagher, but he remained concerned about how society decided who was, and who was not, a typical American child. Beyond the grandstanding and hyperbole at the hearing, one of its most notable features was how little Gallagher and the other legislators seemed to know about basic issues surrounding American drug policy. No one mentioned, for example, the fact that their questions about pediatric drug development were similar to those raised earlier by Kefauver, Humphrey, and others. Moreover, Gallagher seemed to lack basic information about ongoing FDA efforts to address pediatric safety and efficacy-related questions, nor did he seem clear on what the agency actually did. Dorothy Dobbs, Director, Division of Neuropharmacological Drug Products at FDA, for example, had to explain to Gallagher that NIMH, not FDA, funded drug research into the stimulants.[88] She noted that the issues raised by the the *Washington Post* regarding stimulant use in Omaha children were not even research-related since no investigation had been underway. When Gallagher continued to press FDA to engage in ways outside the agency's regulatory domain, Dobbs's superior, Elliot L. Richardson, secretary of Health and Human Services, subsequently wrote to Gallagher, explaining to him that the FDA had no oversight of physician practice.[89]

Finally, Gallagher did not seem to understand that his concerns about psychoactive medications and children were not a problem isolated to behavioral drugs. For example, he expressed concern about doctors prescribing stimulants and other psychoactive drugs for children outside the age range stipulated on the label without acknowledging that this practice occurred for virtually every drug on the market.[90] Only a very few pediatric dosing metrics were backed by scientifically derived safety and efficacy data. Gallagher's lack of knowledge is not surprising. His interest lay primarily in issues related to the right to privacy in American life.[91] He correctly surmised that a Capitol Hill hearing regarding government overreach wherein school personnel seemed to be intruding on parents' rights would garner significant media attention.[92] Even if he agreed with the racism charges leveled by Omaha parents, emphasizing it did not advance his larger privacy-related concerns. But it was a missed opportunity. Had Gallagher chosen to do so, the hearings could have delved into broader issues, potentially synergizing Harry Shirkey's and Sumner Yaffe's parallel efforts during this time period. While the hearing was awash in rhetoric regarding child protection, their needs were in reality not its primary focus.

In December 1970, Leon Eisenberg took the stage at the American College of Neuropsychopharmacology. Hoping to bring nuance and balance to the past year's media-fueled drug controversy, he reminded his colleagues that "Drugs promise neither the passport to a brave new world nor the gateway to the inferno."[93] Eisenberg drew on Harry Shirkey's therapeutic orphan concept as an organizing framework for his talk, subsequently published in a landmark article.[94] He stressed the fact that most of the challenges in pediatric psychopharmacology differed little from general issues surrounding children and drugs. His discussion of the knowledge deficit regarding pediatric dosing, data extrapolation from animal models, and research design-related issues specific to children's evolving development sounded identical to the problems articulated simultaneously by Shirkey and Yaffe.[95]

But Eisenberg also outlined the additional obstacles faced by those in his field, ones that spoke to the differences between child psychiatry and general pediatrics. When most children were prescribed medications, it was for a discrete period of time and to treat a specific illness. But the rationale for psychoactive drugs in children was not as clear. Moreover, they received the drugs for extended periods of time and information regarding long-term effects was virtually nonexistent. This was true for adults as well, but children risked potentially stunted growth or impeded brain development, issues older people did not face. Finally, Eisenberg noted, as he had in the past, that the perceived need to medicate a child was sometimes the result "of disturbed mothers, inadequate teachers or uninformed judges."[96] Reflecting his growing interest in how social and economic circumstances shaped health and clinical practice, Eisenberg urged his colleagues to consider nonmedical variables that might result in prescribing mood-altering medication to children, such as poverty, racism, and other structural problems.

Now a national leader, Eisenberg was a well-funded NIMH researcher, professor at Harvard Medical School, and chief of psychiatry at Massachusetts General Hospital. His efforts with Conners had made hyperactivity a discrete psychiatric diagnosis, one differentiated from the older, more diffuse "disturbed child" entity. Eisenberg had less success, however, stemming the tide of drug advertisements in medical journals. Ironically, his work provided evidence that companies like CIBA, which manufactured Ritalin, could use to increase their focus on children. As Ilina Singh has shown, until the early 1970s most stimulant advertisements featured a picture of an adult. Eisenberg's research demonstrated, however cautiously, that stimulants improved the behavior and cognitive performance of appropriately diagnosed children. His research meant that CIBA increasingly devoted more attention to children.[97] By the 1970s, in addition to promoting Ritalin to physicians, the company was sending brochures and movies to educators and parent-teacher associations extolling the many ways children benefited socially and academically from stimulant drugs.[98]

The year 1973 brought optimism and fresh challenges to issues surrounding pediatric psychopharmacology. A new set of NIMH Psychopharmacology Research Branch–approved standardized pediatric psychiatric measures for evaluating psychotropic drug outcomes in children provided meaningful tools for researchers.[99] At the same time, Senator Ted Kennedy's highly charged hearings into human experimentation publicized abuses involving institutionalized mentally ill and developmentally disabled populations. A number of the cases involved children.[100] In the aftermath of the Kennedy hearings, lawsuits involving the use of antipsychotics and sedatives in vulnerable populations followed. Although drugs' widespread use in such situations was certainly not limited to children, the litigation filed by public interest law firms made an especially strong argument on their behalf.

More Capitol Hill hearings arose from the flow of lawsuits, repeatedly bringing FDA staffers to Capitol Hill. In one instance, for example, petitioners demanded that the "disturbed child" indication on the package insert for Thorazine be replaced with "more precise language which indicates that the drug is approved for the treatment of only those children who have been diagnosed as having a specifically identified psychotic condition . . . for which the drug has been previously approved."[101] Alexander M. Schmidt, FDA commissioner, reassured litigants and Congress that the agency agreed that more clarity regarding children and psychoactive drug prescription was needed. He empaneled an FDA group to work with stakeholders within NIMH, industry, and the American Academy of Pediatrics (AAP) to do just that.[102] The FDA had recently begun asking for American Academy of Pediatrics Committee on Drugs (COD) consultation regarding psychoactive agents. Whereas few of the COD meetings in the 1960s discussed behavioral drugs, issues regarding their safety and when they should be prescribed now occurred frequently, and the COD issued guidelines for stimulant use in 1973. And just as the agency asked the COD for general guidelines concerning pediatric drug testing, so, too, did FDA want COD assistance for scientific and methodological issues specific to pediatric psychopharmacology.[103]

The mid-1970s creation of the National Commission for the Protection of Human Subjects of Biomedical and Behavioral Research, aimed at codifying issues surrounding medical ethics and informed consent, slowed behavioral drug investigations in children just as it did for other research, as everyone awaited its findings. Given the negative publicity surrounding the Kennedy hearings, anyone who wanted to undertake such work faced difficult obstacles finding subjects for studies. This made it even more difficult to answer a fundamental question: did all children respond to stimulants or just those who were hyperactive? If the attention span improved in all children who received Ritalin, what condition, exactly was the drug treating? Leon Eisenberg had long worried about this issue, but saw no ethical way to address it. He had admitted as much in a 1968 letter to a Harvard colleague, copied to Henry Beecher, whose influential 1966 article about experimentation ethics had ignited much debate within medicine: "I have never been able to persuade myself that it would be legitimate to give drugs to normal children, even were their parents to consent."[104]

One young Harvard-trained child psychiatrist at NIMH, Judith Rapoport, decided to study this question using a novel strategy. Before arriving at NIMH, Rapoport practiced at a clinic where she was struck by stimulants' effects on children who had accidently ingested pills meant for a sibling: "These calm children just got calmer on stimulants!"[105] Now an NIMH staff scientist, Rapoport decided to study their effects in normal children. Perhaps recognizing how difficult it would be to undertake such an investigation in a traditional clinical setting, she decided to approach her NIMH colleagues with children. In an effort to reassure them that the drugs were safe, her own two sons were the first subjects enrolled in her study. Twelve other boys between the ages of six and twelve years whose parents worked at NIMH received one dose of a stimulant or placebo, after which their performance on a variety of psychometric and self-report measures was assessed. Rapoport made sure that none of the families involved fit anyone's definition of powerless: "the parents were doctors, lawyers, and, in one case, president of the local ACLU."[106] Her findings confirmed what she had observed empirically: nonhyperactive children also responded with decreased motor activity and improved test performance. While her research did not yield new information about whether stimulants worked in hyperactive children, she concluded that their "lack of specificity" was "no argument against . . . use."[107] As an example, she reminded readers that diuretics increased urine output in everyone who took them, not just those with congestive heart failure.[108]

As the 1970s ended, those interested in pediatric psychopharmacology grew more optimistic. The perceived need to understand psychoactive drugs in the context of the pediatric patient had helped create a unique niche for child psychiatrists. Newly refined psychometric measures created by Conners and others now allowed clinicians to more clearly differentiate the mentally ill youngster in ways beyond the older "disturbed child" category. Better assessment tools and greater diagnostic specificity meant that outcomes in response to medication could be more reliably evaluated. Moreover, by 1979, just as the FDA accepted the COD scientific guidelines for pediatric drug research, so, too, did the agency distribute its supplement specific to pediatric psychoactive drug investigations. Child psychiatrists who argued that mental illness was rooted in organic causes believed they were on the cusp of a new era. The first pediatric psychopharmacology text, influenced heavily by biology and genetics, had just been published. The third edition of *Diagnostic and Statistical Manual of Mental Disorders*, due out in 1980, reinforced this perspective and significantly expanded the pediatric section. For those who believed in a more biologically oriented framework for child psychiatry, one in which drug therapy played an important role, these changes seemed destined to facilitate the specialty's shift away from the child guidance model even further.[109]

# 7

# Pediatric Drug Development and Policy after 1979

••••••••••••••••••••

As 1980 dawned, there was good reason for stakeholder optimism regarding pediatric drug safety- and efficacy-related issues. In the over-the-counter drug market, protective caps made products safer and aspirin poisoning rates continued to decline. Those with a vested interest in pediatric prescription drugs could look to new scientific and ethical guidelines governing pediatric drug research. And Food and Drug Administration staff affirmed commitment to the 1979 regulation that full clinical trial data supporting claims for children's dosing and administration accompany any pediatric indication in new drug applications (NDAs).

But the 1979 rule, like the 1938 and 1962 laws, did not require pediatric studies. In other words, companies only had to submit pediatric data if they sought its inclusion on the label. In many ways, the rule was only a reiteration of earlier legislation. The intention of both the 1938 Federal Food, Drug, and Cosmetic Act and the 1962 Kefauver-Harris Amendments was to make sure that directions for use were safe and effective for all groups, including children. The decades-long core issue remained unaddressed: who would pay for all the additional steps necessary to assure pediatric drug safety and efficacy? This variable had never been incidental in the United States, but as the pharmaceutical industry continued to comprise a larger sector of the American economy and health care costs escalated in the early 1980s, it became increasingly important. Given the small pediatric market relative to adults, drug companies had few economic incentives to invest in pediatric testing. Ever since the first sulfonamides arrived on the market, clinicians had, through trial and error, adapted them for use in children as quickly as possible. As a result, industry leaders correctly wagered that they would continue to do so. As long as every major firm behaved in a similar fashion, there was no competitive disadvantage to this practice.[1]

Thus, more than one hundred years after Abraham Jacobi had first argued that children could not be considered miniature adults when it came to therapeutics, they remained, as Harry Shirkey had memorably categorized them, "orphaned" in terms of many of the protections afforded to adults. But as this history reveals, it was not because no one had considered children's issues. In the late nineteenth and early twentieth centuries, Jacobi himself as well as other pediatric and public health leaders railed against the risks to infants from soothing syrups. In the 1930s, the Philadelphia Pediatric Society convinced the American Academy of Pediatrics (AAP) to seek more pediatric representation to the USP. In the 1940s, Irvin Kerlan and Robert Stormont at FDA prophetically identified the need for more clarity regarding pediatric drugs. In the 1950s and 1960s, Shirkey's pioneering efforts pressed the AMA, AAP, and USP to work for broad reforms in pediatric drug development, testing, and regulation. Others, including John Nestor, Frances Kelsey, Helen Taussig, Jay Arena, and Leon Eisenberg, strove to spotlight problems surrounding children and drug safety. In the 1970s, researchers such as Allen A. Mitchell and Sumner Yaffe created innovative research and practice initiatives to propel pediatric pharmacology knowledge forward.

All these efforts focused attention on the problem and resulted in some legislative successes. In 1906, fears of soothing syrups and other patent medicines that maimed or killed children helped create the modern FDA. In 1938 and 1962, respectively, robust new laws increased federal oversight of the pharmaceutical industry in the wake of the Elixer Sulfanilamide and thalidomide crises. Yet, by and large, adults benefited disproportionately from these statutes because the laws did not mandate anyone to address children's issues specifically. And just as had occurred in the past, an analysis in the wake of the FDA's 1979 pediatric regulation revealed that it, too, failed to reduce the pediatric drug knowledge gap. Despite Marion Finkel's best efforts to "pressure companies to do pediatric studies of certain products undergoing the approval process," the regulation remained "voluntary but encouraged." Thus, only a small percentage of new drug applications submitted to FDA with potential for use in children included pediatric clinical trial data.[2]

Moreover, by 1980, those who sought more robust governmental oversight of the pharmaceutical industry in the United States knew they faced an uphill battle. Sharp declines in manufacturing in the 1970s and an oil embargo that sent gasoline prices sharply upward stalled the economy. The resulting recession shook Americans' optimism and ended the postwar economic boom. Watergate and other political scandals disillusioned many Americans' belief in governmental solutions. As a result, Ronald Reagan's small government philosophies resonated with voters in the 1980 presidential election.[3]

## A New Template for Pediatric Drug Development: The Orphan Drug Act

It was in this clinical, economic, and political context that Connecticut mother Abbey S. Meyers began fighting on behalf of her son David. David suffered from Tourette Syndrome (TS), a complex neurological disorder characterized by repetitive movements and vocal tics. As his symptoms worsened in the late 1970s, David's doctor suggested he try an investigational drug for schizophrenia, Orap (pimozide). Meyers felt very relieved when the drug improved David's symptoms. But in 1979, McNeil Laboratories, a division of Johnson and Johnson, decided to stop its manufacture. Their tests revealed it was not useful for schizophrenia and that not enough people suffered from TS to make the drug financially worthwhile to produce. As a result, Orap became a drug with only "orphan" potential, a term referring to drugs that might be used in either adults or children, but in numbers so small that their manufacture would not prove profitable. Several companies did make a few targeted products as a philanthropic gesture, but the scale was small and there was no organization to these efforts. Unfortunately, Orap was not one of those drugs. Aghast that David's treatment had disappeared overnight, Meyers began contacting other parents in the Tourette Foundation. Because it was a small organization, she also reached out to the growing number of advocacy groups for other rare diseases, ultimately uniting them into what became the National Organization for Rare Diseases (NORD).[4]

When a mother who lived in the district of powerful California Democratic Representative Henry Waxman faced a problem obtaining an orphan drug for her child, she contacted Meyers, NORD's president. Meyers, the self-proclaimed "housewife from Connecticut," seized an opportunity.[5] She organized a group of parents who, in 1980, convinced Waxman, chair of the House Commerce Committee, to convene a hearing focused on orphan drugs. Meyers testified eloquently, using arguments rich with themes of both gender and social class that garnered media attention:

> As a mother, when I realized that my son could no longer get Pimozide, I was devastated. Without medication . . . he could not write, feed, or dress himself. I panicked. I began to study drug policy in foreign countries in order to find a way to smuggle the drug into the United States. I, a law-abiding, middle class mother began to contemplate breaking the law in order to circumvent the needless

suffering of my child. I learned that the practice was not new and that if I were affluent I could easily get this drug from Mexico. But I was not affluent.[6]

Meyers saw the issue starkly, as good versus evil. She implored the committee "in the name of my children" and "millions of others like them" to intervene on their behalf with legislation to protect them from "profit margins and red tape."[7] Meyers's words and the way in which she framed the issue as corporations versus children captured attention on and off Capitol Hill. It is unlikely, however, that her efforts would have gotten very far without Waxman's deft legislative hand, which guided an orphan drug bill through Congress and the quiet leadership of the FDA's Marion Finkel. Finkel and her colleagues at FDA had been studying problems related to orphan drugs for years. She bolstered Meyers's emotional testimony with concrete policy recommendations.[8]

The drug industry had refused Waxman's offer to testify. After the hearing's negative publicity, companies scrambled to undo Meyers's characterization of them as greedy and unfeeling toward desperately ill children. The industry made sure that their interests were well represented in subsequent Capitol Hill discussions. But the drug industry had little interest in an orphan drug law. At one 1981 hearing, for example, Louis A. Engman, president of the Pharmaceutical Manufacturers Association, argued that the private sector could effectively address the issue, and was already doing so.[9] But the bill Waxman introduced not only featured savvy activist parent Abbey Meyers, it attracted celebrity attention. Television star Jack Klugman's brother suffered from a rare disease and the actor reached out to Meyers. At her urging, Klugman subsequently testified on Capitol Hill and devoted two episodes of his popular TV show *Quincy* to orphan drugs. With effort, the bill passed both houses of Congress just before Christmas 1982. Nonetheless, it appeared that President Reagan planned to ignore the bill until Congress adjourned, killing it using a legislative procedure known as a pocket veto. The Orphan Drug Act arrived on Reagan's desk just before Christmas. According to Meyers, in an effort to appeal to the president's emotions and reach out to him directly, NORD purchased a large advertisement in the Palm Springs, California, newspaper (close to the southern California ranch where the president spent his holiday) and the *Washington Post*. Worded to make him feel like "Scrooge" by ignoring those "doomed to an early death" or suffering from "painful and disabling sicknesses," the advertisement begged him to not to ignore the bill.[10]

In January 1983, Reagan quietly signed the Orphan Drug Act into law despite his professed antipathy for governmental expansion and to the dismay of the pharmaceutical industry. The statute created a new FDA branch, the Office of Orphan Products Development, with Finkel as its first director. The law offered incentives for companies that invested in drug development for conditions afflicting only small numbers of people, subsequently defined as fewer than 200,000 individuals each year. It also offered lucrative rewards in an attempt to generate industry interest in developing and manufacturing orphan drugs, among them tax credits for research-related expenses. Importantly, the Orphan Drug Act also authorized an exclusive right to market the drug for seven years.[11]

No one anticipated the financial windfall the Orphan Drug Act would afford to manufacturers. Health and Human Services Secretary Margaret Heckler had suggested that the law would make developing drugs for rare conditions financially feasible, but admonished that it would "make nobody rich."[12] She could not have been more wrong. The exclusivity provision protected the producer of an orphan product from competition, but was silent on what it could charge. This meant that companies retained a seven-year monopoly on their drug and could set the price at whatever they chose. As a result, the profits for some orphan drugs reached a billion dollars. Newly created biotechnology and niche drug companies raced to develop orphan drugs.[13]

While the drugs were often expensive and generated enormous profits for some companies, the Orphan Drug Act also meant that, for the first time, children with rare conditions such as pediatric genetic metabolic disorders lived healthier lives.[14] Given that many such diseases were genetic or congenital anomalies, children benefited disproportionately from the law. Because so many of the orphan drugs focused on children, the Office of Orphan Products Development became the central place for discussions regarding pediatric drug-related issues within the agency in the 1980s. Finkel's successor Marlene Haffner noted, soon after she became its director in 1986, that she and her office "view[ed] the problem of the inadequate study of products for pediatric indications as an orphan issue."[15]

## American Childhood in the 1980s: New Fears Concerning Protection

By the 1980s, American children and families were also experiencing the effects of broad and deep changes in the social and economic landscape over the course of the previous decade. While indigent and working-class mothers had always worked outside the home, a majority of middle-class mothers now did so as well, by necessity as the United States moved from a manufacturing economy to one more focused on services, which lowered the wages of many, or by choice, as a result of second wave feminism.[16] Rising divorce rates also altered traditional notions of family life. Partly because many parents were busier, children's lives became more structured and some worried that they suffered as a result. During the 1980s, fears about children's safety and protection escalated in the United States. While the numbers of "missing children," for example, were relatively few, their stories were featured again and again on television and in books and magazines, stoking anxiety.[17]

At the same time, all children now received more scrutiny for behavioral and learning disorders than in the past. This was due, in part, to legislative mandates. The 1967 Early and Periodic Screening Diagnostic and Treatment Act screened Medicaid-enrolled children for developmental conditions. The 1975 Education for All Handicapped Children Act mandated that every American child receive a free education appropriate to his or her needs. Taken together, the numbers of children diagnosed with learning disabilities, behavioral conditions, and mental illness began to rise. As their incidence escalated, inpatient psychiatric hospital stays by children quadrupled relative to earlier decades. Managers of the new for-profit private psychiatric units quickly realized that children's length of stay averaged 50 percent longer than those of adults, making them lucrative customers.[18]

Children and parents in the 1980s faced a number of other crises that further heightened anxiety about American youngsters' well-being. Aspirin became linked in the early 1980s to Reye's syndrome, a terrifying brain disorder that caused profound neurological dysfunction and was often fatal.[19] The pediatric antipyretic market supremacy afforded to St. Joseph Aspirin for Children was challenged in much the way it had been by the rapid rise in aspirin poisoning in young children in the 1950s. In 1981, the Centers for Disease Control recommended warning labels advising against aspirin's use in children. The aspirin industry responded by employing all the tactics it had developed to delay safety caps. It fomented confusion about the problem, challenged the science based on technicalities, argued that warning labels did not serve children well, and funded its own "consumer" groups to fight against the parent-founded National Reye's Syndrome Foundation and AAP campaigns.[20] The resulting stalemate lasted five years. The aspirin industry finally lost the scientific and legislative battle in 1986. After warning labels were placed on every bottle advising against aspirin's use in children, the incidence of Reye's syndrome declined dramatically. Unfortunately, however, the delay resulted in the death of almost fifteen hundred children, and probably permanent cognitive disabilities in many more.[21]

The AIDS epidemic brought another unanticipated risk to children. Although the numbers of children afflicted by the disease relative to adults were always very small in the United States and concentrated in a few cities, it raised frightening new fears. Misinformation abounded about the likelihood of disease transmission from casual contact with body fluids such as saliva. Like adults, children suffering from AIDS had few treatment options beyond supportive medical and nursing care. But in 1987 the FDA approved the antiretroviral drug Zidovudine (azidothymidine), also known as AZT. Children were, however, orphaned once again because the drug had been tested only in adults and, as such, was not approved for use in pediatrics, even for dying youngsters.[22]

Activists had successfully hastened the drug evaluation process so adults could gain access to experimental antiretroviral drugs. Whether this course of action was in the best interests of children with AIDS weighed heavily on families, clinicians, and the FDA. Old questions emerged. While physicians could legally prescribe the drug to children, how could they be sure youngsters got a dose that was large enough to be effective but not so high as to be toxic? Could any of the ample adult data regarding the drug be extrapolated to children? And how should issues surrounding proxy consent be addressed? That many of the infants and children who stood to benefit from (or be harmed by) experimental AIDS medicines hailed from indigent minority backgrounds complicated the problem, as did the fact that a large number resided in hospitals or foster homes as wards of the state because one or both parents had died from the disease. The legacy of past experimentation in vulnerable populations loomed large in these debates.[23]

## A Home for the Therapeutic Orphan

It was in this context in 1990 that representatives from the FDA and the National Institute of Child Health and Human Development (NICHD) once again came together with members of the pharmaceutical industry, the AAP Committee on Drugs (COD), and other leading stakeholders. The Institute of Medicine-sponsored conference signaled "renewed interest in finding solutions to the longstanding difficulties in making drug therapy as available to children as to adults, and in eliminating the barriers to drug testing in the pediatric population so that children are not therapeutic orphans."[24] This gathering differed from earlier ones. First, there was less finger pointing than in the past as to whether industry, FDA, or academic medicine was to blame for the situation. Second, attendees were encouraged by the Orphan Drug Act's success at stimulating drug companies to invest in treatments even if the targeted population was small. Third, pediatric-specific drug development barriers and costs were more frankly and openly discussed than at past meetings. Finally, the conference was held in the context of the urgency surrounding how best to balance issues of risk and protection with regard to antiretroviral therapy for HIV positive children.[25]

Paula Botstein, FDA pediatrician and deputy director for medical affairs, worked on pediatric issues in the 1980s and 1990s. She and her colleagues were trying to shift FDA thinking from the agency's all or nothing approach that mandated full pediatric clinical trials before approving a pediatric indication to one that allowed waiver of a complete trial in certain instances.[26] Just as it was wrong to assume children were just small adults and that dosing was always proportional, so, they reasoned, was it incorrect to ignore adult data if evidence "exists to show that the course of the disease and the drug response are sufficiently similar in adults and children to permit extrapolation."[27] Botstein was part of a group that created a pilot initiative allowing, in certain instances, for adult research to be considered in place of full pediatric trials.

Notwithstanding the AIDS and Reye's syndrome epidemics and societal angst concerning children's well-being, by the early 1990s American children were, as a group, healthier than ever before. Pediatric morbidity and mortality rates continued to decline, although disparities according to race, social class, and ethnicity persisted.[28] Better chemotherapeutic regimens for cancer, improved surgical techniques for congenital anomalies, and more sophisticated medical and nursing care made it easier to save ill and injured children and those born very prematurely. But improved survival rates meant that there were larger numbers of medically fragile and chronically ill youngsters than in the past. As a result, more children received more drugs relative to earlier decades.[29] In 1994, the FDA codified the pediatric waiver, debuting what became known as the Pediatric Rule. This regulation requested that industry include pediatric data when submitting a new drug application and strove to make it easier for them to do so by permitting extrapolation from adults in certain instances.

So long as evidence suggested that a disease's course and a drug's effects were similar in children and adults, data from adult clinical trials could be cautiously considered for children, especially when accompanied by all available pediatric pharmacokinetic and safety data.[30] The new guideline was launched with great optimism and fanfare. Health and Human Services Secretary Donna E. Shalala celebrated its promise stating "taking care of our children is our top priority. . . . These measures promise the kind of quality medical care our children deserve."[31] FDA commissioner pediatrician David A. Kessler, affirmed the agency's commitment to youngsters. "We have a duty to our children," he professed. "We can get the information we need to treat our children safely and effectively if we think creatively and are willing to commit resources to the challenge."[32]

At about the same time, the NICHD launched an effort that everyone hoped would make it easier to build a national pediatric pharmacology database. Sumner Yaffe, now director of the NICHD Center for Research for Mothers and Children inaugurated a federal funding structure to create Pediatric Pharmacology Research Units (PPRUs). Located in academic medical centers, PPRUs linked drug companies to pediatricians and their patients. The inability to access child subjects was a factor companies had identified as inhibiting pediatric drug development.[33] Shortly afterward, the National

Institute of Mental Health (NIMH) replicated Yaffe's initiative, funding Research Units in Pediatric Psychopharmacology (RUPPs) to facilitate psychoactive drug research in children. The pediatric population was an increasingly attractive one for companies that manufactured mood-altering agents. There had been a sharp rise in costs for child mental illness in the 1980s, as the numbers of inpatient beds and pediatric lengths of stay increased. Insurers in the 1990s responded to financial pressures by turning toward a managed care model for psychiatric treatment. Drug therapy was much cheaper than a hospital stay.[34]

Unfortunately, however, despite the government's request for a voluntary effort on the part of industry and the NICHD- and NIMH-funded research units to facilitate access to children and investigators, only a few drug companies initiated pediatric drug studies. Stakeholders within the FDA and AAP became convinced that a drug company mandate was the only way to assure that every new application for any drug that might be used in children included relevant pediatric information. The agency issued this requirement in 1998. In an effort to generate more pediatric data for agents already approved by FDA, government also offered a lucrative incentive. Six additional months of patent protection before another company could compete by making a similar generic product stood to be worth billions of additional revenue on a blockbuster drug.[35]

While the idea of patent extensions for voluntarily undertaking pediatric research proved popular with drug companies, the mandatory Pediatric Rule was less so. Those who opposed the regulation framed their concern in the language that supporters on all sides of pediatric drug regulation had long done: child protection. Henry I. Miller, for example, a representative of the conservative Hoover Institution at Stanford University, argued that mandating pediatric testing as part of a new drug application to FDA was not only "unnecessary," it was "inimical to free market forces."[36] Such action was, he stipulated "detrimental to kids" because it stood to make it more expensive to develop new drugs and take longer to bring them to market.[37] Instead, he suggested (without acknowledging that this practice had represented the status quo for decades) the drugs should be tailored to adults but contain labels that stressed the product had not been tested for safety and efficacy in children. Miller also recommended that FDA "publish a list of such drugs," so that "parents and physicians could exert moral and economic pressure on drug companies."[38] He either did not know or deliberately obfuscated the fact that attempts had been underway in one form or another without success to do just that ever since the Philadelphia Pediatric Society drew attention to the lack of pediatric dosing information in the 1930s. When the FDA's authority to create the Pediatric Rule was successfully challenged in federal court, Congress, with input from the FDA and AAP COD, crafted new legislation to give the agency the statutory power to do so. While many drug companies remained opposed to pediatric legislation, some in industry now looked to capitalize on children's market potential in recognition that new regulation was forthcoming. As Ronal Keeney reminded her colleagues in the trade journal *Pharmaceutical Executive*, "half the world's six billion people are under the age of 15. Clearly there is a vast market opportunity for pediatric products."[39]

All this effort culminated in the 2002 Best Pharmaceuticals for Children Act (BPCA) and the Pediatric Research Equity Act (PREA). Together, the laws provided a clear "carrot" and "stick" and created an Office of Pediatric Therapeutics within FDA to centralize all efforts related to children. The BPCA "carrot" continued patent extensions in an effort to encourage drug companies to generate pediatric data for drugs FDA had already approved. The PREA "stick" mandated pediatric data for a new drug application in which the medication might be used in children. By 2006, the statutes had resulted in 115 label changes updating pediatric information, twelve new pediatric formulations of drugs already on the market, and adverse effects information in more than fifty agents. In 2012, President Barack Obama signed legislation making these laws permanent. Since then, the numbers of drugs carrying pediatric information on their labels has continued to expand.[40]

## Conclusion

There are parts of this story where it can be argued that, despite fits and starts, pediatric drug development fits the progressive, triumphalist narrative common among those who wrote about the history of health care until the social history transformation of the 1960s. As a nurse who has observed children near death from overwhelming infection thrive after receiving the correct antibiotic, for example, I cannot help but marvel at what I witnessed. The history of pediatric pharmacotherapeutics is replete with heroic clinicians and researchers who advocated for children's interests, undertook important research, and reconfigured clinical practice at particular moments in time and in ways that made children healthier and saved lives. At the same time, within the FDA and other branches of government, again and again policy entrepreneurs strove to use all the tools available to them to protect children. They deserve recognition and praise for their efforts.

But the past, like the present, is freighted with nuance and contingency. The history of pediatric drug development and testing is also a messy one, full of florid rhetoric regarding children's importance to American society, followed by little or no effective action. It is further complicated by the fact that the people and events in this book cannot be removed from the cultural, scientific, and ethical contexts in which children became ill, parents sought advice and care for them, health care providers practiced, investigators undertook research, and drug companies developed medications. As such, there are no easy "lessons" that can be mapped directly onto today's concerns.

Nonetheless, the story does suggest a few conclusions worth contemplating. Competing agendas resulted in missed opportunities to act on children's behalf. In the 1930s, the AAP, for example, identified the problem of children and drug safety but also used the issue as a tool through which to seek legitimacy for the organization. Its approach led the American Medical Association to conclude that the AAP was trying to develop a rival power base for drug-related issues and to conflict rather than action on behalf of children. In the early postwar era the AAP and Children's Bureau battled one another for finite resources instead of working together on common issues such as pediatric drug safety. Pediatric drug research also advanced the academic careers of the physicians involved. Horace Hodes, Julius Richmond, Leon Eisenberg, and William Silverman, for example, benefited from testing drugs on children, but in many instances so did the children who received the medications. Pharmacotherapeutics improved ill children's lives and reduced pediatric mortality in the postwar era. But hindsight was often the only way physicians knew whether their experiments would be celebrated as an effective treatment for an almost universally fatal condition—as Hodes's bacterial meningitis sulfonamide research at Sydenham and Sidney Farber's and Emil Freireich's cancer research was—or whether they would yield important information but have no statistically significant effect—as Silverman's research into retinal damage in premature babies treated with ACTH showed.

Yet, in at least some instances, we can measure and adjudicate the morality of early postwar pediatric drug experimentation. Silverman carefully drew on all the data at his disposal to design his studies. When his trial revealed that the babies who received ACTH had no less retinal damage from oxygen than untreated infants, he was surprised because preliminary animal research suggested a different outcome, as had his clinical observations. Richmond's case is a particularly resonant example of the power of the context in shaping practice standards. One of the twentieth century's most venerated pediatricians, he served as the first director of Project Head Start, the acclaimed 1960s federally funded enrichment program for disadvantaged children, and as surgeon general during the Carter administration. Richmond subsequently taught at Harvard Medical School, which endowed a chair in his honor. How can his activism on behalf of children be reconciled with what today seems like disregard for the risks to healthy newborn babies to whom he administered sulfonamides to ascertain more pharmacokinetic information? It is illogical to believe that Richmond callously put children in harm's way in 1950, only to commit himself to the nation's most vulnerable youngsters a little more than a decade later. Rather, his history provides a potent reminder of how invisible and unacknowledged clinical norms and ethical values can be, both to practitioners and to the public. Like most physicians in the early postwar period, Richmond believed it was his responsibility to balance issues of risk and protection for individual children, and many Americans agreed.[41]

Like Richmond, Hodes, Eisenberg, and Silverman were young men when they undertook the pediatric drug research that launched their academic careers. They, too, subsequently played significant roles in addressing research-related pediatric ethical and social justice issues. Many years later Hodes oversaw the AAP Pediatric Research, Informed Consent, and Medical Ethics (PRIME) committee; Eisenberg became a civil rights activist and later used his perch as chair of social medicine at Harvard to press for more rigorous ethical standards in research and practice. Silverman talked freely and wrote prolifically about the challenges inherent in balancing issues surrounding risk and protection. Their trajectories can be viewed through the lens, not just of shifting research and consent standards, but of their evolving personal and professional development.[42]

The benefit and risk calculus for children also changed over time, further clouding issues of risk and protection. In 1940, despite a paucity of information about sulfonamide dosing and metabolism in children, it made sense for Hodes to expose children critically ill with bacterial infections to the drugs and, through trial and error, to try to save their lives from almost universally fatal infections. But clinical decision making became more complicated in the wake of penicillin and broad spectrum antibiotics. Once a drug that works fairly well is available for children with a specific condition, for example, when is it worth trying a newer, potentially better agent about which much less is known? The growing appreciation in the postwar era for infants' and toddlers' physiological differences from older children and adults complicated this question even more. It also made the need for more drug research both more urgent and more challenging.

But even according to the research ethics of the era in which they undertook their research, some investigators' studies are, like Richmond's sulfonamide research, less justifiable. Elmer H. Loughlin, Louverture Alcindor, and Aurele A. Joseph, for example, administered the broad spectrum antibiotic Terramycin (oxytetracycline) to indigent Haitian children for a protracted period of time simply to see how it affected their growth. Samuel O. Sapin's, Ephraim Donoso's, and Sidney Blumenthal's intrusive and risky digoxin experimentation on healthy infants posed a high risk to those babies. Lauretta Bender expressed few qualms about exposing children to mood-altering agents and LSD for protracted periods of time. Her research questions were often vague and not designed to answer a specific question. Bender rejected the idea of the randomized trial, despite sturdy evidence that it provided robust information. The metrics she drew upon to base her conclusions that children improved after treatment with psychopharmaceuticals were rarely defined.

A close analysis of the historical record with regard to pediatric drug research from the 1930s through the 1970s also suggests another professional group whose research participation deserves more attention—nurses. As Silverman's anecdote in Chapter 3 about the nurse whose interventions confounded his attempts at randomization shows, nurses participated in almost every aspect of drug research. They usually administered the drugs and tracked children's responses and adverse reactions. And they almost surely reassured parents and educated them about their child's treatment protocol. Historians and bioethicists have largely ignored nurses' participation in drug research. Perhaps scholars are loath to attack a professional group that they perceive as lacking agency. Nurses have struggled for autonomy and societal recognition and, as such, may fear that a full accounting of their profession's participation in twentieth-century research does not serve their twenty-first-century agenda for more political clout and professional autonomy. It is true that nurses had significantly less power than physicians. Moreover, many of those caring for children at the hospital bedside in the early postwar era were nursing students. But, like physicians, nurses practice under a code of ethics. Although the early codes focused more on professional conduct, they articulated nurses' duty to patients. Surely the nurses administering sulfonamides to Richmond's patients or those participating in the hepatitis studies at Willowbrook should have known that their actions could not be easily reconciled with their profession's ethical guidelines. In any case, American nursing has yet to grapple with its participation in what many today consider unethical drug experimentation.[43]

But if the lessons are subtle in some places, in others the uses—and abuses—of child protection rhetoric are hard to ignore and can serve as a stark example of the ways a weakly regulated drug economy failed children. In the 1950s, manufacturers of broad spectrum antibiotics implied through their promotional materials that they created pediatric formulations not for profit, but out of beneficence, despite evidence to the contrary. Sometimes industry also used the issue of child protection disingenuously. Nowhere is this more evident than the case of children's aspirin. The aspirin industry co-opted the child protection rhetoric to defend its action (and inaction) on aspirin poisoning in young children, and many died as a result. From the mid-1950s to the early 1970s, aspirin manufacturers confounded every attempt to mandate safety caps and standardize pill size to prevent poisoning, parental confusion, and dosing error. On numerous occasions, industry representatives obfuscated or outright rejected the overwhelming evidence that aspirin poisoning represented a significant threat to young children. When denying the existence of aspirin poisoning in young children became impossible because of insurmountable evidence, companies blamed parents for inadequate supervision of their youngsters and, in the audacious case of Maurice L. Tainter, toddlers and preschoolers themselves.

While Plough, Inc. did fund Jay Arena's safety cap research after aspirin poisoning rates in children skyrocketed, his company's executives continued to publicly fight increased regulation. They subsequently used the company's voluntary investment in the safety cap to try to fend off a mandate and as proof that it cared about children's well-being. Parents, health care providers, public health officials, and FDA officials who argued for new aspirin-related laws were no match for manufacturers' stance that youngsters' best interests were served by growing up in a nation unfettered by safety caps and other common sense mandates such as a standardized dosage for children's aspirin. As a result of industry opposition, it took almost two decades to legislate a solution to the problem of children's aspirin poisoning.

The history of low dose flavored aspirin also reveals the ways in which its invention, marketing, and research into the subsequent problem of aspirin poisoning in young children was freighted with notions of gender, race, and social class. Advertisements in magazines such as *Parents* emphasized white middle-class families and showed boys and girls playing with toys that reinforced stereotypes. African American and other minority children were underrepresented in early aspirin poisoning research. Safety cap tests gathered information about parents' marital status, presumed proxies for social class or morality. It is an exemplar of the ways these variables suffuse American life and research in often unacknowledged ways.

The candy aspirin case is not just about the forces behind the product's creation and its unintended consequences. It also reveals something important about the history of children and childhood—that children have more agency and power in the marketplace than is generally recognized. Plough's St. Joseph Aspirin for Children and all its competitors could not have succeeded if children did not find it more palatable than a bitter pill or liquid. Plough spent considerable time and money worrying about how to appeal to children, and his product's phenomenal success reveals how children's choices inarguably shaped the postwar drug economy. Finally, the St. Joseph example also shows how, once branded, a drug can carry significant cultural power. When children's aspirin was ingeniously renamed "low dose" and remarketed as a heart disease preventive agent for older people in the wake of Reye's syndrome, sales improved. Its iconic imprint on American baby boomers was such that one of their own became a pitchman in 2011, former child actor Ken Osmond ("Eddie Haskell" on the classic 1950s TV show *Leave It to Beaver*). And the St. Joseph Aspirin website today attempts to evoke nostalgia in baby boomers by reminding them that "your mom gave you St. Joseph Children's Aspirin when you were a child. You felt better and were reassured that St. Joseph took care of you."[44]

When I began this research, several pediatricians suggested informally that no one had really tried to address the issue of pediatric drug safety from a policy or scientific perspective until the latter part of the twentieth century because the issues were considered too complicated. As this book shows, that is not accurate at all. While few devoted their careers to the problem in the way Harry Shirkey and Sumner Yaffe did, this story reveals repeated instances in which leading pediatricians, organizations, Congress, and the FDA attempted to address pediatric drug safety- and efficacy-related issues. While they were successful in describing how and why children did not benefit in the same way as adults from American drug laws, this acknowledgment did little to help children. Since the issue was never one of recognition, the solution lay not merely in trying to raise awareness of it. While that may not have been clear to most stakeholders in 1938, a time when it was uncommon for physicians to prescribe drugs to children, it was certainly evident by 1975, when Caspar Weinberger openly acknowledged that children did not receive the same legislative protection as adults from the post-thalidomide 1962 Kefauver-Harris Amendments.

While not focused on children specifically, youngsters benefited from the early postwar academic, industry, and government partnerships that generated new cancer therapeutics. And just as it invested in cancer drug treatments, the federal government sought to bring organization and leadership to discussions concerning the risks and benefits of mood-altering drugs in children during this time. Although pediatric cancer and child mental illness had little in common, both received focused federal attention because of societal interest in these areas. But with regard to drug safety for agents used much more frequently in American children, such as antibiotics, government seemed to have no vehicle to generate pediatric pharmacokinetic knowledge beyond market mechanisms and informal partnerships between investigators and drug companies.

Although many people recognized the ways in which drug laws disenfranchised children from safety and efficacy provisions benefiting adults, almost everyone tried to balance what was optimal with what seemed feasible. As the Cold War deepened, the importance of distinguishing the United States from its communist adversaries convinced most stakeholders that more robust statutory oversight, in the form of child-specific laws, for a leading industry were untenable. In a country that embraced the rhetoric of the 1930 Children's Charter, but did not seek an action plan to bring its promises to fruition, and rejected numerous nonpoverty child-related statutes such as the 1949 Children's Research Act and the 1973 Comprehensive Child Development bill, they were probably not wrong. Given the numbers of children treated with antibiotics or steroids for common pediatric illnesses by the 1950s, more governmental safety and testing regulations for drugs with potential for pediatric use would have challenged the narrative that limited regulation protected children better than robust governmental oversight. This belief was not new in the 1950s and it endures today. Many Americans remain ambivalent about child-focused legislation because of fears of state intrusion into family life and parental rights. President Obama's stalled universal preschool initiative is just one recent example of resistance to stand-alone, public investments in child well-being.[45]

This story also provides an opportunity to study the unintended consequences of regulatory action. The 1938 Federal Food, Drug, and Cosmetic Act did not contain child-specific language. The legislators' intent is clear from the surviving documentation; they intended drugs used in children to contain the same degree of safety information as for adults. Absent the direct mandate, however, drug companies remained free to determine how they would test new drugs. While the 1962 Kefauver-Harris Amendments added more governmental oversight of industry it, too, was silent on children. The law also made it more expensive to bring a new drug to market, providing yet another disincentive to undertake pediatric testing. It mandated adequate and well-controlled trials in an era when the scientific understanding of how to do so for the pediatric patient was rapidly evolving, presenting another challenge. The law's well-intended requirement for informed consent created confusion about who should make such decision, which only worsened in the aftermath of Beecher's article, the Kennedy hearings, and subsequent debates concerning fetal research and legalized abortion.

The consequences of drug laws remain dynamic. Some believe that the market exclusivity afforded to companies that undertake pediatric testing has incentivized them to move research offshore to areas with less regulation, media oversight, and fewer empowered parents. In other words, it is possible that some of the new knowledge benefiting American children has been derived from testing those in the global south. Other analyses contradict this finding, showing robust pediatric research in the United States, except for infectious diseases primarily found in the countries in which drugs or immunizations are being studied.[46]

Nowhere in pediatric drug development have there been more unintended consequences than in the area of pediatric psychopharmacology. In 1979, most physicians and parents seemed in broad agreement with Leon Eisenberg, who argued that psychoactive medications should be used cautiously and only after rigorous testing. Few could have foreseen that within a generation American children would be awash in prescriptions for behavioral and mood-altering drugs. There is an entire body of literature analyzing this phenomenon. Some suggest that the increase is the result of better case-finding and shifting disease definitions that have broadened the numbers of children who fit diagnostic categories for a behavioral or mental condition. Others have argued that there is growing willingness on the part of insurers to pay for medication because it is less expensive than psychotherapy. Still others maintain that newer, more effective drugs mean fewer side effects and risks to children and, as a result, a healthier childhood for those who need medication. Finally, some believe that the reason children receive more mood-altering drugs today is rooted in ongoing changes to American society, child-rearing, and childhood. They suggest that the drug industry successfully capitalizes on anxious parents who seek every competitive advantage for their children in an era of growing economic inequality, or a collective forgetting on the part of parents, teachers, health care providers and others that healthy children sometimes act out, need to be disciplined, or cannot sit still in school.[47]

No matter the reason, the media regularly sounds alarm about the phenomenon in ways designed to stimulate parental and societal concern: "Still in a Crib Yet Being Given Antipsychotics" blares a December 2015 *New York Times* headline. In this case journalist Alan Schwarz charts the rise of the antipsychotic drug Risperdal (risperidone). Although the drug is not approved for use in children under the age of five years (and then only for a very specific indication, irritability associated with autism), almost 20,000 children under the age of two years old received a prescription in 2014.[48] Finally, perhaps no other class of drugs reflects the social class prism through which American society views children than mood-altering drugs. As of 2015, Pennsylvania youngsters insured by Medicaid, for example, are prescribed psychoactive drugs more often than those with commercial insurance. And those in foster care, almost all of whom are very poor, have even higher rates; they are prescribed antipsychotics at three times the rate of other Medicaid-enrolled Pennsylvania children.[49]

While the Best Pharmaceuticals for Children Act and the Pediatric Research Equity Act have substantively improved pediatric drug safety and efficacy, challenges remain. In October 2016, pediatrician Dianne Murphy, former director of the FDA Office of Pediatric Therapeutics, reminded Americans how far the nation had come with regard to drug regulation and children: "the biggest accomplishment is that pediatrics is no longer an afterthought in terms of product development, it's become part of the process of developing therapeutic products." At the same time, she also cautioned, "we haven't tackled the really hard stuff yet, such as therapies for neonates."[50] New data continue to emerge regarding old, presumed to be safe drugs for children. On April 20, 2017, the FDA issued a Drug Safety Communication requiring a labeling change for any drug containing the opioids codeine or tramadol. A review of decades of adverse events reports revealed dozens of incidences of breathing problems in children and two dozen deaths between 1969 and

2015. While the FDA recommendations regarding use of both drugs in the pediatric population had been made more stringent in 2015, they were now strengthened.[51]

Another problem impacting pediatric pharmacology knowledge and clinical practice is the fact that not all drug study results are well disseminated, and analyses of this phenomenon focus mostly on the adult population.[52] Finally, because the newly generated pediatric dosage formulations receive extended patent protection as a result of the BPCA incentives, they are usually much more expensive than drugs in pill form. The branded liquid form of the generic antihypertensive Lisinopril, Qbrelis, for example, costs 775 times more than the generic tablet. Because it usually requires less investment to create a liquid formulation of an already existing medication than it does to invent a new drug, some argue that reformulation profits are outsized.[53]

Novel techniques for drug development will require fresh approaches to assure pediatric safety and efficacy. If the relatively new field of pharmacogenomics evolves as some predict, we have begun a paradigm shift almost as profound as the beginning of the antibiotic era. The old rubrics for determining drug doses will be retired, as medications for everyone will be tailored to individual needs based on one's genetic make-up. In January 2015, President Obama committed hundreds of millions of federal dollars to this initiative.[54] Although precision medicine holds great promise, history suggests that it will be more difficult to operationalize than might appear right now. There will be unintended consequences and unforeseen challenges, and progress will not be linear, for children or adults. Most likely, legislators, politicians, and interest groups, as they have in the past, will look for ways to frame their efforts as benefiting children, considered noncontroversial and deserving of investments in their welfare. Many of those initiatives will serve youngsters well. But others may be narrowly focused, grounded in what is considered politically or economically practicable at the moment, using children as political props, rather than what the evidence suggests they actually need. But children benefit most when, in the words of Stephen P. Spielberg, pediatrician, former FDA deputy commissioner, medical school dean, and industry executive, those who care about them think broadly, engage with both scientific and political issues, and "align . . . with all the things going on out there from the molecular to the economic."[55]

Our actions on children's behalf also need to be informed by a social justice framework, one that acknowledges our moral duty—and fulfills the nation's enduring rhetorical promise—to all youngsters. This does not mean that children always need stand-alone laws tailored specifically to them. Mandates for clean water, milk, safe highways, and thousands of other measures benefit children just as they do everyone else. But sometimes there is sturdy evidence that laws need to be tailored to their unique needs. Early in the postwar period, a preponderance of data suggested that pharmaceutical policy was one of those instances. For decades, however, there was a lack of political will to apply the growing historical and scientific evidence indicating this was the case to policymaking because of drug industry opposition and Americans' ambivalence regarding government regulation. As a result, in the twentieth century, the most important changes in the way we control our medications were reactive, not proactive, and were built on the bodies of Elixir Sulfanilamide children, aspirin-poisoned toddlers and preschoolers, and thalidomide babies.

As I sit here writing in early 2017, it appears that the United States is headed toward a betrayal of all three precepts—science, history, and social justice—with regard to children and drug safety. The new administration's professed goal to undo decades of drug laws threatens the knowledge and other gains wrought by the Best Pharmaceuticals for Children Act and the Pediatric Research Equity Act. Even if these statutes remain in place, significant changes to the regulatory apparatus in which they are nested may decrease their effectiveness. Adults can make their support for, or opposition to, the president's agenda known. But children cannot speak for themselves, and ignoring past experience and present knowledge related to children and drug safety neglects our obligation to them and would be an abrogation of responsibility to our nation's most vulnerable citizens.

# Appendix

# Primary Sources and
# Archival Collections

● ● ● ● ● ● ● ● ● ● ● ● ● ● ● ● ● ● ● ● ●

American Academy of Child and Adolescent Psychiatry Archives, Washington, DC
    History Series

American Academy of Pediatrics, Pediatric History Center, Elk Grove Village, Illinois
    Committee on Accident Prevention Records
    Committee on Drugs Records
    George M. Wheatley Papers
    Oral History Collection
        Thomas E. Cone
        Joan E. Hodgman
        Milton Markowitz
        William A. Silverman
        George M. Wheatley

American Institute of the History of Pharmacy, University of Wisconsin School of Pharmacy, Madison, Wisconsin
    Harry C. Shirkey Bibliographic File
    Drug Topics Photography Collection
    Selected Drug Company Annual Reports

American Medical Association, Archives and Manuscripts Division, Chicago
    Historical Health Fraud and Alternative Medicine Collection

Archives and Special Collections, Columbia University Medical Center,
    Columbia University, New York City
    Hattie Alexander Papers
    Babies Hospital Case Histories

Boston Children's Hospital Archives, Boston, Massachusetts
    Annual Reports
    Department of Nursing Archives

Brooklyn College Library Archives and Special Collections, Brooklyn,
    New York
    Lauretta Bender Papers

Center for the Study of the History of Neuropsychopharmacology, American College of Neuropsychopharmacology Records, History and Special Collections, Louise M. Darling Biomedical Library, UCLA, Los
    Angeles
    Frank Berger Papers
    Oral History Collection
        Frank Berger
        C. Keith Conners
        Barbara Fish
        Judith L. Rapoport

College of Physicians of Philadelphia, Historical Medical Library, Philadelphia
    Children's Hospital of Philadelphia Records
    Philadelphia Pediatric Society Records

Duke University Medical Center Archives, Durham, North Carolina
    Jay M. Arena Papers
    Duke Poison Control Center Records

Food and Drug Administration Library, Rockville, Maryland: Selected
    Pediatric Speeches, Files, and Reports

Harvard Medical Library, Francis A. Countway Library of Medicine, Boston, Massachusetts
    Henry K. Beecher Papers
    Maxwell Finland Papers

Icahn School of Medicine at Mount Sinai, Archives, Gustave L. and
    Janet W. Levy Library, New York City
    Horace L. Hodes Papers

Johns Hopkins Hospital Medical Records, Baltimore, Maryland

Johns Hopkins University, Alan Mason Chesney Medical Archives of
    The Johns Hopkins Medical Institutions, Baltimore, Maryland
    Edwards A. Park Papers
    Helen B. Taussig Papers

Mandeville Special Collections Library, Geisel Library, University of
    California, San Diego, La Jolla, California
    Charles C. Edwards Papers

Manuscript Division, Library of Congress, Washington, D.C.
    Frances Oldham Kelsey Papers

MD Anderson Special Collections, Research Medical Library, History of
    Cancer Collections, University of Texas MD Anderson Cancer Cen-
    ter, Houston, Texas
    Oral History Collection
        Emil J. Freireich
    Research Reports

Medical Center Archives of New York-Presbyterian/Weill Cornell, New
    York City
    Harry Gold Papers

Miner Library Archives, University of Rochester, Rochester,
    New York
    Edward C. Atwater Collection of American Popular Medicine
    Rochester Pediatric Society

National Academies Archives, Washington, DC
    Drug Efficacy Study Records

National Archives and Record Administration, College Park,
    Maryland
    Federal Trade Commission Records, RG 122
    Food and Drug Administration Records, RG 88
    Office of the NIH Director, RG 443

National Library of Medicine, History of Medicine Division, Bethesda,
    Maryland
    John Adriani Papers
    Harry Filmore Dowling Papers
    Milton J. E. Senn Papers
    Sydenham Hospital Records
    FDA Oral History Series
        Marlene Haffner
        Wallace F. Janssen
        Frances Oldham Kelsey
        Helen B. Taussig

Northwestern University Archives Deering Library, Evanston, Illinois
    Isaac Arthur Abt Papers

Pratt History Library, Children's Hospital Medical Center, Cincinnati,
    Ohio
    Harry C. Shirkey Oral History
    Harry C. Shirkey Curriculum Vitae and Newspaper Clippings

Rush Rhees Library, University of Rochester, Rochester, New York
    Louis C. Lasagna Papers

University Archives, University of Minnesota, Minneapolis, Minnesota
    Wesley W. Spink Papers

University of Utah, J. Willard Marriott Library, Special Collections and
    Archives, Salt Lake City, Utah
    Louis S. Goodman Papers

Wisconsin Historical Society, Madison, Wisconsin
    United States Pharmacopeial (USP) Convention Archives

# Acknowledgments

I first became interested in the history of children and pharmacotherapeutics in 2002 when I served as a legislative fellow on Capitol Hill in the office of Minnesota Senator Paul Wellstone, and, by chance, attended a hearing related to the Best Pharmaceuticals for Children Act (BPCA). Christopher Dodd, then a senator from Connecticut and the hearing's chair, emphasized our weak knowledge base with regard to pediatric drug dosing, side effects, adverse reactions, and other important scientific information. I was shocked. At that point, I had been a pediatric nurse and nurse practitioner for more than twenty years, and I had administered hundreds of different drugs to thousands of children. I had always assumed that the books and pediatric pharmacists I relied upon for my practice possessed evidence-based answers. But I had never really thought about the processes through which such evidence was generated. Senator Dodd and other BPCA supporters were convinced that, because of the limited legislative success of earlier laws, the nation needed a new one designed to address children's unique needs. This topic seemed an ideal way to engage the nursing part of my life, in which I focus on twenty-first-century child health care delivery, and my historian's propensity to examine the events, people, and beliefs that forged the contemporary template in which that care is delivered.

I had little idea how complicated this topic would be when I started what became *Children and Drug Safety: Balancing Risk and Protection in Twentieth Century America* in 2010. In fact, I was not even sure I could find enough material to write a book. Early support from the University of Pennsylvania Research Foundation, Trustees' Council of Penn Women, American Institute of the History of Pharmacy at the University of Wisconsin School of Pharmacy (Sonnedecker Visiting Scholar Award for Pharmaceutical Historical Research), American Association for the History of Nursing, and the Karen

Buhler-Wilkerson fellowship from the Barbara Bates Center for the Study of the History of Nursing allowed me to gather enough preliminary archival data to convince me there was a story worth telling.

The historical actors who had considered pediatric drug-related issues and their ongoing debates, frustrations, and successes, gradually became visible when I received support in the form of a Robert Wood Johnson Foundation Investigator Award. This generous and unusually flexible funding allowed me to piece together the story in ways not otherwise possible. It is fascinating how the documents "dialogue" with one another, often referencing the same events, but from different perspectives. For example, in the Food and Drug Administration (FDA) records in the National Archives, letters from parents detail concerns about the safety of specific drugs prescribed or recommended for their children. At the same time, the American Academy of Pediatrics Committee on Drugs and United States Pharmacopeia records reflect organizational perspectives on pediatric drug development, safety, and efficacy. The FDA records reveal staffers' attempts to address parents' and clinicians' concerns and a number of attempts to use the regulatory apparatus to make drugs safer for children. The papers of individual physicians such as Jay M. Arena and Horace L. Hodes illuminate pediatricians' painstaking research and their interactions with regulatory agencies and drug companies. Fortunately, primary source data generated by the pharmaceutical industry can be found in all the above archives and were critical to piecing together the story, since I received no response to my queries to specific drug companies seeking access to relevant historical records. Finally, a National Endowment for the Humanities fellowship provided the time to draw all the threads together and complete the narrative.

I want to thank the many librarians and archivists without whose help I would never have located the sources I used over the course of many years. Russell S. Koontz, Duke Medical Center Library and Archives; Phoebe Letocha, Alan Mason Chesney Medical Archives, The Johns Hopkins Medical Institutions; Gregory Higby and Gregory Bond, American Institute of the History of Pharmacy; Tab Lewis, National Archives and Records Administration; Susan Bolda Marshall and Christopher Kwiat, American Academy of Pediatrics Division of Library and Archival Services; Jessica Murphy, Francis A. Countway Library of Medicine, Harvard University; Christopher Hoolihan, University of Rochester's Miner Library Archives; Beth Lander, College of Physicians of Philadelphia; Marcia Meldrum and Russell Johnson, UCLA's Center for the Study of the History of Neuropsychopharmacology, History and Special Collections, Louise M. Darling Biomedical Library; Sheila Spaulding, Boston Children's Hospital; Barbara Niss and Nicholas Webb, Icahn School of Medicine at Mount Sinai Archives, Gustave L. and Janet W. Levy Library; Stephen Greenberg, John P. Rees, and Crystal Smith, History of

Medicine Division, National Library of Medicine; and Andrew Peters at the American Academy of Child & Adolescent Psychiatry.

I owe a special debt of gratitude to Patricia D'Antonio, who read multiple drafts of this manuscript, listened to me talk through my thoughts and arguments, and provided continual encouragement. John Swann gave generously of his time to review chapters, locate relevant materials, and tutor me in the complicated nuances of the FDA and American drug policy. Gregory Higby and John Parascandola facilitated my understanding of the history of pharmacy. Scott Podolsky suggested meaningful archival sources I would not have otherwise located and was a valuable sounding board on numerous occasions. A conversation with Susan Lederer sparked the idea for this project and her critique of the human experimentation chapters was very beneficial. My discussions with Julie Fairman surrounding the ways in which history is embedded in contemporary policy and practice deepened my analysis. Naomi Rogers's insightful suggestions helped me plumb my data in new ways. Janet Golden offered a tireless sounding board for my ideas and I always left our time together with a deeper understanding of the history of children's health care in the United States. I am especially grateful to the individuals with expertise in pediatric drug policy who made time to give me their perspective including Cheston Berlin, Dianne Murphy, Edward G. Feldmann, Marlene Haffner, Samuel Maldonado, Abbey Meyers, Allen A. Mitchell, Stephen P. Spielberg, Robert Ward, Sidney Wolfe, and Sumner Yaffe.

Colleagues whose support was invaluable along the way include Rima Apple, Joel Braslow, James Colgrove, David Herzberg, Joan Lynaugh, Lewis Leavitt, Beth Linker, Thomas Maeder, Gerald Oppenheimer, Heather Munro Prescott, David Rosner, Dominique Tobbell, Barbra Mann Wall, and John Harley Warner. Conversations with Jeffrey Baker, Jeffrey Brosco, Naixue Cui, Cindy Christian, Kara Finck, Richard Gelles, Janet Golden, Richard Meckel, Edward Schor, and Debra Schilling Wolfe sharpened my thinking about this history in the context of past and present children's health care delivery and policy. Peter Mickulas, my editor at Rutgers University Press, continually encouraged me, was always available to listen, and was patient when circumstances delayed the manuscript's completion.

This book could not have been completed without the collegiality, intellectual energy, and laughter that makes the Barbara Bates Center for the Study of the History of Nursing such a special place. It is my distinct honor to have been able to call each successive Bates Center director, Joan Lynaugh, Karen Buhler-Wilkerson, Julie Fairman, and now Patricia D'Antonio, a mentor and a friend. The vision and enthusiastic support of Penn Nursing dean emerita, Afaf Meleis, and my current dean Antonia Villarruel, create an academic space for the humanities to flourish and their support has transformed my personal and professional life. Bates Center colleagues Elisa Stroh and Jessica Clark are never too busy to answer a question or help with something. Both make the Bates Center a fun and lively space. Current and former students John Barbieri, Jason Chernesky, Briana Ralston Smith, Virginia Schieck, and Benjamin Schneider provided assistance at various junctures of this project. Kimberley Byrd, Seymour Sejour and all the information technology staff at Penn Nursing responded to my numerous computer-related emergencies speedily and calmly, keeping my research and writing on track. The assistance of colleagues Christine Eisler, Sherri Kaplan, Jake Rutkowski, and Denise Scala also facilitated my ability to complete this book.

Friends who distracted, listened, supported, nurtured, and fed me during the many years it took to complete *Children and Drug Safety* include Carol Albert, Michael Albert, Michael Berthold, Gary Blum, George Bradt, Thomas Butler, Robert Elfont, Jeffrey Hartzell, Carolyn Reiners, Jeffrey Snyder, Lisa Stern, and Sharon Wolfson. Finally, I am deeply grateful to my family, my late parents Nicholas and Mary Connolly, sister Jackie, brother Nick, sister-in-law Linda, nephew Nicholas, and niece Lauren, whose sense of humor and love always keep me going.

This study received approval from the University of Pennsylvania Institutional Review Board. All Oral History Association guidelines were followed for interviews cited in this study. I received Privacy Board approval to view archival records in which Protected Health Information might be included from the Countway Library, The Johns Hopkins Medical Institutions, and the Duke University Medical Center. While the Sydenham Hospital records are open to researchers, the History of Medicine Division of the National Library of Medicine screens requests to review case files. I applied for and received permission. All names of patients or parents in archival records have been abbreviated or anonymized.

Portions of the following articles have been used with permission of the publishers: "Mother: Here's the Aspirin Tablet That 'Fits' Your Child's Needs: Candy Aspirin and Children, 1947–1960," *Nursing History Review* 25 (2017): 103–116 and (co-authored with Janet Golden and Benjamin Schneider) "A Startling New Chemotherapeutic Agent: Pediatric Infectious Disease and the Introduction of Sulfonamides at Baltimore's Sydenham Hospital," *Bulletin of the History of Medicine* 86 (2012): 66–93.

# Notes

## Chapter 1    Drug Therapy: From "Baby Killers" to Baby Savers, 1906–1933

1   The laws have generated pediatric-related information on more than 400 drugs. Dianne Murphy, MD, "Overview and Impact of the Pediatric Legislation (since 1997)," "Comments on Specific Tasks: Drug Labeling, Tasks 1 and 2," *Meeting 1: Pediatric Studies Conducted under BPCA and PREA*, Institute of Medicine, Washington, DC, 17 December 2010; Powerpoint of talk, accessed August 1, 2016, http://www.nationalacademies.org/hmd/Activities/Children/PediatricStudiesBPCAPREA/2010-DEC-17.aspx.

2   Institute of Medicine of the National Academies, *Addressing the Barriers to Pediatric Drug Development* (Washington, DC: National Academies Press, 2008), 1.

3   Abraham Jacobi, *Report on the Clinic for Diseases of Children, Held in the New York Medical College, Session 1860–61* (New York: Ballière, 1861), as cited in Russell Viner, "Abraham Jacobi and German Medical Radicalism in New York," *Bulletin of the History of Medicine* 72 (1998): 434–463, quote page 457.

4   See, for example, Steven Mintz, *Huck's Raft: A History of American Childhood* (Cambridge, MA: Belknap Press of Harvard University Press, 2004); Richard A. Meckel, *Save the Babies: American Public Health Reform and the Prevention of Infant Mortality, 1850–1929* (Baltimore: The Johns Hopkins University Press, 1990); Viviana Zelizer, *Pricing the Priceless Child: The Changing Social Value of Children* (New York: Basic Books, 1985); Judith Sealander, *The Failed Century of the Child: Governing America's Young in the Twentieth Century* (Cambridge: Cambridge University Press, 2003); Stephanie Coontz, *The Way We Never Were: American Familes and the Nostalgia Trap* (New York: Basic Books, 1993).

5   The recent study that most directly engages with children's health in the early postwar period in terms of federal policy is Marilyn Irvin Holt, *Cold War Kids: Politics and Childhood in Postwar America, 1945–1960* (Lawrence: University of Kansas Press, 2014). Other recent scholarly works addressing Cold War childhood include Ann Marie Kordas, *The Politics of Childhood in Cold War America* (Brookfield, VT: Pickering & Chatto, 2013) and Margaret Peacock, *Innocent Weapons: The Soviet and American Politics of Childhood in the Cold War* (Chapel Hill: University of North Carolina Press, 2014).

6 See, for example, James Harvey Young, *Pure Food: Securing the Federal Food and Drugs Act of 1906* (Princeton, NJ: Princeton University Press, 1989); Harry Marks, *The Progress of Experiment: Science and Therapeutic Reform in the United States, 1900–1990* (Cambridge: Cambridge University Press, 1997); Philip J. Hilts, *Protecting America's Health: The FDA, Business, and 100 Years of Regulation* (New York: Knopf, 2003); Arthur Daemmrich, *Pharmacopolitics: Drug Regulation in the United States and Germany* (Chapel Hill: University of North Carolina Press, 2004); John E. Lesch, *The First Miracle Drugs: How the Sulfa Drugs Transformed Medicine* (New York: Oxford University Press, 2007); Lara Marks, *Sexual Chemistry: A History of the Contraceptive Pill* (New Haven, CT: Yale University Press, 2001); Jeremy A. Greene, *Prescribing by Numbers: Drugs and the Definition of Disease* (Baltimore: The Johns Hopkins University Press, 2006); Jeremy A. Greene, *Generic: The Unbranding of American Medicine* (Baltimore: The Johns Hopkins University Press, 2014); Elizabeth S. Watkins, *The Estrogen Elixir: A History of Hormone Replacement Therapy* (Baltimore: The Johns Hopkins University Press, 2007); Andrea Tone and Elizabeth Siegel Watkins, eds., *Medicating Modern America: Prescription Drugs in History* (New York: New York University Press, 2007); Daniel Carpenter, *Reputation and Power: Organizational Image and Regulation at the FDA* (Princeton, NJ: Princeton University Press, 2010); Dominique Tobbell, *Pills, Power, and Policy: The Struggle for Drug Reform in Cold War America and Its Consequences* (Berkeley: University of California Press, 2011); Heather Munro Prescott, *The Morning After: A History of Emergency Contraception in the United States* (New Brunswick, NJ: Rutgers University Press, 2011); and Scott H. Podolsky, *The Antibiotic Era: Reform, Resistance, and the Pursuit of a Rational Therapeutics* (Baltimore: The Johns Hopkins University Press, 2015).

7 Charles E. Rosenberg, "Anticipated Consequences: Historians, History, and Health Policy," in *History and Health Policy in the United States*, ed. Rosemary Stevens, Charles E. Rosenberg, and Lawton R. Burns (New Brunswick, NJ: Rutgers University Press, 2006), 28.

8 Elizabeth Wright Burak, "Children's Health Coverage in Arizona: A Cautionary Tale for the Future of the Children's Health Insurance Program (CHIP)," Center for Children and Families, January 2015, accessed August 1, 2016, http://ccf .georgetown.edu/; "2016 Election Results and the Future of Child Health Policy," November 11, 2016, www.childrens.hospitals.org.

9 Joseph M. Hawes and N. Ray Hiner, "Reflections on the History of Children and Childhood in the Postmodern Era," in *Major Problems in the History of American Families and Children*, ed. Anya Jabour (New York: Houghton Mifflin, 2005), 23–30.

10 Lainie Friedman Ross, *Children in Medical Research: Access versus Protection* (Oxford: Oxford University Press, 2006), 17–24.

11 Marcel J. Casavant and Jill R. K. Griffith, "Pediatric Pharmacotherapy Part 1: The History of Pediatric Drug Therapy: Learning from Errors, Not Trials" (update 7/28/2010), in *Goodman & Gilman's The Pharmacological Basis of Therapeutics*, 12th edition, ed. Laurence L. Brunton, Bruce A. Chabner, and Bjorn C. Knollmann (New York: McGraw-Hill's AccessMedicine Clinical Library), accessed February 10, 2012, http://www.accessmedicine.com/updatesContent.aspx?aID=1001636 &searchStr=casavant.

12 I. Glenn Cohen, "Therapeutic Orphans, Pediatric Victims? The Best Pharmaceuticals for Children Act and Existing Pediatric Human Subject Protection," *Food and*

*Drug Law Journal* 58 (2003): 661–710; Jonathan M. Davis and Mark A. Turner, "Global Collaboration to Develop New and Existing Drugs for Neonates," *JAMA Pediatrics* 169, no. 10 (October 2015): 887–888; Sabrina Tavernise, "Study of Babies Did Not Disclose Risks, U.S. Finds," *New York Times*, April 10, 2013.

13 These topics have also received scholarly treatment. On vitamins, see Rima Apple, *Vitamania: Vitamins in American Culture* (New Brunswick, NJ: Rutgers University Press, 1996). On vaccines, see James Colgrove, *State of Immunity: The Politics of Vaccination in Twentieth-Century America* (Berkeley: University of California Press, 2006) and Elena Conis, *Vaccine Nation: America's Changing Relationship with Immunization* (Chicago: University of Chicago Press, 2014). For a thoughtful analysis of how smallpox vaccine influenced, and was influenced by, changing ideas about childhood in eighteenth- and nineteenth-century England, see Lydia Murdoch, "Carrying the Pox: The Use of Children and Ideals of Childhood in Early British and Imperial Campaigns Against Smallpox," *Journal of Social History* 48 (Spring 2015): 511–535. For more on the history of children's cancer, especially leukemia, see Gretchen Krueger, *Hope and Suffering: Children, Cancer, and the Paradox of Experimental Medicine* (Baltimore, The Johns Hopkins University Press, 2008).

14 Steven Epstein briefly discusses issues of children's participation in drug trials as part of his valuable analysis, what he calls the emergence of a "biopolitical paradigm" that influenced clinical practice as well as state policy. Children, like women, minorities, and the elderly, are among the many groups recognized to have special pharmacological needs. Epstein, however, focuses largely on the 1980s and 1990s, when the problem I describe in this book is well entrenched. Moreover, children are not the central focus of his study. Steven Epstein, *Inclusion: The Politics of Medical Difference* (Chicago: University of Chicago Press, 2007), 61, 116–122.

15 For brief overviews of the development of drug policy in industrialized countries, see Philip R. Lee and Jessica Herzstein, "International Drug Regulation," *Annual Review of Public Health* 7 (1986): 217–235. For a U.S. government commissioned analysis of drug development and policies in developing countries, see U.S. Congress, Office of Technology Assessment, *Drug Labeling in Developing Countries*, OTA-H-464 (Washington, DC: U.S. GPO, 1993).

16 "Dr. James' Soothing Syrup Cordial," *Pittsburgh Press*, August 27, 1900, accessed August 1, 2016, https://news.google.com/newspapers?nid=1144&dat=19000827&id=xPwaAAAAIBAJ&sjid=iEgEAAAAIBAJ&pg=6255,3327113&hl=en.

17 For a history of narcotics regulation, see David F. Musto, *The American Disease: Origins of Narcotic Control* (New Haven, CT: Yale University Press, 1973). On heroin, see David F. Musto, Pamela Korsmeyer, and Thomas W. Maulucci, Jr., eds., *One Hundred Years of Heroin* (Westport, CT: Auburn House, 2002).

18 Glenn Sonnedecker, *Kremer and Urdang's History of Pharmacy*, 4th edition (Philadelphia: J. P. Lippincott, 1976), 157, 339–345; Young, *Pure Food*, 44–59. There were no laws barring the sale or advertising of any drug in the United States in the nineteenth century. In 1879 the first federal bill regulating food and drugs was introduced. This early bill had more to do with food adulteration than with drugs. It did not pass, nor did any of the dozens of similar bills between 1879 and 1906. Mitchell Okun, *Fair Play in the Marketplace: The First Battle for Pure Food and Drugs* (Dekalb: Northern Illinois University Press, 2006).

19 For more on the history of Mrs. Winslow's Soothing Syrup, see Denise M. Kohn, "Laura Jane Curtis Bullard," *Legacy* 21 (2004): 74–82. Soothing syrups were among

the most common patent medications, so named because the recipes were proprietary, imported from England, where they were manufactured under "patents of
royal favour." By the early twentieth century, health almanacs and advice books had
recommended narcotics for children for almost two hundred years in the United
States. James Harvey Young, "'Even to a Suckling Infant': Nostrums and Children,"
*Transactions and Studies of the College of Physicians of Philadelphia* 5th ser. 1 (1979):
5–32. For more on the history of patent medicines, see J. Worth Estes, "The Pharmacology of Nineteenth-Century Patent Medicines," *Pharmacy in History* 30, no. 1
(1988): 3–18. For more on the history of health almanacs, see Louise Hill Curth,
"Medical Advertising in the Popular Press: Almanacs and the Growth of Proprietary Medicines," *Pharmacy in History* 50, no. 1 (2008): 3–15.

20 Young, "'Even to a Suckling Infant,'" 5–32.

21 Jacobi, *Report on the Clinic for Diseases of Childre*, 457. Physicians at the newly
founded hospitals specializing in the care of sick youngsters, such as Children's
Hospital of Philadelphia, founded in 1855, administered narcotics frequently to
treat pain and suppress cough. Children's Hospital of Philadelphia Records, Series
VI, Bound Volumes, Subseries E, Patient Histories, Doctor's Case Book, 1879–1899,
MSS 6/0014–0, College of Physicians of Philadelphia, Historical Medical Library.
They are also a fixture in the surviving Children's Hospital of Philadelphia Prescrib-
ing Manuals for 1862, 1882, and 1890 for use in a variety of ailments, found in the
book collection at the College of Physicians of Philadelphia, Historical Medical
Library. For more about the founding of children's hospitals, see Charles R. King,
*Children's Health in America: A History* (New York: Twayne, 1993), 59; Janet
Golden, Introduction to *Infant Asylums and Children's Hospitals: Medical Dilem-
mas and Developments, 1850–1920: An Anthology of Sources*, ed. Janet Golden (New
York: Garland, 1989), i–xviii.

22 Horatio C. Wood, "The Origin of Young's Rule," *Journal of the American Pharmaceutical Association* 8 (1947): 36–39.

23 Thomas Lauder Brunton, *Experimental Investigation of the Action of Medicines,
Part 1* (London: Churchill, 1875), 9; Thomas Lauder Brunton, *Pharmacology and
Therapeutics or, Medicine Past and Present* (London: Macmillan, 1880), 206; Oswald
Schmiedenberg, *Elements of Pharmacology* (Edinburgh: Young J. Pentland, 1887),
113. On the history of pharmacology in the United States, see John Parascandola,
*The Development of American Pharmacology: John J. Abel and the Shaping of a
Discipline* (Baltimore: The Johns Hopkins University Press, 1992); John P. Swann,
*Academic Scientists and the Pharmaceutical Industry: Cooperative Research in
Twentieth-Century America* (Baltimore: The Johns Hopkins University Press, 1988),
12–20; John P. Swann, "The Evolution of the American Pharmaceutical Industry,"
*Pharmacy in History* 37, no. 2 (1995): 76–86; Sonnedecker, *Kremer and Urdang's
History of Pharmacy*, 189–212, 226–241.

24 Abraham Jacobi, "The Relations of Pediatrics to General Medicine," *Transactions
of the American Pediatric Society* 1 (1889): 15–17; Abraham Jacobi, "Introduction," *American Journal of Dieases of Children* 1 (January 1911): 1–5; Sydney Halpern, *American Pediatrics: The Social Dynamics of Professionalism, 1880–1980* (Berkeley: University of California Press, 1988), 35; Charles R. King, *Children's Health in
America: A History* (New York: Twayne, 1993), 91; Meckel, *Save the Babies*, 46. On
nursing, see Cynthia A. Connolly, "Growth and Development of a Specialty: The
Professionalization of Child Health Care," *Pediatric Nursing* 31 (2005): 211–215.

25  For a case study of one city, see the essays in David Rosner, ed., *Hives of Sickness: Public Health and Epidemics in New York City* (New Brunswick, NJ: Rutgers University Press, 1995). See also Jeffrey P. Brosco, "The Early History of the Infant Mortality Rate in America: 'A Reflection upon the Past and a Prophecy of the Future,'" *Pediatrics* 103 (February 1999): 478–485; George B. Mangold et al., "Infant Mortality in American Cities," *Annals of the American Academy of Political and Social Science* 31 (1908): 184–192; Samuel H. Preston and Michael R. Haines, *Fatal Years: Child Mortality in Late Nineteenth-Century America* (Princeton, NJ: Princeton University Press, 1991); Meckel, *Save the Babies*, 104–106.

26  On the rabies vaccines, see Gerald L. Geison, *The Private Science of Louis Pasteur* (Princeton, NJ: Princeton University Press, 1995); Suzanne White Junod, "Biologics Centennial: 100 Years of Biologics Regulation," Food and Drug Law Institute (November–December 2002), accessed August 1, 2016, http://www.fda.gov/AboutFDA/WhatWeDo/History/ProductRegulation/ SelectionsFromFDLIUpdateSeriesonFDAHistory/ucm091754.htm; Ramunas A. Kondratas, "Biologics Control Act of 1902," in *The Early Years of Federal Food and Drug Control*, ed. James Harvey Young (Madison, WI: American Institute of the History of Pharmacy, 1982), 8–27. For descriptions of the disaster, see "Fatal to Eleven Children: Result of Inoculation with Diphtheria Antitoxin," *Washington Post*, November 2, 1901; Philip J. Hilts, *Protecting America's Health: The FDA, Business, and 100 Years of Regulation* (New York: Knopf, 2003), 69. For changing pedical practice during the nineteenth century, see John Harley Warner, *The Therapeutic Perspective: Medical Practice, Knowledge, and Identity in America, 1820–1885* (Cambridge, MA: Harvard University Press, 1986).

27  Samuel Hopkins Adams, *The Great American Fraud* (New York: Collier & Son, 1906); Young, "'Even to a Suckling Infant,'" 5–32. See also Elizabeth Fee, "Samuel Hopkins Adams (1871–1958): Journalist and Muckraker," *American Journal of Public Health* 100, no. 8 (August 2010): 1390–1391; Hilts, *Protecting America's Health*, 46, 48; W. Steven Pray and Dennis B. Worthen, *A History of Nonprescription Product Regulation* (Binghamton, NY: Pharmaceutical Products Press, 2003), 78–84.

28  On the history of the Council on Pharmacy and Chemistry, see Austin Smith, "The Council on Pharmacy and Chemistry and the Chemical Laboratory," in *The American Medical Association, 1847–1947*, ed. Morris Fishbein (Philadelphia: W. B. Saunders, 1947), 865–886, and Harry F. Dowling, "The American Medical Association's Policy on Drugs in Recent Decades," in *Safeguarding the Public: Historical Aspects of Medicinal Drug Control*, ed. John B. Blake (Baltimore: The Johns Hopkins University Press, 1970), 123–132; Marks, *Progress of Experiment*, 22–27. For letters to the AMA, see "More Deaths from Soothing Syrups," *JAMA* 48, no. 6 (1907): 535; For an overview of the evolution of experimental pharmacology as a discipline and its relationship to clinical medicine, see John Parascandola, "From Germs to Genes: Trends in Drug Therapy, 1852–2002," *Pharmacy in History* 44, no. 1 (2002): 3–11.

29  These guidelines assured a common nomenclature and chemical composition for all drugs. The USP set standards for strength, quality, and purity for drugs and the National Forumulary set standards for "unofficial" drugs such as botanicals, elixers, and excipients. The organizations merged in the 1970s. For a history of the USP and NF, see Lee Anderson and Gregory J. Higby, *The Spirit of Voluntarism: A Legacy of Commitment and Contribution: The United States Pharmacopeia, 1820–1995* (Rockville, MD: United States Pharmacopeial Convention, 1995); Glenn Sonnedecker,

"The Founding Period of the U.S. Pharmacopeia," *Pharmacy in History* 36, no. 3 (1994): 3–122.

30  Young, "'Even to a Suckling Infant,'" 5–32.

31  James Marten, "Introduction," in *Children and Youth during the Gilded Age and Progressive Era*, ed. James Marten (New York: New York University Press, 2014), 1–15; Michael B. Katz, *In the Shadow of the Poorhouse: A Social History of Welfare in the United States* (New York: Basic Books, 1986); Sealander, *The Failed Century of the Child*, 105–106; "The White House Conference on Children," *Charities* (January 1909): 766–768; Matthew A. Crenson, *Building the Invisible Orphanage: A Prehistory of the American Welfare System* (Cambridge, MA: Harvard University Press, 1998), 2, 3, 7–9; *Proceedings of the Conference on the Care of Dependent Children, Held at Washington, D.C., January 25, 26, 1909: Special Message of the President of United States Recommending Legislation Desired by the Conference on the Care of Dependent Children . . . and Transmitting the Proceedings of the Conference. Communicated to the Two Houses of Congress on February 15, 1909*, 60th Congress, 2nd Session (Washington, DC: GPO, 1909), accessed January 17, 2017, http://hdl .handle.net/2027/hvd.32044005543723.

32  "National Fight on Baby Killers," *The Survey* 25 (October 1, 1910): 3–5; *American Association for the Study and Prevention of Infant Mortality, Transactions of the First Annual Meeting*, Baltimore, November 9–11, 1910, Johns Hopkins University, 334.

33  Lyman F. Kebler, *Habit-Forming Agents: Their Indiscriminate Sale and Use a Menace to the Public Welfare* Farmer's Bulletin no. 393 (Washington, DC: GPO, 1910), 4; Emmett Campbell Hall, "Deadly Drugs and Beverages," *Good Housekeeping* 51 (November 1910): 582–584.

34  Young, "'Even to a Suckling Infant,'" 5–32. On the Harrison Narcotic Act, see Musto, *The American Disease*, 3–5. On the Federal Trade Commission, see Carpenter, *Reputation and Power*, 83.

35  Molly Ladd-Taylor, *Raising a Baby the Government Way: Mothers' Letters to the Children's Bureau, 1915–1932* (New Brunswick, NJ: Rutgers University Press, 1986), 72, 100–101.

36  U.S. Department of Labor, Children's Bureau, *Infant Care*, Publication no. 8 (Washington, DC: GPO, 1929), 39.

37  See discussion of the importance of "electrolytes debates" in this era in Horace L. Hodes's 1976 Presidential Address to the American Pediatric Society, Box 3, Folder 8, Horace L. Hodes papers, Icahn School of Medicine at Mt. Sinai, New York, New York (hereafter cited as Hodes papers). On electrolytes, see, for example, M. W. McKim Marriott, "The Pathogenesis of Certain Nutritional Disorders," *American Journal of Diseases of Children* 20 (December 1920): 461–485; Lawrence T. Weaver, "Kinderheilkunde and Continental Connections in Child Health: The 'Glasgow School Revisited'—Again," *Journal of the History of Medicine and Allied Sciences* 68, no. 4 (2012): 583–626. More refined measurement of the electrolyte glucose also facilitated diabetic children's treatment with the pancreatic extract insulin. Chris Feudtner, *Bittersweet: Diabetes, Insulin, and the Transformation of Illness* (Chapel Hill: University of North Carolina Press, 2003). On the evolution of children's hospitals, see Golden, ed., *Infant Asylums and Children's Hospitals*, iv ff; and Stafford McLean, "Standards for a Children's Hospital," *Modern Hospital* 10 (1918): 324–328. On the child as a scientific focus during this era, see Alice Boardman Smuts, *Science in the Service of Children 1893–1935* (New Haven, CT: Yale University Press, 2008).

38  Elnora E. Thomson, "Public Health Nursing and Child Care in the United States," *Annals of the American Academy of Political and Social Science* 151 (September 1930): 116–120; Howard Childs Carpenter, "Health Services for Preschool Children," *Annals of the American Academy of Political and Social Science* 151 (September 1930): 102–109; Harriet L. Leete, "The Maternity and Infancy Law and State Nurse Directors," *American Journal of Nursing* 22 (March 1922): 453–457; Alexandra Minna Stern, "Making Better Babies: Public Health and Race Betterment in Indiana, 1920–35," *American Journal of Public Health* 92 (May 2002): 742–752; Naomi Rogers, "Vegetables on Parade: American Medicine and Child Health Education in the Jazz Age," in *Children's Health Issues in Historical Perspective*, ed. Cheryl Krasnick Warsh and Veronica Strong-Boag (Waterloo: Wilfred Laurier University Press, 2005), 23–71; Meckel, *Save the Babies*, 214–219. On school nursing, see Richard A. Meckel, *Classrooms and Clinics: Urban Schools and the Protection and Promotion of Child Health, 1870–1930* (New Brunswick, NJ: Rutgers University Press, 2013); On public health nurses' efforts to promote health and prevent tuberculosis in at-risk children, see Cynthia A. Connolly, *Saving Sickly Children: The Tuberculosis Preventorium in American Life, 1909–1970* (New Brunswick, NJ: Rutgers University Press, 2008). On the development of well-child care and pediatricians, see Jeffrey P. Brosco, "Weight Charts and Well-Child Care: How the Pediatrician Became the Expert in Child Health," *Archives of Pediatric and Adolescent Medicine* 155 (2001): 1385–1389; Halpern, *American Pediatrics*, 9; and Howard Markel and Janet Golden, "Successes and Missed Opportunities in Protecting our Children's Health: Critical Junctures in the History of Children's Health Policy in the United States," *Pediatrics* 115 (April 2005): 1129–1133.

39  Proceedings of the St. Louis Session, Minutes of the Seventy-third Annual Session of the American Medical Association, Held at St. Louis, May 22–26, 1922, House of Delegates, May 23, "Resolution on Sheppard-Towner Law," *JAMA* 78, no. 3 (1922): 1709.

40  Lee Forrest Hill, "The American Academy of Pediatrics—Its Growth and Development," *Pediatrics* 1 (1948): 1–8; Jeffrey P. Baker and Howard A. Pearson, eds., *Dedicated to the Health of All Children* (Chicago: American Academy of Pediatrics, 2005), 32–35.

41  Marks, *The Progress of Experiment*, 75.

42  "Protection of Children First: Aim of Federal Caustic Poison Act," *California and Western Medicine* 46 (January 1937): 68; Marion Moser Jones and Isidore Daniel Benrubi, "Poison Politics: A Contentious History of Consumer Protection Against Dangerous Household Chemicals in the United States," *American Journal of Public Health* 103 (May 2013): 801–812.

43  *White House Conference on Child Health and Protection* (New York: Century Publications, 1930).

44  On the Philadelphia Pediatric Society, see Jeffrey P. Brosco, "Sin or Folly: Child and Community Health in Philadelphia, 1900–1930" (PhD Dissertation, University of Pennsylvania, 1994), 81–82.

## Chapter 2   New Drugs, Old Problems in Pediatrics: From Therapeutic Nihilism to the Antibiotic Era, 1933-1945

1  J. P. Crozer Griffith and A. Graeme Mitchell, *The Diseases of Infants and Children* (Philadelphia: W. B. Saunders, 1933), 176; this book is still in print in its 20th

edition, now titled *Nelson Textbook of Pediatrics*. For a history of early pediatric dosing, see Horatio C. Wood, "The Origin of Young's Rule," *Journal of the American Pharmacists Association* 8 (1947): 36–39.

2  Charles A. Janeway to Estes Kefauver, 23 July 1962, Box 62, Folder 13, Helen B. Taussig papers, Alan Mason Chesney Archives of the Johns Hopkins Medical Institutions, Baltimore, Maryland.

3  Thomas E. Cone Oral History, interviewed by Howard A. Pearson, July 17, 1996, American Academy of Pediatrics, Pedriatic History Center, Oral History Collection, Elk Grove Village, Illinois (hereafter cited as AAP Oral History Collection), quote page 41, accessed August 1, 2016, https://www.aap.org/en-us/about-the-aap/Pediatric-History-Center/Pages/Oral-Histories.aspx.

4  "Resolution Presented to Board of Directors Meeting of the Philadelphia Pediatric Society," 17 January 1933, Philadelphia Pediatric Society Records, Box 16, Folder 8, College of Physicians of Philadelphia, Historical Medical Library, Philadelphia, Pennsylvania (hereafter cited as PPS records). Under the 1906 Federal Food and Drugs Act, the USP and NF standards became statutory. John P. Swann, "The Evolution of the American Pharmaceutical Industry," *Pharmacy in History* 37, no. 2 (1995): 76–86.

5  In 1934, only 1,734 full-time pediatricians practiced in the United States; almost all of them were in large cities such as Boston, New York, Philadelphia, Baltimore, and Chicago. Sydney Halpern, *American Pediatrics: The Social Dynamics of Professionalism, 1880–1980* (Berkeley: University of California Press, 1988), 83.

6  "Dear Doctor" Cover letter, William N. Bradley and H. Harris Perlman, September 20, 1933, Box 16, Folder 8, PPS records.

7  Pediatric societies around the country quickly gave their full support to the Philadelphia physicians' proposal; for example, see Minutes of meeting, October 20, 1933, Rochester Pediatric Society Miner Library Archives, Academy of Medicine Collection, University of Rochester, Rochester, New York. See also "Pediatricians Heard from to Date" [undated, appears to be late 1933 or early 1934], Box 16, Folder 8, PPS records.

8  "Resolution Presented to Board of Directors Meeting of the Philadelphia Pediatric Society," January 17, 1933, Box 16, Folder 8, PPS records.

9  Isaac Arthur Abt, *Baby Doctor* (New York: McGraw Hill, 1944), 16–17, 29. For an example of public health nurses' medication recommendations, see Arlene W. Keeling, *Nursing and the Privilege of Prescription, 1893–2000* (Columbus: Ohio State University Press, 2007), 22–23; On pharmacists' scope of practice, see John P. Swann, "FDA and the Practice of Pharmacy: Prescription Drug Regulation Before the Durham-Humphrey Amendment of 1951," *Pharmacy in History* 36, no. 2 (1994): 55–70.

10  "Comments," *Journal of Pediatrics* 5 (September 1934): 432.

11  On decisions regarding representation to the USP revision committees, see Lee Anderson and Gregory J. Higby, *Spirit of Voluntarism: A Legacy of Commitment and Contribution—The United States Pharmacopeia 1820–1995* (Rockville, MD: United States Pharmacopeial Convention, 1995), 202–207.

12  Isaac Abt to H. Harris Perlman, July 27, 1933, Box 16, Folder 8, PPS records.

13  On the history of the Council, see Austin Smith, "The Council on Pharmacy and Chemistry and the Chemical Laboratory," in *The American Medical Association, 1847–1947*, ed. Morris Fishbein (Philadelphia: W. B. Saunders, 1947), 865–886 and Harry F. Dowling, "The American Medical Association's Policy on Drugs in Recent

Decades," 123–132; Glenn Sonnedecker, *Kremer and Urdang's History of Pharmacy*, 4th edition (Philadelphia: J. P. Lippincott, 1976), 282.

14 "Report of the Committee on Revision of the Pharmacopeia" as it outlined its work for the coming year. Document undated but included with items from 1936. Committee on Revision of the Pharmacopeia, Committee on Drugs records, American Academy of Pediatrics, Pediatric History Center, Elk Grove Village, Illinois (hereafter cited as COD archives).

15 Folder: "Committee on Drugs: History": Minutes of the Executive Board of the AAP, June 8, 1938; COD archives. There is nothing in the USP Executive Committee minutes about the AAP request, or any recorded vote on the matter, MSS 149, Box 160, United States Pharmacopeial Convention Archives, Wisconsin Historical Society, Madison, Wisconsin.

16 On the Children's Bureau in the 1930s, see United States Children's Bureau, *The Children's Bureau Yesterday, Today and Tomorrow* (Washington, DC: GPO, 1937) and United States Children's Bureau, *The Children's Bureau and Its Relationship with Other Agencies* (Washington, DC: GPO, 1939). On women in medicine and gender-related issues, see Ellen S. More, *Restoring the Balance: Women Physicians and the Profession of Medicine, 1850–1995* (Cambridge, MA: Harvard University Press, 1999), 149–153, 161. On relationships between pediatricians and government physicians, see Howard Markel, "For the Welfare of Children: The Origins of the Relationship between US Public Health Workers and Pediatricians," *American Journal of Public Health* 6 (2000): 893–899. The AAP was also caught between the pro-governmental forces within the AAP and Children's Bureau and those in the AMA that opposed public involvement in health care, such as national health insurance. Jeffrey P. Baker and Howard A. Pearson, eds., *Dedicated to the Health of All Children: 75 Years of Caring, 1930–2005* (Elk Grove Village, IL: American Academy of Pediatrics, 2005), 42.

17 Daniel Carpenter, *Reputation and Power: Organizational Image and Regulation at the FDA* (Princeton, NJ: Princeton University Press, 2010), 80.

18 Gwen Kay, "Healthy Public Relations: The FDA's 1930s Legislative Campaign," *Bulletin of the History of Medicine* 75, no. 3 (2001): 446–487; Arthur Kallet and F. J. Schlink, *100,000,000 Guinea Pigs: The Dangers in Everyday Foods, Drugs, and Cosmetics* (New York: Vanguard Press, 1933).

19 "Copeland Exhibits Drug Law 'Horrors,'" *New York Times*, April 3, 1935.

20 On Lamb and a discussion of Hazel Fay Brown and correspondence between Lamb and FDA colleagues regarding how to use Musser's letter, see Kay, "Healthy Public Relations," 474. Letter also published in Ruth deForest Lamb, *American Chamber of Horrors: The Truth about Food and Drugs* (New York: Grosset & Dunlap, 1936), 327.

21 A. McGehee Harvey, "The Story of Chemotherapy at Johns Hopkins: Perrin H. Long, Eleanor A. Bliss, and E. Kennerly Marshall, Jr.," *Bulletin of the Johns Hopkins Hospital* 138 (February 1976): 54–60; Perrin H. Long and Eleanor A. Bliss, "Para-Amino-Benzene-Sulfonamide and Its Derivatives," *JAMA* 108, no. 1 (January 1937): 32–37. For sulfa and childbed fever, see John E. Lesch, *The First Miracle Drugs: How the Sulfa Drugs Transformed Medicine* (New York: Oxford University Press, 2007), 85–89.

22 Julius H. Hess, "The Present Status of Serum Therapy in Pediatrics," *New Orleans Medical and Surgical Journal* 90 (1937): 134–142. On the use of serum and antitoxin in diphtheria control, see Evelyn Hammonds, *Childhood's Deadly Scourge: The*

*Campaign to Control Diphtheria in New York City, 1880–1930* (Baltimore: The Johns Hopkins University Press, 1999). On the history of serum therapy, see Scott H. Podolsky, *Pneumonia before Antibiotics: Therapeutic Revolution and Evaluation in Twentieth-Century America* (Baltimore: The Johns Hopkins University Press, 2006).

23 For an example of a meningococcal serum reaction, see "Patient Records, 1935–1936," Series II, Box 19, Case 31671, Sydenham Hospital, Baltimore, Sydenham Hospital Records, 1909–1962, Modern Manuscripts Collection, History of Medicine Division, National Library of Medicine, Bethesda, Maryland (MS C 243) (hereafter cited as Sydenham records). For an example of a case of fatal serum reaction in a pediatric patient elsewhere, see Case 973, Babies Hospital Case Histories, 1932–1955, Archives and Special Collections, Columbia University Medical Center, Columbia University, New York. For a review of clinicians' concerns about the complexity of drawing blood from, and administering intravenous injections to, infants, see Alice Haehnlen, "A Simple Method of Procuring Blood for Diagnosis from Infants," *American Journal of Nursing* 21 (August 1921): 786–788.

24 "Conquering Streptococci," *New York Times*, December 18, 1936, 24.

25 Baker and Pearson, eds., *Dedicated to the Health of All Children*, 111–112. On the relationship between the Harriett Lane Home and Sydenham Hospital, see Edwards A. Park, John W. Littlefield, Henry M. Seidel, and Lawrence S. Wissow, *The Harriet Lane Home: A Model and a Gem* (Baltimore: Department of Pediatrics, School of Medicine, The Johns Hopkins University, 2006), 62, 69, 236.

26 For the development of sulfanilamide, see Lesch, *The First Miracle Drugs*, 126–132, for Prontosil's cost see page 147; Morton N. Swartz, "Bacterial Meningitis—A View of the Past 90 Years," *New England Journal of Medicine* 351 (October 2004): 1826–1828, and Barron H. Lerner, "Scientific Evidence versus Therapeutic Demand: The Introduction of the Sulfonamides Revisited," *Annals of Internal Medicine* 15, no. 4 (August 1991); 315–320.

27 The treatment protocol is detailed in Memorandum from Dr. Francis F. Schwentker, July 1, 1936, Series IV, "Minutes of staff meetings," 1935–1937, Box 81, Folder 7, Sydenham records.

28 For concerns about Sydenham serum relative to Johns Hopkins, see Thomas R. Boggs to Huntingdon Williams, May 15, 1935, Series IV, Box 81, Folder 7; Minutes of Staff Meetings, 1935–1937, Sydenham records. Francis F. Schwentker attended Union College and The Johns Hopkins University School of Medicine, graduating in 1929. After completing a residency at Hopkins in pediatrics, he accepted a position at the Rockefeller Institute. He stayed at Sydenham for three years, leaving in 1938 to go to Romania on behalf of Rockefeller. Francis F. Schwentker (Obituary), *Pediatrics* 16 (July1995): 132–134; Park et al., *The Harriet Lane Home*, 224–238.

29 Francis F. Schwentker, M. D. Freeman, P. Clason, William A. Morgan, Janvier W. Lindsay, and Perrin H. Long, "The Use of Para-Amino-Benzene-Sulphonamide or Its Derivatives in the Treatment of Beta Haemolytic Streptococcal Meningitis," *Bulletin of Johns Hopkins Hospital* 60, no. 4 (1937): 297–306, quote page 299.

30 Arthur B. Musgrave, "Medical Science Conquers a Foe," *Baltimore Sun*, June 6, 1937. Schwentker used Long's mice-based dosing recommendations as a beginning guide to estimate pediatric doses. Long and Bliss, "Para-Amino-Benzene-Sulfonamide and Its Derivatives"; Long and Bliss, "Observations on the Mode of Action of Sulfanilamide," *JAMA* 109, no. 19 (1937): 1524–1527, commentary on page 1527 for Schwentker's discussion of Sydenham patients.

31  Harry Haller, "Sydenham Checks Two Scourges," *Baltimore Sun*, August 6, 1939.

32  Frances F. Schwentker, Sidney Gelman, and Perrin H. Long, "The Treatment of Meningococcic Meningitis with Sulfanilamide: Preliminary Report," *JAMA* 108, no. 17 (1937): 1407–1408.

33  During the second decade of the twentieth century, for example, whooping cough (pertussis) mortality was three to six times higher in Baltimore's black infants than in white; Samuel K. Roberts, *Infectious Fear: Politics, Disease and the Health Effects of Segregation* (Chapel Hill: University of North Carolina Press, 2009), 69.

34  Memorandum, Myron G. Tull Sydenham, superintendent to Huntingdon Williams (Baltimore health commissioner), "Report of Visit to Hospitals in the South," Series IV, Box 81, May 31, 1935, Sydenham records. For a discussion of race, medicine, and American society, see Keith A. Wailoo, *Dying in the City of the Blues: Sickle Cell Anemia and the Politics of Race and Health* (Chapel Hill: University of North Carolina Pess, 2001). For history of origins of ideas about race and science in the twentieth century, see Michael Yudell, *Race Unmasked: A 20th Century Struggle to Define Human Difference* (New York: Columbia University Press, 2014). I am not arguing that racial disparities did not exist in Baltimore, only discussing pediatric sulfonamide access at Sydenham during the late 1930s and early 1940s. For research that suggests that use of the sulfonamides diffused more slowly to the black population in general, see Seema Jayachandran, Adriana Lleras-Muney, and Kimberly V. Smith, "Modern Medicine and the 20th Century Decline in Mortality: Evidence on the Impact of the Sulfa Drugs" (June 2009), National Bureau of Economic Research Working Paper No. 15089, accessed March 30, 2011, http://www.nber.org/papers/w15089.

35  The Children's Hospital, "Report of the Medical Service," *Annual Report, Part II, Medical Statistics for 1936*, 18, Boston Children's Hospital Archives, Boston, Massachusetts.

36  Ibid.

37  Francis F. Schwentker, "The Use of Sulfanilamide in the Treatment of Infections," *Medical Clinics of North America* 21 (September 1937): 1449–1460; Frances F. Schwentker and Sidney Gelman, "Sulfanilamide Rash," *Bulletin of the Johns Hopkins Hospital* 61, no. 2 (1937): 138–139.

38  Perrin H. Long and Eleanor A. Bliss, "Observations upon the Experimental and Clinical use of Sulphanilamide," 1937. For examples of other researchers studying age-specific issues surrounding the sulfonamides in the late 1930s, see Benjamin W. Carey, Jr., "The Use of Para-Aminobenzenesulfonamide and Its Derivatives in the Treatment of Infections Due to Streptococcus Hemolyticus of the Meningococcus and the Gonococcus: Report of 38 Cases," *Journal of Pediatrics* 11 (August 1937): 202–211; Rustin McIntosh, Daniel A. Wilcox, and Howell F. Wright, "Results of Sulfanilamide Treatment at Babies Hospital, New York City; Survey of 58 Cases Observed Prior to June 10, 1937," *Journal of Pediatrics* 11 (August 1937): 167–182; Julius M. Waghelstein, "Sulfanilamide in the Treatment of One Hundred and Six Patients with Meningococcic Infection," *JAMA* 11 (September 1939): 2172.

39  Musgrave, "Medical Science Conquers a Foe." The pace of change from serum to serum and sulfa to sulfa only is not clearly documented for the years 1937 to 1940. By 1941, however, the annual report noted, "All cases of meningococcus meninigitis received one of the several sulfonamides but anti-meningococcus serum was not used." City of Baltimore, *One Hundred and Twenty-Seventh Annual Report of the Department of Health* (Baltimore, Health Department, 1941), 121.

40 Daniel Carpenter, *Reputation and Power: Organizational Image and Regulation at the FDA* (Princeton, NJ: Princeton University Press, 2010), 73–85.

41 "'Death Drug' Hunt Covered 15 States," *New York Times*, November 26, 1937, 42.

42 Carpenter, *Reputation and Power*. 8, 90–100, 104, 111; Daniel Carpenter and Gisela Sin, "Policy Tragedy and the Emergence of Regulation: The Food, Drug, and Cosmetic Act of 1938," *Studies in American Political Development* 21 (Fall 2007): 149–180; Carol Ballentine, "Taste of Raspberries, Taste of Death: The 1937 Sulfanilamide Incident," *FDA Consumer* (June 1981), accessed July 2, 2015, http://www.fda.gov/AboutFDA/WhatWeDo/History/ProductRegulation/SulfanilamideDisaster/default.htm; James Harvey Young, "Sulfanilamide and Diethylene Glycol," in *Chemistry and Modern Society: Historical Essays in Honor of Aaron J. Ihde*, ed. John Parascandola and James C. Whorton (Washington, DC: American Chemical Society, 1983), 105–125.

43 United States Department of Agriculture, "Elixir Sulfanilamide: Letter from the Secretary of Agriculture Transmitting in Response to Senate Resolution No. 194," in *A Report on Elixir Sulfanilamide-Massengill 75th Congress November 26, 1937* (Washington, DC: GPO, 1937); see also "Plea for U.S. Regulation follows 'Elixir' Deaths," *Washington Post*, October, 29, 1937, 9; "Elixir Victim's Mother Asks President to Aid Death Fight," *Los Angeles Times*, November 28, 1937, 5.

44 *A Report on Elixir Sulfanilamide*, 1937.

45 Federal Food, Drug, and Cosmetic Act of 1938, Section 502, Pub. L. No. 717, 52 STAT. 1040, quote page 1052; Carpenter and Sin, "Policy Tragedy and the Emergence of Regulation," 149–180. See also Charles O. Jackson, *Food and Drug Legislation in the New Deal* (Princeton, NJ: Princeton University Press, 1970). For contemporaneous discussion of efforts by consumers' and women's groups in the 1920s and 1930s, see James F Corbett, "The Activities of Consumers' Organizations," *Law and Contemporary Problems* 1 (December 1933): 61–66.

46 Peter Temin, "The Origin of Compulsory Drug Prescriptions," *Journal of Law & Economics* 22, no. 1 (1979): 91–105; Harry M. Marks, "Revisiting 'The Origins of Compulsory Drug Prescriptions,'" *American Journal of Public Health* 85, no. 1 (1995): 109–115. Under a law enacted just after the 1938 drug legislation, the Wheeler-Lea Act, the Federal Trade Commission's powers were enlarged to protect consumers from inappropriate advertising. Milton Handler, "The Control of False Advertising under the Wheeler-Lea Act," *Law and Contemporary Problems* 6, no. 1 (1939): 91–110 and Kay, "Healthy Public Relations," 485. On the confusion in proprietary industry about safety, see James F. Hoge, "An Appraisal of the New Drug and Cosmetic Legislation from the Viewpoint of Those Industries," *Law and Contemporary Problems* 6, no. 1 (1939): 111–128.

47 For the 1934 bill, see U.S. Senate, "Food, Drugs, and Cosmetics," *Report to Accompany S. 2800, 73rd Congress, March 19, 1934* (Washington, DC: GPO, 1934). On the 1938 law's lack of specificity with regard to children and new drugs, see Federal Food, Drug, and Cosmetic Act of 1938. For detailed overview of the legislation as it was viewed by those who observed the sulfanilamide crisis and legislative debates specific to the language in the final bill, see David F. Cavers, "The Food, Drug, and Cosmetic Act of 1938: Its Legislative History and Its Substantive Provisions," *Law and Contemporary Problems* 6, no. 1 (1939): 2–42.

48 John P. Swann, "FDA and the Practice of Pharmacy: Prescription Drug Regulation before the Durham-Humphrey Act of 1951," *Pharmacy in History* 36 (1994): 55–70.

49  Excellent histories that discuss the serum to sulfa transition for pneumonia in adults include Podolsky, *Pneumonia before Antibiotics*, 60–90; Lesch, *The First Miracle Drugs*, 160–169, 225–227. On the development of pneumococcal serum, see Harry Marks, *The Progress of Experiment: Science and Therapeutic Reform in the United States, 1900–1990* (Cambridge: Cambridge University Press, 1997), 60–62. On the disease in children, see Jesse G. M. Bullowa and Evelyn Greenbaum, "Pneumococcic Pneumonia in Infants and Children," *American Journal of Diseases of Children* 53 (January 1937): 22–31; Camille Kereszturi and David Hauptmann, "The Serum Treatment of Pneumonia in Children," *Journal of Pediatrics* 4 (March 1934): 331–41; Roderick Heffernon, *Pneumonia* (New York: Commonwealth Fund, 1939), 514, 617, 703, 834–835.

50  Horace L. Hodes, William E. Stifler, Jr., Ethel Walker, Maclyn McCarty, and Robert G. Shirley, "The Use of Sulfapyridine in Primary Pneumococcic Pneumonia and in Pneumococcic Pneumonia Associated with Measles," *Journal of Pediatrics* 14 (April 1939): 417–446, quote page 427.

51  Stafford McLean and Charles A. Lane, "Fluid Injections in Dehydrated Infants," *American Journal of Diseases of Children* 19 (May 1920): 359–368; Griffith and Mitchell, *Pediatrics* (1937): 718–719; Langley Porter and William F. Carter, *Management of the Sick Infant and Child* (St. Louis: Mosby, 1938), 579; Luther E. Holt, John Howland, and Rustin McIntosh, *Holt's Diseases of Infancy and Childhood: A Textbook for the Use of Students and Practitioners,* 11th edition (New York: Appleton-Century, 1939), 56.

52  On the sulfapyridine application, see Marks, *The Progress of Experiment,* 84–87. On the regulatory environment between 1938 and 1951, see John P. Swann, "FDA and the Practice of Pharmacy: Prescription Drug Regulation before the Durham-Humphrey Act of 1951," *Pharmacy in History* 36 (1994): 55–70. Hodes was appointed to Sydenham in 1938. A graduate of the University of Pennsylvania undergraduate and medical school (1931), Hodes completed an internship at the Children's Hospital of Philadelphia followed by a pediatric residency at Johns Hopkins Hospital's Harriett Lane Home. He arrived at Sydenham and Johns Hopkins in 1938 after a research position at the Rockefeller Institute for Medical Research. Hodes pioneered pediatric sulfapyridine research in the United States. He left Sydenham in 1949 when it closed and went to New York's Mount Sinai, where he spent the rest of his career. He died in 1989. Park, Littlefield, Seidel, and Wissow, *The Harriet Lane Home,* 189–192; Helen B. Taussig, "Horace L. Hodes—The Man," *Journal of Pediatrics* 67 (December 1975): 1057–1061; (Obituary) "Horace L. Hodes, A Pediatrician; Linked Virus to Gastroenteritis," *New York Times,* April 25, 1989. See also biographical note in the Finding Aid (Hodes papers).

53  Series II, Box 27, Case 25484, 1938, Sydenham records.

54  Hodes et al., "The Use of Sulfapyridine," 435.

55  Ibid., 429.

56  Ibid., 439. It is unclear whether children and parents were even aware of the nature of the experimental drugs they received. At some point, Sydenham developed a consent form that parents signed at their child's admission. The form provided blanket consent for any treatment that physicians deemed necessary during the course of the hospitalization, but it does not appear that individual therapeutics, even those being used for the first time, required parental approval. For discussions of research in children and consent in the interwar period, see Susan E. Lederer, *Subjected to Science: Human Experimentation in America before the Second World*

*War* (Baltimore: The Johns Hopkins University Press, 1995), 103–110 and Susan E. Lederer, "Orphans as Guinea Pigs: American Children and Medical Experimenters, 1890–1930," in *In the Name of the Child: Health and Welfare, 1880–1940,* ed. Roger Cooter (London: Routledge, 1992), 96–124. For a Sydenham Hospital consent form, see the record for Series II, Box 52, Case 46384, 1947, Sydenham records.

57  Harry Haller, "Sydenham Checks Two Scourges," *Baltimore Sun,* August 6, 1939.

58  Horace L. Hodes, James F. Ziegler, and Helen D. Zepp, "Development of Antibody Following Vaccination of Infants and Children Against Pneumococci," *Journal of Pediatrics* 24 (1944): 641–649, quote page 641. For examples of other studies in children, see Henry L. Barnett, Alexis F. Hartmann, A. M. Perley, and M. B. Ruhoff, "The Treatment of Pneumococcic Infections in Infants and Children with Sulfapyridine," *JAMA* 112, no. 21 (1939): 518–527. For tests of sulfapyridine around that same time to demonstrate efficacy and work out dosing, see also Henry S. Christian, Gilbert M. Jorgensen, and Catherine Ellis, "Treatment of Pneumococcic Infections in Children with Sulfapyridine," *American Journal of Diseases of Children* 59 (January 1940): 1–18; Glenn E. Cullen and Armine T. Wilson, "Levels of Sulfapyridine in Blood of Children Following Dosage by Body Weight," *American Journal of Diseases of Children* 60 (October 1940): 891–896.

59  Cullen and Wilson, "Levels of Sulfapyridine in Blood of Children," 894.

60  Ibid., 891.

61  "Pneumonia, America's No. 1 Killer, Declared Conquered," *Los Angeles Times,* March 3, 1939.

62  "Sulfa Drug Saves Baby," *New York Times,* February 23, 1943. See also "Sulfa Saves Newborn," *Science News Letter,* September 25, 1943, 197; Waldemar Kaemffert, "The Growing Miracle of Sulfa Drugs," *New York Times,* July 19, 1942; and Lois Mattox Miller, "Sulfa-Miracles," *Hygeia* 18 (September 1940): 776–778.

63  City of Baltimore, *One Hundred and Thirty-Third Annual Report of the Department of Health* (Baltimore, Health Department, 1947), 103.

64  John P. Swann, "The 1941 Sulfathiazole Disaster and the Birth of Good Manufacturing Practices," *Pharmacy in History* 41, no. 1 (1999): 16–25. The FDA also sought new ways to protect patients in the aftermath of the 1938 law. For example, it disseminated public policy statments, known as "trade correspondence" because they often rose in response to industry queries. These communiques specified labeling, directions for use, and other rules governing drug sales. Where data were available, pediatric directions for use or warning labels were provided, but this occurred very infrequently. See, for example, pediatric dosing and instructions for chinchona alkaloids (TC-392, August 20, 1942) in Vincent A. Kleinfeld and Charles Wesley Dunn, *Federal Food, Drug, and Cosmetic Act: Judicial and Administrative Records 1938–1949* (New York: Commerce Clearing House, 1950), 728.

65  Harry F. Dowling, *Fighting Infection: Conquests of the Twentieth Century* (Cambridge, MA: Harvard University Press, 1977), 122; Lesch, *The First Miracle Drugs,* 216–220; City of Baltimore, *One Hundred and Twenty-Seventh Annual Report* (Baltimore, Health Department, 1941) 28; City of Baltimore, *One Hundred and Twenty-Eighth Annual Report* (Baltimore, Health Department, 1942), 30. The *Annual Reports* show that new sulfa drugs were introduced very quickly: 1936 para-amino-benzene-sulfonamide, 1937 sulfanilamide, 1938 sulfapyridine, 1939 sulfathiazole, 1941 sulfadiazine, 1943 and sulfapyrazine.

66  Dowling, *Fighting Infection,* 125. For histories of penicillin, see Robert Bud, *Penicillin: Triumph and Tragedy* (New York: Oxford University Press, 2007); Scott H.

Podolsky, *The Antibiotic Era: Reform, Resistance, and the Pursuit of a Rational Therapeutics* (Baltimore: The Johns Hopkins University Press, 2015).

67  Gladys L. Hobby, *Penicillin: Meeting the Challenge* (New Haven, CT: Yale University Press, 1985), 110; David P. Adams, *Greatest Good to the Greatest Number: Penicillin Rationing on the American Homefront, 1940–1945* (New York: Peter Lang, 1991), 25–27.

68  Marks, *The Progress of Experiment*, 106; "Set Plans to Rule Penicillin Supply," *New York Times*, September 26, 1943, 52, accessed December 24, 2010, http://proquest .umi.com/pqdweb?index=1&did=83943893&SrchMode=1&sid=2&Fmt=10& VInst=PROD&VType=PQD&RQT=309&VName=HNP&TS=1293503200& clientId=63417.

69  Chester S. Keefer to Wesley W. Spink, July 1, 1942; D. F. Robertson, Associate Medical Director Merck & Co, to Wesley W. Spink, July 10, 1942; Airmail Receipt Merck & Co to Wesley Spink, July 9, 1942, Box 32, Folder, "Penicillin Miscellaneous," Wesley W. Spink papers, University Archives, University of Minnesota, Minneapolis. For a citation that Spink was the first to use penicillin in an American child, see also Historical Archives Advisory Committee, "Committee Report: American Pediatrics: Milestones at the Millennium," *Pediatrics* 107 (June 2001): 1482–1491.

70  "Proposal for Investigations with Penicillin," [undated]; Letter June 22, 1942, Perrin H. Long to Wesley W. Spink; Undated Case Report from Wesley W. Spink to Chester S. Keefer summarizing July 1942 case, Wesley W. Spink papers.

71  Adams, *Greatest Good to the Greatest Number*, 31; Johns Hopkins Medical Institutions, Patient A. Medical Record numbers are anonymized to protect patient privacy per Johns Hopkins Hospital Medical Institutions' Privacy Board requirements.

72  Cone Oral History, AAP Oral History, 42.

73  City of Baltimore, *One Hundred and Twenty-Ninth Annual Report* (Baltimore, Health Department, 1943), 28.

74  Lawrence Weld Smith and Ann Dolan Walker, *The Penicillin Decade, 1941–1951: Sensitizations and Toxicities* (Washington, DC: Arundel Press, 1951), 33.

75  Dowling, *Fighting Infection*, 122.

76  For examples of working out the dose in children, see Series II, Box 51, Case 45877 for 1946 and Case 45054 for 1947, Sydenham records. See also George S. Husson, "Oral Penicillin in Infants," *Journal of Pediatrics* 41 (December 1947): 651–657; Smith and Walker, *Penicillin Decade*, 34; Henry A. Reisman, Arthur A. Goldfarb, Molly Malloy, "Oral Administration of Penicillin in Pediatrics," *American Journal of Diseases of Children* 74 (July 1947): 19–31.

77  Dowling, *Fighting Infection*, 137–139.

78  Stella Goostray, "School of Nursing and Nursing Service," *Annual Report for 1945*, 57, Boston Children's Hospital Archives, Boston, Massachusetts.

79  City of Baltimore, *One Hundred and Thirtieth Annual Report* (Baltimore, Health Department, 1944), 23.

80  *Mitchell-Nelson, Textbook of Pediatrics*, ed. Waldo E. Nelson, 4th edition (Philadelphia: W. B. Saunders, 1945), 183.

## Chapter 3  The Child as Drug Development Problem and Business Opportunity in a New Era, 1945–1961

1  "Vital Statistics—Death Rates, Infant and Maternal Mortality: 1915–1945," *Bureau of Census Historical Statistics of the United States, Colonial Times to 1945* (Washington, DC: GPO, 1949), 39–44, 56; Robert D. Grove and Alice M. Hetzel, *Vital Statistics of the United States, 1940–1960* (Washington, DC: GPO, 1968), 20, 25, 778, 780.

2  Vannevar Bush, *Science, the Endless Frontier: A Report to the President on a Program for Postwar Scientific Research* (Washington, DC: GPO, 1945), 54–55, quote page 55.

3  Rosemary Stevens, *In Sickness and in Wealth: American Hospitals in the Twentieth Century* (New York: Basic Books, 1989), 216–223; Myron E. Wegman, "Infant Mortality in the Twentieth Century, Dramatic but Uneven Progress," *Journal of Nutrition* 131 (February 2001): 401S–408S; Paul W. Beaven, "The Weapon of Truth: The Influence of the Study of Child Health Services Conducted in 1946–1948," *Pediatrics* 14 (July 1954): 64–73; Jeffrey P. Brosco, "Weight Charts and Well-Child Care: How the Pediatrician Became the Expert in Child Health," *Archives of Pediatric and Adolescent Medicine* 155 (December 2001): 1385–1389.

4  Katharine F. Lenroot, Edwin F. Daily, and Melvin A. Glasser, "Health and the Child," *Public Health Reports* 65, no. 46 (November 17, 1950): 1525–1528.

5  Dominique Tobbell, *Pills, Power, and Policy: The Struggle for Drug Reform in Cold War America and Its Consequences* (Berkeley: University of California Press, 2011), 23, 45.

6  Walton Van Winkle, Robert P. Herwick, Herbert O. Calvery, and Austin Smith, "Laboratory and Clinical Appraisal of New Drugs," *JAMA* 126, no. 15 (December 1944): 968–961. Drug companies could also avoid expensive and lengthy testing and trials for new products by marketing them as prescription only, since the 1938 law did not require specific dosing and administration information for drugs prescribed by a physician, who presumably knew treatment standards. Federal Food, Drug, and Cosmetic Act of 1938, Section 502, Pub L. No. 717, 52 STAT. 1040.

7  Marilyn Irvin Holt, *Cold War Kids: Politics and Childhood in Postwar America, 1945–1960* (Lawrence: University of Kansas Press, 2014), 118–119. For the Child Research Act proposals, see *National Child Research Act: Hearings before the Subcommittee on Labor and Public Welfare*, U.S. Senate, 81st Congress, 1st Session, S.904 (May 11, 12, 1949) (Washington, DC: GPO, 1949). For more on postwar children's health policy, see Howard Markel and Janet Golden, "Successes and Missed Opportunities in Protecting Our Children's Health: Critical Junctures in the History of Children's Health Policy in the United States," *Pediatrics* 115 (April 2005): 1129–1133.

8  Tobbell, *Pills, Power, and Policy*, 7.

9  Executive Board meeting, February 3, 1947, p. 50, Committee on Drugs Records, Pediatric History Center, American Academy of Pediatrics, Elk Grove Village, Illinois (hereafter cited as COD archives).

10  Ibid. For penicillin dosage discussions in children in this era, see George S. Husson, "Oral Penicillin in Infants," *Journal of Pediatrics* 41 (December 1947): 651–657; Henry A. Reisman, Arthur A. Goldfarb, and Molly Malloy, "Oral Administration of Penicillin in Pediatrics," *American Journal of Diseases of Children* 74 (July 1947): 19–31.

11  AAP Executive Board meeting, February 3, 1947, pp. 50–51, COD archives.

12 Ibid., p. 53.

13 Ibid., p. 54.

14 Katherine Bain and Harold C. Stuart, "Facts and Figures about Child Health in the United States," *American Journal of Public Health* 39 (September 1949): 1091–1098; American Academy of Pediatrics, *The Road Ahead for Better Child Health* (Elk Grove Village, IL: AAP, 1948); Lee Forrest Hill, "The American Academy of Pediatrics—Its Growth and Development," *Pediatrics* 1, no. 1 (1948): 1–8; James L. Wilson, "The Committee for Improvement of Child Health," *Pediatrics* 1, no. 5 (1948): 657–661; Committee for the Study of Child Health Services, *Child Health Service and Pediatric Education* (New York: Commonwealth Fund, 1949).

15 AAP Executive Board meeting, February 3, 1947, COD archives.

16 Henry G. Poncher, "Committee on Drug Dosage," March 24, 1953, COD archives.

17 Scott H. Podolsky, *The Antibiotic Era: Reform, Resistance, and the Pursuit of a Rational Therapeutics* (Baltimore: The Johns Hopkins University Press, 2015), 19; Thomas Maeder, *Adverse Reactions* (New York: William Morrow, 1994), 182.

18 Scott H. Podolsky and Jeremy A. Greene, "A Historical Perspective of Pharmaceutical Promotion and Physician Education," *JAMA* 300, no. 7 (August 2008): 831–833.

19 Paula S. Fass, "The Child Centered Family? New Rules in Postwar America," *Reinventing Childhood after World War II*, ed. Paula S. Fass and Michael Grossberg (Philadelphia: University of Pennsylvania Press, 2011), 5, 11; Holt, *Cold War Kids*, 22–23.

20 On parenting advice, see Julia Grant, *Raising Baby by the Book: The Education of American Mothers* (New Haven, CT: Yale University Press, 1998), 218–233; Thomas Maier, *Dr. Spock: An American Life* (New York: Basic Books, 2003); Ann Hilbert, *Raising America: Experts, Parents, and a Century of Advice about Children*, (New York: Knopf, 2003). On child development's impact on health care delivery and American ideas about childhood, see Ruth Frank Baer, "The Sick Child Knows," in *Should the Patient Know the Truth?*, ed. Samuel Standard and Helmuth Nathan (New York: Springer, 1955), 100–106; Peter N. Stearns, "Childhood Emotions in Modern Western History," in *Routledge History of Childhood in the Western World*, ed. Paula S. Fass (London: Routledge, 2013), 157–158; Kathleen Jones, "A Sound Mind for the Child's Body: The Mental Health of Children and Youth," in *Children and Youth in Sickness and in Health: A Historical Handbook and Guide*, ed. Janet Golden, Richard A. Meckel, and Heather Munro (Westport, CT: Greenwood Press, 2004), 43–67.

21 May, 1953 Wide World Photo, Drug Topics Photograph Collection, Folder "Babies," American Institute of the History of Pharmacy, University of Wisconsin School of Pharmacy, Madison.

22 "They Get a Taste of Their Own Medicine," *Lilly Review*, November 1953, 2–3, Eli Lilly and Company Archives, Indianapolis, Indiana.

23 "Babies Mean Business," *Advertising Age* 9 (August 1948): 22–23; "More than Two Million New Customers a Year," *Business Week* (August 29, 1953): 28–30.

24 *Hearings before the Subcommittee on Antitrust and Monopoly of the Committee on the Judiciary*, U.S. Senate, 86th Congress, 2nd Session (September 7, 1960), Part 24, Administered Prices in the Drug Industry (Antibiotics) (Washington, DC: GPO, 1960), 13843.

25 Gladys Hobby to Maxwell Finland, May 15, 1950, Box 19, Folder 24, Maxwell Finland papers, 1916–2003, H MS c153. Harvard Medical Library, Francis A. Countway Library of Medicine, Boston, Massachusetts (hereafter cited as Finland papers).

For an overview of Finland's career, see Podolsky, *Antibiotic Era*, 6–7 and Jerome O. Klein, "Maxwell Finland: A Remembrance," *Clinical Infectious Diseases* 34 (March 2002): 725–729.

26  Finland to Hobby, June 3, 1950; Hobby to Finland, June 5, 1950, Box 19, Folder 24, Finland papers.

27  Hobby to Finland, June 5, 1950, Box 19 Folder 24, Finland papers.

28  Finland to Hobby, June 9, 1950, Box 19, Folder 24, Finland papers.

29  Ray A. Patelski to Finland, September 5, 1950, Box 19, Folder 24, Finland papers. For information about Finland and relationship with Pfizer, see Podolsky, *Antibiotic Era*, 65–66.

30  "Children's Medication Products Face Imminent Danger," *F-D-C Reports* 15 (January 9, 1954): 1.

31  March 15, 1955, Memorandum to H. R. Stewart from Robert Bittner, Federal Trade Commission Archives, RG 122, Box 245, National Archives and Record Administration, College Park, MD (hereafter cited as FTC archives, NARA).

32  Undated Memorandum from Howard J. Taylor to Pfizer leadership (among them H. R. Stewart), RG 122, Box 245, FTC archives, NARA.

33  December 26, 1951, Interoffice Correspondence to main office of Lederle from T. B. Van Stone re Terramycin Comic Strip in Bert Thomas, "Wylde and Wooly," *Southern Democrat*, Oneonta, Alabama, September 20, 1951, Box 20, Folder 1, Finland papers. The early 1950s also saw another new law, the 1951 Durham-Humphrey Amendment. This law set parameters for how decisions would be made with regard to how a drug would be sold. After the Harrison Narcotic Act of 1914, for example, all opiates needed a prescription from a physician. The 1938 Federal Food, Drug, and Cosmetic Act referenced, but did not define or set standards for deciding, which drugs needed a doctor's prescription and which could be purchased over the counter. Between the 1938 and 1951 statutes, considerable confusion ensued about how this determination would be made. For more on the law, see Harry M. Marks, "Revisiting 'The Origins of Compulsory Drug Prescriptions,'" *American Journal of Public Health* 85 (January 1995): 109–115; Jeremy A. Greene and Elizabeth Siegel Watkins, "Introduction: The Prescription in Perspective 1–23," in *Prescribed: Writing, Filling, Using, and Abusing the Prescription in Modern America*, ed. Jeremy A. Greene and Elizabeth Siegel Watkins (Baltimore: The Johns Hopkins University Press, 2012); Dominique A. Tobbell, "'Eroding the Physician's Control of Therapy': The Postwar Politics of the Prescription," in Tobbell, *Prescribed*, 91–117, and John P. Swann, "FDA and the Practice of Pharmacy: Prescription Drug Regulation before the Durham-Humphrey Act of 1951," *Pharmacy in History* 36 (1994): 55–70.

34  Lederle (pharmaceutical branch of American Cyanamid) District Manager's Weekly Report, August 19, 1955, RG 122, Box 254, FTC archives, NARA.

35  The Squibb tetracycline also added an antifungal antibiotic because antibiotic treatment sometimes resulted in fungal infections. "Dear Doctor" letter from C. B. Richardson of Squibb, July 6, 1956, Box 254, FTC archives, NARA.

36  See, for example, advertisement for E. R. Squibb, *Parents Magazine* 24, no. 1 (1949): 98. The Wheeler-Lea Act, enacted just after the 1938 Federal Food, Drug, and Cosmetic Act, gave the Federal Trade Commission (FTC) the authority to police advertising. Advertisements in medical journals were permitted because regulators deemed physicians less susceptible to advertising claims. Julie Donohue, "A History of Drug Advertising: The Evolving Roles of Consumers and Consumer Protection," *Milbank Quarterly* 84 (December 2006): 659–699.

37  On the use of children as a Cold War weapon, see Margaret Peacock, *Innocent Weapons: The Soviet and American Politics of Childhood in the Cold War* (Chapel Hill: University of North Carolina Press, 2014), 3. On the history of advertising in this era through the lenses of race, class, and gender, see Kathy Peiss, *Hope in a Jar: The Making of America's Beauty Culture* (New York: Metropolitan Books, Henry Holt, 1998); Jason Chambers, *Madison Avenue and the Color Line: African Americans in the Advertising Industry* (Philadelphia: University of Pennsylvania Press, 2009); Lizabeth Cohen, *A Consumers' Republic: The Politics of Mass Consumption in Postwar America* (New York: Vintage Books, 2003); Nancy Tomes, *Remaking the American Patient: How Madison Avenue and Modern Medicine Turned Patients into Consumers* (Chapel Hill: University of North Carolina Press, 2016).

38  Advertisement, Parke-Davis, *Life* 10 (March 5, 1956): 29.

39  No Author, *The Story of Parke-Davis, 1886–1966* (Detroit: Parke-Davis, 1966), 69; American Institute of the History of Pharmacy, Madison, Wisconsin, Annual Report for 1954 (Syracuse, NY: Bristol Myers, 1954), 14–16.

40  "The National Council on Infant and Child Care, Inc, Code for Advertising" August 13, 1956, FDA History Office, White Oak, Maryland (hereafter cited as FDA History Office); see also "National Council on Infant and Child Care," *New England Journal of Medicine* 295 (October 25, 1956): 827.

41  Quote from Leslie A. Falk, [Letter], "Will Penicillin Be Used Indiscriminately?" *JAMA* 127, no. 11 (March 17, 1945): 672; see also Herman Goodman [Letter], "Will Penicillin Be Used Indiscriminately?" 672.

42  Editorial, "Antibiotics-Whither?" *Journal of Pediatrics* 39 (November 1951): 641–643.

43  Isaac Arthur Abt, *Baby Doctor* (New York: McGraw Hill, 1944), 16–17, 29.

44  Harry Bakwin, "Common Errors in Pediatric Practice," *New York State Journal of Medicine* 49 (February 1949): 391–396; quote page 396. John Craig is a Discussant at the end of the article.

45  James C. Whorton, "Antibiotic Abandon: The Resurgence of Therapeutic Rationalism," In *The History of Antibiotics: A Symposium*, ed. John Parascandola (Madison, WI: American Institute of the History of Pharmacy, 1980), 125–136, quote page 129.

46  Hattie Alexander, Untitled Lecture, "The Problem of Microbial Resistance to Chemotherapeutic Agents," March 25, 1948, Series III, "Lectures," 7, Box 2, Folder 8, Hattie Alexander Papers, Archives and Special Collections, Columbia University Health Sciences Library, Columbia University, New York.

47  Milton J. E. Senn, "It's the Doctor's Job: Let Him Do It," *Woman's Home Companion* 80 (February 1953): 112–113.

48  Milton Markowitz, AAP Oral History Collection, Interviewed by Howard A. Pearson, July 17, 1988, 20, AAP archives.

49  Ibid.

50  Ibid.

51  Lloyd Miller Notes (undated but included with materials from 1952), MSS 149, MAD 4/27/D1-F7 Box 149, Folder 8, U.S. Pharmacopeial Convention Records, Wisconsin Historical Society, Library-Archives Division, Madison (hereafter cited as USP archives).

52  John L. Harvey, Associate Commissioner FDA, to Lloyd C. Miller, October 8, 1953, Box 149 Folder 8, USP archives.

53  William T. Alter to Philip C. Jeans, December 5, 1950, Box 175 Folder 1, USP archives.

54 Jeans was also well known for his research on malnutrition and vitamin deficiency. Genevieve Stearns, "Philip Charles Jeans," *Journal of Nutrition* 64 (January 1958): 1–12; Anonymous eulogy of Philip C. Jeans, December 16, 1952, Box 175, Folder 1, USP records; Jeffrey P. Baker and Howard A. Pearson, *Dedicated to the Health of All Children: 75 Years of Caring, 1930–2005* (Elk Grove Village IL: American Academy of Pediatrics, 2004), 20–21.

55 Other members included Henry L. Barnett of Cornell University; Erling Platou of the University of Minnesota, Alexis F. Hartman of Washington University, and Harry C. Shirkey of the University of Cincinnati. Philip C. Jeans to William T. Salter, March 1, 1951, Box 175, Folder 1, USP archives.

56 Adley B. Nichols to Windsor C. Cutting, January 17, 1952, Box 149, Folder 8, Committee on Posology, USP archives. For uses of calcium chloride in this era, see Katharine Dodd, "Special Reviews: Hypocalcemic States," *Pediatrics* 2 (December 1948): 737–743.

57 Lloyd C. Miller to Harry Shirkey offering him the position, April 18, 1953; Shirkey acceptance to Miller, April 24, 1953, Box 175, Folder 1, USP archives.

58 The CV Shirkey attached to the letter sent to Miller on April 24, 1953, indicated that he was also an associate professor at Cincinnati College of Pharmacy. Harry C. Shirkey CV, Box 175, Folder 1, USP archives. Shirkey's mentor Ashley Weeks had been asked by Jeans to join. He delegated the assignment to his mentee Shirkey. Oral History of Harry C. Shirkey by William Gerhardt, 1988, Heritage Series Oral History Collection, Pratt History Library, Children's Hospital Medical Center, Cincinnati, Ohio.

59 Miller to Shirkey, October 13, 1953, Box 149 Folder 8, USP archives.

60 Ibid.

61 Lloyd Miller's handwritten notes of a meeting with USP president Windsor Cutting, October 24, 1953, Box 149, Folder 8, USP archives.

62 Ibid.

63 Ibid.

64 Harry C. Shirkey to Windsor C. Cutting, August 31, 1953, Box 149, Folder 8, USP archives.

65 Lloyd C. Miller to Harry Shirkey, October 14, 1953, Box 149, Folder 8, USP archives.

66 Morris A. Wessel, John C. Cobb, Edith B. Jackson, George S. Harris, and Ann C. Detwiler, "Paroxysmal Fussing in Infancy, Sometimes Called 'Colic,'" *Pediatrics* 14 (November 1954): 421–435. M. B. Emanuel, "Histamine and the Antiallergic Antihistamines: A History of Their Discoveries," *Clinical and Experimental Allergy* Supplement 3 (July 29, 1999): 1–12.

67 Shirkey was interested in body surface area, which he and others thought might be a more precise metric than weight or certainly age. Harry C. Shirkey to Lloyd C. Miller, January 22, 1957, Box 175, Folder 1, USP archives.

68 Harry C. Shirkey and William P. Barba, II, "Drug Therapy," in *Textbook of Pediatrics*, ed. Waldo E. Nelson, 7th edition (Philadelphia: W. B. Saunders, 1959): 205–227.

69 A. J. Thompson, Manager of Standards and Analytical Research, Merck to Lloyd C. Miller, April 29, 1958, Box 175, Folder 1, USP archives.

70 Shirkey to Miller, June 4, 1958, Box 175, Folder 1, USP archives.

71 Ibid.

72 Shirkey to Miller, June 10, 1958, Box 175, Folder 1, USP archives.

73 Ibid.

74 Ibid.

75 The AMA renamed its Council on Pharmacy and Chemistry the Council on Drugs in the mid-1950s. "A.M.A. Council and Publication Renamed," *JAMA* 163 no. 8 (February 1957): 649–650.

76 For discussion of development of attempts to develop rational therapeutics in this era, see Podolsky, *Antibiotic Era*, 61–64; Harry Marks, *The Progress of Experiment: Science and Therapeutic Reform in the United States, 1900–1990* (Cambridge: Cambridge University Press, 1997), 136–163.

77 Edwards A. Park Collection, Series I Correspondence 1920–1939, Box 1, Folder 3, Calco Chemical; Box 8, Folder 8, Eli Lilly; Box 11, Folder 11 (Pfizer). Alan Mason Chesney Medical Archives of the Johns Hopkins Medical Institutions, Baltimore, Maryland.

78 For more on clinical trial research in the interwar period see Joseph M. Gabriel, "The Testing of Sanocrysin: Science, Profit, and Innovation in Clinical Trial Design, 1926–1931," *Journal of the History of Medicine and Allied Sciences* 69 (October 2014): 604–632; Marks, *The Progress of Experiment*, 42–70; For the development of academic and industry partnerships during the interwar period, see John Swann, *Academic Scientists and the Pharmaceutical Industry: Cooperative Research in Twentieth-Century America* (Baltimore: The Johns Hopkins University Press, 1988), 24–56; Nicolas Rasmussen, "The Drug Industry and Clinical Research in Interwar America: Three Types of Physician Collaborator," *Bulletin of the History of Medicine* 79 (Spring 2005): 50–80; John Parascandola, *The Development of American Pharmacology: John J. Abel and the Shaping of a Discipline* (Baltimore: The Johns Hopkins University Press, 1992), 91–125; Jeffrey L. Furman and Megan J. MacGarvie, "Academic Science and the Birth of Industrial Research Laboratories in the U.S. Pharmaceutical Industry," *Journal of Economic Behavior and Organization* 63 (August 2007): 756–776; Tobbell, *Pills, Power, and Policy*, 8, 38, 54.

79 For letters between Hodes and industry representatives, see "Bicillin-Correspondence, Research Material, 1952–1954," Series I Medical Subject Files, 1930–1983, Box 1, Folder 2, Horace L. Hodes Papers, Mount Sinai Archives, Gustave L. and Janet W. Levy Library, Icahn School of Medicine at Mount Sinai, New York (hereafter cited as Hodes papers). For more on Hodes's career, see Joan Cook, "Horace Hodes, a Pediatrician, 81; Linked Virus to Gastroenteritis," *New York Times*, April 25, 1989; Helen B. Taussig, "Horace L. Hodes—The Man," *Journal of Pediatrics* 87 (December 1975): 1057–1061, 1930–1983.

80 Wyeth Director of Clinical Investigation Edward F. Roberts MD to Horace L. Hodes, July 10, 14, 1952, Box 1, Folder 2, Hodes papers.

81 On children with disabilities in the postwar era and the issues families faced, see Allison C. Carey, "Citizenship and the Family: Parents of Children with Disabilities, the Pursuit of Rights, and Paternalism," in *Civil Disabilities: Citizenship, Membership, and Belonging*, ed. Nancy J. Hirschmann and Beth Linker (Philadelphia: University of Pennsylvania Press, 2015), 165–186; Kathleen W. Jones, "Education for Children with Mental Retardation: Public Policy and Family Ideology in the 1950s," in *Mental Retardation in America: A Historical Reader*, ed. Steven Noll and James Trent (New York: New York University Press, 2004), 322–350; Diane B. Paul and Jeffrey P. Brosco, *The PKU Paradox: A Short History of a Genetic Disease* (Baltimore: The Johns Hopkins University Press, 2013); Keith Wailoo and Stephen Pemberton, *The Troubled Dream of Genetic Medicine: Ethnicity and Innovation in*

*Tay-Sachs, Cystic Fibrosis, and Sickle Cell Disease* (Baltimore: The Johns Hopkins University Press, 2004).

82  Undated manuscript (but referencing the year 1952 in the manuscript), "Gonococcal Ophthalmia," Box 1, Folder 43, Hodes papers.

83  Susan E. Lederer, *Subjected to Science: Human Experimentation in America before the Second World War* (Baltimore: The Johns Hopkins University Press, 1995), 103–108; Sydney A. Halpern, *Lesser Harms: The Morality of Risk in Medical Research* (Chicago: University of Chicago Press, 2004). For more on medical research in this era see Robert Baker, *Before Bioethics: A History of American Medical Ethics from the Colonial Period to the Bioethics Revolution* (New York, Oxford University Press, 2013), 232–274, 274–319, and David J. Rothman, *Strangers at the Bedside: A History of How Law and Bioethics Transformed Medical Decision Making* (New York: Basic Books, 1991), 38–39.

84  Rothman, *Strangers at the Bedside*, 62; Susan E. Lederer and Michael A. Grodin, "Historical Overview: Pediatric Experimentation," in *Children as Research Subjects: Science, Ethics, and the Law*, ed. Michael A. Grodin and Leonard H. Glantz (New York: Oxford University Press, 1994), 3–29. Moreover, just as in earlier eras, if physicians thought a drug held promise, they often employed it first on their own children—as Harvard pediatrician Thomas Cone did when he fought to get penicillin during World War II for his sick child. These physicians would hardly have done so if they did not believe the potential benefit justified the risk. Thomas E. Cone oral history, interviewed by Howard A. Pearson, July 17, 1996, American Academy of Pediatrics Oral History Collection, Elk Grove Village, IL, quote page 42 (hereafter cited as AAP Oral History Collection). Another prominent researcher in this era who experimented on his own children was Jonas Salk, Charlotte DeCroes Jacobs, *Jonas Salk: A Life* (Oxford: Oxford University Press, 2015), 220.

85  For an overview of the introduction of steroids, see Harry Marks, "Cortisone, 1949: A Year in the Political Life of a Drug," *Bulletin of the History of Medicine* 66, no. 3 (1992): 419–440.

86  William A Silverman, MD, interviewed by Lawrence M. Gartner, MD, June 10, 1997, AAP Oral History Collection, 11.

87  Ibid.

88  Ibid.

89  Ibid.

90  Ibid.

91  Ibid., 12.

92  Silverman Oral History, 12–13. The grouping together of babies into neonatal intensive care units (NICUs) created cohorts of babies available for experimentation and physicians and nurses together. Jeffrey P. Baker, *The Machine in the Nursery: Incubator Technology and the Origins of Newborn Intensive Care* (Baltimore: The Johns Hopkins University Press, 1996). For nursing's role in their development, see Briana Ralston, "We Were the Eyes and Ears: Nursing and the Development of Neonatal Intensive Care Units in the United States, 1955–1982" (PhD Dissertation, 2015, University of Pennsylvania).

93  Julius B. Richmond, Harvey Kravitz, and William E. Segar, "Sulfonamide Dosage in Early Infancy," *Journal of Pediatrics* 36 (May 1950): 539–549.

94  Samuel O. Sapin, Ephraim Donoso, and Sidney Blumenthal, "Digoxin Dosage in Infants," *Pediatrics* 18 (November 1956): 730–738.

95  On dosing and digoxin, see Gold to Robert F. Ziegler of the Cardiac Clinic at Harriet Lane Home, Harry Gold, MD (1899–1972), March 10, 1947, Papers, Box 12, Folder 9, Medical Center Archives of New York-Presbyterian/Weill Cornell, New York.

96  Sapin, Donoso, and Blumenthal, "Digoxin Dosage."

97  Lederer, *Subjected to Science*, 70–106. For more on the context of research ethics discussion in the 1950s, see Susan E. Lederer, "Research Without Borders: The Origins of the Declaration of Helsinki," in *History and Ethics of Human Experimentation: The Twisted Road to Helsinki*, ed. Ulf Schmidt and Andreas Frewer (Stuttgart: Franz Steiner, 2007), 145–164.

98  Joel D. Howell and Rodney A. Hayward, "Writing Willowbrook, Reading Willowbrook: The Recounting of an Experiment," in *Useful Bodies: Humans in the Service of Medical Science in the Twentieth Century*, ed. Jordan Goodman, Anthony McElligott, and Lara Marks (Baltimore: The Johns Hopkins University Press, 2003), 190–213; David J. Rothman, "Were Tuskegee and Willowbrook 'Studies in Nature?'" *Hastings Center Report* 12 (April 1982): 5–7; David J. Rothman and Sheila M. Rothman, *The Willowbrook Wars* (New York: Harper and Row, 1984). See also Saul Krugman, "The Willowbrook Hepatitis Studies Revisited: Ethical Aspects," *Reviews of Infectious Diseases* 8 (January–February 1986): 157–162.

99  Elmer H. Loughlin, Louverture Alcindor, and Aurele A. Joseph, "Extended Low Level Dosage of Terramycin," Fifth Antibiotic Symposium, October 2–4 1957, RG 88 File 512 (Antibiotics) Box 2890, FDA archives, National Archives and Record Administration, College Park, Maryland (hereafter cited as FDA archives, NARA). For a history of adding antibiotics to animal feed to stimulate growth and increase profits, see W. Boyd, "Making Meat: Science, Technology, and American Meat Production," *Technology and Culture* 42, no. 4 (2001): 631–664. And their research was no secret. For a celebratory article about the research published in a Haiti newspaper, see "Haiti Experiment in Tropical Malnutrition Produces a New Approach," *Haiti Sun*, February 23, 1958. On international discussions about research during this era, see Lederer, "Research Without Borders."

100 Loughlin, Alcindor, and Joseph, "Extended Low Level Dosage."

101 Sidney Farber, Louis K. Diamond, Robert D. Mercer, Robert F. Sylvester, Jr., and James A. Wolff, "Temporary Remissions in Acute Leukemia in Children Produced by Folic Acid Antagonist, 4-Aminopteroyl-Glutamic Acid (Aminopterin)," *New England Journal of Medicine 238* (June 1948): 787–793. For more on the history of children's cancer, especially leukemia, see Gretchen Krueger, *Hope and Suffering: Children, Cancer, and the Paradox of Experimental Medicine (*Baltimore, The Johns Hopkins University Press, 2008). For discussions regarding the industry, FDA, academic partnership by participants, see *First Session on the Causes, Control, and Remedies of the Principal Diseases of Mankind: Hearings before the Committee on Interstate and Foreign Commerce, House of Representatives 83rd Congress*, Part I (October 1, 2, 3, 1953) (Washington, DC: GPO), 96, 251, 3.

102 Quote from Emil J. Freireich Oral History, interviewed by Lesley W. Brunet, July 23, 30, August 13, 2001, History of Cancer Collections, MD Anderson Special Collections, Research Medical Library, University of Texas MD Anderson Cancer Center, Houston. For one cancer hospital's developing pediatric research program see MD Anderson's annual *Research Reports*, 1955–1970, located at History of Cancer Collections, MD Anderson Special Collections.

103 Maeder, *Adverse Reactions*, 116–117.

104 Ibid., 190.

105 Ibid., 115–118.

106 Ibid., 26.

107 Ibid., 19–45. For an example of one FDA investigator's report, see William T. Robinson report from January 19, 1954, about the death of an Ohio infant from chloramphenicol, RG 88, File Number 512.103, Box 2891, FDA archives, NARA.

108 Lincoln E. Wilson, M. S. Harris, H. H. Henstell, O. O. Witherbee, and Julius Kahn, "Aplastic Anemia Following Prolonged Administration of Chloramphenicol: Report of Two Cases, One Fatality," *JAMA* 149, no. 3 (1952): 231–234.

109 Marvin Miles, "Antibiotics Studied as Cause of Anemia: Death of La Canada Doctor's Son Brings Scrutiny of 'Wonder Drug,'" *Los Angeles Times*, May 28, 1952, A1; on nuclear testing in the United States during these years, see *United States Nuclear Tests July 1945 through September 1992 DOE/NV–209-REV*, December 15, 2000, U.S. Department of Energy Nevada Operations Office, accessed January 24, 2016, available electronically at http://www.doe.gov.bridge.

110 An appalled Mrs. J.N.R. (full name abbreviated for privacy purposes) of Lansing, Michigan, for example, wrote to FDA Commissioner George Larrick in February 1960, providing a list of deceased children in her town that she feared had received the drug for "minor infections," RG 88, File 512.103 (Chloromycetin)1960 Box 2891, FDA archives, NARA; for evidence that parental fears concerning chloramphenicol-related aplastic anemia reached policymakers, see *Administered Prices in the Drug Industry (Antibiotics): Hearings before the Subcommittee on Antitrust and Monopoly of the Committee on the Judiciary,* U.S. Senate, 86th Congress, 2nd Session (September 7, 1960), Part 24; Kefauver references, pp. 14044, 14045, concerning letters he received from parents whose children suffered from chloramphenicol-related aplastic anemia.

111 Lafayette E. Burns, Joan E. Hodgman, and Alonzo B. Cass, "Fatal Circulatory Collapse in Premature Infants Receiving Chloramphenicol," *New England Journal of Medicine* 261 (December 1959): 1318–1321.

112 Maeder, *Adverse Reactions*, 198–205.

113 Quote from ibid., 204.

114 Joan E. Hodgman, MD, interview by Lawrence M. Gartner, February 14, 2004, AAP Oral History Collection, 53–54.

115 For use of chloramphenicol in newborns and young infants in this era and its abrupt cessation at the Harriet Lane Home, see Edwards A. Park Papers, Series: Pediatric Diagnostic Index, 1920s–1950s, [Card division 433591662/51] Folder "Therapy, Chloromycetin," Alan Mason Chesney Medical Archives of the Johns Hopkins Medical Institutions, Baltimore, Maryland. It is not known whether the deaths in these files were related to the drug, from an underlying infectious disease for which the child was receiving the drug, or for some other reason.

116 Personal Conversation, John Swann PhD, FDA History Office, June 8, 2016.

117 Robert H. Moser, *Diseases of Medical Progress*, 2nd edition (Springfield, IL: Charles C. Thomas, 1964), 260–261; John E. Lesch, *The First Miracle Drugs: How the Sulfa Drugs Transformed Medicine* (New York: Oxford University Press, 2007), 276–277.

118 Letter to Maxwell Finland from Parke Davis and Company Research laboratories Anthony Glazko, September 14, 1960, Box 4 Folder 20, Finland papers.

119 Letter from Glazko to Rudi Schmid at Boston City Hospital, July 14, 1959, Box 4, Folder 20, Finland papers.

120 "Research Activities of the FDA Relating to Child Health," June 11, 1957; both items at FDA History Office.

121 Speech given by FDA Commissioner Paul S. Dunbar at Tulane University, February 5, 1958, revealed the limits of the FDA's authority specific to children. Dunbar emphasizes poison prevention and promoting broad public health measures. *The Child and the Law*, RG 88, Box 125, Acc 62a379, FDA archives, NARA.

122 Allan M. Butler and Robert H. Richie, "Simplification and Improvement in Estimating Drug Dosage and Fluid and Dietary Allowances for Patients of Varying Sizes," *New England Journal of Medicine* 262, no. 1 (May 1960): 903–908. For more on Butler's career, see Nathan B. Talbott, "Presentation of Howland Award to Allan M. Butler," *Pediatric Research* 3 (September 1969): 471–474 and obituary by Glenn Fowler, "Dr. Allan Butler, Pioneer in Health," *New York Times*, October 9, 1986.

123 "Pharmacy," *Boston Children's Hospital Annual Report for 1960*, Arthur Thompson, Chief Pharmacist, page 142, Children's Hospital Medical Center, Boston Children's Hospital Archives, Boston, Massachusetts.

124 For data on the decline of compounding, see Gregory J. Higby, "Evolution of Pharmacy," in *Remington: The Science and Practice of Pharmacy*, 21st edition, ed. Randy Hendrickson (Philadelphia: Lippincott, Williams & Wilkins, 2006), 7–20.

125 Thompson, "Pharmacy," 142.

126 Ibid., 143.

127 *Nursing Procedure Manual for 1958–1959*, Box 1, Folder 1, Department of Nursing Archival Collection, Children's Hospital Medical Center, Boston Children's Hospital Archives, Boston, Massachusetts.

128 Harry C. Shirkey to Robert W. Elkas (Assistant to Director of Revision, USP), May 26, 1959, Box 175, Folder 1, USP archives; Shirkey to Lloyd C. Miller, May 25, 1960, Box 175, Folder 1, USP archives.

129 Panel on Pediatrics, "Drug Evaluations," 1959–1960, p. 5, Box 175, Folder 2, USP archives.

130 Ibid., 9.

131 Ibid., 11.

132 Windsor Cutting, March 28, 1960, "The Pharmacopeia and the Physician," Box 160, Folder 1, USP archives.

133 AAP Executive Board Meeting Minutes, October 14, 1960, COD archives.

134 Harry Shirkey to Lloyd C. Miller, May 10, 1961, Box 175, Folder 1, USP archives.

135 William L. Nyhan, "Toxicity of Drugs in the Neonatal Period," *Journal of Pediatrics* 59 (July 1961): 1–20; quote page 16; "FDA's New Pediatric Look," 21.

136 "FDA's New Pediatric Look at Drug Uses & Doses May Result in 'Not for Pediatric Use' Labeling in Absence of Specific Work," *F-D-C Reports*, September 25, 1961, 21.

137 Ibid., 21.

138 Ibid., 22.

139 Ibid., 21.

140 "New Controls Proposed for Drug Industry," in *CQ Almanac 1961*, 17th edition, 290–92 (Washington, DC: Congressional Quarterly, 1961), accessed December 27, 2016, http://library.cqpress.com/cqalmanac/cqal61-1373191.

## Chapter 4  The Growth and Development of the Therapeutic Orphan, 1961–1979

1  Harry C. Shirkey to Lloyd C. Miller, May 10, 1961, Box 175, Folder 1, U.S. Pharmacopeial (USP) Convention Records, Wisconsin Historical Society, Madison, Wisconsin.

2  On birth rates during this era, see Robert D. Grove and Alice M. Hetzel, *Vital Statistics of the United States, 1940–1960* (Washington, DC: GPO, 1968), 20, 25, 778, 780; Steven Mintz, *Huck's Raft: A History of American Childhood* (Cambridge, MA: Belknap Press of Harvard University Press, 2004), 276; Paula S. Fass, "The Child-Centered Family? New Rules in Postwar America," in *Reinventing Childhood after World War II*, ed. Paula S. Fass and Michael Grossberg (Philadelphia: University of Pennsylvania Press, 2012), 11.

3  Gardner Murphy and Lois Barclay Murphy, "The Child as Potential," in *Golden Anniversary White House Conference on Children and Youth*, ed. Eli K. Ginzberg (New York: Columbia University Press, 1960), 107; Eli K. Ginzberg, *The Nation's Children*, 3 vols. (New York: Columbia University Press, 1960); George M. Wheatley, "The 1960 White House Conference on Children and Youth," *Pediatrics* 27 (February 1961): 337–339.

4  Tonse N. K. Raju, Robert Bock, and Duane Alexander, "Renaming of the National Institute of Child Health and Human Development in Honor of Mrs. Eunice Kennedy Shriver," *Pediatrics* 122 (October 2008): 948–949; The Birth of an Institute, accessed July 12, 2014, http://www.nichd.nih.gov/about/overview/history/.

5  "Annual Report for 1959," *Food and Drug Administration Annual Reports, 1950–1974* (Washington, DC: GPO, 1976), 193.

6  Paul de Haen, "New Products Parade," *Drug and Cosmetic Industry* 90 (1962): 141–142. For growing concerns about the issue of drug costs, see "Big Pill to Swallow: The Wonder-Drug Makers Get Handsome Profits from Their Captive Consumers," *Life* 48 (February 1960): 97–104; "Annual Report for 1961," *Food and Drug Administration Annual Reports, 1950–1974* (Washington, DC: GPO, 1976), 294.

7  Sydney Mathes, Harry Gold, Raymond Marsh, Theodore Greiner, Frank Palumbo, and Charles Messeloff, "Comparison of the Tolerance of Adults and Children to Digitoxin," *JAMA* 150, no. 3 (September 1952): 191–194. See also "All NDAs with Pediatric Implications Routed to New Dr. Nestor," *F-D-C Reports,* September 25, 1961, 21–22.

8  The effort to think about dosing in preemies and newborns in the post–"gray baby" world was one of many supported by infant formula giant Ross Laboratories at a conference held on November 16 and 17, 1961, and published in *Forty-First Conference on Pediatric Research: Ross Conference on Perinatal Pharmacology* (Columbus, OH: Ross, 1962). On the history of the Ross conferences, see Dewey A. Sehring, "Continuing Physician Education: The Ross Conference Approach," *American Journal of Clinical Nutrition* 46 (July 1987): 192–197.

9  Committee on the Fetus and Newborn, "Effect of Drugs upon the Fetus and the Infant," *Pediatrics* 28 (October 1961): 678.

10  Richard E. McFadyen, "Thalidomide in America: A Brush with Tragedy," *Clio Medica* 11, no. 2 (1976): 79–93; Scott H. Podolsky, *The Antibiotic Era: Reform, Resistance, and the Pursuit of a Rational Therapeutics* (Baltimore: The Johns Hopkins University Press, 2015), 73.

11  Kelsey was born in British Columbia in 1914. She earned a PhD in pharmacology and an MD from the University of Chicago. During World War II she studied antimalarial drugs and observed that quinines crossed the placental barrier and affected fetuses differently from adults. She accepted a job at the FDA when she accompanied her husband, also a pharmacologist, to Washington in 1960 when he was offered a post at the NIH, accessed January 5, 2017, http://www.nlm.nih.gov/changingthefaceofmedicine/physicians/biography_182.html; McFadyen, "Thalidomide in America."

12  Morton Mintz, "Heroine of the FDA Keeps Bad Drug Off of Market," *Washington Post*, July 15, 1962; John Mulliken, "A Woman Doctor Who Would Not Be Hurried," *Life* 10 (August 1962): 28–29; Linda Bren, "Frances Oldham Kelsey: FDA Medical Reviewer Leaves Her Mark on History," *FDA Consumer* (March–April 2001): 24–29; John Lear, "Doctor Frances Kelsey's Struggle against Thalidomide as Described in a Memo from FDA's Official Files," *Saturday Review* 45 (1962): 36–37.

13  Daniel Carpenter, *Reputation and Power: Organizational Image and Regulation at the FDA* (Princeton, NJ: Princeton University Press, 2010), 213–226, 240–251. By 1962 thalidomide had been removed from use in Germany because of its link to birth defects, although this had not yet been reported in the American press. Taussig graduated from the Johns Hopkins University Medical School in 1927. In 1930 she was named director of the Harriett Lane Home Cardiac Clinic. By the time of the thalidomide scandal she was internationally renowned for co-developing a surgical treatment for a deadly heart defect, Tetralogy of Fallot, with Alfred Blalock in 1945. For an overview of her German trip, see Helen B. Taussig Oral History, interviewed by Charles A. Janeway, September 15, 1976, History of Medicine Division, National Library of Medicine, Bethesda, Maryland, 39–47 (hereafter cited as Taussig Oral History), 74. For more on Taussig's life and career, see Ellen S. More, *Restoring the Balance: Women Physicians and the Profession of Medicine 1850–1995* (Cambridge, MA: Harvard University Press, 2009), 178–179.

14  Memorandum of Conference, Helen Taussig, Frances O. Kelsey, and John Nestor, April 6, 1962, Frances Oldham Kelsey papers, Box 34, Folder 6, Library of Congress, Washington, DC (hereafter cited as Kelsey papers); Frances O. Kelsey, "Thalidomide Update: Regulatory Aspects," *Teratology* 38 (September 1988): 221–226; McFadyen, "Thalidomide in America," 79–93.

15  *Drug Industry Antitrust Act: Hearings before the Antitrust Subcommittee (Subcommittee No. 5) of the Committee on the Judiciary*, House of Representatives, 87th Congress, 2nd Session, on *H.R. 6245, A Bill to Amend and Supplement the Antitrust Laws with Respect to the Manufacture and Distribution of Drugs and for Other Purposes* (May 17, 18, 23, 24, 1962) (testimony by Helen B. Taussig) (Washington, DC: GPO 1962), 417–442.

16  "Dear Doctor" template for a letter generated by Taussig and sent to leading pediatricians to build support for pediatric drug-related legislation, June 26, 1962, Box 62, Folder 7, Helen B. Taussig Collection, The Alan Mason Chesney Medical Archives of The Johns Hopkins Medical Institutions, Baltimore, Maryland (hereafter cited as Taussig Collection).

17  Philip S. Barba to Helen B. Taussig, July 18, 1962, Box 62 Folder 7, Taussig Collection. For more on American medicine in the 1950s and early 1960s and the fears of socialized medicine, see Rosemary Stevens, *American Medicine and the Public Interest: A History of Specialization* (New Haven, CT: Yale University Press, 1971).

18 Letter, Morris Fishbein, to *New York Times*, May 12, 1962, 22. For more on Fishbein, see Jonathan Engel, *Doctors and Reformers: Discussion and Debate over Health Policy 1925–1950* (Charleston: University of South Carolina Press, 2002), 291–295.

19 Ibid.

20 Helen B. Taussig, "Dangerous Tranquility: Congenital Malformations," *Science* 136 (May 25, 1962): 683; Helen B. Taussig, "Thalidomide Syndrome," *Scientific American* 207 (August 1962): 29–33. Boxes 34 and 35 of Taussig's papers contain material concerning her television appearances. On her efforts to generate media support, see, for example, Taussig to Norman Cousins (editor of *Saturday Review*), July 18, 1962, Box 62, Folder 13, Taussig Collection. For evidence of her work with Kefauver's committee, see Taussig Oral History, page 46. For other drug-related political work in this era, see Hubert Humphrey, Subcommittee Chair on Government Operations for the Senate to Helen Taussig, October 3, 1962, Box 62, Folder 8, Taussig Collection. Box 62, Folder 17, holds other letters between Taussig and Humphrey.

21 *Drug Industry Antitrust Act: Hearings before the Antitrust Subcommittee*, Taussig testimony, 418.

22 Ibid., 419.

23 Ralph Smith Presentation at the National Meeting of the Drug and Allied Products Guild, Inc., at Ellenville, New York, June 14, 1962, quote page 8, FDA History Office, White Oak Campus, Silver Spring, Maryland (hereafter cited as FDA History Office).

24 *Interagency Coordination in Drug Research and Regulation: Hearings before the Subcommittee on Reorganization and International Organizations of the Committee on Government Operations, Agency Coordination Study: Review of Cooperation on Drug Policies Among Food and Drug Administration, National Institutes of Health, Veterans' Administration, and Other Agencies Part 1*, 87th Congress, 2nd Session (hereafter *Agency Coordination Study*) (August 1, 9, 1962) (Washington, DC: GPO, 1962), 229.

25 For years Kelsey received letters from women, thanking her and confiding in her about drug- and health-related issues. Letters for the years 1963–1967 in Box 1, Folders 2, 4, and 8 The thalidomide controversy and lawsuits would continue for decades. It was ultimately estimated that the drug maimed 20,000 and killed 80,000 fetuses. Although the criminal trials of Chemie-Grunenthal, the German company that created and marketed thalidomide beginning in 1957 under the name Contergan, came to an end in 1970, a large number of documents discovered in 2014 revealed secret meetings in 1969 between the company and the German federal health ministry. These materials reveal behind the scenes deal making that disadvantaged thalidomide-afflicted children and their families. They also document a more fulsome account of high level Nazis who served on the Board. Harold Evans, "Thalidomide: How Men Who Blighted Lives of Thousands Evaded Justice," accessed November 14, 2014, http://www.theguardian.com/society/2014/nov/14/-sp-thalidomide-pill-how-evaded-justice.

26 House of Representatives, Report no. 2526, *Drug Amendments of 1962*, October 2, 1962, 87th Congress, 2nd Session, 3.

27 "Memorandum to the Executive Board from the Committee on Drug Dosage and Cooperating Organizations," October 28, 1962, Committee on Drugs records, Pediatric History Center, American Academy of Pediatrics, Elk Grove Village, Illinois (hereafter cited as COD archives); reprinted in *Agency Coordination Study,*

*Part 4*, 88th Congress, 1st Session (March 21, 1963) (Washington, DC: GPO, 1964), 1356–1357.

28 Ibid., 1706; a sampling of responses to Humphrey's query letter are included in the transcripts on pages 1708–1726.

29 Ibid., 1729; letter of 3/12/63, Humphrey to Luther Terry.

30 Ibid.

31 *Agency Coordination Study, Part 3*, 88th Congress, 1st Session (March 20, 1963) (Washington, DC: GPO, 1963), 782; undated letter from Nestor to Humphrey outlining what he would say is Reprinted in Committee on Government Operations, *Agency Coordination Study, Part 4*, 1706–1707.

32 *Agency Coordination Study, Part 3*, 783.

33 Ibid., 783.

34 Ibid.

35 Ibid., 783–784

36 Ibid., 784.

37 Charles D. May testimony, Committee on Government Operations, *Agency Coordination Study: Part 3*, 1031; Charles D. May written comments to Humphrey (undated); reprinted in *Agency Coordination Study, Part 4*, 1708.

38 *Agency Coordination Study, Part 3*, "Statements by the Commissioner of Food and Drugs Regarding Charges Made by John O. Nestor M.D," 1018–1020; "Initial Comments by Senator Hubert H. Humphrey Responding to Statement of March 20, 1963, by Food and Drug Administration on Testimony of Dr. Nestor: Initial Rebuttal to the Rebuttal," 1020–1021; subsequent letters, 1021–1024. There is also a more formally crafted FDA response to Nestor's testimony in the record "Observations of the Food and Drug Administration on Testimony Presented to the Subcommittee on Government Operations, U.S. Senate, on March 20, 1963," 1024–1028.

39 *Agency Coordination Study, Part 4*, 1322–1356.

40 Ibid., 1355.

41 Ibid., 1343, 1345; Norman Kretchmer, "Primum Non Nocere," *Pediatrics* 30 (October 1962): 513–515.

42 Ibid., 1354.

43 Ibid.

44 Letter to Humphrey from Stuart M. Sessoms, Deputy Director, NIH, dated February 27, 1963, *Agency Coordination Study, Part 4*, 1703.

45 Letter writer's name is withheld; letter, March 29, 1963, *Agency Coordination Study: Part 3*, 1242.

46 Ibid.

47 Harry C. Shirkey Oral History, interview by William Gerhardt, 1988, Heritage Series Oral History Collection, Children's Hospital Medical center, Cincinnati, Ohio (hereafter cited as Shirkey Oral History).

48 Ibid. Shirkey details his FDA consultations to the FDA in a letter to Robert G. Frazier, Secretary AAP, December 28, 1964, COD archives.

49 Robert G. Frazier, Secretary AAP to Shirkey, November 21, 1963; see also COD meeting minutes October 1963, both in COD archives.

50 Shirkey Oral History. "FDA's New Pediatric Look at Drug Uses & Doses May Result in 'Not for Pediatric Use' Labeling in Absence of Specific Work," *F-D-C Reports*, September 25, 1961, 21.

51 Shirkey Oral History. According to pharmacologist and scientist Edward G. Feldmann, the term therapeutic orphan was coined in late 1963 or early 1964

when Feldmann was Director, Scientific Division, American Pharmaceutical Association and worked closely with Shirkey on the problem of pediatric dosing. The phrase was deliberately designed to be provocative and to capture attention. Personal communication with Edward G. Feldmann by author, February 7, 2011. The first published reference to the therapeutic orphan can be found in Harry C. Shirkey, *Preface to Dosage-Posology Handbook: Usual Doses for Infants and Children* (Washington, DC: American Pharmaceutical Association, 1965), 6.

52  B. Harvey Minchew, "Pediatric Dosage Labeling," Memorandum of Meeting, November 9, 1965. The AMA Council on Drugs enacted a resolution in May 1964 requesting that manufacturers include pediatric dosing information. This resolution is described in Joseph F. Sadusk, Jr., MD, to J. F. Palmer, MD, November 2, 1965, both items in Box 11, Folder "Medical Advisory Board Fifth Meeting, FDA Agenda for December 14 and 15, 1965," Wesley W. Spink papers, University Archives, University of Minnesota, Minneapolis.

53  On Shirkey's concerns, see COD Minutes, December 2, 1966, COD archives.

54  There is little emphasis on specific pediatric issues in the surviving DESI records, Drug Efficacy Study of the National Research Council's Division of Medical Sciences, National Academies Archives Collection, Washington, DC. One DESI participant, Edward G. Feldmann, does not recall any discussion of pediatric issues; personal communication February 7, 2011. On the DESI initiative, see Dominique A. Tobbell, "Allied Against Reform: Pharmaceutical Industry–Academic Physician Relations in the United States, 1945–1970," *Bulletin of the History of Medicine* 82, no. 4 (2008): 878–912; Carpenter, *Reputation and Power*, 351–355.

55  The monthly COD Minutes document variants of these questions were raised repeatedly between 1964 and the late 1960s; see, for example, Minutes, December 2, 1966, COD archives. On NICHD, see Memorandum, Betty Barton to Donald Harting, July 9, 1965, Record Group 443, Office of the NIH Director, Box 104, National Archives and Records Administration, College Park, Maryland (hereafter cited as NARA)

56  Arthur Eidelman, Letter to the Executive Director, American Academy of Pediatrics, *Pediatrics* 17 (January 1966): 138–139.

57  Ibid.

58  Ibid.

59  Clement A. Smith, "Editor's Reply," *Pediatrics* 17 (January 1966): 139.

60  Ibid.

61  Susan E. Lederer, "Research without Borders: The Origins of the Declaration of Helsinki," in *History and Theory of Human Experimentation: The Declaration of Helsinki and Modern Medical Ethics*, ed. Ulf Schmidt and Andreas Frewer (Stuttgart: Franz Verlag, 2007), 145–164. Lainie Friedman Ross, "Children in Medical Research: Balancing Protection and Access: Has the Pendulum Swung Too Far?" *Perspectives in Biology and Medicine* 47, no. 4 (2004): 519–536.

62  "Statement of Investigator," FDA Form FD 1573, Box 1, Folder 69, "Lincomycin-Correspondence, Research Material, 1964," Horace L. Hodes, Papers, Mount Sinai Archives, Gustave L. and Janet W. Levy Library, Icahn School of Medicine at Mount Sinai, New York, New York (hereafter cited as Hodes papers).

63  Rosemary Stevens, *American Medicine and the Public Interest: A History of Specialization*, 2nd edition (Berkeley: University of California Press, 1998), 437–443, 473–479.

64 Henry K. Beecher "Ethics and Clinical Research," *New England Journal of Medicine* 274 (June 1966): 1354–1360.

65 Howard E. Ticktin and Hyman J. Zimmerman, "Hepatic Dysfunction and Jaundice in Patients Receiving Triacetyloleandomycin," *New England Journal of Medicine* 267 (November 1962): 964–968, quote page 964.

66 Ibid.

67 For historical discussions of the work and impact of Beecher, see Susan E. Lederer and Michael A. Grodin, "Historical Overview: Pediatric Experimentation," in *Children as Research Subjects: Science, Ethics, and the Law*, ed. Michael A. Grodin and Leonard H. Glantz (New York: Oxford University Press, 1994), 3–29; Lainie Friedman Ross, *Children in Medical Research: Access versus Protection* (New York: Oxford University Press, 2006), 4–15; David J. Rothman, *Strangers at the Bedside: A History of How Law and Bioethics Transformed Medical Decision Making*, 2nd edition (New York: de Gruyter, 2003), 70–84. Rothman identifies the studies on 273–274. Beecher's 22 studies were culled from a much larger number; David S. Jones, Christine Grady, and Susan E. Lederer, "'Ethics and Clinical Research': The 50th Anniversary of Beecher's Bombshell," *New England Journal of Medicine* 374, no. 24 (2016): 2393–2398.

68 Evan Charney to Henry K. Beecher, June 21, 1966. Along with his letter to Beecher he included his original letter to A. Ashley Weech dated October 8, 1963; both items in Box 30, Folder 2, Henry K. Beecher papers, 1848–1976, HMS c64, Harvard Medical Library, Francis A. Countway Library of Medicine, Boston, Massachusetts (hereafter cited as Beecher papers). The article Charney expressed concern about is D. A. Fisher, H. R. Pyle, J. C. Porter, A. G. Beard, and T. C. Panos, "Control of Water Balance in the Newborn," *American Journal of Diseases of Children* 106 (August 1963): 137–146. Weech was chief of staff at Cincinnati Children's Hospital in the 1940s and became Harry Shirkey's mentor. For more on his career, see Rustin McIntosh "Alexander Ashley Weech, An Appreciation," *American Journal of Diseases of Children* 105 (June 1963): 535–541.

69 A. Ashley Weech to Evan Charney, October 15, 1963, Box 30, Folder 2, Beecher papers.

70 Ibid.

71 A. Ashley Weech to Evan Charney, February 10, 1964, Box 30, Folder 2, Beecher papers.

72 Henry K. Beecher to Evan Charney, June 24, 1966, Box 30, Folder 2, Beecher papers.

73 Thomas Hayes to Hugh H. Hussey, January 18, 1967, "Trip Report: FDA Meeting Washington, DC, January 11, 1967," Box 27, Folder 7, "Council on Drugs, Meeting Agendas, May 1967," John Adriani papers, MS C 453, Modern Manuscripts Collection, History of Medicine Division, National Library of Medicine, Bethesda, Maryland (hereafter cited as Adriani papers).

74 Notes and drafts for *Pharmacological Basis of Therapeutics (PBOT)*; see Louis S. Goodman Papers, Accession 937. For 1965 *PBOT*, 3rd edition (London: Macmillan, 1965), Box 21, Folder 2; for 1970 *PBOT*, 4th edition (London: Macmillan, 1970), Box 31, Folder 3, Special Collections and Archives, University of Utah, J. Willard Marriott Library, Salt Lake City, Utah.

75 Clem O. Miller, Foreword, Conference Coordinator, Coordinator of Scientific Committees, Office of the Commissioner, FDA; *Conference on Pediatric*

*Pharmacology* (Washington, DC: U.S. Department of Health, Education, and Welfare, 1967), iii.

76  For conference planning discussion and letters of invitation, see "Working Papers File Regarding Pediatric Pharmacology Conference," FDA archives, Record Group 88, Accession Number 71A-3473, Box 2, Proceedings of Conferences and National Advisory Food & Drug Council Records, 1963–1968, Folders 8–9, NARA (hereafter cited as FDA archives NARA).

77  Charles N. Christensen, "Presentation of an Ideal Industry Program for Determining Safety and Efficacy of Drugs for Use in the Perinatal Period, Infancy and Childhood," *Conference on Pediatric Pharmacology*, 74.

78  Ibid.

79  Ibid., 80.

80  Ibid.

81  Charles F. Weiss, *Conference on Pediatric Pharmacology*, 82.

82  Ibid.

83  Charles U. Lowe, "Conference Objectives and Plans," *Conference on Pediatric Pharmacology*, 7.

84  Mildred Spencer, "Medical Editor for the Buffalo Evening News," *Conference on Pediatric Pharmacology*, 105.

85  Minutes of COD Workshop Meeting, October 21 and 22, 1967, *Committee on Drugs Annual Report*, October 1967. Harry C. Shirkey to Stanley L. Harrison, AAP Secretary for Committees, November 10, 1967, COD archives. Harry C. Shirkey, "American Academy of Pediatrics Committee on Drugs Statement of Purpose, Scope and Functions," *Pediatrics* 41 (February 1968): 534.

86  Alan K. Done, ed., *Problems of Drug Evaluation in Infants and Children: Report of the Fifty-Eighth Ross Conference on Pediatric Research* (Columbus, OH: Ross Laboratories, 1968), 9.

87  Ibid., 10.

88  Ibid., 11.

89  Ibid., 33.

90  Ibid., 13.

91  Ibid.

92  Melissa A. Warfield to Herbert L. Ley, Director, Bureau of Medicine, 11 April 1967; Letter O. M. Carroll, FDA Acting Deputy Division of Endocrine & Metabolic Drugs to John J. Jennings, Director of Drug Surveillance, May 9, 1967; B. Harvey Minchew, Acting Deputy Director of Bureau of Medicine to Melissa A. Warfield, 23 June 1967, All RG 88, File Number 500.133 (Dosage and Warning Children and Infants) Box 4233, FDA archives, NARA.

93  James L. Goddard, "Child Health and Adult Investigation," April 11, 1968, 7, FDA History Office.

94  Ibid., 8.

95  Ibid., 7.

96  Ibid.

97  Paul S. Dunbar, "The Child and the Law," Speech at Tulane University, February 5, 1958, RG 88, Box 125, Acc 62a379 Folder "Articles and Speeches," FDA archives, NARA.

98  Jean D. Lockhart, MD, "FDA Bureau of Medicine Activities, 1969," in Harry Filmore Dowling Papers, 1908–1979, MS 372, Box 5, Folder 5, "Bureau of

Medicine Activities, Board Meeting, 1969," Modern Manuscripts Collection, History of Medicine Division, National Library of Medicine, Bethesda,
Maryland.

99  Ibid., 6. For more internal discussion of FDA's perceptions of its limited regulatory
authority for pediatric specific issues, see letter, Medical Officer Martha M. Freeman, to John Jennings, Acting Deputy Director, Bureau of Medicine, May 1, 1969,
RG 88, File number 500.133 "Dosage and Warning Children and Infants," Box 4233,
FDA archives, NARA.

100  COD Meeting Minutes: April 30, October 9, 1968; April 7, August 28,
October 20, 21, 1969; February 23, 24, June 11, 12, October 22, 23, 1970; "Progress
Report on Activities of the COD for 1970," COD archives. For a published sum-
mary of the problem as perceived by a FDA physician and COD member see
Jean D, Lockhart, "The Information Gap in Pediatric Drug Therapy," *Modern
Medicine* 38 (November 16, 1970): 56, 57, 60, 68.

101  Jeffrey P. Baker and Howard A. Pearson, eds., *Dedicated to the Health of All Children: 75 Years of Caring, 1930–2005* (Elk Grove Village, IL: American Academy of
Pediatrics, 2005), 54–59.

102  Sumner J. Yaffe, Harry C. Shirkey, Arnold P. Gold, Frederick M. Kenny, Mary Ellen
Avery, Harris D. Riley, Irwin Schafer, Leo Stern, Henry L. Barnett, Alfred M. Bon-
giovanni, and Robert J. Haggerty, "Committee on Drugs: Statement of Purpose,
Scope, and Function," *Pediatrics* 41 (February 1968): 534.

103  Harry C. Shirkey to Irwin A. Schafer, Associate Professor of Pediatrics, Cleveland
Metropolitan General Hospital, June 12, 1969, Box 33, Folder 14, Adriani papers.

104  Ibid.

105  William J. Curran and Henry K. Beecher, "Experimentation in Children: A Reex-
amination of Legal Ethical Principles," *JAMA* 210, no. 1 (January 1969): 77–83.

106  Beecher consulted a number of physician and lawyers to inform his stance. The
notes and correspondence that helped frame his thinking are found in Boxes 8, 10,
11, and 12, and 30, Beecher papers; Edward J. Rourke, "Experimentation in Children," *JAMA* 211, no. 2 (1970): 301; Ruth R. Faden, Tom L. Beauchamp, and
Nancy R. P. King, *A History of Informed Consent* (New York: Oxford University
Press, 1986). For a cogent synthesis of late 1960 and early 1970s debates see Ross,
*Children in Medical Research*, 17–24.

107  Sumner J. Yaffe, Mary Ellen Avery, Arnold P. Gold, Frederick M. Kenny,
Harris D. Riley, Jr, Irwin A. Schafer, Leo Stern, Harry Shirkey, Jeffrey Bishop,
Louis A. Farchione, Jean Lockhart and Charles F. Weiss, "Drug Testing in Children:
FDA Regulations," *Pediatrics* 43 (March 1969): 463–465, quote page 464.

108  "Memorandum of Conference," November 9, 1970, Box 26, Folder 3, Kelsey papers;
see also COD Meeting Minutes, February 26, 27, 1971, COD archives. On Finkel,
see "Marion J. Finkel, Leader in Orphan Product Development," accessed May 19,
2016, http://www.fda.gov/AboutFDA/WhatWeDo/History/ucm346388.htm.

109  "Drugs Likely to be Used in Children Must Be Tested in Them," *F-D-C Reports* 32
(October 5, 1970): 17.

110  Robert Warren to FDA, January 13, 1971, FDA RG 88 File number 500.133 [Dosage
and Warning Children and Infants] Box 4847, FDA archives, NARA.

111  John W. Winkler to Robert Warren from March 4, 1971, ibid.

112  Warren to Winkler, March 10, 1971, ibid.

113  COD Minutes, June 10–11, September 23–24, 1971, COD archives.

114 On conference planning, see letter dated August 5, 1971 from Duke C. Trexler, Drug Research Board, to Harry C. Shirkey; Duke C. Trexler, "Notes, Atlantic City Planning Meeting, Conference on Pediatric Pharmacology," May 7, 1971; Duke C. Trexler, "Planning Meeting, Conference on Pediatric Pharmacology," April 12, 1971; all from Folder on Conference on Pediatric Pharmacology, National Academies Archives Collection, Washington, DC.

115 Drug Research Board, *Preliminary Report, Conference on Pediatric Pharmacology*, 15, November 8–9, 1971, National Academies Archives Collection, Washington, DC. For skepticism within the AAP about this latest gathering's ability to address pediatric drug-related issues, see COD Minutes, January 10–12, 1972, COD archives.

116 "General Information Scope and Organization of Evaluations," 6, Box 28, Folder 5, Adriani papers. On the AMA disbanding the Council on Drugs, see Glenn Sonnedecker, *Kremer and Urdang's History of Pharmacy*, 4th edition (Philadelphia: J. P. Lippincott, 1976), 282. Shirkey subsequently returned to Cincinnati Children's Hospital. He retired in 1984 and died in 1995. William Gerhardt, "Harry Shirkey Eulogy," provided to author by Dr. Gerhardt.

117 Charles F. Weiss, "Statement of Purpose," *Pediatrics* 49 (March 1972): 452. For data on pediatric expertise at FDA, see *Bureau of Drugs Weekly*, Special Edition, May 1, 1972, Box 12, Folder 7, Kelsey papers. Weiss had recently left Parke Davis and Company and was now on the faculty at the University of Florida Departments of Pediatrics and Pharmacology.

118 Charles C. Edwards, "American Academy of Pediatrics Keynote, October 16, 1972," 11, MSS O447, Box 4, Folder 1, Charles C. Edwards papers, Mandeville Special Collections Library, Geisel Library, University of California, San Diego, La Jolla, California.

119 Ibid., 11.

120 Ibid.

121 For an overview of Nelson's hearings, see Dominique Tobbell, *Pills, Power, and Policy: The Struggle for Drug Reform in Cold War America and its Consequences* (Berkeley: University of California Press, 2011), 175–177; and Podolsky, *Antibiotic Era*, 120.

122 *Competitive Programs in the Drug Industry: Hearings before the Subcommittee on Monopoly of the Select Committee on Small Business*, "Present Status of Competition in the Pharmaceutical Industry," U.S. Senate, 93rd Congress, 1st Session, Part 23 (Tuesday, February 6, 1973) (Washington, DC: GPO, 1973), 9581.

123 Ibid., 9581.

124 Ibid.

125 On the concept of drug lag see Tobbell, *Pills, Power, and Policy*, 184–185, and Arthur Daemmrich, "Invisible Monuments and the Costs of Pharmaceutical Regulation: Twenty-Five Years of Drug Lag Debate," *Pharmacy in History* 45, no. 1 (2003): 3–17.

126 Subcommittee on Monopoly, *Competitive Programs in the Drug Industry*, 9582.

127 Ibid., 9583.

128 Ibid., 9585

129 Ibid., 9588.

130 Ibid., 9587.

131 For more on children's rights during this period see Mintz, *Huck's Raft*, 323–338; Michael Grossberg, "Liberation and Caretaking: Fighting over Children's Rights

in Postwar America," in *Reinventing Childhood After World War II*, ed. Fass and Grossberg, 19–38.

132 Joseph M. Hawes, *The Children's Rights Movement: A History of Advocacy and Protection* (Boston: Twayne, 1991), 26–39; Mintz, *Huck's Raft*, 341–342.

133 On the history of child abuse, see Linda Gordon, *Heroes of Their Own Lives: The Politics and History of Family Violence* (New York: Viking Press, 1988). For efforts to optimize Medicaid for children, see Sara Rosenbaum, D. Richard Mauery, Peter Shin, and Julia Hidalgo, *National Security and U.S. Child Health Policy: The Origins and Continuing Role of Medicaid and EPSDT*, Policy Brief, George Washington University School of Public Health and Health Services, 2005, accessed August 18, 2016, http://hsrc.himmelfarb.gwu.edu/sphhs_policy_briefs/36/. For juvenile justice reform, see Judith Sealander, *The Failed Century of the Child: Governing America's Young in the Twentieth Century* (New York: Cambridge University Press, 2003), 41–43. On advocacy for disabled children in this era, see Rothman, *Strangers*, 192–200, 204; and Allison C. Carey, "Citizenship and the Family: Parents of Children with Disabilities, the Pursuit of Rights, and Paternalism," in *Civil Disabilities: Citizenship, Membership, and Belonging*, ed. Nancy J. Hirshmann and Beth Linker (Philadelphia: University of Pennsylvania Press, 2015), 165–186.

134 "Child Development Legislation Dies in House," in *CQ Almanac 1972*, 28th edition, 03–914–03–918, Washington, DC: *Congressional Quarterly*, 1973, accessed February 17, 2016, https://library.cqpress.com/cqalmanac/document.php?id=cqal72-1249564; Editorial, The Comprehensive Child Development Bill and Its Veto, *American Journal of Public Health* 62 (April 1972): 462–463.

135 Hawes, *Children's Rights*, 120–121.

136 COD Meeting, November 26–28, 1973. Final draft included in minutes, *General Guidelines for the Evaluation of Drugs to be Approved for Use during Pregnancy and for the Treatment of Infants and Children*, 3, COD archives.

137 COD, *General Guidelines*, 18. The FDA reviewed the guidelines and accepted them at the October 24–27, AAP COD meeting 4, COD archives.

138 James H. Jones, *Bad Blood: The Tuskegee Syphilis Experiment* (New York: Free Press, 1981); Susan M. Reverby, *Tuskegee's Truths: Rethinking the Tuskegee Syphilis Study* (Chapel Hill: University of North Carolina Press, 2009).

139 *Quality of Health Care—Human Experimentation, 1973: Hearings before Subcommittee on Health of the Committee on Labor and Public Welfare*, U.S. Senate, 93rd Congress, 1st Session (Part 1 February 21, 22; Part 2 February 23, March 6; Part 3 March 7, 8; Part 4 April 30, June 28, 29, July 10) (Washington, DC: GPO 1973).

140 "Fact Sheet," November 15, 1972, *Quality of Health Care—Human Experimentation, 1973*, 307; "Kennedy Says 45 Babies Died in a Test," *New York Times* 12 October 1972, 22.

141 *Quality of Health Care—Human Experimentation, 1973*, Part 1, February 21, quote page 29; Edwards testimony, 13, Schweiker queries to Simmons, 31.

142 Ibid.

143 The AAP Committee on Drugs trod lightly on the issue of pregnant women. Although documents such as the group's 1974 guidelines emphasized the need for testing drugs in pregnant women, pediatricians had little authority in this domain because obstetricians oversaw the care of pregnant women. A new medical specialty of maternal-fetal medicine was emerging during this era, but it was not yet recognized. The AAP Committee on the Fetus and Newborn did raise the issue of pregnant women wherever possible. See, for example, *Biomedical Ethics and the*

*Protection of Human Research Subjects: Hearings before the Subcommittee on Public Health and Environment of the Committee on Interstate and Foreign Commerce*, House of Representatives, 93rd Congress, 1st Session (September 27, 28, 1973) (Washington, DC: GPO, 1974), 272–275. This was not the first time that a health issue seemingly unrelated to abortion became tangled in its politics. An earlier German measles epidemic had created demand for the procedure in middle-class women infected during pregnancy. Leslie J. Reagan, *Dangerous Pregnancies: Mothers, Disabilities, and Abortion in Modern America* (Berkeley: University of California Press, 2010).

144 Harry C. Shirkey, "Ethical Limits of Pharmacological Research on Children," *Pediatricia XIV: Proceedings 3* (Buenos Aires: Medica Panamericana, 1974): 206–217, quote page 212.

145 Ibid., 208.

146 Ibid.

147 On the development of bioethics, see Robert Baker, *Before Bioethics: A History of American Medical Ethics from the Colonial Period to the Bioethics Revolution* (New York: Oxford University Press, 2013). On the changing context of children, parents, and disability rights in this era, see Tamar W. Carroll and Myron P. Gutmann, "The Limits of Autonomy: The Belmont Report and the History of Childhood," *Journal of the History of Medicine and Allied Sciences* 66, no. 1 (2010): 82–115.

148 COD Minutes October 24–October 27, 1974, COD archives; Minutes, PRIME meeting December 2, 1974, Box 3, Folder 4, "American Academy of Pediatrics-Task Force on Pediatric Research Informed Consent and Medical Ethics," Hodes papers.

149 Yaffe to Chief, Institutional Relations Branch, Division of Research Grants, NIH, November 18, 1974; Appended to COD Minutes October 24–27, 1974, COD archives,

150 Thomas C. Smith, MD, PhD, Director, Clinical Pharmacologist at Parke Davis and Company to Jean Lockhart, MD, AAP, November 25, 1974, Box 3, Folder 4, "American Academy of Pediatrics-Task Force on Pediatric Research Informed Consent and Medical Ethics," Hodes papers.

151 Ibid.

152 Avrum L. Katcher to Horace L. Hodes, January 13, 1975; letter and statements on the importance of fetal research by physician groups in Box 3, Folder 4, "American Academy of Pediatrics-Task Force," Hodes papers.

153 The COD's Sanford L. Cohen testified before the National Commission, December 14, 1975. His testimony is appended to January 12–14, 1975, COD minutes, COD archives.

154 Conference Committee on Fetal Research and Applications, Institute of Medicine, *Fetal Research and Applications: A Conference Summary* (Washington, DC: National Academies Press, 1994), 8.

155 Paoli L. Morselli, "Pediatric Clinical Pharmacology: Routine Monitoring or Clinical Trials?" in *Clinical Pharmacy and Pharmacology*, ed. William A. Gouvei, Gianni Tognoni, and Eppo van der Kleijn (New York: Elsevier/North-Holland, 1976), 277–287.

156 Lawrence K. Altman, "Ethics of Human Experimentation are Debated at Science Forum," *New York Times*, February 23, 1975: 30.

157 Ibid.

158 COD Minutes, October 22–24, 1975; December 13–15, 1976, COD archives.

159 Barbara Resnick Troetel, "Three Part Disharmony: The Transformation of the Food and Drug Administration in the 1970s" (PhD Dissertation, City University of New York, 1996), 307–310.

160 Lester Soyka, COD Minutes, December 13–15, 1976, COD archives.

161 Issues surrounding generic drugs in children had been noted as early as 1957; Editorial, "The Trade-Name for a Drug Dilemma," *Journal of Pediatrics* 50 (February 1957): 267–269. For 1960s debates on this issue, see Harry C. Shirkey, "Generic Versus Therapeutic Equivalency for Drugs," Box 36, Folder 9, "FDA Background materials 196[?]–1979," Adriani papers. For 1970s COD discussions, see COD Committee on Bioavailability, April 4–6, 1974, January 7–9, April 1–3 1975, COD archives. For the broader history of generic drugs, see Jeremy A. Greene, *Generic: The Unbranding of Modern Medicine* (Baltimore: The Johns Hopkins University Press, 2014), 93–134.

162 Committee on Drugs, "Generic Prescribing," *Pediatrics* 57 (February 1976): 275–277, quote page 276.

163 Ibid.

164 Boston Children's Hospital Department of Clinical Pharmacology, *1975/1976 Research Report*, Boston Children's Hospital Archives, Boston, Massachusetts, 9–10. For a history of institutional review boards, see Laura Stark, *IRBs and the Making of Ethical Research* (Chicago: University of Chicago Press, 2012).

165 Boston Children's Hospital Archives, *1975/1976 Research Report*, 16–17; Allen A. Mitchell interview with author, May 8, 2012; A Report from the Boston Collaborative Drug Surveillance Program of the Boston University Medical Center, "Drug Surveillance: Problems and Challenges," *Pediatric Clinics of North America* 19 (February 1972): 117–131; Allen A. Mitchell, Peter Goldman, Samuel Shapiro, and Dennis Slone, "Drug Utilization and Reported Adverse Reactions in Hospitalized Children," *American Journal of Epidemiology* 110, no. 2 (1979): 196–204; Allen A. Mitchell, Peter Goldman, Samuel Shapiro, Victor Siskind, and Dennis Slone, "Intensive Drug Surveillance in a Pediatric Hospital," in Gouvei et al., *Clinical Pharmacology*, 311–317. The PeDS program ran for fourteen years and ultimately enrolled a total of 11,500 children. Louis Vernacchio and Allen A. Mitchell, "Epidemiology of Adverse Effects," in *Neonatal and Pediatric Pharmacology: Therapeutic Principles in Practice*, ed. Sumner J. Yaffe and Jacob V. Aranda, 4th edition (Philadelphia: Lippincott, Williams, and Wilkins, 2011), 892.

166 Sumner Yaffe, Correspondence to Steven Sawchuk, MD, Director of Medical Services Johnson and Johnson, August 14, 1975; Johnson and Johnson Institute for Pediatric Service Correspondence "Plan for the Development of Clinical Pharmacology" (undated but attached to the letter from Yaffe to Sawchuck), Box 4, Folder 48, "Johnson and Johnson Institute for Pediatric Service, Correspondence, Board Meeting minutes, 1969–1981," Hodes papers; Sumner Yaffe interview with author, November 1, 2010.

167 Samuel D. Maldonado, MD, MPH, FAAP, Vice-President and Head, Pediatric Drug Development Center of Excellence, Johnson & Johnson interview with author, January 6, 2011; Gretchen Krueger, *Hope and Suffering: Children, Cancer, and the Paradox of Experimental Medicine* (Baltimore: The Johns Hopkins University Press, 2008), 98, 118. For an overview of childhood leukemia's declining mortality, see Sandra C. Steinhorn and Max H. Myers, "Progress in the Treatment of Childhood Acute Leukemia: A Review," *Medical and Pediatric Oncology* 9, no. 4 (1981): 333–346.

168 National Commission for the Protection of Human Subjects of Biomedical and Behavioral Research, *Report and Recommendations: Research Involving Children* (Washington, DC: GPO, 1977). Susan E. Lederer, *Subjected to Science: Human Experimentation in America before the Second World War* (Baltimore: The Johns Hopkins University Press, 1995), 139–142; Ross, *Children in Medical Research*, 17–24; Carroll and Gutmann, "The Limits of Autonomy," 82–115; National Commission for the Protection of Human Subjects of Biomedical and Behavioral Research, *The Belmont Report: Ethical Principles and Guidelines for the Protection of Human Subject of Research* (Washington, DC: GPO, 1979).

169 "Requirement for Pediatric Studies (Retrospective Analysis) Drugs Approved 1972–1978," Box 28, Folder 3, "Subject Studies in Vulnerable Populations, Folder Fetuses, Infants, and children, 1961–1999," Kelsey papers.

170 FDA, *General Consideration for the Clinical Evaluation of Drugs in Infants and Children* (Washington, DC: GPO, 1977); Marion J. Finkel, "Drug Studies in Children," *Pediatric Pharmacology* 1, no. 1 (1980): 7–14; "Specific Requirements on Content and Format of Labeling for Human Prescription Drugs; Revision of 'Pediatric Use' Subsection in the Labeling; Final Rule," 21 CFR Part 201, Department of Health and Human Services Food and Drug Administration, accessed January 5, 2017, http://www.fda.gov/ohrms/dockets/ac/01/briefing/3778b1_Tab6 _7-21CFR%20Part%20201.pdf; FDA, "Labeling and Prescription Drug Advertising; Content and Format for Labeling for Human Prescription Drugs; Final Rule," *Federal Register* 44, no. 124 (June 26, 1979): 37434–37467.

171 Sumner J. Yaffe, "Introduction and Historical Perspectives," in *Pediatric Pharmacology: Therapeutic Principles in Practice*, ed. Sumner J. Yaffe (New York: Grune & Stratten, 1980), 3–5.

## Chapter 5 A "Big Business Built for Little Customers": Candy Aspirin, Children, and Poisoning, 1947–1976

1 Eugene Whitmore, "Big Business Built for Little Customers," *American Business* 8 (December 1951): 32–34.

2 Aspirin was created in 1899 by Bayer chemist Felix Hoffmann. Plough did not invent the first flavored aspirin; at least one version entered the market in the early 1930s. Advertised to adults, it made few profits. For histories of aspirin, see Diarmuid Jeffreys, *Aspirin: The Remarkable Story of a Wonder Drug* (New York: Bloomsbury, 2004); Charles C. Mann and Mark L. Plummer, *The Aspirin Wars: Money, Medicine, and 100 Years of Rampant Competition* (Brighton, MA: Harvard Business School Press, 1993); and Jan McTavish, "What's in a Name? Aspirin and the American Medical Association," *Bulletin of the History of Medicine* 61 (Fall 1987): 343–366. While these histories provide an excellent historical context for aspirin's role in twentieth-century American health care and business, the role of children's aspirin in the development of the American aspirin industry is largely absent.

3 Born in 1891 in Tupelo, Mississippi, Plough dropped out of school in the eighth grade. He began his career as an entrepreneur at age sixteen, when he borrowed money from his father to produce "Plough's Antiseptic Healing Oil." Made of camphor, carbolic acid, and cottonseed oil stirred in an old kettle, the teenager went up and down the streets of Memphis in a horsedrawn wagon selling his new product. With aggressive advertising and creative marketing, he soon turned a profit. He

began buying up failing drug businesses and turning them around with shrewd marketing. "The Abe Plough Story: One Brick at a Time," *Schering-Plough People* 7 (Spring 1974): 2–3; located in the Jay M. Arena papers, Box 11, Folder "Plough, Inc.," Duke University Medical Center Archives, Durham, North Carolina (hereafter cited as Arena papers); Abe Plough, "Abe Plough Recalls His 53 Years in Drug Field," *Advertising Age* 32 (October 1961): 86–100; "A Man to Watch in Ethical Drugs," *Chemical Week* 81 (November 10, 1957): 53–54; Thomas Michael, "Abe Plough Celebrates a Business Romance," *Memphis Commercial Appeal*, March 2, 1958, section I, *Press-Scimitar* Clippings File, Preservation and Special Collections/ Mississippi Valley Collection Department, McWherter Library, University of Memphis, Memphis; "Abe Plough, Founder of Medicinal Concern," *New York Times*, September 15, 1984; Robert E. Bedingfield, "Personality: A Medicine Man from Tupelo," *New York Times*, October 5, 1958. For more on Plough's sometimes ruthless labor practices and business strategies, see Michael K. Honey, *Southern Labor and Black Civil Rights* (Champaign: University of Illinois Press, 1993), 74–75, 82, and Alfred D. Chandler, Jr., *Shaping the Industrial Century* (Cambridge, MA: Harvard University Press, 2005), 217–218. On his skin bleaching products for African Americans and analysis of his advertising strategies, see Kathy Peiss, *Hope in a Jar: The Making of America's Beauty Culture* (New York: Metropolitan Books, 1998), 111–113. On his involvement in funding the first sickle cell anemia clinic in Memphis, see Keith Wailoo, *Dying in the City of the Blues: Sickle Cell Anemia and the Politics of Race and Health* (Chapel Hill: University of North Carolina Press, 2001), 34. On Plough in the context of Southern Judaism, see Selma S. Lewis, *A Biblical People of the Bible Belt: The Jewish Community of Memphis, Tennessee, 1840s–1960s* (Macon, GA: Mercer University Press, 1998), 86–89.

4 For historical examples of formulating drugs to appeal to children, see Roni Grad, "Cod and the Consumptive: A Brief History of Cod-Liver Oil in the Treatment of Pulmonary Tuberculosis," *Pharmacy in History* 46, no. 3 (2004): 106–120. For lollipop aspirin, see "Lollipops Containing Aspirin, TC-130 dated March 7, 1940," in Vincent A. Kleinfeld and Charles Wesley Dunn, *Federal Food, Drug, and Cosmetic Act: Judicial and Administrative Records 1938–49* (New York: Commerce Clearing House, 1950), 620.

5 Kathryn Jackson and Corinne Malvern, *Nurse Nancy* (New York: Simon & Schuster, 1952); Susan E. Lederer, "Playing Doctor, Playing Nurse: Perspectives on the Origins of the Toy Doctor and Nurse Kits," *Nursing History Review* 25 (2017): 117–129. There is a robust literature about consumer culture in the postwar era as it relates to children and parenting. For examples, see Steven Mintz, *Huck's Raft: A History of American Childhood* (Cambridge, MA: Harvard University Press, 2004), 274–277; Daniel Thomas Cook, *The Commodification of Childhood: Personhood, the Children's Wear Industry and the Rise of the Child Consumer, 1917–1962* (Durham, NC: Duke University Press, 2004); Stephen Kline, *Out of the Garden: Toys and Children's Television in the Age of TV Marketing* (London: Verso 1993); Nicholas Sammond, *Babes in Tomorrowland: Walt Disney and the Making of the American Child, 1930–1960* (Durham, NC: Duke University Press, 2005); David Nasaw, "Children and Commercial Culture," in *Small Worlds: Children and Adolescents in America, 1850–1950*, ed. Elliott West and Paula Petrick (Lawrence: University of Kansas Press, 1992), 14–25; Jodi Vandenberg-Davies, *Modern Motherhood: An American History* (New Brunswick, NJ: Rutgers University Press, 2014). On mothers, see Rima D. Apple, *Perfect Motherhood: Science and Childrearing in America*

(New Brunswick, NJ: Rutgers University Press, 2006); Victoria D. Alexander, "The Image of Children in Magazine Advertisements from 1905–1990," *Communication Research* 21 (December 1994): 742–765; Lisa Jackson, ed., *Children and Consumer Culture in American Society: A Historical Handbook and Guide* (Westport, CT: Praeger, 2008). On postwar consumerism in general in the United States, see Lizabeth Cohen, *A Consumers' Republic: The Politics of Mass Consumption in Postwar America* (New York: Vintage Books, 2003).

6  Lawrence M. Hughes, "Plough Plows It Back," *Sales Management* 66 (June 1951): 37–39, 106–110.

7  Steven Schlossman, "Perils of Popularization: The Founding of 'Parents Magazine,'" in *History and Research in Child Development*, ed. Alice Boardman Smuts and John W. Hagen (Chicago: Chicago Society for Research in Child Development, 1986), 65–78.

8  See, for example, a comparison of St. Joseph's ads to others in *Parents* 24 (January–June 1949).

9  It would not be until 1964 that *Ebony* magazine could purchase a St. Joseph advertisement featuring an African American mother and child; see *Ebony* 19 (February 1964): 40. For more on racial integration in advertising, see Jason Chambers, *Madison Avenue and the Color Line: African Americans in the Advertising Industry* (Philadelphia: University of Pennsylvania Press, 2008), 119–145.

10  For Mrs. Donald Crow's testimonial, see *Parents* 29 (November 1954): 19. For white male physician and celebrity endorsement, see *Parents* 33 (December 1958): 3. For another example of using physicians to sell St. Joseph's, see "Thousands of Doctors Approve," *New York Times*, November 30, 1952.

11  For the little girl putting on evening gown, see *Parents* 24 (January 1949): 46; the little boy putting on the pants of an adult man is in *Parents* 24 (February 1949): 59.

12  Marilyn Irvin Holt, *Cold War Kids: Politics and Childhood in Postwar America, 1945–1960* (Lawrence: University of Kansas Press, 2014), 22–23; Peter N. Stearns, "Childhood Emotions in Modern Western History," in *Routledge History of Childhood in the Western World*, ed. Paula S. Fass (London: Routledge, 2013), 158–173; Kathleen Jones, "A Sound Mind for the Child's Body: The Mental Health of Children and Youth," in *Children and Youth in Sickness and in Health: A Historical Handbook and Guide*, ed. Janet Golden, Richard A. Meckel, and Heather Munro Prescott (Westport, CT: Greenwood, 2004), 43–67.

13  Whitmore, "Big Business Built for Little Customers," 33. For more on St. Joseph Aspirin for Children's profitability, see "Production and Profit Trends, Wall Street Journal Report on Corporate Sales, Earnings, and Dividend Prospects," *Wall Street Journal*, September 22, 1949, and "St. Joseph's Aspirin Cures Memphis Headache," *Business Week*, January 29, 1949, 37.

14  Maximillian Berkowitz, Jerome E. Lasser, and Douglas E. Johnstone, "The Incidence of Allergy to Drugs in Pediatric Practice," *Annals of Allergy* 11 (September/October 1953): 561–566. On the crowded competitive aspirin market and children, see Nancy Tomes, *Remaking the American Patient: How Madison Avenue and Modern Medicine Turned Patients into Consumers* (Chapel Hill: University of North Carolina Press, 2016), 83.

15  "Plough Estimates 1956 Net at New High, 50% above 1955," *Wall Street Journal*, February 25, 1957.

16  "Double-Use Calendar," *New York Times*, November 17, 1953. For the story about hiring women, see "Abe Plough," *Advertising Age*, 86–100.

17 Charles O. Jackson, *Food and Drug Legislation in the New Deal* (Princeton, NJ: Princeton University Press, 1970).

18 A review of surviving case records from 1930 to 1949 for children with meningitis or pneumonia reveals that aspirin was not part of the standard treatment protocol for either condition. Sydenham Hospital Records, 1909–1962, MS C 243 Archives and Modern Manuscripts Program, History of Medicine Division, National Library of Medicine, Bethesda, MD. For examples of its use in children early in the twentieth century, see "Growing Pains," *JAMA* 37 (August 1901): 468–471; A. L. Skoog, "Treatment of Acute Anterior Poliomyelitis," *JAMA* 55, no. 21 (November 1910): 1804; "New and Nonofficial Remedies: Chorea," *JAMA* 50 (April 1910): 1142–1143. On aspirin in children with rheumatic fever, see Peter C. English, *Rheumatic Fever in America and Britain: A Biological, Epidemiological, and Medical History* (New Brunswick, NJ: Rutgers University Press, 1999), 86–87, 136–138.

19 One of many discussions on the growing role in aspirin in pediatrics as a result of children's flavored small dose aspirin was held on October 7, 1955, at the AMA Committee on Toxicology: see AMA Committee on Toxicology, "Minutes," AMA Committee on Toxicology Records, Box 7, vol. 1, 93, 147–148, Arena papers.

20 Benjamin Spock, *The Common Sense Book of Baby and Child Care* (New York: Duell, Sloan, and Pearce, 1946); Benjamin Spock, *Baby and Child Care*, 2nd edition (New York: Pocket Books, 1957), 444.

21 Maximillian Berkowitz, Jerome Lasser, and Douglas E. Johnstone, "The Incidence of Allergy to Drugs in Pediatric Practice," *Annals of Allergy* 11 (September/October 1953): 561–566.

22 "Plough Estimates 1956 Net at New High, 50% above 1955," *Wall Street Journal*, February 25, 1957. For growing profits during the 1950s, see *Plough, Incorporated Annual Reports*, 1949–1959, ProQuest Historical Annual Reports.

23 *Children's Hospital of Philadelphia Prescribing Manual* (Philadelphia: Collins, 1882), available at College of Physicians of Philadelphia, Historical Medical Library, Philadelphia. See also John Burnham, "How the Discovery of Accidental Child Poisoning Contributed to the Development of Environmentalism in the United States," *Environmental History Review* 19, no. 3 (1995): 57–81; Marion Moser Jones and Isidore Daniel Benrubi, "Poison Politics: A Contentious History of Consumer Protection against Dangerous Household Chemicals in the United States," *American Journal of Public Health* 103, no. 6 (2013): 801–812.

24 George M. Wheatley Oral History, interviewed by David Annunziato, MD, August 7, 1996, AAP Oral History Collection (hereafter cited as Wheatley Oral History); Harry Dietrich, George Wheatley, Slidden Brooks, Robert Kotte, and Dorothy Wyvell, "Round Table Discussion: Childhood Accidents and Their Prevention," *Pediatrics* 8, no. 3 (1951): 426–430; Katharine Bain, "Death Due to Accidental Poisoning in Young Children," *Journal of Pediatrics* 44 (June 1954): 616–623, and "Are Home Accidents in Children Preventable?" *Pediatrics* 13, no. 6 (1954): 568–575. For more articles documenting the problem of aspirin poisoning in this era, see W. Ray Shannon, "Aspirin Poisoning in Children," *Minnesota Medicine* 35 (June 1952): 555; Editorial, "Infant Deaths from Aspirin," *Journal of Pediatrics* 42 (February 1953): 276; Emily Gardner, "Aspirin Poisoning," *Virginia Medicine Monthly* 80 (March 1953): 147–151; Harry J. Lawler, "Aspirin Poisoning in Children," *Rocky Mountain Medical Journal* 50 (April 1953): 326–328; and Robert W. Winters, "Salicylate Intoxication in Infants and Children," *General Practitioner* 10 (August 1954): 67–72. On the American Academy of Pediatrics

Committee on Accident Prevention, see Harry F. Dietrich, "Clinical Application of the Theory of Accident Prevention in Childhood," *American Journal of Public Health* 42 (July 1952): 849; Jeffrey P. Baker and Howard A. Pearson, eds., *Dedicated to the Health of All Children* (Chicago: American Academy of Pediatrics, 2005), 60–61; and Paul A. Palmisano, "Targeted Intervention in the Control of Accidental Drug Overdoses by Children," *Public Health Reports* 96 (March–April 1981): 150–156.

25 Jay Arena, "Poisoning in Infants and Children," *Pediatric Clinics of North America* 1 (November 1954): 771–785.

26 For discussions of the problem regarding the lack of standardized dosing, see the Memorandum from January 1955, Folder, Committee on Accident and Poison Prevention, entitled "Precautions Regarding Salicylates, Including Aspirin"; see also a letter from George Wheatley to AAP Executive Director E. H. Christopherson, February 17, 1955, AAP Folder: Committee on Accident and Poison Prevention Correspondence American Academy of Pediatrics, Pediatric History Center, Elk Grove Village, Illinois (hereafter cited as AAP archives). On the early poison control movement, see also Jay M. Arena Oral History by James Gifford, February 28 and March 14, 1984, Duke University Medical Center Archives, Durham, NC (hereafter cited as Arena Oral History) and Wheatley Oral History. For a more recent history of the poison control movement, see Committee on Poison Prevention and Control, *Forging a Poison Prevention and Control System*, Institute of Medicine of the National Academies (Washington, DC: National Academies Press, 2004): 80–105.

27 W. H. Moses, Houston Inspection Statement to Chief, New Orleans District, June 14, 1954, entitled "Deaths of Infants Following Ingestion of 'Baby' Aspirin"; this and other similar letters and reports are in File No. 500.23, Box 1991, Poison Series, Records of the Food and Drug Administration, Record Group 88, National Archives and Records Administration College Park, College Park, MD (hereafter cited as Poison Series, FDA records); For an early history of poison control from the perspective of the FDA, see Wallace F. Janssen, "Warning: Hazardous to Children," *FDA Consumer* 7 (March 1973): 16–23.

28 Ibid.

29 H. B. Solmson, Plough Executive Vice President, to George Wheatley, May 3, 1954, File No. 500.23, Box 1991, Poison Series, FDA records.

30 Ibid.

31 A. Dale Console at Squibb to George Wheatley, May 5, 1954, File No. 500.23, Box 1991, Poison Series, FDA records. In this folder there is a similar letter from Bayer vice president Harry M. Mauss to George Wheatley, February 24, 1954, stressing the importance of parent education.

32 Jerome F. Grattan at Carroll Dunham Smith to Wheatley, May 20, 1954, File No. 500.23, Box 1991, Poison Series, FDA records.

33 Allan M. Brandt, *The Cigarette Century: The Rise, Fall, and Deadly Persistence of the Product That Defined America* (New York: Basic Books, 2007), 5, 159–169; David Michaels, *Doubt Is Their Product: How Industry's Assault on Science Threatens Your Health* (New York: Oxford University Press, 2008), x–xi, 4–6. The lead industry was also engaged in a similar campaign blaming poverty, not lead, when children became ill. Gerald Markowitz and David Rosner, "'Cater to the Children': The Role of the Lead Industry in a Public Health Tragedy, 1900–1955," *American Journal of Public Health* 90 (January 2000): 36–46. For more on this history of the strategy

of science denial and attempts to change mount a public relations war and shift the issue away from the health risk in question, see also Naomi Oreskes and Erik M. Conway, *Merchants of Doubt: How a Handful of Scientists Obscured the Truth on Issues from Tobacco Smoke to Global Warming* (New York: Bloomsbury, 2010), and Gary Taubes, *The Case Against Sugar* (New York: Knopf, 2016).

34  Paul S. Dunbar, "The Child and the Law," Speech at Tulane University, February 5, 1958, Box 125, RG 88, Food and Drug Administration Archives, National Archives, College Park, MD, 8 (hereafter cited as FDA archives RG 88). On FDA advisory meetings, see Susan L. Moffitt, *Making Policy Public: Participatory Bureaucracy in American Democracy* (Cambridge: Cambridge University Press, 2014), 112–113.

35  Handwritten notes by Kerlan on January 3, 1955, File No. 500.23, Box 1991; Poison Series, FDA records. On Public Health Service attempts to safeguard poisons in household products, see Jones and Benrubi, "Poison Politics."

36  George Wheatley's concerns about industry's willingness to take action on behalf of pediatric aspirin poisoning can be found in the Minutes for the Committee on Accident Prevention in August 1954, American Academy of Pediatrics Archives.

37  "Precautions Regarding Salicylates, Including Aspirin," January 1955, Folder: Committee on Accident and Poison Prevention; see also letter from Wheatley to. Christopherson, February 17, 1955; also [undated] Background Information prepared for "Medical Advisory Panel on the Accidental Ingestion and Misuse of Salicylate Preparations by Children," File No. 500.23, Box 1991, Poison Series, FDA records.

38  "Accidental Aspirin Poisoning," *F-D-C Reports* 16 (January 31, 1955): 1, 13–15, quote page 13.

39  "Salicylate Warning Statement," *F-D-C Drug Letter* 4 (February 21, 1955): 12–15, 16; "Advisory Panel Considers Aspirin Safety Measures," *Food and Drug Review* 32 (March 1955): 1, 50. For informal summaries of the aspirin hearing by FDA staff, see documents in File Number 500.23, Box 1991, FDA records. See also "Candy Medication and Accidental Poisoning," *JAMA* 158 (May 1955): 44–45; For final recommendations in which FDA "asks" companies to put warning labels on bottles, see FDA Press Release, Aspirin Advisory Ruling, Thursday, October 20, 1955 Files, FDA History Office, White Oak Campus, Silver Spring, Maryland.

40  "Salicylate Warning Statement," *F-D-C Drug Letter* 4 (February 21, 1955): 13.

41  Ibid., 14.

42  Margaret Peacock, *Innocent Weapons: The Soviet and American Politics of Childhood in the Cold War* (Chapel Hill: University of North Carolina Press, 2014), 1–3; *Juvenile Delinquency (Comic Books): Hearings before the Subcommittee to Investigate Juvenile Delinquency* 83rd Congress, 2nd Session (1954); Paul Ringel, "Reforming the Delinquent Child Consumer: Institutional Responses to Children's Consumption from the late Nineteenth Century to the Present," in *Children and Consumer Culture in American Society: A Historical Handbook and Guide*, ed. Lisa Jacobson (Westport, CT: Praeger, 2008), 43–62.

43  Wheatley to Christopherson, February 17, 1955.

44  *Bulletin of the Committee on Toxicology*, AMA Committee on Toxicology, Discussions re: AMA statement, "Candy Medication and Accidental Poisoning," vol. 1, quote March 16, 1955, 209–210, Committee on Toxicology Bulletins, Box 7, Arena papers.

45  Arnold Gesell, "Developmental Pediatrics: Its Tasks and Possibilities," *Pediatrics* 1 (March 1948): 331–335; Howard Markel and Janet Golden, "Successes and Missed Opportunities in Protecting Our Children's Health: Critical Junctures in the

History of Children's Health Policy in the United States," *Pediatrics* 115 (April 2005): 1129–1133; Florence Blake, *The Child, His Parents, and the Nurse* (Philadelphia: Lippincott, 1954).

46 "Candy Medication and Accidental Poisoning," *JAMA* 158 (May 1955): 44–45.

47 Robert B. Mellins, Joseph R. Christian, and Herman N. Bundesen, "The Natural History of Poisoning in Childhood," *Pediatrics* 17, no. 3 (1956): 314–326, quote page 321.

48 Arena attended Duke University medical school, interned at the Harriet Lane Home at Johns Hopkins Hospital and then returned to Duke for residency and to spend the rest of his career. Arena's interest in poison arose during his medical school days at Duke University in the early 1930s. The numbers of children seriously injured from ingesting common household products had made a lasting impression, Arena Oral History, 16; Arena, "Poisoning in Infants and Children"; Jay M. Arena, "The Pediatrician's Role in the Poison Control Movement and Poison Prevention," *American Journal of Diseases of Children* 137 (September 1983): 870–873; and Wheatley Oral History. For a more recent history of the poison control movement, see Committee on Poison Prevention and Control, *Forging a Poison Prevention and Control System*, 80–105.

49 Arena Oral History, 16.

50 Ibid., 17.

51 Ibid.

52 Jay M. Arena to Ray L. Sperber, September 13, 1955, Duke Poison Control Center Records, Series: Jay M. Arena Records, 1951–1976, Box 6, Safety Closure Cap Correspondence 1957–1958 (folder labeled 1957 and 1958, but includes materials from earlier), Duke University Medical Center Archives, Durham, North Carolina (hereafter cited as DPCC records).

53 Arena Oral History, 16–17; Jay M. Arena, "Safety Closure Caps," *JAMA* 169, no. 11 (March 1959): 1187–1188. Even before it developed a safety cap, Plough's public reputation had not suffered for refusing to engage with the FDA and pediatricians at the 1955 meeting. Beyond featuring the company's paid advertising, *Parents* even promoted St. Joseph Aspirin for Children and other Plough products through its Consumer Service Bureau. After director Barbara Daly Anderson visited Plough's Memphis plant, she raved about the company in her column, lauding its "elaborate system of controls and counter controls that leave no possibility for error." Barbara Daly Anderson, "Visit to Plough, Inc.," *Parents' Magazine & Family Home Guide* 32 (December 1957): 24, 28.

54 For Plough safety cap advertisement, see *Parents* 22 (December 1958): 3.

55 For Bayer ad, see *Parents* 34 (November 1959): 24.

56 For mortality rates in the late 1950s and early 1960s, see Wallace F. Janssen, "Warning: Hazardous to Children," *FDA Consumer* 7 (March 1973): 16–23. Tracking measures for poisoning continued to grow more sophisticated. Beginning in 1957, The U.S. Public Health Service accumulated data from poison control centers and health departments and created a national poisoning database. Howard M. Cann, Albert P. Iskrant, and Dorothy S. Neyman, "Epidemiologic Aspects of Poisoning Accidents," *American Journal of Public Health* 50 (December 1960): 1914–1924; Henry L. Verhulst and Howard McCann, "Poison Control Activities," *Journal of the American Pharmaceutical Association* 21 (March 1960): 122–125; see also letters that continue to arrive at the FDA, Box 2158 and Box 2159, File No. 500.23, Poison Series, FDA records. On growing media coverage, see "Physicians Call Aspirin a

Major Childhood Peril," *New York Times*, April 5, 1957 and "Children, Curious, Are Easy Poison Victims," *Los Angeles Times*, January 5, 1959. See also Case Reports from the late 1950s, Box 5, DPCC records.

57  Harold E. Heldreth, "Childhood Accidents and Their Prevention," *Reference Papers on Children and Youth Prepared for the 1960 White House Conference on Children and Youth* (Washington, DC: Golden Anniversary of the White House Conference on Children and Youth, 1960), 174–177.

58  Letter dated February 19, 1960, from Barbara Moulton to Kenneth D. Campbell, page 13927, in *Administered Prices: Part 23: Administered Prices in the Drug Industry, Hearings before the United States Committee on the Judiciary, Senate Subcommittee on Antitrust and Monopoly*, 86th Congress, 2nd Session (Washington, DC: GPO, 1960).

59  Paul Wehrle, L. DeFreest, J. Penhollow, and Virginia Goddard Harris, "The Epidemiology of Accidental Poisoning in an Urban Population: The Repeater Problem in Accidental Poisoning," *Pediatrics* 27 (April 1961): 614–620.

60  Roger J. Meyer, "Acetylsalicylic (Aspirin) Poisoning: Epidemiology," *American Journal of Diseases of Children* 102 (July 1961): 17–24, quotes pages 22–23.

61  *Federal Hazardous Substances Labeling Act, Report to Accompany S. 1283*, Report Number 1861, 86th Congress, 2nd Session (June 14, 1960).

62  At the time the 1962 Drug Amendments Act was passed, an estimated 100,000 to 300,000 over-the-counter drug products on the market needed to be reviewed for efficacy to meet the new law; aspirin was one of them. For a brief summary of this history, see "Over-the-Counter Acetaminophen-Containing Drug Products in Children Background Package," Joint Nonprescription Drugs Advisory Committee and Pediatric Advisory Committee Meeting, May 17–18 2011, FDA, accessed April 20, 2016, http://www.fda.gov/downloads/AdvisoryCommittees/CommitteesMeetingMaterials/Drugs/NonprescriptionDrugsAdvisoryCommittee/UCM255306.pdf.

63  *An Omnibus Bill to Rewrite the Food, Drug, and Cosmetic Act of 1938*, H.R. 1235, 89th Congress, 1st Session, *Congressional Record*, vol. 111 (January 26, 1965), 1345 (Statement of Representative Leonor K. Sullivan); "Candy Aspirin," *Consumer Reports* 29 (March 1964): 12.

64  (Statement of Representative Leonor K. Sullivan), *Congressional Record*, vol. 111, 1341; Section 14 of the Sullivan bill pertained to aspirin.

65  Jack Anderson, "'Inborn Leak' at Top: Aspirin Deaths," *Washington Post*, February 14, 1965.

66  *Children's Aspirin Amendment of 1965*, S. 2404, 89th Congress, 1st Session, *Congressional Record*, vol. 111, part 15 (August 12, 1965), 20155–20157; "A Curb on Infants' Aspirin," *New York Times*, August 14, 1964; Jean R. Halley, "Sen. McGovern Urges Controls on Sale of Aspirin for Children," *Washington Post*, August 16, 1965.

67  For Subcommittee discussion, see Subcommittee on Accidental Poisoning Meeting, Minutes for 25 October 1965, Committee on Accident Prevention Archives, AAP archives. Arena's editorial of support was published under the title "Aspirin Packaging Amendment," *Clinical Pediatrics* 4 (November 1965): 654.

68  There was also more research on how to treat aspirin poisoning by age. The evolving scientific understanding of the infant kidney in this era, for example, helped explain how and why the metabolic sequelae of aspirin poisoning varied by age and other developmental factors. Because young infants' kidneys could not metabolize and excrete aspirin as readily, for example, toxicity, in the form of dehydration and

metabolic acidosis, occurred more rapidly. Older children, on the other hand, were more likely to present with a respiratory alkalosis from too much aspirin. Alan K. Done, "Salicylate Poisoning," *JAMA* 192, no. 9 (May 1965): 770–772.

69   Janssen, "Warning: Hazardous to Children."

70   "Poison Information Unit Keeps Death Rate Low," *Los Angeles Times*, April 11, 1966, A3. See also "Valley to Join in on Drive on Poisons," *Los Angeles Times*, March 20, 1966.

71   Wallace F. Janssen Oral History, interview by James Harvey Young, Fred L. Lofs-vold, and Robert G. Porter, January 30–31, 1984, National Library of Medicine, Bethesda, MD, 46 (hereafter cited as Janssen Oral History).

72   Janssen Oral History; a copy of the comic book is filed as an addendum.

73   Ibid., "Child Protection." In *CQ Almanac 1966*, 22nd edition, 325–327; Washington, DC: Congressional Quarterly, 1967, accessed September 17, 2016, http://library .cqpress.com/cqalmanac/cqal66-1301508.

74   Speech, Lyndon Baines Johnson, "Special Message to the Congress on Consumer Interests," March 21, 1966, *American Presidency Project*, accessed January 20, 2015, http://www.presidency.ucsb.edu/ws/index.php?pid=27505#axzz1zfPFs3sS.

75   John D. Pomphret, "Johnson Asks New Laws for Consumer Protection," *New York Times*, March 22, 1966.

76   James F. Hoge, "Rendezvous with Destiny," *Food, Drug, Cosmetic Law Journal* 21 (August 1966): 431–436, quote page 435.

77   Ibid., 431.

78   The Hearings were officially called the Child Safety Act and Personnel Training, but the law became known as the Child Protection Act. Examples of statements regarding children's best interest pages 13 and 107; *Child Safety Act and Person-nel Training: Hearing on H.R. 13884, H.R. 14634, H.R. 13886, H.R. 14557, H.R. 14632, June 24; August 15, 29; September 12, 29, 1966, Before Subcommittee on Public Health and Welfare of the Committee on Interstate and Foreign Commerce* (Serial No. 89–43), 89th Congress, 2nd Session (Washington, DC: GPO, 1966) (hereafter cited as *Child Safety Act Hearings*).

79   *Child Safety Act Hearings*, June 24, 1966, 14.

80   Ibid., 23.

81   Ibid.

82   *Child Safety Act Hearings*, August 15, 1966, Leonor K. Sullivan testimony, 41–43. "National Clearinghouse for Poison Control Centers," 47, "Aspirin Most Frequently Ingested by All Ages, by Trade Name, 1961, Only," 48–49; detailed breakdown of poison statistics by year beginning in the early 1950s on pages 55–58.

83   *Child Safety Act Hearings*, Lynn E. Stalbaum, August 29, 1966, 119.

84   Ibid.

85   Ibid., C. Joseph Stetler, August 15, 1966, 91.

86   Ibid., 86.

87   Ibid., Richard E. Fisher, August 15, 1966, 107.

88   Ibid., 116.

89   Ibid., Harry B. Solmson, August 29, 1966, 134.

90   Ibid., 134.

91   Ibid., Maurice L. Tainter, September 12, 1966, 179.

92   Ibid., 186.

93   Ibid., 173.

94   Ibid.

95  Ibid., 178, 189.
96  Ibid., James F. Hoge, September 12, 1966, 204.
97  Ibid., 266.
98  Ibid., 209.
99  Ibid., Macpherson letter to Rep. John Jarman, Chair, Subcommittee on Public Health and Welfare, Committee on Interstate and Foreign Commerce, August 16, 1966, 331.
100 Ibid., Blasingame to Jarmon, Chair, September 13, 1966, 307–308.
101 Ibid., Leo O'Brien, September 12, 1966, 262.
102 Ibid.
103 Ibid.
104 Ibid., 274.
105 Ibid., September 19, 1966, 283, 291, 295.
106 Ibid., 277.
107 Ibid.
108 Child Protection Act of 1966, 89th Congress, 2nd Session (H Rpt. 2166) (Washington, DC: GPO, 1966). Plough played little price with the publishers of *Parents* (now named *Parents' Magazine and Better Homemaking*) for its lack of support for new aspirin laws. In September 1966, St. Joseph Aspirin for Children once again received a commendation from the magazine for its "quality standards" and its child-protection feature, the safety cap. Marjorie B. Keiser, "Consumer's Service Bureau Report," *Parents' Magazine and Better Homemaking* 41 (September 1966): 40, 42.
109 *Consumer Bulletin*, September 1966, 2, "Aspirin: Major Menace to Health in both Old and Young," Jay M. Arena Series, Box 6, DPCC records.
110 Joseph M. Pisani, "Safety in the Use of Home Medicines" *Proceedings of the Committee on Scientific Development, The Proprietary Association*, Meeting held December 8 1966 (Washington, DC: Proprietary Association, 1966), 4.
111 Ibid., 12.
112 Shirkey did acknowledge poisoning's risks to young children, highlighting preventive and treatment measures in his publications. Harry C. Shirkey, "The New United States Pharmacopeia (XVII) and National Formulary (XII): New and Vital Changes, for Children," *Journal of Pediatrics* 67 (November 1965): 833–835.
113 "Prevention of Accidental Ingestion of Salicylate Products by Children," *FDA Papers* (March 1967): 4–8, quote page 4.
114 Ibid.
115 Edward Press, April 11, 1967, Memorandum of Record: Summary of conference on Safety Closures with Mr. Charles Sullivan of Plough, Inc., and Mr. Al Johnson of Owens-Illinois [glass manufacturer]. This memorandum and correspondence related to all meetings in Arena Series, Box 6, Folder: "Safety Closure Caps Correspondence, 1967," DPCC records. For AAP perspective, see "Minutes of Meeting of the Subcommittee on Accidental Poisoning" for October 17, 1967, and October 22, 1968. For more about Subcommittee work from industry's perspective, see Maurice L. Tainter, "The Realities of Safety Packaging," in Proprietary Association Scientific Development Committee, *Safety Packaging in the '70s: Proceedings of a Conference Sponsored by the Scientific Development Committee*, December 9, 1970 (Washington, DC: Proprietary Association, 1970), 14–30. On the design of research tools, see Edward Press, "Performance Standards Development-A Chronicle of Government-Industry-Medicine Joint Effort," *Safety Packaging in the '70s*, 63–76.

116 Wyeth Laboratories Press Release, Sunday, March 19, 1967, "Safer Packaging for Aspirin," Folder entitled "Safety Closure Caps, Correspondence 1967," Jay M. Arena Series, Box 6, DPCC records.

117 This plan assuaged Sterling's Maurice L. Tainter, who restated his call to study poisoned toddler "repeaters." "Prevention of Accidental Ingestion of Salicylate Products by Children," *FDA Papers* (March 1967): 4–8, quote page 5.

118 Unfortunately for Plough, however, a large percentage of the recorded overdoses had used St. Joseph Aspirin for Children, despite the fact it was already packaged with a safety cap. John J. Crotty, "The Epidemiology of Salicylate Poisoning," *Clinical Toxicology* 1, no. 4 (1968): 381–386.

119 For discussions of the work in progress, see Robert C. Scherz, "Performance Standards Development: A Chronicle of Government-Industry-Medicine Joint Effort-II," 79–91; and Alan K. Done, "Performance Standards Development: A Chronicle of Government-Industry-Medicine Joint Effort-III, both in Proprietary Association Scientific Development Committee," *Safety Packaging in the '70s*. Appendices I and II include reports of the safety closure committee work, pp. 111–144. Details of the work are also "Experimental Protocol: Evaluation of Safety Packaging Forms in Prevention of Ingestions by Children" and "American National Standard Specifications for Child-Resistant (or Safety) Closures for Containers of Solid-Type Medications, Z66 Standards Committee," 1969–1974, Box 8, Jay M. Arena papers.

120 Mrs. C.H. (full name abbreviated for privacy purposes) in Oregon to James Goddard, November 24, 1966. For one mother's ideas for safety caps, see Mrs. P.M., January (no date) 1967 to FDA, both in Box 3991. Many other letters from parents and other consumers offering support and ideas for safety caps can be found in Box 1991 as well as Boxes 4137, 4244, and 4520 in File # 501 (safety caps), FDA archives.

121 Harry E. Buttee. Asst to the Director, Bureau of Regulatory Compliance, FDA, March 13, 1968 to Mr. R.S.P, File # 501, Box 4137, FDA archives.

122 *Federal Hazardous Substance Act: Hearings Before the Senate Committee on Commerce* (Serial No. 91–35), 91st Congress, 1st Session (October 1, 2, 1969), 1.

123 Ibid. (Statement of Alan K. Done), 77.

124 Ibid., 77; Shirkey to Frank E. Moss, Chair Subcommittee for Consumers on September 29, 1969, 265–269.

125 Ibid., Maurice L. Tainter, 194, 170.

126 Robert Kostello to Phillip Lee, October 6, 1969, RG 88, File number 500.133, "Dosage and Warning Children and Infants," Box 4233, FDA archives, NARA.

127 John M. Gowdy, MD, Acting Deputy Associate Director for Medical Review, Bureau of Medicine, FDA to Robert T. Kostello, November 12, 1969, RG 88, File number 500.133, "Dosage and Warning Children and Infants."

128 Ibid.

129 Gregory B. Rodgers, "The Effectiveness of Child-Resistant Packaging for Aspirin," *Archives of Pediatric and Adolescent Medicine* 156 (September 2002): 929–933; A. Clark and William W. Walton, "Effect of Safety Packaging on Aspirin Ingestion by Children," *Pediatrics* 63 (May 1979): 687–693; Georg S. Maisel, "Poison Prevention Packaging: New Protection for Children," *FDA Consumer* 7 (March 1973): 24–26.

130 Malcolm W. Jensen, "Child Safety," *FDA Consumer* 6 (June 1972): 4–10.

131 Charles Edwards, "Statement to National Commission on Product Safety," undated but included with materials from 1970, Jay Arena papers.

132 "Annual Report, 1968," 626; "Annual Report, 1970," 729; "Annual Report, 1971," 792, *Food and Drug Administration Annual Reports, 1950–1974* (Washington, DC: GPO, 1976); Jensen, "Child Safety," 4–10.

133 "Annual Report, 1968," 626.

134 Subcommittee for Consumers, Committee on Commerce, Richard O. Simpson, Chairman, Consumer Product Safety Commission, *Consumer Product Safety Commission Oversight, Hearing on S. 644 and S. 1000, February 21, 26, 27, 28, and April 18, 1975* (Serial No. 94–12), U.S. Senate, 94th Congress, 2nd Session (Washington, DC: GPO, 1975), 305; William W. Walton, "An Evaluation of the Poison Prevention Packaging Act," *Pediatrics* 69 (March 1982): 363–370.

135 Lorne K. Garrettson, "The Child Resistant Container: A Success and a Model for Accident Prevention," *American Journal of Public Health* 67 (February 1977): 135–136; Richard A. Schieber, Julie Gilchrist, and David A. Sleet, "Legislative and Regulatory Strategies to Reduce Childhood Unintentional Injuries," *The Future of Children* 19 (Spring/Summer 2000): 111–136; John C. Burnham, "How the Discovery of Accidental Childhood Poisoning Contributed to the Development of Environmentalism in the United States," *Environmental History Review* 10 (Autumn 1995): 57–81.

136 For other examples of this strategy, see David Michaels and Celeste Monforton, "Manufacturing Uncertainty: Contested Science and the Protection of the Public's Health and Environment," *American Journal of Public Health* 95 (S1) (July 2005): S39–S48; Oreskes and Conway, *Merchants of Doubt*; Jones and Benrubi, "Poison Politics"; Gerald Markowitz and David Rosner, *Lead Wars: The Politics of Science and the Fate of America's Children* (Berkeley: University of California Press, 2013); Markowitz and Rosner, "'Cater to the Children.'" On tobacco, see Brandt, *The Cigarette Century*.

## Chapter 6    Children and Psychopharmacology in Postwar America

1 Recent histories include Rick Mayes, Catherine Bagwell, and Jennifer Erkulwater, *Medicating Children: ADHD and Pediatric Mental Health* (Cambridge, MA: Harvard University Press 2009); Matthew Smith, *Hyperactive: The Controversial History of ADHD* (London: Reaktion Books, 2012); Matthew Smith, "Cold War Politics, the Brain Race, and the Origins of Hyperactivity in the United States, 1957–1968," in *Locating Health: Historical and Anthropological Investigations of Place and Health*, ed. Erika Dyck and Christopher Fletcher (London: Pickering and Chatto, 2010), 57–69. Most of the recent and robust historiography of psychopharmacology positions a particular drug or drug class at the study's center. Children are often mentioned but are not the central focus. See, for example, Nicolas Rasmussen, *On Speed: The Many Lives of Amphetamine* (New York: New York University Press, 2008); Ilina Singh, "Not Just Naughty: 50 Years of Stimulant Drug Advertising," in *Medicating Modern America: Prescription Drugs in History*, ed. Andrea Tone and Elizabeth Siegel Watkins (New York: New York University Press, 2007), 131–156; Andrea Tone, *The Age of Anxiety: A History of America's Turbulent Affair with Tranquilizers* (New York: Basic Books, 2009); David Healy, *The Creation of Psychopharmacology* (Cambridge, MA: Harvard University Press, 2002); and David L. Herzberg, *Happy Pills in America: From Miltown to Prozac* (Baltimore: The Johns Hopkins University Press, 2009).

2 Advertisement (designed to look like letter to the editor from a mother), Mrs. Winslow's Soothing Syrup, *New York Times*, December 1, 1860; James Harvey Young, "'Even to a Suckling Infant': Nostrums and Children," *Transactions and Studies of the College of Physicians of Philadelphia* 1 (1979): 5–32.

3 Leo Kanner, *Child Psychiatry* (Springfield, IL: Charles C. Thomas, 1935), 95; J. P. Crozer Griffith and A. Graeme Mitchell, *The Diseases of Infants and Children* (Philadelphia: W. B. Saunders, 1933). On Kanner, see Lauretta Bender, "In Memoriam Leo Kanner, MD, June 13, 1894–April 4, 1981," *Journal of the American Academy of Child Psychiatry* 21 (January 1982): 88–89.

4 Margo Horn, *Before It's Too Late: The Child Guidance Movement in the United States, 1922–1945* (Philadelphia: Temple University Press, 1989); Kathleen W. Jones, *Taming the Troublesome Child: American Families, Child Guidance, and the Limits of Psychiatric Authority* (Cambridge, MA: Harvard University Press, 1999); Kathleen W. Jones, "A Sound Mind for the Child's Body: The Mental Health of Children and Youth," in *Children and Youth in Sickness and in Health: A Historical Handbook and Guide*, ed. Janet Golden, Richard A. Meckel, and Heather Munro Prescott (Westport, CT: Greenwood Press, 2004), 43–67; and Paula S. Fass, *The End of American Childhood: A History of Parenting from Life on the Frontier to the Managed Child* (Princeton, NJ: Princeton University Press, 2016), 99–100.

5 Walter R. Miles, *Arnold Lucius Gesell, 1880–1961* (Washington, DC: National Academy of Sciences, 1964).

6 Charles Bradley, "The Behavior of Children Receiving Benzedrine," *American Journal of Psychiatry* 94 (November 1937): 577–585, quote page 577.

7 Ibid., 578, 582, 583.

8 For more, see Rasmussen, *On Speed*, 30; Smith, *Hyperactive*, 41–44; Madeline P. Strohl, "Bradley's Benzedrine Studies on Children with Behavioral Disorders," *Yale Journal of Biology and Medicine* 84, no. 1 (2011): 27–33. For a discussion of inpatient psychiatric care for children in this era, see Deborah Blythe Doroshow, "Residential Treatment and the Invention of the Emotionally Disturbed Child in Twentieth-Century America," *Bulletin of the History of Medicine* 90 (Spring 2016): 92–123.

9 Gerald N. Grob, *The Mad among Us: A History of the Care of America's Mentally Ill* (New York: Free Press, 1994), 210–215.

10 Marilyn Irvin Holt, *Cold War Kids: Politics and Childhood in Postwar America, 1945–1960* (Lawrence: University of Kansas Press, 2014), 22–24.

11 Leo Kanner, "Autistic Disturbances of Affective Contact," *Nervous Child* 2 (1943): 217–250, quote page 217. For more on the history of child psychiatry, see Irving N. Berlin, "The History of the Development of the Subspecialty of Child & Adolescent Psychiatry in the United States," Box 144, American Academy of Child and Adolescent Psychiatry Archives, Washington, DC.

12 Mayes, Bagwell, and Erkulwater, *Medicating Children*, 79; Gerald N. Grob, "Origins of DSM-I: A Study in Appearance and Reality," *American Journal of Psychiatry* 148 (April 1991): 421–431.

13 After an internship and psychiatry residency at the University of Chicago and Boston Psychopathic Hospital, she arrived at Johns Hopkins in 1928 as a research associate for Adolf Meyer. In 1930 she accepted a position at Bellevue Hospital's Child Psychiatric Division. Lauretta Bender, "Childhood Schizophrenia," *Nervous Child* 1 (Spring 1942): 138–140; Lauretta Bender Curriculum Vitae dated January 22, 1973, Box 18, File 4, Lauretta Bender Papers (accession number #90–012), Brooklyn College Library Archives and Special Collections, Brooklyn, New York

(hereafter cited as Bender papers). Bender moved to New York City to accompany her husband, Viennese psychiatrist Paul Schilder. For an autobiographical summary, see Lauretta Bender, "A Career of Clinical Research in Child Psychiatry," in *Explorations in Child Psychiatry*, ed. E. James Anthony (New York: Plenum Press, 1975), 419–462.

14 Jones, "A Sound Mind for the Child's Body," 43–67; Lauretta Bender and Frances Cottington, "The Use of Amphetamine Sulphate (Benzedrine) in Child Psychiatry," *American Journal of Psychiatry* 99 (July 1942): 116–121; Lauretta Bender, "Children's Reactions to Psychotomimetic Drugs," in *Psychotomimetic Drugs*, ed. Daniel H. Efron (New York: Raven Press, 1970), 265–272; Wanda Wright, "Special Schoolroom Attitudes and Activities for the Problem Child," in *Child Psychiatric Techniques*, ed. Lauretta Bender (Springfield, IL: Charles C. Thomas, 1952), 277–286. On drugs and the legitimization of psychiatry as a medical specialty, see Edward Shorter, *Before Prozac: The Troubled History of Mood Disorder in Psychiatry* (New York: Oxford University Press, 2009), 192.

15 *Background Material for Preparatory Committees on Personnel and Treatment, Conference on In-Patient Treatment for Children*, June 24, 1956, Box 1, Folder 9, Bender papers. See also Lauretta Bender, "A Longitudinal Study of Schizophrenic Children with Autism," *Hospital and Community Psychiatry* 20 (August 1969): 230–237; Archie A. Silver, "Report on Somatic Therapies Prepared for Conference on In-Patient Treatment for Children," June 25, 1956, Box 1, Folder 5, Bender papers.

16 Robert L. Gatski, "Chlorpromazine in the Treatment of Emotionally Maladjusted Children," *JAMA* 157, no. 9 (April 1955): 1298–1300; Brian R. Hunt, Thomas Frank, and Thaddeus P. Crush, "Chlorpromazine in the Treatment of Severe Emotional Disorders of Children," *American Journal of Diseases of Children* 91 (March 1956): 268–277. For more on the history of tranquilizers, see Lawrence C. Rubin, "Merchandising Madness: Pills, Promises, and Better Living through Chemistry," *Journal of Popular Culture* 38, no. 2 (2004): 369–383; Tone, *Age of Anxiety*, 83, 106, 135.

17 *Background Material for Preparatory Committees*, 6.

18 The six drugs they tested included Benadryl, Ambodryl, Thorazine, Tolserol, Artane, and Serpasil; Alfred M. Freedman, Abraham S. Effron, and Lauretta Bender, "Pharmacotherapy in Children with Psychiatric Illness," *Journal of Nervous and Mental Disease* 122 (November 1955): 479–486, quote page 486.

19 Ibid., 479.

20 On behavior problems including juvenile delinquency in girls, see Jones, "A Sound Mind for the Troubled Child," 57; Wini Breines, "The Other Fifties: Beats and Bad Girls," in *Not June Cleaver: Women and Gender in Postwar America, 1945–1960*, ed. Joanne Meyerowitz (Philadelphia: Temple University Press, 1994), 382–409; and Rickie Solinger, *Wake Up Little Susie: Pregnancy and Race before Roe v. Wade* (New York: Routledge, 1992).

21 Lauretta Bender, "Treatment of Children in an Outpatient Child Guidance Clinic," September 22, 1960, Box 13, File 3, page 3, Bender papers.

22 Ibid., 3. For more of her thoughts on race, see Lauretta Bender, "Behavior Problems in Negro Children," *Psychiatry* 2 (May 1939): 213–228. For a critique of Bender and race, see Dennis Doyle, "'Racial Differences Have to be Considered': Lauretta Bender, Bellevue Hospital, and the African American Psyche, 1936–1952," *History of Psychiatry* 21, no. 2 (2010): 206–223.

23 Lauretta Bender and Sol Nictern, "Chemotherapy in Child Psychiatry," *New York State Journal of Medicine* 56 no. 18 (1956): 2791–2795, quote page 2791.

24  C. Keith Conners Oral History by Dr. Burt Angrist, December 10, 1997, page 3, American College of Neuropsychopharmacology, Center for the Study of the History of Neuropsychopharmacology, History and Special Collections, Louise M. Darling Biomedical Library, UCLA, Los Angeles, California (hereafter cited as Conners Oral History).

25  Lawrence Galton, "A New Drug Brings Relief for the Tense and Anxious," *Cosmopolitan* (August 1955): 82–83, quote page 82. For growing concerns about these and other psychoactive drugs' addictive potential in the mid-1950s, see Herzberg, *Happy Pills in America*, 90–93.

26  Harry R. Lichtfield, "Clinical Evaluation of Meprobamate in Disturbed and Prepsychotic Children," *Annals of the New York Academy of Sciences* 67 (May 1957): 828–832, quote page 828.

27  *Miltown: The Tranquilizer with Muscle Relaxant Action* (New Brunswick, NJ: Wallace Laboratories), quote page 20, in Frank Berger Papers, American College of Neuropsychopharmacology, Center for the Study of the History of Neuropsychopharmacology, History and Special Collections, Louise M. Darling Biomedical Library, UCLA, Los Angeles, California (hereafter cited as Berger papers). For more on the history of Miltown and minor tranquilizers, see Herzberg, *Happy Pills in America*, 30–38; Jonathan Metzl, "'Mother's Little Helper': The Crisis of Psychoanalysis and the Miltown Resolution," *Gender and History* 15 (August 2003): 240–267; Frank J. Ayd, "The Early History of Modern Psychopharmacology," *Neuropsychopharmacology* 5, no. 2 (1991): 71–84; Shorter, *Before Prozac*, 36–46; and Andrea Tone, "Tranquilizers on Trial: Psychopharmacology in the Age of Anxiety," in *Medicating Modern America*, ed. Tone and Watkins, 156–183.

28  Ibid., 20.

29  Ibid.

30  The *Physician's Drug Reference* does mention Miltown as a therapy for muscle spasm from cerebral palsy and for seizures, conditions that can occur in children, although not exclusively. Nonetheless, the Miltown marketing materials made a case for its pediatric use far beyond its FDA-approved label. *Physician's Desk Reference to Pharmaceutical Specialties and Biologicals*, 10th edition (Oradell, NJ: Medical Economics, 1956), 583; *Miltown: The Tranquilizer with Muscle Relaxant Action*, 18–19, 42.

31  Milton W. Talbot, "The Use of Reserpine in Irritable and Hypertonic Infants," *Annals of the New York Academy of Sciences* 61, no. 1 (1955): 188–197, quote page 188.

32  Herzberg, *Happy Pills in America*, 31. Amphetamines were recommended as appetite suppressants to treat obesity in children, just as they were in adults. Leo Kanner and Leon Eisenberg, "Childhood Problems in Relation to the Family," *Pediatrics* 20 (July 1957): 155–164. For an overview of the drugs in the context of childhood obesity, see Laura Dawes, *Childhood Obesity in America: Biography of an Epidemic* (Cambridge, MA: Harvard University Press, 2014), 100–107.

33  Ann Marie Kordas, *The Politics of Childhood in Cold War America* (London: Pickering and Chatto, 2013), 83.

34  *Miltown: The Tranquilizer with Muscle Relaxant Action*, 19–20. On mothering judgments, see Jodi Vandenberg-Davies, *Modern Motherhood: An American History* (New Brunswick, NJ: Rutgers University Press, 2014); Marga Vicedo, *The Nature and Nurture of Love: From Imprinting to Attachment in Cold War America* (Chicago: University of Chicago Press, 2013). On marketing psychoactive drugs in this era, see Rubin, "Merchandising Madness," 369–383. For a general overview of prescription drug advertising, see Jeremy A. Greene and David Herzberg, "Hidden

in Plain Sight: Marketing Prescription Drugs to Consumers in the Twentieth Century," *American Journal of Public Health* 100 (May 2010): 793–803.

35 *Background Material for Preparatory Committees on Personnel and Treatment, Conference on In-Patient Treatment for Children*, 6, Bender papers. For an overview of the conference, see *Psychiatric Inpatient Treatment of Children: Report of the Conference on Inpatient Psychiatric Treatment for Children held at Washington, D.C., October 17–21, 1956* (Washington, DC: American Psychiatric Association, 1957). For media coverage of the conference, see "Caution Advised in Drug Therapy," *New York Times*, March 16, 1956, 18.

36 For more on the development of the Psychopharmacology Service Center, see Grob, *The Mad among Us*, 210–215, and Tone, *Age of Anxiety*, 82.

37 R. H. Felix, "Foreword," in *Child Research in Psychopharmacology*, ed. Seymour Fisher (Springfield, IL: Charles C. Thomas, 1959), vii–viii, quote page vii.

38 Ibid., vii.

39 Ibid., vii.

40 Leo Kanner and Leon Eisenberg, "Childhood Problems in Relation to the Family," *Pediatrics* 20 (July 1957): 155–164. Eisenberg received his medical education at the University of Pennsylvania and his psychiatric training at New York's Mt. Sinai and at Johns Hopkins Hospital. For more on his career as well as his decades of social activism, see Benedict Carey, "Dr. Leon Eisenberg, Pioneer in Autism Studies, Dies at 87," *New York Times*, September 23, 2009; Leon Eisenberg, Harvard University Office of Faculty Affairs, accessed January 9, 2017, http://www.fa.hms.harvard.edu/about-our-faculty/memorial-minutes/e/leon-eisenberg/Leon Eisenberg; Society for Research in Child Development Oral History Project, interviewed May 19, 1998, by Emily Cahan, accessed January 9, 2017, http://www.srcd.org/about-us/oral-history-project (hereafter cited as Eisenberg Oral History).

41 Leon Eisenberg, "Basic Issues in Drug Research with Children: Opportunities and Limitations of a Pediatric Age Group," in *Child Research in Psychopharmacology*, ed. Fisher, 31.

42 Ibid., 22.

43 Ibid., 31.

44 Lauretta Bender, "Discussion," in ibid., 35.

45 Ibid., 40.

46 Ibid.

47 Milton J. E. Senn, "Closing Remarks," in ibid., 168.

48 Ibid.

49 Ibid.

50 Ibid.

51 The study investigated tranquilizers for what was then known as minimal brain dysfunction, http://www.fa.hms.harvard.edu/about-our-faculty/memorial-minutes/e/leon-eisenberg/Eisenberg, Society for Research in Child Development Oral History http://www.srcd.org/about-us/oral-history-project, both accessed January 9, 2017; Ronald S. Lipman, "NIMH–PRB Support of Research in Minimal Brain Dysfunction and Other Disorders of Childhood," *Psychopharmacology Bulletin* (Washington, DC: GPO, 1973), 1–8.

52 Leon Cytryn, Anita Gilbert, and Leon Eisenberg, "The Effectiveness of Tranquilizing Drugs plus Supportive Psychotherapy in Treating Behavior Disorders of Children: A Double-Blind Study of Eighty Outpatients," *American Journal of Orthopsychiatry* 30 (January 1960): 113–129, quote page 115.

53 Leon Eisenberg, Roy Lachman, Peter A. Molling, Arthur Lockner, and James D. Mizelle, "A Psychopharmacologic Experiment in a Training School for Delinquent Boys: Methods, Problems, and Findings," *American Journal of Orthopsychiatry* 33 (April 1963): 431–447.

54 Anonymous mother (EH), "Drugs for Children" *Ladies Home Journal*, February 1960, 4. For discussions of the growing public concern about tranquilizers in this era, see Susan L. Speaker, "From 'Happiness Pills' to 'National Nightmare': Changing Cultural Assessment of Minor Tranquilizers in America, 1955–1980," *Journal of the History of Medicine and Allied Sciences* 52 (July 1997): 338–376.

55 EH, "Drugs for Children."

56 Ibid.

57 There were eleven other federally funded units at this time. For a description of Fish's early experiments, see Barbara Fish Oral History by Marcia Meldrum and Beth Bromley, September 11, 2008, 41–42, Center for the Study of the History of Neuropsychopharmacology, History and Special Collections, Louise M. Darling Biomedical Library, UCLA, Los Angeles, California. Fish's close colleague for much of this work was her first research assistant, Dr. Theodore Shapiro, later a professor of pediatrics and psychiatry at Cornell Medical College. He later reminisced about her work at Bellevue: Theodore Shapiro, "Barbara Fish: The Bellevue Years," *Journal of Child and Adolescent Psychopharmacology* 15 (November 3, 2005): 344–347.

58 For an examination of medical experimentation with LSD in adults, see Erika Dyck, *Psychedelic Psychiatry: LSD from Clinic to Campus* (Baltimore: The Johns Hopkins University Press, 2008).

59 Lauretta Bender, "Children's Reactions to Psychotomimetic Drugs," in *Psychomimetic Drugs*, ed. Efron, 265–272, quote page 268.

60 Ibid., 269.

61 Ibid., 268.

62 Ibid.

63 Gloria Faretra and Lauretta Bender, "Autonomic Nervous System Responses in Hospitalized Children Treated with LSD and UML," in *Recent Advances in Biological Psychiatry: Proceedings of the Nineteenth Annual Convention and Scientific Program of the Society of Biological Psychiatry, Los Angeles, California, May 1–3*, ed. Joseph Wortis (New York: Plenum Press, 1964), 1–8, quote page 6.

64 Ibid., 8.

65 Bender, "Children's Reactions to Psychotomimetic Drugs," 270.

66 Lauretta Bender and D. V. Siva Sankar, "Chromosome Damage Not Found in Leukocytes of Children Treated with LSD-25," *Science* 159, no. 3816 (February 16, 1968): 749.

67 Bender, "Psychotomimetic Drugs," 270.

68 *Research Program of the Children's Unit, Creedmoor State Hospital*, March 15, 1968, page 11, Box 2, File 7, Bender papers.

69 Emma Harrison, "LSD Drug Found to Aid Children," *New York Times*, November 10, 1963, 46.

70 Conners oral history; Leon Eisenberg oral history.

71 Letter dated May 24, 1963, from Leon Eisenberg to Senator Hubert Humphrey; *Interagency Coordination in Drug Research and Regulation: Hearings before the Subcommittee on Reorganization and International Organizations of the Committee on Government Operations, Agency Coordination Study: Review of Cooperation on*

*Drug Policies Among Food and Drug Administration, National Institutes of Health, Veterans' Administration, and Other Agencies Part 3*, 88th Congress, 1st Session (March 20, 1963) (Washington, DC: GPO, 1963), 1726.

72 Ibid.

73 Leon Eisenberg, "Role of Drugs in Treating Disturbed Children," *Children* 2, no. 5 (1964): 167–173, quote page 167.

74 Ibid., 168.

75 Lipman, "NIMH–PRB Support of Research," quote page 2.

76 Leon Eisenberg, "Commentary with a Historical Perspective by a Child Psychiatrist: When 'ADHD' was the 'Brain-Damaged' Child," *Journal of Child and Adolescent Psychopharmacology* 17 no. 3 (2007): 279–283.

77 Lipman, "NIMH–PRB Support of Research," cites all the studies, as does the *Hearing before the Federal Involvement in the Use of Behavior Modification Drugs on Grammar School Children of the Right to Privacy Inquiry: Subcommittee of the Committee on Government Operations, House of Representatives*, 91st Congress, 2nd Session (September 29, 1970) (Washington, DC: GPO, 1970), 4–5. On the development of the development of better pediatric psychometric measure, see Conners oral history, 5–6; "Selected Progress Reports by Grantees of the Psychopharmacology Research Branch," *Psychopharmacology Bulletin* (Washington, DC: GPO, 1973), 9–23; "Background and Preliminary Components of the Children ECDEU Battery," *Psychopharmacology Bulletin* (Washington, DC: GPO, 1973), 24–85.

78 Ad Hoc Committee on the Report of the Joint Commission on the Mental Health of Children, *Crisis in Child Mental Health: Challenge for the 1970s: Report of the Joint Commission on Mental Health of Children* (New York: Harper & Row, 1970).

79 Ibid., 288.

80 Robert C. Maynard, "Omaha Pupils Given 'Behavior' Drugs: 5 to 10% of Omaha Pupils Given Drugs to Improve Behavior," *Washington Post*, June 29, 1970, A1; Mayes et al., *Medicating Children*, 60. Maynard was a crusading young African American journalist. For more on Maynard see "Robert C. Maynard: Life and Legacy," Maynard Foundation, accessed August 4, 2016, http://mije.org/robertmaynard.

81 Ibid.

82 Robert Reinhold, "Rx for Child's Learning Malady: Rx for Learning Malady in Child Gaining in U.S.," *New York Times*, July 3, 1970, 27–28, quote page 28.

83 Ibid., 27.

84 Subcommittee of the Committee on Government Operations, House of Representatives, *Federal Involvement in the Use of Behavior Modification Drugs on Grammar School Children*, 2–3.

85 Ibid., 72.

86 Ibid., 58.

87 Ibid., 13.

88 Ibid., 24–25.

89 Ibid.; letter from Elliot L. Richardson, secretary, Health and Human Services, to Cornelius E. Gallagher, November 3, 1970, 110–112.

90 Ibid., 71.

91 For an overview of Gallagher's interest in the right to privacy, see Al Sullivan, "Looking for a Little Truth: Former Representative Neil Gallagher Recounts His Battle for Privacy Rights," *Hudson Reporter*, April 26, 2007.

92 See, for example, testimony Gallagher invited from a mother, Mrs. Daniel Youngs, who charged that school officials diagnosed her child with minimal brain dysfunction, tried to force him to take medication, and harassed the family when they resisted, 77–86.

93 Leon Eisenberg, "Principles of Drug Therapy in Child Psychiatry with Special Reference to Stimulant Drugs," *American Journal of Orthopsychiatry* 41 (April 1971): 371–379, quote page 371.

94 Ibid., 371.

95 Ibid., 372–373.

96 Ibid., 374.

97 Singh, "Not Just Naughty," 131–156, 131–156.

98 Smith, *Hyperactive*, 94.

99 "Background and Preliminary Components of the Children ECDEU Battery," *Psychopharmacology Bulletin*, National Clearinghouse for Mental Health Information (Washington: GPO, 1973): 24–85.

100 *Quality of Health Care—Human Experimentation, 1973: Hearings before the Subcommittee on Health of the Committee on Labor and Public Welfare*, U.S. Senate, 93rd Congress, 1st Session, Part 1, February 21, 22; Part 2, February 23, March 6; Part 3, March 7, 8; Part 4, April 30, June 28, 29, July 10 (Washington, DC: GPO, 1973). Issues surrounding experimentation on developmentally disabled and mentally ill institutionalized populations arose at every hearing.

101 Statement of Dennis J. Lehr, *Drugs in Institutions: Hearings before the Subcommittee to Investigate Juvenile Delinquency of the Committee on the Judiciary, United States Senate, The Abuse and Misuse of Controlled Drugs in Institutions, Volume II, the Improper Drugging of Mentally Ill and Mentally Handicapped Persons*, 94th Congress, 1st Session (July 31, August 18, 1975) (Washington, DC: GPO, 1977), 10.

102 Ibid.; undated letter from Alexander M. Schmidt to Dennis Lehr, 400–408.

103 See, for example, Committee on Drugs Minutes for April 13–15, June 19–22, 1972; February 15–17, June 21–23, October 11–13, 1973; October 11–13, 1975; January 12–14, 1976, Committee on Drugs Records, American Academy of Pediatrics, Pediatric History Center, Elk Grove Village, Illinois. In 1974 the FDA convened a subcommittee within its Neuropharmacology group to work on pediatric-specific issues. The AAP COD provided consultation to this group. Robert L. Sprague, "Principles of Clinical Trials and Social, Ethical and Legal Issues of Drug Use in Children," in *Pediatric Psychopharmacology: The Use of Behavior Modifying Drugs in Children*, ed. John S. Werry (New York: Brunner/Mazel, 1978), 109–135. For AAP position statements in the early 1970s on stimulants, see Sumner J. Yaffe, Charles W. Bierman, Howard M. Cann, et al., "Use of Amphetamine and Related Central Nervous System Stimulants in Children," *Pediatrics* 51 (February 1973): 302–305. With regard to the hyperactivity diagnosis, the FDA faced another daunting challenge. Dr. Ben Feingold's claim that food additives caused hyperactivity and other behavioral disorders in children attracted intense media coverage and still more Capitol Hill hearings that put the agency on the defensive because it did not have ready data to bolster or refute Feingold's thesis. Matthew Smith, *An Alternative History of Hyperactivity: Food Additives and the Feingold Diet* (New Brunswick, NJ: Rutgers University Press, 2011).

104 Leon Eisenberg to Fred H. Frankel, January 31, 1968, Box 8, Folder 61, Henry K. Beecher papers, 1848–1976, H MS c64, Harvard Medical Library, Francis A. Countway Library of Medicine, Boston, Massachusetts.

105 Judith L. Rapoport Oral History by David Healy, December 1998, page 6, American College of Neuropsychopharmacology, Center for the Study of the History of Neuropsychopharmacology, History and Special Collections, Louise M. Darling Biomedical Library, UCLA, Los Angeles, California.

106 Ibid., 6.

107 Judith L. Rapoport, Monte S. Buchsbaum, Theodore P. Zahn, Herbert Weingartner, Christy Ludlow, and Edwin J. Mikkelsen, "Dextroamphetamine: Cognitive and Behavioral Effects in Normal Prepubertal Boys," *Science* 199, no. 4328 (February 1978): 560–563, quote page 562. See also Gina Bari Kolata, "Childhood Hyperactivity: A New Look at Treatments and Causes," *Science* 199, no. 4328 (February 1978): 515–517.

108 Rapoport has had a long and distinguished career. She is currently chief, Section on Childhood Neuropsychiatric Disorders, Child Psychiatry Branch, at NIMH, accessed August 8, 2016, http://www.nimh.nih.gov/labs-at-nimh/principal -investigators/judith-rapoport.shtml.

109 On new metrics for assessment and diagnosis, see William Guy, *ECDEU Assessment Manual for Psychopharmacology* (Rockville, MD: Psychopharmacology Research Branch, National Institute of Mental Health, 1976). On pediatric psychopharmacology texts, see Jerry M. Wiener, *Psychopharmacology in Childhood and Adolescence* (New York: Basic Books, 1978) and Werry, ed., *Pediatric Psychopharmacology*. On growing diagnostic specificity, see Joaquim Puig-Antich, Stephen Blau, Nola Marx, Laurence L. Greenhill., and William Chambers, "Prepubertal Major Depressive Disorder: A Pilot Study," *Journal of the American Academy of Child Psychiatry* 17, no. 4 (1978): 695–707. On the guidelines for pediatric psychoactive drug research, see Bureau of Drugs of the Food and Drug Administration, *Guidelines for the Clinical Evaluation of Psychoactive Drugs in Infants and Children* (Washington, DC: GPO, 1979). On DSM-III preparation and children, see Judith L. Rapoport and Deborah R. Ismond, *DSM-III Training Guide for Diagnosis of Childhood Disorders* (New York: Brunner/Mazel, 1984), 6–7. For the history of DSM-III, see Hannah S. Decker, *The Making of DSM-III: A Diagnostic Manual's Conquest of American Psychiatry* (New York: Oxford University Press, 2013).

## Chapter 7   Pediatric Drug Development and Policy after 1979

1 Christopher-Paul Milne, "Exploring the Frontiers of Law and Science: FDAMA's Pediatric Study Initiative," *Food and Drug Law Journal* 57 (2002): 491–517.

2 Memorandum, "Issues in Pediatric Indications," from Marlene E. Haffner, Director Office, Orphan Products Development to sixteen FDA staffers, August 30, 1988, Box 28 Folder 5, Frances Oldham Kelsey papers, Library of Congress, Washington, DC (hereafter cited as Kelsey papers).

3 Peter N. Carroll, *It Seemed like Nothing Happened: America in the 1970s* (New Brunswick, NJ: Rutgers University Press, 1982); Kim Phillips-Fein, *Invisible Hands: The Businessmen's Crusade against the New Deal* (New York: Norton, 2009).

4 On orphan drugs, see Lisa Ruby Basara and Michael Montagne, *Searching for Magic Bullets: Orphan Drugs, Consumer Activism, and Pharmaceutical Development* (New York: Pharmaceutical Products Press, 1994), 131–133. For more on Tourette Syndrome, see *Tourette Syndrome Fact Sheet*, accessed January 16, 2017, http://www .ninds.nih.gov/disorders/tourette/detail_tourette.htm. Meyers has published her story in a number of places, including Abbey S. Meyers, *Orphan Drugs: A Global*

*Crusade* (2016), accessed January 16, 2017, available at https://www.abbeysmeyers .com.; Abbey S. Meyers, "Working Toward Passage of the Orphan Drug Act: An Example of Determination," *American Medical Writers Association* 3 (March 1988): 3–8; Abbey S. Meyers, "Orphan Drugs: The Current Situation in the United States, Europe, and Asia," *Drug Information Journal* 31 (1997): 101–104. There have been numerous historical analyses of disease-related advocacy. For examples, see Beatrix Hoffman, Nancy Tomes, Rachel Grob, and Mark Schlesinger, eds., *Patients as Policy Actors* (New Brunswick, NJ: Rutgers University Press, 2011), and Barron H. Lerner, *The Breast Cancer Wars: Hope, Fear, and the Pursuit of a Cure in Twentieth-Century America* (New York: Oxford University Press, 2003).

5  Meyers, *Orphan Drugs*, 50.

6  *Volume II Drug Regulation Reform—Oversight Orphan Drugs: Hearing before the Subcommittee on Health and the Environment, Committee on Interstate and Foreign Commerce*, House of Representatives, 96th Congress, 2nd Session (June 26, 1980) (Washington, DC: GPO, 1980), 18.

7  Ibid., 19, 20.

8  Ibid., Marion J. Finkel, 29–33.

9  *Health and the Environment Miscellaneous—Part 2: Subcommittee on Health and the Environment, Committee on Energy and Commerce*, House of Representatives, *Orphan Drugs*, 97th Congress, 1st Session (March 9, 1981) (Washington, DC: GPO, 1981), 76. On industry opposition to the Orphan Drug Act, see Henry Waxman, *The Waxman Report: How Congress Really Works* (New York: Hachette, 2009).

10  Meyers, *Orphan Drugs*, 85–89, quote page 88; Abbey Meyers interview with author, January 10, 2012.

11  Marlene Haffner interview with author, February 9, 2012; Oral History of Marlene Haffner by Suzanne Junod and Robert A. Tucker, December 6, 2011, March 13, 2012, National Library of Medicine, accessed June 27, 2016; available at www.fda .gov. For an overview of the Orphan Drug Act's impact since the 1980s, see Aaron S. Kesselheim, "Innovation and the Orphan Drug Act, 1983–2009: Regulatory and Clinical Characteristics of Approved Orphan Drugs," in *Institute of Medicine (US) Committee on Accelerating Rare Diseases Research and Orphan Product Development*, ed. Marilyn J. Field and Thomas F. Boat (Washington, DC: National Academies Press, 2010), 291–308.

12  Geeta Anand, "How Drugs for Rare Diseases Became Lifeline for Companies," *Wall Street Journal*, November 15, 2005.

13  For example, see Aimee Medeiros, *Heightened Expectations: The Rise of the Human Growth Hormone Industry in America* (Tuscaloosa: University of Alabama Press, 2016).

14  Kathleen L. Miller and Michael Lanthier, "Trends in Orphan New Molecular Entities, 1983–2014: Half Were First in Class, and Rare Cancers Were the Most Frequent Target," *Health Affairs* 35 (March 2016): 464–470.

15  Marlene Haffner, "Issues in Pediatric Indications," Box 28, Folder 5, Kelsey papers.

16  On changes to family life and childhood in this era, see Robert D. Putnam, *Our Kids: The American Dream in Crisis* (New York: Simon & Schuster, 2015); Paula S. Fass, *The End of American Childhood: A History of Parenting from Life on the Frontier to the Managed Child* (Princeton, NJ: Princeton University Press, 2016); and Steven Mintz, *Huck's Raft: A History of American Childhood* (Cambridge, MA: Belknap Press of Harvard University Press, 2004).

17  Paula S. Fass, "The Child Centered Family? New Rules in Postwar America," in *Reinventing Childhood after World War II*, ed. Paula S. Fass and Michael Grossberg (Philadelphia: University of Pennsylvania Press, 2011), 11; Fass, *The End of American Childhood*, 173; Kate Springer, "Etan Patz: A Brief History of the 'Missing Child' Milk Carton Campaign," *Time*, April 20, 2012.

18  Rick Mayes, Catherine Bagwell, and Jennifer Erkulwater, *Medicating Children: ADHD and Pediatric Mental Health* (Cambridge, MA: Harvard University Press, 2009), 61–95; Paul. H. Dworkin, "Coming Full Circle: Reflections at the Interface of Developmental-Behavioral and General Pediatrics," *Journal of Developmental and Behavioral Pediatrics* 28 (April 2007): 167–172; Sara Rosenbaum, D. Richard Mauery, Peter Shin, and Julia Hildalgo, *National Security and U.S. Child Health Policy: The Origins and Continuing Role of Medicaid and EPSDT*, Policy Brief, George Washington University School of Public Health and Health Services, 2005, accessed August 18, 2016, http://hsrc.himmelfarb.gwu.edu/sphhs_policy_briefs/36/; and Judith Sealander, *The Failed Century of the Child: Governing America's Young in the Twentieth Century* (New York: Cambridge University Press, 2003).

19  *NINDS Reye's Syndrome Information Page*, accessed August 18, 2016, http://www.ninds.nih.gov/disorders/reyes_syndrome/reyes_syndrome.htm. On the history of Reye's syndrome, see Mark A. Largent, *Keep Out of Reach of Children: Reye's Syndrome, Aspirin, and the Politics of Public Health* (New York: Bellevue Literary Press, 2015).

20  By now Plough was Schering Plough as a result of the merger of the two companies. On the campaign against the science by industry for a number of conditions, including aspirin and Reye's syndrome, see David Michaels and Celeste Monforton, "Manufacturing Uncertainty: Contested Science and the Protection of the Public's Health and Environment," *American Journal of Public Health* 95, S1 (July 2005): S39–S48. For other examples of science denialism, see Naomi Oreskes and Erik M. Conway, *Merchants of Doubt: How a Handful of Scientists Obscured the Truth on Issues from Tobacco Smoke to Global Warming* (New York: Bloomsbury, 2010); Allan M. Brandt, *The Cigarette Century* (New York: Basic Books, 2007); Gerald Markowitz and David Rosner, *Lead Wars: The Politics of Science and the Fate of America's Children* (Berkeley: University of California Press, 2013).

21  "Delay on Aspirin Warning Label Cost Children's Lives, Study Says," *New York Times*, October 23, 1992; Devra Lee Davis and Patricia Buffler, "Reduction of Deaths after Drug Labeling for Risk of Reye's Syndrome," *The Lancet* 340 (October 24, 1992): 1042.

22  "FDA Panel Urges AZT for Children," *New York Times*, March 31, 1990.

23  Timothy Ross and Anne Lifflander, *The Experiences of New York City Foster Children in HIV/AIDS Clinical Trials* (New York: Vera Institute of Justice, 2009), accessed June 28, 2016, http://www.vera.org/.

24  *Drug Development and the Pediatric Population: Report of a Workshop* (Washington, DC: National Academies Press, 1991), 1.

25  Ibid.

26  Paula Botstein, "Drugs for Use in Children," prepared for April 23 and 24, 1990, *Institute of Medicine Meeting on Drug Development and Pediatric Populations*, 1. See also Paula Botstein, "Drug Studies in Children," Society of Clinical Trials Presentation, Atlanta, May 17–19, 1987.

27  Diane P. Goyette, Division of Regulatory Affairs/OC/CEDR, FDA, "Pediatric labeling Preliminary Draft," April 2, 1991, Box 28, Folder 5, Kelsey papers.

28  Gopal K. Singh, *Child Mortality in the United States, 1935–2007: Large Racial and Socioeconomic Disparities Have Persisted over Time* (Rockville, MD: Department of Health and Human Services, 2010); Gopal K. Singh and Michael D. Kogan, "Widening Socioeconomic Disparities in US Childhood Mortality, 1969–2000," *American Journal of Public Health* 97 (September 2007): 1658–1665.

29  Lara J. Akinbami, "The State of Childhood Asthma United States—1980–2005," *Advance Data from Vital and Health Statistics* 381 (Hyattsville, MD: National Center for Health Statistics, 2006); Albert P. Rocchini, "Childhood Obesity and a Diabetes Epidemic," *New England Journal of Medicine* 346, no. 11 (March 2002): 854–855.

30  "Specific Requirements on Content and Format of Labeling for Human Prescription Drugs: Revision of 'Pediatric Use' Subsection in the Labeling," *Federal Register* 59, no. 238 (December 13, 1994): 64240–64250.

31  FDA Press Release, "FDA Announces New Rules for Children's Medicines," December 13, 1994.

32  Ibid.

33  "Why FDA Is Encouraging Drug Testing in Children," *FDA Consumer Special Report on New Drug Development in the United States* (January 1995), 63–66; Sumner Yaffe interview by author, November 1, 2010; Sanford N. Cohen, "The Pediatric Pharmacology Research Unit Network (PPRU) and Its Role in Meeting Pediatric Labeling Needs," *Pediatrics* 104 (September 1999): 644–645.

34  Mark A. Riddle, Elizabeth A. Kastelic, and Emily Frosch, "Pediatric Psychopharmacology," *Journal of Child Psychology and Psychiatry* 42 (January 2001): 73–90. Mayes, Bagwell, and Erkulwater, *Medicating Children*, 91.

35  "Regulations Requiring Manufacturers to Assess the Safety and Effectiveness of New Drugs and Biological Products in Pediatric Patients," *Federal Register* 63, no. 231 (December 2, 1998): 66632–66672.

36  Henry I. Miller, "Kids and FDA Drug Trials? Not a Good Idea," *Baltimore Sun*, December 21, 1998.

37  Ibid.

38  Ibid.

39  Ronal Keeney, "Pediatric Mandate: FDA Final Rule Forces the Pharma Industry to Change Its Clinical Trial Culture," *Pharmaceutical Executive* (April 2001): 98–106.

40  *Addressing the Barriers to Pediatric Drug Development* (Washington, DC: National Academies Press, 2008); *Safe and Effective Medicines for Children: Pediatric Studies Conducted Under BPCA and PREA*, ed. Marilyn J. Field and Thomas F. Boat (Washington, DC: National Academies Press, 2012); "Dianne Murphy: A Unique Insight into the World of Pediatric Medicine," *FDA Consumer Update*, October 19, 2016, accessed January 2, 2017.

41  On Richmond. see Bruce Weber, "Dr. Julius B. Richmond, Who Led Head Start and Battled Tobacco Dies at 91" [Obituary], *New York Times*, July 30, 2008.

42  I appreciate historian Susan E. Lederer's suggestion that it was not just the era in which the research was occurring, but the age of the experimenter. Lederer argues that their ethical acumen deepened with age and professional maturity (personal communication, Monday, August 8, 2016). My many conversations with historian Janet Golden also shaped my analysis and thinking about this topic. Silverman spent the latter part of his career critiquing early postwar medical research ethics and drawing attention to both the problems and possibilities raised by new therapeutics. See, for example, William A. Silverman, *Retrolental Fibroplasia: A Modern*

*Parable* (New York: Grune & Stratton, 1980); William A. Silverman, *Human Experimentation: A Guided Step into the Unknown* (New York: Oxford University Press, 1985); and William A. Silverman, *Where's the Evidence? Debates in Modern Medicine* (New York: Oxford University Press, 1998). In addition to Silverman's oral histories and publications, I gained insight about his decades' long attempt to grapple with research ethics from historian Gerald Oppenheimer, who spoke with him about this topic. He shared with me his sense that Silverman spent a great deal of time thinking about how to adjudicate the risks and benefits of research. Leon Eisenberg and Lawrence B. Guttmacher, "Were We All Asleep at the Switch? A Personal Reminiscence of Psychiatry from 1940 to 2010," *Acta Psychiatrica Scandinavica* 122 (August 2010): 89–102; Box 3, Folder 4, "American Academy of Pediatrics Task Force on Pediatric Research Informed Consent and Medical Ethics," Hodes papers; Kurt Hirschhorn, "Horace L. Hodes (1907–1989)," *Journal of Pediatrics* 128, no. 3 (1996): 436–437.

43  A notable exception to the absence of historical research into nurses and human experimentation is Susan Reverby's work on Eunice Rivers and her role as nurse in the long running Tuskegee experiment, in which indigent African American men were denied penicillin treatment when it became available. Reverby treats Rivers as a significant historical actor and analyzes her in the context of Tuskegee and Public Health Service physicians. Susan M. Reverby, *Examining Tuskegee: The Infamous Syphilis Study and Its Legacy* (Chapel Hill: University of North Carolina Press, 2009) and Susan M. Reverby, ed., *Tuskegee's Truths: Rethinking the Tuskegee Syphilis Study* (Chapel Hill: University of North Carolina Press, 2000). But because so little other historical research explores the role of nurses, it becomes easier to assume that Rivers was an outlier which may or may not be accurate. On nursing ethical codes, see "A Suggested Code: A Code of Ethics Presented for the Consideration of the American Nurses' Association," *American Journal of Nursing* 26 (August 1926): 599–601. See also Guy Philbin and David M. Keepnews, "Edward L. Bernays and Nursing's Code of Ethics: An Unexplored History," *Nursing History Review* 22 (2014): 144–158.

44  "St. Joseph Aspirin Taps Iconic TV Character Eddie Haskell to Relaunch the Improved Brand," July 28, 2011, accessed June 25, 2016, https://www.thestreet .com/story/11202636/1/st-joseph-aspirin-taps-iconic-tv-character-eddie-haskell-to -relaunch-the-improved-brand.html; http://stjosephaspirin.com/about-us/.

45  Lindsey Burke and Rachel Sheffield, "Universal Preschool's Empty Promises," accessed September 23, 2016, http://www.heritage.org/research/reports/2013/03/ universal-preschools-empty-promises.

46  Sara K. Pasquali, Danielle S. Burstein, Daniel K. Benjamin, P. Brian Smith, and Jennifer S. Li, "Globalization of Pediatric Research: Analysis Clinical Trials Completed for Pediatric Exclusivity," *Pediatrics* 126 (September 2010): 687–692; Julia Donne, M. Dianne Murphy, and William J. Rodriguez, "The Globalization of Pediatric Clinical Trials," *Pediatrics* 130 (December 2012): 1583–1591; Adriana Petryna, *When Experiments Travel: Clinical Trials and the Global Search for Human Subjects* (Princeton, NJ: Princeton University Press 2009), 50–52.

47  Thomas Insel, "Director's Blog: Are Children Overmedicated?" accessed January 16, 2017, http://www.nimh.nih.gov/about/director/2014/are-children-overmedicated .shtml; Mayes, Bagwell, and Erkulwater, *Medicating Children*; Matthew Smith, *Hyperactive: The Controversial History of ADHD* (London: Reaktion Books, 2012); Ilina Singh, "Not Just Naughty: 50 Years of Stimulant Drug Advertising," in

*Medicating Modern America: Prescription Drugs in History*, ed. Andrea Tone and Elizabeth Siegel Watkins (New York: New York University Press, 2007), 131–156; Judith Warner, *We've Got Issues: Children and Parents in the Age of Medication* (New York: Riverhead Books, 2010); Gary Greenberg, "The Psychiatric Drug Crisis," *New Yorker,* September 3, 2013; John Jureidini and Leemon B. McHenry, "Key Opinion Leaders and Pediatric Antidepressant Overprescribing," *Psychotherapy and Psychosomatics* 78 (2009): 197–201; *The Ritalin Explosion,* http://www.pbs.org/wgbh/pages/frontline/shows/medicating/experts/explosion.html airdate April 10, 2001; transcript retrieved August 1, 2016.

48  Alan Schwarz, "Still in a Crib Yet Being Given Antipsychotics," *New York Times,* December 10, 2015; Mark Olfson, Marissa King, and Michael Schoenbaum, "Treatment of Young People with Antipsychotic Medications in the United States," *Journal of the American Medical Association Psychiatry* 72, no. 9 (2015): 867–874. Johnson and Johnson's Janssen Pharmaceuticals agreed to pay more than two billion dollars in 2014 in response to charges that it misleadingly marketed Risperdol. Under the terms of the agreement, the company did not admit to any crimes. Katie Thomas, "J & J to pay $2.2 Billion in Risperdol Settlement," *New York Times,* November 4, 2013.

49  Meredith Matone, Sarah Zlotnik, Kathleen Noonan, Dorothy Miller, and David Rubin, *Antipsychotic Prescribing to Children: An In-Depth Look at Foster Care and Medicaid Populations,* CHOP Policy Lab, Spring 2015, accessed July 18, 2016, http://policylab.chop.edu/project/growing-use-and-safety-concerns-antipsychotic-medication-among-medicaid-enrolled-children; Stacy Burling, "Too Many Pa. Foster Children Are on Psychiatric Medications," *Philadelphia Inquirer,* February 25, 2016. See also Guido Cataife, and Daniel A. Weinberg, "Racial and Ethnic Differences in Antipsychotic Medication Use among Children Enrolled in Medicaid," *Psychiatric Services* 66 (September 2015): 946–951; Tumaini R. Coker, Marc N. Elliott, Sara L. Toomey et al., "Racial and Ethnic Disparities in ADHD Diagnosis and Treatment," *Pediatrics* 138 (September 2016): originally published online August 23, 2016.

50  "Dianne Murphy," *FDA Consumer Update,* 1.

51  "FDA Drug Safety Communication," April 20, 2017, accessed online April 24, 2017, https://www.fda.gov/Drugs/DrugSafety/ucm549679.htm; Catherine Saint Louis, "F.D.A Strengthens Warnings for Painkillers in Children," *New York Times,* April 20, 2017.

52  Natalie Pica and Florence Bourgeois, "Discontinuation and Nonpublication of Randomized Clinical Trials Conducted in Children," *Pediatrics* 138 (September 2016) originally published online August 4, 2016.

53  Luke A. Probst and Thomas R. Welch [Letter], "Pediatric Drug Formulations: Unintended Consequences of Legislation," *New England Journal of Medicine* 376 (February 23 2017: 795–796).

54  Allison Proffitt, "Obama Announces $215m Precision Medicine Investment for NIH, FDA," accessed June 29, 2016, http://www.bio-itworld.com/2015/1/30/obama-announces-215m-precision-medicine-investment.html; FACT SHEET: President Obama's Precision Medicine Initiative, https://www.whitehouse.gov/the-press-office/2015/01/30/fact-sheet-president-obama-s-precision-medicine-initiative.

55  Stephen P. Spielberg interview by author, January 18, 2013.

# Index

abortion, 90, 158; and drug development, 91;
    *Roe v. Wade*, 90–92
Abt, Isaac Arthur, 17–18, 44
Achromycin (tetracycline), 38, 42
acute lymphocytic leukemia (ALL), 56, 94
adrenocorticotropic hormone (ACTH),
    52–54, 153
adults: appeal to children, 4, 20, 38, 51; dos-
    age, modified for children, 7, 30, 74, 89;
    and flavored drugs, 40; pharmacothera-
    peutic differences from children, 2–3,
    11, 16–17, 24, 26–27, 35, 48, 65–66, 68,
    70–71, 82, 86–87
advertising: and AAP, 36; and African
    Americans, 210n.9; and antibiotics, 38;
    of aspirin, 7–8, 96–99, 100–101fig., 105;
    and candy aspirin, 7–8; and Children's
    Bureau, 13; and child well being, 108; and
    drug industry, 13, 42–43; and drug safety,
    116; instead of drug testing, 72; in medical
    journals, 36–37, 74–75; and Miltown, 130;
    and opium, 13; in pediatrics, 75; phar-
    maceutical, 36; and prescription drugs,
    42–43, 99; and psychoactive drugs, 136;
    race, class, and gender stereotypes in, 7–8,
    43, 96–99, 156; and safety caps, 109; and
    soothing syrups, 9–10; and stimulants,
    140; of St. Joseph Aspirin for Children,
    96–99, 100–101fig.
*Advertising Age* (magazine), 39
Affordable Care Act (2010), 3

African Americans: and advertising, 210n.9;
    and aspirin poisoning, 108–9, 156; and
    Bender's study, 128; dramatic recovery
    with sulfapyridine, 27; and drug research,
    137; and health care, 35; and hospital
    admission, 23; poison-related information
    and, 108–9; and Ritalin, 137
AIDS (acquired immunodeficiency syn-
    drome), 9, 148–49
Alcindor, Louverture, 55, 154
Alexander, Hattie, 44
American Academy of Pediatrics (AAP):
    and advertising, 36; annual confer-
    ence (1962), 69; and Children's Bureau,
    153–54; Committee on Accident Preven-
    tion, 102, 104–6; Committee on Drug
    Dosage, 38, 63; Committee on Fetus and
    Newborn, 65–66; Committee on Revi-
    sion of Pharmacopeia, 18–19; Committee
    to Cooperate with FDA, 37; and dosage
    study, 60; and drug development, 144;
    and drug safety, 67, 153; on experimenta-
    tion on human subjects, 91; and FDA,
    5, 36–37, 95; formation of, 14–15; and
    health care delivery, 19; and pediatric
    curriculum, 37; PRIME task force, 91–92,
    94, 154; and psychoactive drugs, 140; and
    Reye's syndrome, 148; Section on Pediat-
    ric Pharmacology, 79; Subcommittee on
    Accidental Poisoning, 111; and USP, 62;
    on well child care, 33–34

American Academy of Pediatrics (AAP), Committee on Drugs (COD), 64, 73, 78–80, 82–85, 89, 91–95; and drug safety, 64; on drug testing, 82; and FDA regulation, 95; on generic drugs, 93; guidelines for drug research, 140, 142; mandate of, 82; and Pharmaceutical Manufacturers Association, 79; on pregnant women, 205n.143; scientific guidelines for pediatric drug research, 142; and stimulants, 140

American Academy of Child Psychiatry, 130–32

*American Chamber of Horrors* (Lamb), 20

*American Journal of Diseases of Children*, 77

American Medical Association (AMA), 6; on all drugs except pediatrics, 62; Committee on Toxicology, 102, 107; Council on Drugs, 49; Council on Pharmacy and Chemistry, 18, 34; and drug safety, 25; and pediatrics, 11; in pharmaceutical policy, 12; and Sheppard-Towner Act, 14

American Nurses Association, 25

American Pediatric Society (APS), 67; and fetal research, 92

American Pharmaceutical Association (APhA), 5

American Psychiatric Association (APA), 130–32

Aminopterin, 56

amphetamines, 8, 126, 222n.32

Anderson, Jack, 111

Anthony, Susan B., 11

antibiotics: and advertising, 38; antifungal, 188n.35; benefits of, 33–34, 64, 152; broad spectrum, 38, 44, 58; Chloramphenicol, 38, 58; and clinical decision making, 154; drug resistance, 44; in early Cold War era, 6–7; growing pediatric market for, 38–44; and increasing mortality rates, 58; parental demand for, 44–45; and pediatric care, 34; and profits, 38

Antibiotic Symposium, Fifth (1957), 55

antihistamines, 45, 48, 71

antipsychotics, 140

aplastic anemia, 57–58, 60, 194n.110

Arena, Jay M., 108, 111, 119, 144, 156, 214n.48

aspirin: advertising of, 7–8, 96–99, 105; and Child Protection Act hearings, 114–16; and child protection rhetoric, 155; Children's Aspirin Amendment (1965), 111; development of industry for, 208n.2; FDA regulation of, 112; FDA-sponsored conference on (1967), 118; formulated for children, 97; labeling for, 102, 106, 109, 148; most common drug in pediatrics, 99, 102; pediatric morbidity and mortality from, 113; and pills per bottle standard, 111, 113–14, 118–19; regulation of, 111–12; research on, 111–12; and Reye's syndrome, 9, 148; and safety caps, 108–9, 123; standardization of, 106, 109, 111; total dosage per unit of sale, 115. *See also* candy aspirin; St. Joseph Aspirin for Children

aspirin poisoning, 8, 102–5, 110fig.; and African Americans, 108–9, 156; and child-rearing practices, 107; conference on (1955), 105–9, 111; deaths related to, 107–9, 111–12; decline of, 123, 143; epidemiology of, 113; most common household poison, 104; parents blamed for, 115–17, 155–56; in pediatric population, 119; and public health, 156; as public health problem, 105, 109; and race, 119–20; research on, 111–12; statistics on, 104, 107, 112; symptoms of, 104; in young children, 102–3. *See also* candy aspirin; dosage; labeling; parents

Aureomycin (chlortetracycline), 38

AZT, 148–49

baby boom, 33–34, 96–97; and demand for children's products, 97; and drug market, 39; and population statistics, 64

"baby killers", 6

"baby-saving" movement, 13

*Baltimore Sun* (newspaper), 24, 28

Banes, Daniel, 80

Barba, Philip S., 67

Barba, William P., 48

Bayer (German company): and aspirin, 99, 104, 115–16; aspirin created by, 208n.2; Dr. James' Soothing Syrup, 10, 12–13; and heroin, 10; and safety caps, 109

Beecher, Henry, 83, 95, 141, 158; on research ethics, 76–77

behavior: conditions, on the rise, 148; and drug safety, 140; drugs for, growth of, 9; medicalization of, 132; normal, 8, 124, 130,

138; problems, 129. *See also* hyperactivity; mood-altering drugs

Bellevue Hospital (New York), 126–34; Children's Psychopharmacology Research Unit, 133–34

Benadryl, 221n.18

Bender-Gestalt Visual Motor test, 126

Bender, Lauretta, 8, 126–29, 131–34, 137, 220n.13; diagnostic patterns used by, 128; LSD experiments of, 134–35, 154–55; and racism, 128

benzedrine sulfate, 126

Best Pharmaceuticals for Children Act (BPCA) (2002), 1, 9, 152, 159, 161

Bicillin, 51

Biologics Control Act (1902), 12

Bittner, Robert, 42

"black box" warning, 60

Blasingame, F.J.F., 116

Bliss, Eleanor A., 20–21, 24

Blumenthal, Sidney, 54, 154

Boston Children's Hospital, 16, 23–24, 31, 43, 46, 56, 60–62, 76, 93–94, 109

Botstein, Paula, 149–50

Bowman, Philip I., 40

Bradley, Charles, 125–27

Bristol Laboratories, 40

Brown, Hazel Fay, 20

Bullard, Laura Curtis, 11

Bundesen, Herman N., 107–8

Bureau of Product Safety (BPS), 122

Burroughs Welcome Fund, 93–94

Bush, Vannevar, 33

*Business Week* (magazine), 39

Butler, Allan M., 43, 60

cancer, 5, 56, 72, 94, 150, 153, 157

candy aspirin: and advertising, 7–8; aspirin "lollipop", 97; deaths related to, 107–9, 111–12; flavor of, 96, 99, 104, 106–7; overdose of, 108, 111–16, 119–20; for pediatric patient, 97; and safety caps, 8; unintended consequences of, 102–5. *See also* aspirin; flavored drugs

Carpenter, Daniel, 25

Carroll Dunham Smith Pharmaceuticals, 105

cerebral palsy, 51

Chain, Ernst, 29

Charney, Evan, 76–77

child abuse, 82, 88

Child Abuse Prevention and Treatment Act (1974), 88

child development, 38–39, 51; and NICHD, 65; and Soviet threat, 88–89. *See also* developmental psychology

child labor, 13, 88

child protection: and aspirin, 106; defining, 88–89; and drug development, 152–53; fears about, 147; and free enterprise, 11; and government, 92; and labeling, 102. *See also* names of individual agencies and legislation

Child Protection Act (1966), 112, 117, 216n.78

Child Protection Act hearings, 8, 112–18; and aspirin, 114–16

Child Protection and Toy Safety Act (1969), 122

child psychiatry, 8, 125, 139, 141; drug of choice in, 129; and drug therapy, 131; and psychopharmacology, 127–28, 131, 141–42; and research, 132

children: definition of, 81–82; emotional needs, 98–99; government commitment to, under Kennedy, 65; increased attention on, 38–39; influence of, 4, 65, 156; and profits, 146; public sympathies for, 20; well being of, 33–34, 38, 51, 64, 69, 88, 106, 108, 139, 152

Children's Act (1949), 35

Children's Aspirin Amendment (1965), 111

Children's Bureau, 13–14, 37, 68, 125; and advertising, 13; and American Academy of Pediatrics (AAP), 153–54; on drug therapy, 34; and health care delivery, 19; and psychopharmacology, 136; struggling for resources, 153

Children's Charter (1930), 15, 35, 157

Children's Defense Fund, 88–89

Children's Health Insurance Program (CHIP), 3, 172n.8

Children's Hospital of Philadelphia (CHOP), 94–95, 102, 174n.21

Children's Psychopharmacology Research Unit (Bellevue Hospital), 133–34

Children's Research Act (1949), 157

Child Research in Psychopharmacology Conference (1958), 130

"child-saving" movement, 13, 15, 125

Chloramphenicol (chloromycetin), 56–60; aplastic anemia associated with, 57–58, 194n.110; catastrophes of, 7; deaths caused by, 59–60; epidemiology of, 57–58; FDA investigation, 57–58; first antibiotic on market, 38; and infant mortality, 194n.115; and labeling, 60; and profits, 56–57; research, 90
Christensen, Charles, 78–80, 84
Christian, Joseph R., 107–8
Christopherson, E. H., 107
CIBA (Chemical Industry Basel), 43, 139–40
class: and advertising, stereotypes in, 7–8, 43, 96–99, 156; and health care, 35; and mood-altering drugs, 159
clean water, 160
clinical trials: adult vs. pediatric, 150; drug approval process for, 68; FDA-mandated, 149; pediatric drug, 69; in pediatric pharmacology, 133; in pediatric psychopharmacology, 132; randomized controlled, 50, 53–54, 191n.78
clysis, 27
codeine, 10, 27, 159
colic, 9, 48, 71
Columbia-Presbyterian Babies Hospital, 52
The Common Sense Book of Baby and Child Care (Dr. Spock), 39
Compazine (prochlorperazine): in clinical trials, 133; introduction of, 49; and profits, 49; Shirkey on, 62; side effects of, 72
Comprehensive Child Development bill (CCDB) (1973), 88–89, 157
Cone, Thomas E., 16, 30
Conference on Pediatric Pharmacology (1967), 78
Conference on Pediatric Pharmacology (1971), 78, 85
Conference on Perinatal Pharmacology (1961), 65
Congressional hearings. See Child Protection Act hearings; Gallagher hearings; Humphrey hearings; Kefauver hearings; Kennedy hearings; Nelson hearings; Poison Prevention Act hearings
Conners, C. Keith, 135–37, 139, 141
consent. See informed consent; parents
Console, A. Dale, 105
Consumer Bulletin, 118

consumer movement, 19–20
Consumer Product Safety Commission (CPSC), 122
Consumer Reports (magazine), 111
Consumers' Research, Inc., 20
Copeland, Royal S., 20, 24, 26
Cosmopolitan (magazine), 129
Craig, John, 44
Creedmoor State Hospital (New York), 132, 134–35
Crisis in Child Mental Health (Joint Commission), 137
Crotty, John J., 120
Cullen, Glenn E., 28
Curnan, William J., 83
Cutting, Windsor, 46–48, 62

Decadron (dexamethasone), 75
Declaration of Helsinki, 75
dehydration, 14
Delvex (dithiazanine iodide), 77
Denhoff, Eric, 137
developmental psychology, 51, 107. See also child development
Diagnostic and Statistical Manual of Mental Disorders, 126, 136, 142
Diamond, Louis, 56
diethylene glycol, 24–25
digitalis, 27, 62
digitoxin, 65
digoxin, 19; experiments, 154; potentially dangerous, 62; research, 54
dipenicillin G, 51
The Diseases of Infants and Children (Griffith and Mitchell), 16
Diseases of Medical Progress (Moser), 60
Dobbs, Dorothy, 138
Done, Alan K., 80, 120–21
Donoso, Ephraim, 54, 154
dosage: for children, 3, 7, 11, 23–24, 28, 30, 35, 54, 62, 65, 68; and chloramphenicol catastrophe, 59–60; controversy, 62; and drug industry, 138; and drug safety, 1, 15, 25; guidelines, 3, 95; overdose, 13, 103–5, 108, 111–16, 119–20; and over-the-counter drugs, 121; and prescription drugs, 121; reduced, 97; and side effects, 23, 49; standards for, 18, 35; studies of, 60–61; and United States Pharmacopeia (USP), 45–49, 62–63; weak

metrics for, 16–17, 36–38, 41, 77, 84, 92–93, 138; weight-based, 46, 54, 62, 68, 74, 115–16. *See also* labeling; parents

Dover's powder, 27

Downs, Elinor Fosdick, 21

Dr. James' Soothing Syrup Cordial, 9–10, 12

Drug Amendments Act (1962), 215n.62

drug development: and abortion, 91; adult vs. child, 34; and child protection, 152–53; children under-represented in, 72; cost burden of, 74; and drug safety, 34; financial feasibility of, 147; and government, 35, 138; history of, 2–4; and Orphan Drug Act, 145–47; and PPRUs, 150–51; and profits, 145; reforms in, 144; regulation slows, 80; risks and benefits, 88–90; unintended consequences, 158; for unprofitable drugs, 146–47

Drug Efficacy Study Implementation (DESI) program, 73–74, 82

drug industry: advertising of, 63; and dosage, 138; and drug safety, 72, 86; and drug testing, 68, 72, 84; and FDA policy, 70; FDA threatens, 41; *F-D-C Reports* (newsletter), 42, 63, 68, 84, 106; federal oversight of, 144; flourishes in 1930s, 19; focus on children's needs, 40; and governmental oversight, 68, 72–73, 114–18, 144; and health care costs, 143; labels threaten, 42; opportunity for, 152; and orphan drug law, 146; patent drug industry, 12, 19–20; pediatric drug knowledge, 35–38; and pediatrics, 50; and *Pediatrics* (journal), 65; and pharmaceutical policy, 161; poor data from, 82–83; price fixing in, 109; and PRIME task force, 92; and profits, 58, 61, 63; public-private partnerships, 56, 114; regulation of, 58, 65, 73, 161; and research, 50; at Ross conference (1968), 80; wants protection from government regulation, 114

drug research. *See* research

drugs: arguments against, 16, 19; cost of, 86, 93, 160; drug approval process, 9; drug lag, 86–87; drug price list, 97fig.; drug resistance, 44; economy of, 4, 155–56; explosion of, 54, 65, 150; flavored, 39–41; generic drugs, 93; and health, 2; and mental illness, 137; new drugs, as new regulatory category, 25; orphan drugs, 145–47;

pediatric drug database, 94, 150; pediatric drug knowledge, 35–38; rapid growth of market for, 65; regulation, modern era of, 6; research and testing for, 50–56; sleeping pill, 7; socialized medicine, 35; substance abuse, 138; and United States Pharmacopeia (USP), 48–49. *See also* aspirin; dosage; mood-altering drugs; names of individual drugs; new drug applications; over-the-counter drugs; prescription drugs; psychoactive drugs

drug safety: and advertising, 116; and behavior, 140; children not yet included in, 26; and Committee on Drugs, 64; and dosage, 1, 15; and drug development, 34; and drug testing, 1–3, 25, 89; education campaigns, 112, 119; and efficacy, 68–69, 157; fatalities call attention to (1937), 24–25; and FDA, 1–2, 25–26, 63, 67, 86, 93, 112, 138, 144; and FDCA law, 34–35; and Federal Trade Commission, 36; and Food, Drug, and Cosmetic Act (FDCA) (1938), 143; funding for, 37; negotiating mandates, 118–21; ongoing debates over, 62; overdoses, 13, 103–5, 108, 111–16, 119–20; still no progress, 80; and thalidomide, 66–67. *See also* aspirin poisoning; child protection; drug testing; poisoning; safety caps

drug studies: children excluded from, 4–5; children still a mystery for, 70, 74; dissemination of results of, 160; and informed consent, 75–77; pediatric, 151; pregnant women excluded from, 4–5; and psychopharmacology, 134–37; public relations campaign for, 79

drug testing: on children, 31, 79, 89, 92–93, 158; cost of, 67; and drug industry, 68, 72, 87; and drug safety, 1–3, 25, 89; eliminating barriers to, 149; and FDA, 68–69, 73, 84, 90; funding for, 82, 84, 87, 92–93; *General Guidelines for the Evaluation of Drugs to Be Approved for Use during Pregnancy and for Treatment of Infants and Children* (FDA), 89; and government, 68, 87; guidelines for pediatric, 86; Humphrey hearings, 69–73; and informed consent, 68, 85; and mood-altering drugs, 129; moves offshore, 158; and research, 50–56; Shirkey on, 82–83. *See also* drug safety; experimentation; research

Dunbar, Paul B., 81
DuPont, 20, 22

Early and Periodic Screening, Diagnostic, and Treatment Act (1967), 148
*Ebony* (magazine), 201n.9
economy: changing role of women in, 147; of drugs, 4, 155–56; free market/enterprise, 11, 20, 89, 116, 151, 157–58; Great Depression, 15, 19; health care economics, 76; pediatric products, explosion of, 65; recession in, 144–45; weakly regulated drug, 155. *See also* profits
Edelman, Marion Wright, 88–89
Education for All Handicapped Children Act (1975), 148
Edwards, Charles, 85–86, 90, 122
efficacy: Drug Efficacy Study Implementation (DESI) program, 73–74; and drug safety, 68–69, 157
Effron, Abraham S., 128
Eidelman, Arthur, 75
Eisenberg, Leon, 8, 131–33, 135–37, 139, 141, 144, 153–54, 158, 223n.40
electroencephalograph, 34
electrolyte management, 14, 34
Elgar, Edward, 10
Eli Lilly and Co., 43, 77–78, 84; flavored medication, 39, 40fig.
Elixir Sulfanilamide, 6, 24–26, 161
Engman, Louis A., 146
epinephrine, 134
Erikson, Erik, 39
erysipelas, 20
ethics: Declaration of Helsinki, 75; Nuremburg Code, 52; and research, 51–56, 76–77, 83, 90, 92–95, 154. *See also* informed consent
experimentation: to benefit knowledge, 77, 95; on children, 51, 54–55, 90, 134; Declaration of Helsinki, 75; guidelines for, 91; in Haiti, 154, with LSD, 154; on prisoners, 91–92. *See also* drug testing; ethics; informed consent; research

Faber, Harold K., 37
Falk, Leslie A., 44
Farber, Sidney, 56, 153
Faretra, Gloria, 134

*Farmers' Bulletin*, 13
*F-D-C Reports* (drug industry newsletter), 42, 63, 68, 84, 106
Federal Caustic Poison Act (1927), 14–15, 102–3
Federal Trade Commission (FTC): aspirin regulated by, 99; and drug safety, 36; narcotics regulated by, 13
Felix, R. H., 131
feminist movement, 8, 88, 147
fetal research, 90–92, 158
Finkel, Marion J., 83–85, 93, 95, 144, 146
Finland, Maxwell, 41, 50, 60, 76
Fish, Barbara, 133, 136
Fishbein, Morris, 67
Fisher, Richard E., 114–15, 117
flavored drugs, 39–41. *See also* candy aspirin
Fleming, Alexander, 29
Florey, Howard, 29
Food and Drug Administration (FDA): and AAP, 5, 36–37, 95; aspirin conference (1967), 118; aspirin regulation, 112; and chloramphenicol investigation, 57–58; clinical trials mandate, 149–50; creation of, 2, 6, 144; and dosage problem, 45–46, 48–49, 78; and drug safety, 1–2, 25–26, 63, 67, 86, 93, 112, 138, 144; and drug testing, 68–69, 73, 84, 90; expanded authority of, 14, 25, 116; *General Guidelines for the Evaluation of Drugs to Be Approved for Use during Pregnancy and for Treatment of Infants and Children* (1973), 89; and guidelines for drug research, 142; and informed consent, 76, 83; and labeling, 12, 15, 81–82, 95, 102, 109, 129; and new drug applications, 8, 35, 41, 63, 66; Office of Orphan Products Development, 146; Office of Pediatric Therapeutics, 152; and opium products for children, 13; pediatrician hired by, 63; and pediatric pharmacology, 80, 85; and Pediatric Rule, 9, 150–51; and pediatrics, 60; powerlessness of, 120; prescription drug regulation, 113, 122, 140, 143; public policy statements of, 184n.64; on soothing syrups, 13; and therapeutic orphans, 81, 84–85; Toy Safety Review Committee, 122
Food, Drug, and Cosmetic Act (FDCA) (1938), 6, 25, 63, 105, 143; and aspirin

poisonings in children, 104; and broad
spectrum antibiotic market, 41–42; Conference on Accidental Aspirin Poisoning
(1955), 105–9, 111; and Conference on
Pediatric Pharmacology, 78; and drug
safety, 143; efficacy review overseen by, 72;
evidentiary criteria sought for, 34; impact
on children, 158; informed consent guidelines, 83; Kefauver-Harris Amendments
to, 68; and labeling, 81; pediatrician hired
by, 63; pediatric policies of, 70–71; and
therapeutic orphans, 81
Freedman, Alfred M., 128
free enterprise, 11, 89, 116, 151; and government, 158; and health care, 19; and labeling, 20
Freireich, Emil, 56, 153

Gallagher, Cornelius E., 137–38
Gallagher hearings, 137–38
gender: and advertising, 7–8, 43, 96–99;
and health care delivery, 19. *See also*
women
*General Guidelines for the Evaluation of
Drugs to Be Approved for Use during Preg-
nancy and for Treatment of Infants and
Children* (FDA), 89
generic drugs, 93
Gesell, Arnold, 125
Gilman, Alfred, 77
Glazko, Anthony, 60
Goddard, James L., 81, 113, 117–18
Golden, Janet, 230n.42
Gold, Harry, 4
*Good Housekeeping* (magazine), 13
*Goodman & Gilman's Pharmacological Basis
of Therapeutics* (2010), 4
Goodman, Louis S., 77
Goostray, Stella, 128
government: Americans want drug industry
regulation from, 73; Americans wary of,
35, 146, 161; and child protection, 92;
commitment to children under Kennedy, 65; and drug development, 35, 138;
and drug industry, 68, 72–73, 114–18,
144; and drug safety, 67, 86; and drug
testing, 68, 87; and free market, 158;
and health care delivery, 19; lack of collaboration within, 68; limited to market

mechanisms, 157; overlapping work of,
19; public-private partnerships, 56, 114;
research funding, 35, 50. *See also* names of
individual agencies and legislation
Gowdy, John M., 121
Grattan, Jerome F., 105
gray baby syndrome, 59–60, 65
*The Great American Fraud* (Hopkins), 12
Great Depression, 15, 19
Great Society Initiatives, 81, 136–37
Griffith, J. P. Crozer, 16
Gruening, Ernest, 72

Haffner, Marlene, 147, 228n.11
Haggerty, Robert, 62
Haiti, drug research in, 55, 154, 193n.99
Halpern, Sydney, 52
Harriet Lane Home ( Johns Hopkins Hospi-
tal), 20, 22, 30, 50, 59–60, 125
Harrison Narcotics Act (1914), 6, 13
Harvey, John L., 45
Hazardous Substances Labeling Act (1960),
109
Head Start project, 153
health care: costs, 143; delivery of, free enter-
prise vs. government, 19; economics, 76;
and poverty, 35; transformation of, 76
health insurance: employer-based, 34, 76;
and mood-altering drugs, 159
Hecht, George, 98
Heckler, Margaret, 147
hepatitis, 55, 155
heroin, 10, 12
Hess, Alfred F., 52
highways, safe, 160
Hill-Burton Act (1946), 34
history, 3–5; comparative history of pharma-
cotherapeutics needed, 6
HIV, 149
Hobby, Galdys, 41
Hodes, Horace L., 27–29, 50–51, 76, 91,
153–54, 183n.52
Hodgman, Joan, 58–59, 90
Hoffmann, Felix, 208n.2
Hoge, James F., 113, 116–17
Hoover, Herbert, 15
Hoover Institution, 151
Hopkins, Samuel Adams, 12

hospitals: child population in, 23; federal funding for, 34–35; improved outcomes from, 14; transformation of, 6, 29; women's limited access to, 19
Humphrey hearings, 69–73, 135–36
Humphrey, Hubert, 68–73, 138; shocked at lack of collaboration in government agencies, 68
hyperactivity: defining diagnostic criteria for, 136; as discrete psychiatric diagnosis, 139, 226n.103. *See also* behavior; mood-altering drugs
hyperkinesis, 124, 136, 138

infant mortality, 12–13, 33, 88; and Chloramphenicol, 194n.115
informed consent, 51–55, 83, 133, 158; in chloramphenicol study, 59; and drug studies, 75–77; and drug testing, 68, 85; and FDA, 76, 83; National Commission for the Protection of Human Subjects in Biomedical and Behavioral Research, 91; Nuremburg Code, 52. *See also* drug studies; ethics; parents; research
Institute of Medicine (IOM), 149; and drug testing, 1–2
Institute of Medicine Manufacturers, 20
insurance. *See* health insurance
International Congress of Microbiology, 20
International Congress of Pediatrics, 91
International Year of the Child (1979), 95
Irvington House, 51

Jacobi, Abraham, 2, 11, 16, 131, 144
Janeway, Charles A., 16
Janssen, Wallace F., 105, 112
Jeans, Philip Charles, 45–46
Jenson, Malcolm, 122
Johnson and Johnson, 94
Johnson, Lyndon B., 81, 136–37; on aspirin poisoning, 112–13
Joint Commission of Mental Health of Children, 137
Joseph, Aurele A., 55, 154
*Journal of Pediatrics*, 17; and advertising, 36–37; experimentation on children published in, 54
*Journal of the American Medical Association* (JAMA), 12, 18, 67, 83, 107; AMA reports

on Compazine in, 49; chloramphenicol catastrophe ignored in, 58; FDA requirements for drug approval in, 34
juvenile: delinquency, 63, 76, 106, 127, 130, 133, 137; justice, 13, 88, 125, 127

Kanner, Leo, 131, 135
Keefer, Chester S., 29–30
Keeney, Ronal, 152
Kefauver, Estes, 63, 67–68, 109, 138
Kefauver-Harris Amendments (1962), to Federal Food, Drug, and Cosmetic Act, 7, 74, 78–80, 86, 93, 111, 113, 122, 157; drug development slowed by, 80; and drug safety, 143; and informed consent, 75; Kennedy signs, 68–69; limitations of, 158
Kefauver hearings, 67–68
Kelsey, Frances O., 66–68, 72, 144
Kempe, Henry, 62
Kennedy hearings, 90, 92, 140–41, 158, 226n.100
Kennedy, John F., 65, 68–69
Kennedy, Ted, 90, 92, 140
Kerlan, Irvin, 36–37, 105, 112, 144
Kessler, David A., 150
Ketcham, Hank, 112
Kevadon, 66. *See also* thalidomide
Klugman, Jack, 146
Kostello, Robert T., 121
Kretchmer, Norman, 72
Krugman, Saul, 55

labeling: and aspirin, 102, 106, 109, 148; and child protection, 102; and Chloramphenicol, 60; to circumvent drug safety, 73; disclaimer for pediatric use, 85–85; and FDA, 12, 15, 81–82, 95, 102, 109, 129; and free enterprise, 20; Hazardous Substances Labeling Act (1960), 109; and Miltown, 129; mockery of, 118; for new drug applications, 36, 63; and opioids, 159; pediatric information on, 152; and psychoactive drugs, 140; and stimulants, 138; as threat to drug industry, 42; warning labels, 15, 60, 102, 106, 109, 148. *See also* dosage; parents; safety caps
*Ladies Home Journal*, 12, 133
Lamb, Ruth deForest, 20
Larrick, George P., 71

laxatives, 19
*Leave It to Beaver* (TV show), 156
Lederer, Susan E., 52
Lederle, 38, 42–43, 56
Leer, John, 84
Lenroot, Katharine F., 34
leukemia, 56, 94
Ley, Herbert, 82–83
Lichtfield, Harry R., 129, 131
*Life* (magazine), 43
Lipman, Ronald S., 136, 138
Little Golden Book series, 97
Lockhart, Jean, 80
Long, Perrin H., 20–21, 24, 28–30, 107
*Los Angeles Times* (newspaper), 28, 58, 112
Loughlin, Elmer H., 55, 154
Lowe, Charles U., 79
LSD (lysergic acid diethylamide), 137; children's responses to, 134–35; experiments with, 154–55

MacPherson, Archibald R., 116
Maeder, Thomas, 57
malignant diseases, 33
managed care model, for psychiatric treatment, 151
Markowitz, Milton, 45
Massachusetts General Hospital, 60
Massengill Co., 24
May, Charles D., 65, 71
McGovern, George, 111
McIntosh, Rustin, 53
McKhann, Charles F., 28
McNeil Laboratories, 145
Medicaid, 76, 79, 88, 148, 159
medical journals, advertising in, 74–75
*Medical World News* (periodical), 67
Medicare, 76
Mellins, Robert B., 107–8
meningitis, 6, 22–23, 31, 50, 102, 153
mental health: *Crisis in Mental Health* (Joint Commission), 137; differentiation from disorders, 125; National Mental Health Act (1946), 126
mental illness: and drugs, 137; rise in, 148
Merck and Co., 26–27, 29–30, 48, 75
Meyer, Adolf, 127
Meyer, Roger J., 109
Meyers, Abbey S., 8, 145–46

milk, 19, 33, 46, 55, 160
Miller, Henry I., 151
Miller, Lloyd C., 45–48
Miltown (meprobamate), 129–30, 222n.27, 222n.30; and advertising, 130; in clinical trial, 133; FDA approved label for, 129
Minchew, B. Harvey, 81
missing children, 147–48
Mitchell, A. Graeme, 16, 125
Mitchell, Allan A., 93, 144
mood-altering drugs: for child mental illness, 151; for children, 124–25, 157–59; and class, 159; and drug testing, 129; experiments with, 154; and health insurance, 159; over-prescription of, 131–33, 139; and society, 159
Moser, Robert H., 60
Moses, W. H., 104
Moulton, Barbara, 109
Mrs. Winslow's Soothing Syrup, 10fig., 11, 125
Munns, George F., 36
Murphy, Dianne, 1–2, 159

narcotics, 11; Harrison Narcotics Act (1914), 6, 13
National Academy of Sciences (NAS), 84–85; Conference of Pediatric Pharmacology (1971), 78, 85; Drug Research Board, 73; pediatric drug research group, 84
National Child Research Act (1949), 35
National Clearing House for Poison Control Centers, 112
National Commission for the Protection of Human Subjects in Biomedical and Behavioral Research (1974), 91–92, 94–95, 140–41; *Research Involving Children* (1977), 94
National Council on Infant and Child Care (1956), 43
National Formulary (NF), 12, 17
National Institute of Child Health and Human Development (NICHD), 71–72, 85, 95, 137, 149–51; Conference on Pediatric Pharmacology, 78; developmental pharmacology program of, 74; establishment of, 65; and national pediatric pharmacology database, 150

National Institute of General Medical Sciences (NIGMS), 78

National Institute of Mental Health (NIMH), 126, 130–32; Pediatric Psychopharmacology Research Units, 151; and psychopharmacology, 131–41; Psychopharmacology Research Branch, 131

National Institutes of Health (NIH), 50, 65, 68–69, 71–72, 83, 92; founding of, 56; narrow focus of studies by, 72

National League of Women Voters, 25

National Mental Health Act (1946), 126

National Organization for Rare Diseases (NORD), 145

National Research Act (1974), 91

National Research Council, 29; Committee on Chemotherapeutic and Other Agents (COC), 29

National Reye's Syndrome Foundation, 148

Nectadon (noscapine), 48

Nelson, Gaylord, 86; Shirkey spars with, 86–87

Nelson hearings, 86–87

Nelson, Waldo E., 37, 48

neonatology, 65, 159

Nestor, John, 66–68, 144; and drug approval process, 69; FDA hires, 63; on FDA policy, 70–71

new drug applications: clinical trial data in, 143–44; and drug safety, 86; and drug testing, 68; and FDA, 8, 35, 41, 63, 66; and labeling, 36, 63; new drugs, as new regulatory category, 25; and Pediatric Rule, 150; and thalidomide, 66

New England Journal of Medicine, 56, 76

New York Times, 21, 24, 28, 67, 113, 135, 137, 159

Nidiffer, Joan, 25

Nixon, Richard, 88, 122

normal, 8, 124, 130, 138

Nuremburg Code, 52

nurses: American Nurses Association, 25; code of ethics, 155; and pediatric drugs, 61–62; research participation of, 155

Nyhan, William L., 63

Obama, Barack, 9, 152, 158, 160

O'Brien, Leo, 117

100,000,000 Guinea Pigs (Consumers' Research, Inc.), 20

opioids, 159

opium, 6, 12–13, 27

Orap (pimozide), 145

Orphan Drug Act (1983), 8, 145–47, 149

orphan drugs, 145–47; and profits, 147

Osmond, Ken, 156

over-the-counter drugs: dosing confusion, 121; legislation affecting, 116; in pediatric drug market, 96; and regulation, 113; safety caps for, 143

Panos, T. C., 77

parents: blamed for aspirin poisoning, 105, 109, 115–17, 155–56; blamed for child behavior, 131; and consent to research on children, 51, 54, 60, 75–76, 83, 92, 94–95; drug demands of, 44–45; on drug safety issues, 93; education for, 45, 106, 109, 112, 119; and orphan drug law, 145–46

Parents (magazine), 43; advertisements in, 98–99, 109, 116

Parke-Davis and Co., 38, 43, 56–58, 60, 79, 92; Chloramphenicol-related disaster and, 58

Park, Edwards A., 50

Patelski, Ray A., 41

patent drug industry, 12, 19–20

Patient Protection and Affordable Care Act (2010), 3

pediatric drug knowledge, 35–38

Pediatric Drug Surveillance (PeDS) program, 93–94

Pediatric Pharmacology Research Units, 150–51

Pediatric Research Equity Act (2002), 1, 9, 152, 159, 161

Pediatric Research, Informed Consent, and Medical Ethics (PRIME), 91–92, 94, 154

Pediatric Rule, 9, 150–52

pediatrics: advertising in, 75; children rarely saw pediatricians in 1930s, 17; and drug industry, 50; and drug safety, 86; drug standards not representative of, 17; and FDA, 60, 63; growing role of aspirin in, 102–4; increasing number of pediatricians (1949), 37; institutionalization of,

11; new emphasis on, 63; pediatric stages, 89; role of hospital pharmacy in, 61

*Pediatrics* (journal), 71–72, 79; and advertising, 75; on aspirin poisoning, 109; and drug industry, 65; experimentation on children published in, 54; FDA's informed consent guidelines in, 83; "Pharmacology for the Pediatrician" section, 85

penicillin, 3, 29–32, 34, 56; and clinical decision making, 154; compared with sulfonamides, 31; discovery of, 29; early formulation of, 31; impact on American childhood, 32; penicillin G, 51; success of treatment with, 30

Pfizer, 38, 41–42, 50, 55

Pharmaceutical Manufacturers Association (PMA), 80, 114, 146; and AAP, 79; and drug approval process, 69

pharmacists: apothecaries turned into, 10; role of, 61

pharmacogenomics, 160

pharmacokinetics, 72, 77–79, 89–90, 150, 157

*Pharmacological Basis of Therapeutics* (Goodman and Gilman), 77–78

pharmacy, transformation of, 61–62

Philadelphia Pediatric Society (PPS), 17, 26, 62, 144, 151; and pediatric representation, 17

phocomelia, 66

*Physician's Drug Reference*, 92

Piaget, Jean, 39

pilocarpine, 134

Pisani, Joseph M., 118

*Pittsburgh Press* (newspaper), 9

Plough, Abe, 106, 108, 115, 118, 208n.3; and advertising, 96–99, 100–101fig., 102–4

Plough Co., 96, 156

pneumonia, 6, 26–28, 34, 50, 102, 124, 126

poisoning: accidental, 102–3; education campaign, 112, 119; poison prevention poster, 110fig. *See also* aspirin poisoning

Poison Prevention Act hearings (1969), 121

Poison Prevention Packaging Act (1969), 120

Poison Prevention Packaging Act (1973), 122

poverty: effect on children, 137; and health care, 35; and informed consent, 51; and mood-altering drugs, 139; and over-prescription, 159; and Ritalin, 137; War on Poverty, 136–37

premature infants: effect of drugs on, 69–70; retinal damage in, 52–53, 66, 153

prescription drugs: and advertising, 42–43, 99; antibiotics, 7; compounded vs. ready-made, 61; and dosing confusion, 121; explosion of, 65, 158; FDA regulation of, 113, 122, 140, 143; and Harrison Narcotics Act, 13; mood-altering drugs, 132–33, 158–59; over-prescription of, 44, 132, 139, 158–59; and PeDS, 94; and profits, 102; and psychopharmacology, 127; race to secure pediatric formulations, 42; and regulation of new drugs, 25

prisoners, experimentation on, 91–92

profits: and antibiotics, 38; and children, 146; and Chloramphenicol, 56–57; and Compazine, 49; and drug development, 145; and drug industry, 58, 61, 63; FDA and labels threaten, 41–42; and focus on children's needs, 40; and orphan drugs, 147; and prescription drugs, 102; and reformulation, 160; and soothing syrups, 125

Prontosil, 20–21

Proprietary Association, 20, 113–14, 116, 118

protection. *See* child protection

psilocybin, 134

psychiatry. *See* child psychiatry

psychoactive drugs: and advertising, 136; children's responses to, 132, 140; and labeling, 140; measurement tools needed for, 131; rationale for, 124–25, 139. *See also* LSD

psychopharmacology, 124–42; and child psychiatry, 127–28, 131, 141–42; first randomized controlled trial, 133; first review article, 128; history of pediatric, 125–26; in 1960s, 133–37; in 1970s, 137–42; LSD experiments, 134–35; and prescription drugs, 127; unintended consequences in, 158

Psychopharmacology Conference (1958), 131–32

public health, 33; and aspirin poisoning, 156

Public Health Service, 12, 89, 92, 105, 112, 119, 130

*Quincy* (TV show), 146

race: and advertising, stereotypes in, 7–8, 43, 96–99, 156; and aspirin poisoning, 119–20; and Bender's study, 128; and hospital admission, 23; and mood-altering drugs, 139; racialized norms influence research, 109; and Ritalin, 137; Tuskegee Study, 89–90, 92
Ramsey, Paul, 83
randomized controlled trials, 50, 53, 74, 132–33, 154
Rapoport, Judith L., 141
Reagan, Ronald, 8, 145–46
*Report and Recommendations: Research on the Fetus* (National Commission), 92
research: advantages of children for, 31, 151; on aspirin poisoning, 111–12; cancer-related, 56; and child psychiatry, 132; on children, 83, 90–91; Declaration of Helsinki, 75; and drug industry, 50; and drug testing, 50–56; early pediatric, 54–55; and ethics, 51–56, 76–77, 83, 90, 92–95, 154; fetal, 90–92, 158; funding for, 50; government funding for, 35, 50; guidelines for, 140, 142; into child mental illness, 136; moves offshore, 158; norms of, 52; Nuremburg Code, 52; nurses' participation in, 155; and parental consent, 51, 54; parents consent to children in, 75–76; and racialized norms, 109; randomized controlled trials, 50, 53, 74, 132–33, 154; Ross Conference on Pediatric Research (1968), 80. *See also* drug testing; ethics; experimentation; informed consent
*Research Involving Children* (National Commission), 94–95
reserpine, 130
*The Revolution* (periodical), 11
Reye's syndrome, 9, 148, 150, 156
rheumatic fever, 51
Richardson, Elliot L., 138
Richmond, Julius B., 54, 76, 129, 153
Risperdal (risperidone), 159
Ritalin, 137, 139–41; and African Americans, 137
Roberts, Edward F., 51
*Roe v. Wade*, 90–92
Roosevelt, Franklin D., 20, 25–26
Roosevelt, Theodore, 13

Ross Conference on Pediatric Research (1968), 80
Ross Laboratories, 80
Rourke, Edward, 83

safety caps, 8, 108–9, 111, 113–15, 117–20, 123, 148, 155–56; and candy aspirin, 8
Sandoz Co., 134–35
Sansert, 134–35
Sapin, Samuel O., 54, 154
schizophrenia, 126, 134–35, 145
Schmid, Rudi, 60
Schmidt, Alexander M., 140
Schwarz, Alan, 149
Schweiker, Richard S., 90
Schwentker, Francis F., 22–24
scurvy, 52
sedatives, 29, 62, 140
Semm, Milton J. E., 45, 132
serum therapy, 21–22, 24, 26–28, 50
Shaefer, Irwin A., 82
Shalala, Donna E., 150
Sheppard-Towner Maternity and Infancy Act (1921), 14
Shirkey, Harry C., 47fig., 48–50, 62–65, 72–74, 78, 81, 85–91, 94, 115, 118, 121, 135, 139, 144, 157; on child protection, 85, 89; on children's needs, 7; on Compazine, 49; demands Congress force FDA on drug safety, 86; and DESI initiative, 74; on dosage problem, 46–49; on drug testing, 69, 82–83; "Ethical Limits of Pharmacological Research in Children" (speech), 91; at Nelson hearings, 86–87; retirement of, 204n.116; at Ross Conference (1980), 80
Shriver, Eunice Kennedy, 65
Silverman, William A., 52–53, 65–66, 80, 153–55, 230n.42
silver nitrate, 51
Simmons, Henry E., 90
Simpson, Richard, 122
Singh, Ilina, 140
Sin, Gisela, 25
sleeping pill, 7
smallpox, 12
Smith, Austin, 57
Smith, Clement A., 75
Smith, Kline, and French Laboratories, 49–50, 126–27; on Compazine, 62

Smith, Ralph G., 92
socialized medicine, 35
social justice, 154, 160–61
Social Security Act, 35
Solmson, Harry B., 104–5, 115, 117
soothing syrups, 9–14; and advertising,
    9–10; as "baby killers", 13; Dr. James' cor-
    dial, 9–10, 12; opium-laced, 6, 10; patent-
    ing of, 173n.19; and profits, 125; risks to
    infants, 12–14, 144; in 20th century, 11
Soviet threat, 39, 88, 106, 130; and child
    development, 88–89
special needs, 88
Spencer, Mildred, 79
Sperber, Ray L., 108–9
Spielberg, Stephen P., 160
Spink, Wesley W., 30
Spock, Benjamin (Dr. Spock), 39, 102
sputum culture, 27
Squibb, 29, 42, 105
Stalbaum, Lynn E., 114
Stanton, Elizabeth Cady, 11
Sterling Drug, 115–16, 121
steroids, 45, 52, 99, 157
Stetler, C. Joseph, 80, 114, 117
Stewart, H. R., 42
stimulants, 135–41; and advertising, 140; and
    hyperkinesis, 124, 136, 138; and labeling,
    138; research on, 135–36, 138
St. Joseph Aspirin for Children: and adver-
    tising, 96–99, 100–101fig.; in 1980s, 148;
    overdose with, 108; recommended by
    doctors, 102; safety cap protection for,
    109, 115. *See also* aspirin
Stormont, Robert, 36–37, 144
strep throat, 45
substance abuse, 138
sulfa drugs, 6; introduction of new, 184n.65;
    side effects, 28–29, 57; testing, 23, 29
sulfanilamide, 21–26; adverse reactions with,
    23–24; danger of, 6; dosing protocols
    for, 23–24, 180n.30; first trial of, 21–22;
    market competition for, 24–25; for men-
    ingitis, 22–23; unintended consequences,
    28–29
sulfapyridine, 26–29; dramatic recoveries
    with, 27–28; unintended consequences,
    28–29
sulfathiazole, 29

sulfonamides, 6, 20–26, 34, 56, 144; and
    clinical decision making, 154; compared
    with penicillin, 154; effect on childhood,
    32; medical literature on, 31; mortality
    reduced with, 31; as prescription drug, 25;
    research on, 153; testing of, 155
Sullivan, Leonor K., 111, 114
Sydenham Hospital (Baltimore): children's
    ward, 29; experimental drugs at, 183n.56;
    meningitis at, 22, 31; nurse staffing
    problem at, 28; sulfanilamide use at, 22;
    sulfapyridine use at, 27; sulfonamide use
    at, 28–29, 153
syphilis, 89–90

Tainter, Maurice L., 115–17, 121, 218n.117
Talbot, Milton W., 130–31
Taussig, Helen, 94, 144; drug safety cam-
    paign, 66–69
Taylor, Howard J., 42
Terramycin (oxytetracycline), 38, 41–42,
    154; research on children in Haiti with, 55
Terry, Luther, 69
*Textbook of Pediatrics* (Nelson), 48
thalidomide, 4, 7, 66–67, 80, 111, 135, 138,
    144, 157, 161; disaster, 7, 111; and drug
    safety campaign, 66–67
therapeutic nihilists, 17
therapeutic orphans: concept of, 7, 73, 139;
    conferences on, 85; contention over, 78,
    86; and FDA, 81, 84–85; solutions for,
    149
therapeutics, 1–2
Thompson, Arthur, 61
Thorazine (chlorpromazine), 127–29, 133,
    140, 221n.18
Ticktin, Howard E., 76
Tigan (trimethobenzamide hydrochloride),
    80–81
tormadol, 159
Tourette Foundation, 145
Tourette Syndrome, 145
Toy Safety Review Committee, 122
tranquilizers, 127, 129–31, 133, 136
Triacetyloleandomycin, 76
Truman, Harry S., 35
Trump, Donald, 161
Tull, Myron G., 23
Tuskegee Study, 89–90, 92

United States Pharmacopeia (USP), 12, 17, 64; committee on pediatric dosing, 45–46, 190n.55; and dosage, 45–49, 62–63; and drug development, 144; and drugs, 48–49; Panel on Pediatrics, 62–63

vaccines, 52
vital statistics, 11–12

Wallace Laboratories, 129
Wall, Joseph A., 36
*Wall Street Journal* (newspaper), 99
Warfield, Melissa A., 80–81
warning labels. *See* labeling
War on Poverty, 136–37
Warren, Robert, 84
*Washington Post* (newspaper), 66, 111, 137–38, 146
Watergate scandal, 145
Watkins, Albe, 57
Watkins, Geraldine, 57
Waxman, Henry, 145–46
Weech, A. Ashley, 77
Weinberger, Caspar, 92–93, 157
Weiss, Charles F., 79–80, 84–85
Welch, Henry, 57
West, Olin, 18
Wheatley, George M., 102–3, 105, 107

White House: Conference on Child Health and Protection (1930), 15; Conference on Children (1950), 38–39, 99, 126; Conference on Children and Youth (1960), 64–65, 109
William S. Merrell Corp., 66
Willowbrook State School, 55, 155
Wilson, Armine T., 28
Winkler, John W., 84
*Woman's Home Companion* (magazine), 45, 98
women: changing role in economy, 147; drug laws supported by, 25; excluded from drug studies, 4–5; feminist movement, 8, 88, 147; as physicians, 19; *The Revolution* (periodical), 11; special pharmacological needs of, 173n.14; women's rights, 8. *See also* gender
World Medical Association, 75
Wyeth Laboratories, 51, 76

Yaffe, Sumner, 78–79, 84, 87, 89, 92, 94–95, 139, 144, 150–51, 157
Young's Rule, 11
youth unrest, 88

Zidovudine (AZT), 148–49
Zimmerman, Hyman J., 76

# About the Author

CYNTHIA A. CONNOLLY is a pediatric nurse and historian of children's health care. She is associate professor at the University of Pennsylvania School of Nursing where she is the Rosemarie B. Greco Term Endowed Associate Professor in Advocacy. She is associate director at the Barbara Bates Center for the Study of the History of Nursing; a faculty director at the Field Center for Children's Policy, Practice, and Research; and a senior fellow at the Leonard Davis Institute of Health Economics, all at the University of Pennsylvania. She is the author of *Saving Sickly Children: The Tuberculosis Preventorium in American Life, 1909–1970* (Rutgers University Press, 2008).

Mark A. Hall and Sara Rosenbaum, eds., *The Health Care "Safety Net" in a Post-Reform World*

Laura L. Heinemann, *Transplanting Care: Shifting Commitments in Health and Care in the United States*

Laura D. Hirshbein, *American Melancholy: Constructions of Depression in the Twentieth Century*

Laura D. Hirshbein, *Smoking Privileges: Psychiatry, the Mentally Ill, and the Tobacco Industry in America*

Timothy Hoff, *Practice under Pressure: Primary Care Physicians and Their Medicine in the Twenty-first Century*

Beatrix Hoffman, Nancy Tomes, Rachel N. Grob, and Mark Schlesinger, eds., *Patients as Policy Actors*

Ruth Horowitz, *Deciding the Public Interest: Medical Licensing and Discipline*

Powel Kazanjian, *Frederick Novy and the Development of Bacteriology in American Medicine*

Rebecca M. Kluchin, *Fit to Be Tied: Sterilization and Reproductive Rights in America, 1950–1980*

Jennifer Lisa Koslow, *Cultivating Health: Los Angeles Women and Public Health Reform*

Susan C. Lawrence, *Privacy and the Past: Research, Law, Archives, Ethics*

Bonnie Lefkowitz, *Community Health Centers: A Movement and the People Who Made It Happen*

Ellen Leopold, *Under the Radar: Cancer and the Cold War*

Barbara L. Ley, *From Pink to Green: Disease Prevention and the Environmental Breast Cancer Movement*

Sonja Mackenzie, *Structural Intimacies: Sexual Stories in the Black AIDS Epidemic*

Michelle McClellan, *Lady Lushes: Gender, Alcohol, and Medicine in Modern America*

David Mechanic, *The Truth about Health Care: Why Reform Is Not Working in America*

Richard A. Meckel, *Classrooms and Clinics: Urban Schools and the Protection and Promotion of Child Health, 1870–1930*

Alyssa Picard, *Making the American Mouth: Dentists and Public Health in the Twentieth Century*

Heather Munro Prescott, *The Morning After: A History of Emergency Contraception in the United States*

Andrew R. Ruis, *Eating to Learn, Learning to Eat: School Lunches and Nutrition Policy in the United States*

James A. Schafer Jr., *The Business of Private Medical Practice: Doctors, Specialization, and Urban Change in Philadelphia, 1900–1940*

David G. Schuster, *Neurasthenic Nation: America's Search for Health, Happiness, and Comfort, 1869–1920*

Karen Seccombe and Kim A. Hoffman, *Just Don't Get Sick: Access to Health Care in the Aftermath of Welfare Reform*

Leo B. Slater, *War and Disease: Biomedical Research on Malaria in the Twentieth Century*

Paige Hall Smith, Bernice L. Hausman, and Miriam Labbok, *Beyond Health, Beyond Choice: Breastfeeding Constraints and Realities*

Matthew Smith, *An Alternative History of Hyperactivity: Food Additives and the Feingold Diet*

Susan L. Smith, *Toxic Exposures: Mustard Gas and the Health Consequences of World War II in the United States*

Rosemary A. Stevens, Charles E. Rosenberg, and Lawton R. Burns, eds., *History and Health Policy in the United States: Putting the Past Back In*

Barbra Mann Wall, *American Catholic Hospitals: A Century of Changing Markets and Missions*

Frances Ward, *The Door of Last Resort: Memoirs of a Nurse Practitioner*